Brazilian Politics on Trial

Brazilian Politics on Trial

Corruption and Reform Under Democracy

Luciano Da Ros
Matthew M. Taylor

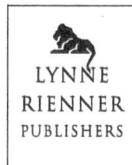

LYNNE
RIENNER
PUBLISHERS

BOULDER
LONDON

Published in the United States of America in 2022 by
Lynne Rienner Publishers, Inc.
1800 30th Street, Suite 314, Boulder, Colorado 80301
www.rienner.com

and in the United Kingdom by
Lynne Rienner Publishers, Inc.
Gray's Inn House, 127 Clerkenwell Road, London EC1 5DB
www.eurospanbookstore.com/rienner

Library of Congress Cataloging-in-Publication Data
Names: Da Ros, Luciano, author. | Taylor, Matthew MacLeod, author.
Title: Brazilian politics on trial : corruption and reform under democracy
   / Luciano Da Ros & Matthew M. Taylor.
Description: Boulder, Colorado : Lynne Rienner Publishers, Inc., [2022] |
   Includes bibliographical references and index. | Summary: "Explores the
   causes of Brazil's numerous corruption scandals, the successes and
   failures of its anticorruption reforms, and the implications of the
   Brazilian experience for reform efforts in countries around the world"—
   Provided by publisher.
Identifiers: LCCN 2021036854 (print) | LCCN 2021036855 (ebook) | ISBN
   9781626379978 (Hardback) | ISBN 9781955055192 (ebook)
Subjects: LCSH: Political corruption—Brazil. | Elite (Social
   sciences)—Brazil. | Government accountability—Brazil. | Judicial
   process—Political aspects—Brazil. | Democratization—Brazil. |
   Brazil—Politics and government—1985–2002. | Brazil—Politics and
   government—2003–
Classification: LCC JL2429.C6 D3 2022 (print) | LCC JL2429.C6 (ebook) |
   DDC 364.1/3230981—dc23/eng/20211115
LC record available at https://lccn.loc.gov/2021036854
LC ebook record available at https://lccn.loc.gov/2021036855

British Cataloguing in Publication Data
A Cataloguing in Publication record for this book
is available from the British Library.

Printed and bound in the United States of America

⊗   The paper used in this publication meets the requirements
    of the American National Standard for Permanence of
    Paper for Printed Library Materials Z39.48-1992.

5 4 3 2 1

*For Marina, for all the beauty, patience, and courage
she brings to my life every day as we navigate together
the turbulent waters of our beloved country*
—LDR

For Dad, who always asked the best questions
—MMT

Contents

Tables and Figures

Tables

Figures

Acknowledgments

Numerous colleagues have generously offered ideas and suggestions that enriched this book. We have also learned a great deal from a promising cohort of recent graduate students whose empirical data has greatly illuminated the issues at hand. We will not attempt to list them all here, for fear of either writing an encyclopedic acknowledgments section or, more likely, inadvertently forgetting someone. But you know who you are.

Various entrepreneurial colleagues organized seminars, conferences, and collective publications that have allowed us to explore our arguments and receive critical feedback over the past few years. An invitation from Robert Rotberg to the American Academy of Arts and Sciences sparked the development of the accountability heuristic in Chapter 3. Fernando Filgueiras spearheaded the two-day conference "Rethinking Anticorruption Efforts in Brazil" that brought together a select group of public servants, anticorruption practitioners, and academics at the Escola Nacional de Administração Pública in Brasília. Sandra Botero, Daniel Brinks, and Ezequiel González-Ocantos held a collegial seminar "Politics and Law in Latin America" at the Universidad del Rosário, which got us thinking about the politics of judicial policy entrepreneurship. Maria Popova, Manuel Balán, and Juan Wang welcomed the presentation of our reflections on *Lava Jato* at the McGill University workshop "Politics of Corruption Prosecutions," which was also the source of a number of comparative insights developed in the pages ahead. Leonardo Avritzer, Fábio Kerche, and

Marjorie Marona welcomed our reflections on the state of account-ability during the government of Jair Bolsonaro in their collected vol-ume on the subject. Rogério Arantes and Diego Werneck Arguelhes pushed us to think about the Supreme Federal Tribunal's role in crim-inal prosecutions in their collected volume. Mariana Prado, Marta Machado, Kevin Davis, and Raquel Pimenta organized a fascinating mix of law faculty and political scientists at the Fundação Getulio Var-gas seminar "Law and Systemic Corruption" that helped us reflect on a key issue we identify in this book: political dominance and how it influences the effective deployment of checks and balances. Bruno Speck and Peter Birle organized an event at the Ibero-American Insti-tute in Berlin that allowed us to develop our thoughts on the demise of the anticorruption agenda within the judiciary during Bolsonaro's presidency. We are grateful to the organizers of all of these projects, as well as the many event participants who introduced new material, raised good questions, and provided unvarnished criticism.

Kate Bersch, Maria Paula Bertran, Manoel Gehrke, Paul Lagunes, Lucio Picci, Radu Pârvulescu, and two anonymous reviewers offered extensive feedback and constructive ideas for improvement of earlier drafts of the book. We are grateful for their help in sharpening our arguments. Luciano thanks his colleagues and students at the Federal University of Santa Catarina and the Federal University of Rio Grande do Sul, where he worked during the development of this proj-ect. Luciano also thanks the Conselho Nacional de Desenvolvimento Científico e Tecnológico for financial support. Matthew thanks his colleagues at the Center for Latin American and Latino Studies and the School of International Service at American University for their encouragement.

Finally, we thank Lynne Rienner, Moorea Corrigan, Diane Foose, Sally Glover, and Shena Redmond for seeing the project through to the finish line.

1

Scandal and Corruption in Brazil

*The corrupt are animals similar to the
non-corrupt. But the latter is a species that is
nearly extinct because it is so easy to capture.*
—Millôr Fernandes, Brazilian satirist

In November 1992, a relatively unknown congressional staffer took his wife out for dinner in Brasília. On their way home, the couple was accosted by two men, and the woman, Ana Elizabeth Lofrano, was driven to a distant suburb and killed. Under pressure from police, her husband, José Carlos Alves dos Santos, claimed that the murder had been orchestrated by his congressional bosses to cover up a fraudulent budget scheme Lofrano had uncovered.

The ensuing budget scandal, referred to tactlessly as the *Anões do Orçamento* (budget dwarves) scandal because of the low rank and short height of the congressmen involved, absorbed all of Brazil during much of 1993. A comissão parlamentar de inquérito (congressional committee of inquiry, CPI) was called to order, and proceeded to find evidence of considerable wrongdoing. Members of the budget committee were found to have written fraudulent budget amendments, with help from Alves dos Santos, favoring construction firms, fraudulent social organizations, and relatives. They received kickbacks and laundered them, including by buying up and cashing winning lottery tickets. The chair of the budget committee, Congressman João Alves, claimed to have won the lottery more than 200 times, prompting incredulous jeers from the audience at the inquiry.

All told, the CPI investigated thirty-seven congressmen and recommended that eighteen be removed from Congress. Of these, six

1

were expelled by their peers, four resigned so as to preserve their political rights, and eight were absolved.[1] Staffer Alves dos Santos served four years of a twenty-year prison sentence for ordering his wife's murder and, twenty-one years later, another two and a half years of an eight-year sentence for his involvement in the budget wrongdoing (Brasília Assombrada 2017; Favero 2013).

The *Anões do Orçamento* scandal led to a review of the budget process and a number of reforms aimed at curbing the feasibility of fraudulent budget amendments. The budget committee chair's discretion was significantly curtailed, and a cap was put on the number and total value of individual representatives' amendments (Praça 2011, 2013).

Fast-forward three decades.

In early 2021, the *Estado de S. Paulo* newspaper revealed that the government was operating a "secret budget" of more than US$560 million to build legislative support (Pires 2021a, 2021b). While investigations are ongoing and it is therefore too soon to declare conclusively that the secret budget was corrupt, several red flags suggested wrongdoing. Perhaps most importantly, most of the amendments allocated funds within the Ministry of Regional Development to purchase heavy equipment for sewage and road construction, and the equipment appeared to have been budgeted at prices substantially higher than the government's own reference price (Praça 2021; Carrança 2021; Valfre and Pires 2021).[2] One Brazilian anticorruption activist, Gil Castello Branco, opined that "this is a scandal that suggests—the investigation will be able to prove it or not—the explicit purchase of political support" (Carrança 2021). Tacitly acknowledging the issues raised by the secret budget, in May 2021 the Jair Bolsonaro administration changed the budget rules once again, formalizing the rapporteur's amendment power in the following year's budget (*O Estado de S. Paulo* 2021).

This pair of budget scandals, nearly thirty years apart, highlights the questions that will guide us in the pages ahead.

First, what explains the seeming constancy of corruption and scandal in democratic Brazil? A Brazilian in the 1990s with a passing acquaintance of the *Anões do Orçamento* scandal and its enormous public repercussion would be shocked to learn that history appears to be repeating itself thirty years later. Not only that, but the secret budget of 2021 would not be the first scandal to repeat a similar script. There had also been a major 2006 *Sanguessugas* (leeches) scandal, which implicated dozens of legislators who were using budget amendments to buy overpriced ambulances. And these are only the scandals that traded *budgetary* side payments for legislative support, to say nothing of other forms of corruption. What are the conditions on the ground that provide constant incentives for corruption in politics and drive the abuse of the public trust for private ends, over and over again?

Second, why have reforms and anticorruption efforts not had the desired effect of lessening political corruption? The democratic regime that began in 1985 has been marked by seemingly continuous reform, including a variety of changes taken in response to specific corruption scandals like the budget troubles above. The country has seen ongoing improvements in the norms, procedures, and agents involved in controlling public sector corruption, whose gradual accumulation over time contributed by the early 2010s to a hopeful perception about the democratic regime's anticorruption progress. In recent years, there has also been a massive anticorruption push associated with the *Lava Jato* investigations, which directly targeted scores of federal politicians and their counterparts in business. *Lava Jato* has been deemed by a range of metrics—such as scope, length, sums involved, prominence of those investigated, and ramifications in other countries—one of the largest criminal investigations into high-level corruption in a democracy anywhere in the world. However, the overall picture is decidedly mixed. The *Lava Jato* case raised hopes that a new era of accountability was arriving, but within seven years the investigations had largely been shuttered and the overall accountability panorama appeared, in many respects, to have regressed. Not only had the *Lava Jato* investigation been pruned to insignificance, but the broader federal accountability infrastructure had also been significantly weakened. Why did these anticorruption efforts and reforms not have the expected dissuasive effect, why did they not accumulate over time into a significant change in the overall patterns of wrongdoing, and why has the pushback been so substantial?

Third, what are the implications of Brazil's experience for anticorruption reformers elsewhere around the world? As the tale of these two budget scandals demonstrates, the Brazilian case is a frustrating example of how anticorruption efforts sometimes fail to sum to an effective change in the overall patterns and prevalence of corruption. What explains this failure, and what can other reformers learn from Brazil's generation-long anticorruption experience?

In sum, this book is an attempt to make sense of Brazil's complex history of corruption and anticorruption since the return to democracy in 1985, and to evaluate its lessons for anticorruption reformers in Brazil and in other large democracies.[3] We evaluate the corruption scandals that erupted and the anticorruption reforms that emerged to consider what it means for anticorruption efforts to succeed, the conditions under which they are more or less likely to prosper, and their multiple potentially sanitizing but also profoundly destabilizing effects on democracy. Throughout the book, we also seek to bring back some of the nuance that has been lost in the fire-hot debates that emerged around *Lava Jato,* the impeachment of Dilma Rousseff, and the election of right-wing provocateur Jair Bolsonaro.

Brazil's Relevance to the Study and Practice of Anticorruption

The Brazilian experience with corruption and accountability is interesting in and of itself. Anticorruption has been one of the central points of contention in politics since the return to democracy in 1985, and the country's accountability trajectory has had consequential and lasting impacts on economic development, political performance, and citizen satisfaction with democracy in Latin America's largest nation. But Brazil's experience with corruption and accountability since 1985 is also extremely relevant to the international literature and practice of anticorruption for at least four reasons.

First, Brazil is a democracy. This is important, because so many of the reforms that are touted as anticorruption remedies emerged in countries that were undemocratic at the time, a fact that limits their broader applicability. For example, Hong Kong's oft-emulated Independent Commission Against Corruption (ICAC), an influential precursor to anticorruption agencies worldwide, was created when Hong Kong was a British colony run from London without direct elections. Robert Klitgaard's (1988) pioneering book on corruption, similarly, derives its lessons predominantly from then nondemocratic nations, including the Philippines under Ferdinand Marcos, Hong Kong and Singapore in the 1970s, South Korea in the 1960s and 1970s, and an unnamed African province in the late 1970s that looked doubtfully democratic. Along similar lines, all five countries deemed "most improved" by Robert I. Rotberg (2017) do not look very democratic: four hybrid regimes and one seemingly authoritarian.[4] To a significant extent, the emphasis on nondemocratic nations is also present in Jon S. T. Quah's (2011) analysis of ten Asian countries and Melanie Manion's (2004) critical comparison of China and Hong Kong.

Unsurprisingly, "political will" or "leadership" often emerges from studies of authoritarian or hybrid regimes as a fundamental variable explaining anticorruption success (Klitgaard 1998; Quah

2010, 2011; Rotberg 2017). But given the choice of cases, this risks tautology: almost by definition, if an autocratic ruler decides to bust graft, his will is going to be crucial to success. The same conditions do not hold in a democracy. By definition, *democracy* is a regime that relies on competition between different wills and whose institutional arrangements are designed to fragment, rather than unify, political leadership. This means that almost by definition, anticorruption efforts in democracies must be a collective endeavor.

The political-electoral calculations of anticorruption reform are much reduced in authoritarian regimes, but this of course results from the fact that, as soon as meaningful investigations become a threat against the regime, they are quashed. In fact, an emerging body of literature in nondemocratic nations shows that anticorruption initiatives have been instrumental in reinforcing rulers' powers, rather than in reducing corruption proper. Additionally, the fact that autocracies are by various comparative accounts more corrupt than democracies (e.g., Treisman 2000, 2007, 2014; McMann et al. 2020), further suggests that the undemocratic nations that managed to reduce corruption are truly exceptional (Mungiu-Pippidi and Johnston 2017). As a result, any broader anticorruption lessons derived from this group of nations should be read with extreme care.

Second, Brazil is a large democracy. There are democratic nations that have recently succeeded in reducing corruption. Some of the "contemporary achievers" discussed by Alina Mungiu-Pippidi and Michael Johnston (2017) include Botswana, Costa Rica, Estonia, Uruguay, and South Korea. Yet except for South Korea, with its population of 52 million, these success stories are small, with populations of fewer than 5 million. How can large Latin American nations such as Argentina (45 million), Colombia (50 million), Mexico (130 million), and Brazil (214 million) learn from the experiences of such small nations? Beyond Latin America, what lessons can other large democratic developing nations, including South Africa (60 million), Indonesia (275 million), and India (1.3 billion) draw from smaller democracies where achieving consensus about the need for reform and the content of reform may be exponentially easier, and where coordinating policy responses is an infinitely simpler task? Large countries may also lack the perception of vulnerability that may help generate political consensus for reform in small countries, especially small countries facing threatening neighbors. Many large democracies, furthermore, are federations, which fragment authority and create problems not often examined in the anticorruption literature, including differing regime types and varied patterns of accountability at the subnational level

(Macaulay 2011; Da Ros 2014; Giraudy, Moncada, and Snyder 2019). While our focus throughout the book is on the federal government, we draw attention to the differing performance of a variety of accountability bodies across the federation and the complications this multi-level diversity may present for a large country such as Brazil.

A third reason to focus on Brazil, especially in the wake of the roughly seven-year arc of *Lava Jato,* is that so much of the corruption literature falls into a classic trap of selection on the dependent variable. Scholars have relied predominantly on success stories to develop recipe-style lists of best practices. These include analyses of Nordic nations such as Sweden, Denmark, and Finland (Rothstein 2011; Johnston 2013; Salminen 2013; Rothstein and Teorell 2015; Teorell and Rothstein 2015); Asian countries such as Hong Kong and Singapore (Quah 2010; Manion 2004); and New Zealand (Gregory and Zirker 2013), as well as a relatively heterogeneous group of "contemporary achievers," including Botswana, Chile, Costa Rica, Estonia, Georgia, Qatar, Rwanda, South Korea, Taiwan, and Uruguay (Mungiu-Pippidi and Johnston 2017) and "most improved" nations, including Liberia, Macedonia, Montenegro, and, again, Georgia and Rwanda (Rotberg 2017; Taylor 2018).

Trying to learn from success is a logical first move. There is, however, a fundamental problem with relying on success stories to learn what works in controlling corruption. "Selecting on the dependent variable" means that the examined cases lack significant variation in the outcome of interest, and therefore lead scholars to overestimate the impact of independent variables on the results of interest (King, Keohane, and Verba 1994; Geddes 2003). Said a bit differently, the conclusions of anticorruption research would likely have been somewhat different had the cases been subject to controlled comparisons between successes and failures. A focus on only successful cases may lead to lists of "best practices," "often selected more because they are found in generally successful societies than for specific reasons why they should work in a given setting," and without giving much thought to "why past reforms have faded or failed" (Johnston and Fritzen 2021: 124). There are some notable exceptions to this focus on success such as studies of *Mani Pulite* in Italy (Colazingari and Rose-Ackerman 1998; Della Porta and Vannucci 1997) and anticorruption reforms in Mexico in the early years of this century (Morris 2009). We hope that a case study of Brazilian democracy—which is at best a mixed case, alternating moments of success and others of failure—will at the very least serve to supply empirical data and generate new hypotheses for future cross-national comparative analyses.

The fourth and final reason to focus on Brazil has to do with the pace of reform, which moved at a slow and incremental pace for much of its first thirty years, before accelerating into a big push during the 2010s. Corruption scholars have devoted a great deal of thought to the pace of reform, in part because of the consensus that corruption is a strategic behavior. Because it is strategic—meaning that citizens' behavior is contingent on how they believe others in society will behave in response to their actions—shifting the corruption equilibrium requires collective action that changes the incentives for a majority of citizens. Can enough people's behavior be changed, and remain changed, so as to ensure that the prevailing equilibrium shifts? The question of pace therefore seems central to shifting from a vicious equilibrium "in which high corruption begets high corruption," to a virtuous "low-corruption equilibrium . . . in which corruption's rarity makes it easier to control" (Stephenson 2020: 193; Mungiu-Pippidi 2013; North, Wallis, and Weingast 2009).

Equilibria are by nature difficult to change: if politicians, business executives, and citizens are used to behaving in a particular way, in response to how they think others will act, it may be difficult to change their behavior in the short term. Further, because the corruption equilibrium is collectively determined, there is a constant danger of reversion: even successful reforms may fail to shift the equilibrium and old preferences or behaviors will reassert themselves. Politicians facing particular electoral incentives, such as high interparty competition, may have strong motivations to collect off-books campaign funds; business executives who face a strong regulatory state may "know" that campaign contributions are necessary to obtain favorable state policies; and citizens who believe the game is rigged may decide there is little reason to get involved in policing the ties between politicians and business interests because the likelihood of changing the system is minimal. Under such conditions, even successful one-off interventions, such as a spectacular jail sentence for a politician or the exemplary firing of a top CEO, may not lead to the changes in broader behavior that move a society out of its equilibrium.

Two prescriptions have vied for dominance in response to this challenge. One group advocates a *big bang* or *big push* (we use these terms interchangeably)—that is, a massive anticorruption effort that concentrates efforts in time and space—in a bid to quickly break equilibrium behaviors. The big push approach has broad goals, ambitious scope, and high visibility. Big push approaches often rely on campaigns, which usually have a "D-Day" for enactment, frequently carried out with some element of surprise. The pace is fast and often abrupt, aimed at overturning the status quo through a massive package of ambitious legislative and administrative initiatives. Katherine Bersch (2019: 2) has referred to the prevailing mentality of such reforms as "powering."

The big push approach, it is argued, may be politically effective in overcoming entrenched opposition because it surprises opponents, takes advantage of moments of political ascendancy, and pushes for quick changes in the equilibrium while the status quo is in flux. Big pushes tend to be legitimated by a shift in political winds such as the arrival of a new government after a period of crisis (e.g., war, revolution, or economic upheaval; Rothstein 2011). Perhaps as a consequence of their rarity, when such a window of opportunity opens, big push advocates are impatient, seeking quick returns and operating with an implicitly short time horizon such as midterm elections or the end of the presidential term. One such example comes from Mexico, where a big anticorruption push by Vicente Fox—the first president in seven decades elected from outside the Partido Revolucionario Institucional (Institutional Revolutionary Party, PRI)—adopted, as his first act in office, the creation of an intersecretarial committee that quickly moved to develop and implement a broad-based anticorruption program (Morris 2009, 4). Until recently, the anticorruption literature fell almost entirely into the big push camp, with the common assumption that without a big push, anticorruption reforms would be overwhelmed by perverse incentives that would pull citizens back into the vicious equilibrium.[5]

A second prescription is incrementalism, whereby small gradual gains are built up on top of each other, accumulating into significant change over the long haul. The pace of incrementalism is slow but ongoing, and reforms tend to be implemented bottom up, often without much coordination. There is no single big package of reforms and, oftentimes, even the road map of reform is unclear, with practitioner learning and problem-solving guiding the reform agenda's various small steps (Bersch 2019). The incremental approach tends to proceed with narrow goals, restricted scope, and visibility only in the impacted policy arenas. Incremental approaches may have no time horizon. This is both their most valuable political feature and their greatest potential political flaw. By moving incrementally (which need not be slowly), they bite off small bits of the problem little by little. Often, having no time horizon goes hand in hand with having no clear long-term plan (or a plan that develops only stepwise, over time). Politically, this can be valuable because the ensuing reforms may not put the back up of entrenched interests and thus may not raise concern among the potentially impacted parties about the long-term accumulation of policy losses. It may also become a flaw, of course, because reforms may be uncoordinated, nonstrategic, and untargeted, leading to expensive, wasteful, and undirected efforts that do not aggregate into long-term gains. But by virtue of its smaller focus, incrementalism does have the advantage of taking place below the radar of potential opposition groups, and it may be possible to make incrementalism more strategic through regular review and coordination. Further, incrementalism may ensure that reforms build on each other, taking into account the unintended consequences of previous changes (Lindblom 1959: 86). Ultimately, as a result of their ongoing nature, their capacity to proceed stepwise to address bottlenecks sequentially, and their narrow breadth, incremental reforms may more easily acquire "value and stability" over time—that is, become "institutionalized" (Huntington 1968: 12)—thereby making them harder to reverse in the future.[6] Further, recent work demonstrates that there is no reason to assume that over time, incremental change cannot produce as much of an equilibrium shift as big bang change (Stephenson 2020).

With regard to the pace of reform, Brazil presents a unique case study because its accountability reforms have followed two distinct strategies over time, one incremental and the other a big push. For nearly three decades, from the outset of democracy until the 2010s, the country adopted a piecemeal, gradual, small-bore reform strategy. This strategy, furthermore, did not become "strategic," in the sense of having predefined and mapped out objectives, until the last decade of this period. Beginning in 2014, Brazil's anticorruption efforts underwent a sea change as the task force of the *Lava Jato* investigation, and many of its allies across government and within civil society, rapidly accelerated the pace of anticorruption efforts, an effort that included investigations, prosecutions of a broad range of elites, public mobilization, and even legislative reforms, in a big push for accountability.

Plan of the Book

The rest of the book turns to the meat of the matter: the Brazilian experience. Chapter 2 describes the prevalent syndrome of corruption in the country, which is marked by what Michael Johnston (2005: 43; 2014) has termed "elite cartel" corruption. We examine four prominent cases of grand corruption that took place in the pre–*Lava Jato* era, which, together, justify the use of the term *elite cartel*: this syndrome has found a fertile home in what we term the *perilous combination* of coalitional presidentialism in a hyperfragmented party system, a large state with a developmentalist economic policy infrastructure, and a loose campaign finance system. These cases demonstrate recurring historical patterns of weak accountability, and begin to illustrate how past failures may have contributed to the emergence of *Lava Jato*.

Chapter 3 explains the heuristic model of accountability that we use as a diagnostic tool to evaluate distinct accountability equilibria at various moments in time. We chart Brazil's incremental progress from a fairly low accountability equilibrium toward a much-improved, if still intermediate, equilibrium over the course of three decades between the 1985 transition to democracy and the onset of *Lava Jato* in 2014. We then evaluate the substantial reforms in the accountability policy set that made these improvements possible, and discuss the paradox of reforms that were implemented by the very political elites who stood to suffer most from reforms' effects.

Chapter 4 assesses the big push represented by *Lava Jato*. Given Brazil's persistent bottleneck with elite impunity before the law, what conditions made *Lava Jato* possible? Our account of this historic event focuses on contingent and highly contextual factors, as well as longer-term institutional changes that had incrementally accumulated over the previous three decades in Brazil. We emphasize the various capacities enjoyed by accountability institutions in the country as a whole, and in *Lava Jato*'s headquarters in Curitiba in particular; the legal and political strategies deployed by the task force of prosecutors and investigators to help judicial cases move forward; and the context of severe political gridlock that prevented any credible threat of political interference in the investigations, especially during the operation's crucial first two years. We further highlight how the task force engaged in a big push, which combined not just legal action but a media push, broad public engagement, and a reform effort that sought ambitious changes in the statutory rules governing corruption prosecutions.

By contrast, Chapter 5 is about the unmaking of *Lava Jato* and its broader ramifications for the "web of accountability institutions" that had developed prior to that investigation.[7] Given its magnitude, it is perhaps unsurprising that *Lava Jato* engendered significant reaction once the political system realigned after President Rousseff's 2016 impeachment. Here, we detail the attempts to derail the investigation, as well as the instances in which such attempts succeeded. We describe the frontal reactions, the effects of political realignment and saturation, and the self-inflicted wounds by the investigators. Importantly, we also describe how, beginning in 2016 and continuing under Bolsonaro after 2018, new governing coalitions targeted not only *Lava Jato,* but also diluted or reversed accountability improvements that had accumulated over the previous decades in Brazil, some of them unrelated to *Lava Jato* proper.

Chapter 6 explores the broader cross-national lessons of *Lava Jato.* Here, we examine three findings. First, although judicial independence has long been praised as an antidote to corruption, successful court-led attempts to engender a big push out of low accountability equilibria have been rare. The problem is that such efforts reproduce in a democracy the powering mentality of reforms that historically have succeeded almost exclusively in autocracies: that of the powerful autonomous anticorruption agency. We show that judicial pushes have not prospered in democracies, drawing on the examples of Italy and France in the 1990s and Indonesia since the 2000s. Second, we describe how one of the regrettable by-products of *Lava Jato* seems to have been a reversion to an equilibrium closer to—if somewhat different from—the old status quo ante before *Lava Jato.* The bottom line for corruption reformers elsewhere can be summarized as follows: big push attempts out of low accountability equilibria can easily lead to a perverse effect whereby the end result is worse than the initial condition. Finally, we argue that the big push approach is especially fraught in large democracies such as Brazil. Country size has a variety of effects, including a higher number of veto players, more difficult collective action, and the heterogeneity of corruption and accountability processes. Together, these make the big push approach less likely to succeed. In a large consolidating democracy like Brazil, big push efforts may also threaten the democratic regime by destabilizing the political system without restructuring the underlying incentives of political engagement that prompted the corruption in the first place.

Chapter 7 concludes with the lessons of the book for anticorruption reformers in Brazil and beyond. We home in on two particularly problematic and long-enduring bottlenecks to the accountability process in Brazil: the degree to which collusion between political and economic elites enabled them to push back against accountability policies and reduce the effectiveness of reform; and the weakness of the sanctioning process, which is plagued by recurring patterns of administrative lassitude and judicial inoperancy in grand corruption cases. Together, these two bottlenecks continue to slow Brazil's forward movement, and may even be contributing to regression. This experience provides a variety of lessons for reformers inside and outside of Brazil on the pace, content, and politics of accountability policies.

Notes

1. Many of those implicated in the scandal later returned to politics, including Edison Lobão (who had not been charged) and Geddel Vieira Lima (who was absolved), both of whom later served as ministers in the Dilma Rousseff and Michel Temer presidential administrations, when they were again touched by scandal. One of the congressmen who was expelled by his peers, Chamber president Ibsen Pinheiro, was cleared of wrongdoing by the courts in 2000 and returned to Congress in 2006.

2. Another red flag was that, relying on a 2019 change in the budget law, the amendments comprising the secret budget were proposed by the budget rapporteur, contravening practices in place since the mid-1990s. Albeit legal in principle, the rapporteur's amendment privilege was far less fiscally transparent and readily visible to the public than other ways of amending the budget, and unlike other types of budget amendment, the rapporteur amendments were not equally distributed among members of Congress, so they represented perks from the government to particular legislators (Rey 2021). Adding to suspicions, the volume of rapporteur amendments rose markedly in the 2020 budget, approved when the Bolsonaro administration was under great pressure from Congress for its failure to address the pandemic, at a moment when there were increasing calls for Bolsonaro's impeachment, and at a time when the executive branch feared that its allies would not be elected to lead the Chamber of Deputies and the Senate.

3. *Corruption* is the abuse of entrusted power for private gain, and *public sector corruption* is the abuse or undue use of public office for the same end. Within public sector corruption, we may further distinguish between *grand corruption,* the abuse of high-level power by the few at the expense of the many, and *petty corruption,* whereby individual low-ranking bureaucrats seek private gain in their everyday interactions with citizens. Grand corruption often involves multiple actors acting in concert, and large sums of money; petty corruption typically involves only a few actors, acting individually or in small groups to perform relatively minor abuses. As the next chapter will demonstrate, while there are examples of both types of public sector corruption in Brazil, grand corruption appears to be the larger and more consequential of the two forms. We base our conceptual definitions around Transparency International's (TI) Anticorruption Glossary (https://www.transparency.org/glossary), although we break with TI in using political corruption and grand corruption interchangeably, in part because of the significant overlap between the two terms, as well as the blurriness of the distinctions between corruption committed for political and personal ends.

4. According to Economist Intelligence Unit (2018).

5. Stephenson (2020) cites, as representative of the big push approach, Collier (2006); Rose-Ackerman (1999); Mauro (2004); Rothstein (2011); Fisman and Golden (2017); Aidt (2003); Akerlof (2016); Bardhan (2006); Garri, Peternostro, and Rigolini (2003); Kingston (2008); Sparrow (2008). Recent work by Davis (forthcoming) is also representative of this approach.

6. This debate is also present in the literature on the politics of economic reform, as for example, in the discussions between gradualists (e.g., Dewatripont and Roland 1995) and shock therapists (e.g., Lipton and Sachs 1990). More generally, see Roland (2001).

7. The term "web of accountability," which we use freely, was coined by Mainwaring (2003: 29–30).

2

The Prevailing Elite
Cartel Syndrome

*It is a big fallacy to affirm that there are campaign
donations in Brazil. In truth, they are true loans to be paid
off at high interest rates when [politicians] are in their
posts. No candidate in Brazil is elected by official
donations alone. Declared campaign expenses correspond
on average to one-third of what is effectively spent.
The rest comes from illicit or undeclared resources.*

—Former Petrobras executive Paulo Roberto Costa[1]

*What the PT [Workers' Party] did from an electoral
perspective is what is done systematically in Brazil.*

—President Luiz Inácio Lula da Silva
discussing the *Mensalão,* 2005[2]

What shape has corruption taken in Brazil? The country is somewhat
puzzling because citizen experiences of petty corruption have been
somewhat lower than their regional peers, even as the volume of
high-level corruption scandals seems out of proportion. This pattern
of simultaneously modest petty corruption and shockingly high grand
political corruption closely resembles the syndrome that Michael
Johnston (2005, 2014) called the "elite cartel" syndrome, in which
networks of political and economic elites develop privileged relations that are protected through corruption.[3] The elite cartel perspective on how graft is distributed between grand and petty corruption is
useful as a starting point for understanding the drivers of corruption,
as well as the difficulties of reaching higher levels of integrity.

With regard to petty corruption, Brazil scored slightly better than most of its peers over the past two decades on Transparency International's Corruption Perceptions Index, and aside from spikes after the *Mensalão* and the eruption of the *Lava Jato* scandal, polls have consistently shown that since 1987 fewer than one in ten Brazilians considered corruption the country's most important problem (Da Ros 2019b; Senters, Weitz-Shapiro, and Winters 2019: 17). Petty corruption is not nonexistent, of course.[4] Police are especially distrusted: in a national victimization poll, more than 61 percent of those polled shared the belief that most police are tolerant of corruption by their colleagues (*Extra* 2013), and there are many examples of corrupt behavior by state police forces. But overall, available data suggests that corruption within the lower ranks of the bureaucracy is perceived as less of a problem than that of the political system: V-Dem, for example, scores public sector corruption within the civil service in Brazil as a less significant problem than corruption by the executive or legislative branches (Coppedge et al. 2020).[5] Cross-national surveys suggest petty corruption is better in Brazil than in most neighboring countries, and "whereas scores for grand corruption are only marginally better for Brazil than they are for most countries in South and Latin America, scores for petty corruption place the country among the group of least corrupt nations in the continent, close to Uruguay and Chile, and better than Costa Rica" (Da Ros 2019b: 238; Transparency International 2017).

Yet at the same time, the volume of high-level corruption scandals and the estimated costs of corruption are enormous. Fully four-fifths of Brazilians polled in 2017 saw the political system as the primary cause of corruption (Ipsos 2017). A 2012 study from the Federation of Industries of the State of São Paulo (FIESP) estimated corruption's cost at 1.38 percent to 2.3 percent of gross domestic product (GDP) (FIESP 2010). This estimate predates the emergence of the *Lava Jato* case, in which defendants estimated the routine cost of bribes at 3 percent of contracts by state-owned enterprises (SOEs) (PGR 2017). It is generally thought, meanwhile, that the SOEs involved in *Lava Jato* were less corrupt than many state and municipal governments, which suggests that the true cost of corruption nationwide may be significantly higher than previous estimates suggested.[6]

Cross-national expert surveys by Yuen Yuen Ang (2020) show a similar pattern, consistent with the elite cartel syndrome. Ang measures perceptions of corruption along two dimensions: elite or nonelite;

theft or exchange. This generates four categories of corruption: petty theft (nonelite, theft); speed money (nonelite, exchanges); grand theft (elite, theft); and access money (elite, exchanges).[7] Ang's surveys of experts across fifteen countries demonstrate that Brazil ranks particularly poorly with regard to the elite forms of corruption: sixth worst in terms of grand theft, with a score 9 percent worse than the sample average; and fifth worst on access money, with a score 14 percent worse than the sample average.[8] This is particularly intriguing because Brazil scores well on petty theft and speed money, placing just behind the advanced developed economies in the sample.

This chapter analyzes the roots of the particular Brazilian variant of the elite cartel syndrome, which is useful for understanding the challenges the country has faced in diminishing corruption. We begin by describing the perilous combination of factors that often seem to jointly contribute to patterns of grand corruption. Then, we analyze four high-profile corruption scandals that offer a window into how the perilous combination has played out over the past two decades. Finally, we take a step back to look at overall patterns of grand corruption, emphasizing ties between politicians, businesspeople, civil servants, and money launderers; recurrent patterns of elite impunity; the high levels of wrongdoing visible among members of all political parties; and the collusive behavior between political elites that have made accountability holding unlikely.

The Perilous Combination

At its core, the syndrome of an elite cartel, in Johnston's (2005) words, or elite forms of corruption such as grand theft and access money, per Ang (2020), have been reinforced in postauthoritarian Brazil by the combination of coalitional presidentialism in a highly fragmented party system, a large developmental state with oligopolistic and intricately intertwined firm structures, and a loosely regulated and opaque yet highly concentrated campaign finance system. This is not to say that any of these factors on their own is determinative of corruption, only that their interaction helps to explain the prevailing modalities of corruption over the past generation. Similarly, this does not mean that other forms of corruption do not exist in Brazil—they obviously do. The elite cartel forms of corruption, however, have been the most prevalent form since redemocratization in the 1980s.[9] Each of these enabling factors merits a brief definition:

- *Coalitional presidentialism* is the "strategy of directly elected minority presidents to build stable majority support in fragmented legislatures, specifically via the coordination of two or more legislative parties by the president" (Chaisty, Cheeseman, and Power 2018: 14). Central to understanding the logic of coalitional presidentialism is the fact that no president's party since 1989 in Brazil has held more than one-fifth of congressional seats; minority presidents must thus seek out a relatively large number of coalition partners and entice them to join a governing coalition using a variety of stratagems (Mainwaring, Power, and Bizzarro 2017). The country has been governed by coalitional presidentialism since the return to democracy in 1985: the system helps to resolve the unique challenges posed by a presidential system mixed with an extremely and increasingly fragmented multiparty legislature and federalism (Abranches 1988, 2018).
- The *developmental state* refers to the idea that the state can serve as an engine of long-term development, by consciously altering investment conditions, tackling market failures, and addressing coordination problems (Haggard 2018; Taylor 2020). The ties between the "state" and the "market" have long been stronger in Brazil than in many of its neighbors, and policymakers deviated significantly from the Washington Consensus of the 1990s, despite a series of reforms (Montero 2014: 100). The developmental state that was inherited from the authoritarian regime has persisted over time at a significant scale: the state consumes more than 10 percent of real GDP per capita in Brazil, by contrast to just over 4 percent in Chile, with a unique institutional combination of a state development bank, a strong state presence in business and finance, five large SOEs that are among the largest companies in the Brazilian economy, and a form of networked capitalism built around state participation and influence in a variety of ostensibly private sector firms (Musacchio and Lazzarini 2014; Lazzarini 2010; Taylor 2020).[10]
- *Campaign finance* in Brazil is governed by a complex set of institutions, including both electoral courts and criminal statutes. But its contribution to the syndrome of corruption is perhaps driven less by these institutions than by the emergent effects of electoral rules that drive party fragmentation, increase the costs of electoral campaigns, and complicate enforcement of campaign finance laws. For most of the examined period, both private

individuals and businesses could make contributions to candidates that were not limited in amount, but were restricted as a proportion of an individual's income or a company's revenue, respectively. This led to an extreme concentration of donors, whereby a few hundred wealthy individuals and large companies with close relations to the government were responsible for the largest share of campaign contributions (Mancuso 2015; Mancuso and Speck 2015; Carazza 2018). Significant portions of these donations were irregular, unregistered with electoral officials, and known by the term *caixa dois,* a so-called second register, referring to the fact that they came from a second, off-the-books, illicit source.

Again, none of these factors on their own is sufficient to explain Brazilian corruption, and it is difficult to prove that the relationship between the three factors is causal rather than simply correlational (Limongi and Figueiredo 2017: 81). For example, neither a developmental state nor a large state is necessarily a predictor of corruption, as Japan and Norway demonstrate; nor is a proportionally small state necessarily a bulwark against corruption, as Mexico and even Chile in their recent scandals have demonstrated (Gerring and Thacker 2005; Persson and Rothstein 2015). Coalitional presidentialism exists in a variety of other countries, and does not always and everywhere lead to the types of scandals seen in recent Brazilian history. Some of them, such as Uruguay, in fact, have had greater success in keeping corruption in check. Expensive political campaigns, likewise, need not lead to corruption per se. In short, in isolation these three factors do not explain corruption, but together they may lead to a perilous combination by generating a series of overlapping incentives for actors in, or close to, the political system.

Among these incentives, the rules governing the Brazilian electoral system play a fundamental role by contributing to significant party fragmentation. The effective number of political parties represented in Congress has increased from 7.1 in 1998 to 13.2 in 2014, and to 16.4 in 2018, the last two being the first- and second-highest scores ever recorded globally (M. A. Melo 2016; Gallagher 2017).[11] Increasing fragmentation has been driven by open list proportional representation (OLPR) electoral rules in large and high-magnitude districts;[12] by the possibility of multiparty electoral coalitions, which benefit small parties; by the ready availability of public campaign funding for parties, which incentivizes party formation; by a high court decision overturning performance thresholds for parties; and by a judicial ban on party switching, except to found new political parties (Samuels 2001; Ames 1995; Marchetti 2008; Marchetti and Cortez 2009).

Because there are so many candidates and representatives per district, the costs to voters of monitoring and punishing corrupt elected representatives are steep (Kunicová and Rose-Ackerman 2005; Tavits 2007). In the electoral realm, voters are only weakly connected to politicians. The information that voters can compile about candidates is fragmented and sparse (Ames, Baker, and Rennó 2008). Studies show that fewer than one-fifth of voters are able to correctly place parties on an ideological scale (Carreirão 2007; Montero 2014: 91). And even though most voters claim in the abstract to wish to punish corrupt politicians, in practice they fail to do so when given the chance (Boas, Hidalgo, and Melo 2019).

Furthermore, large numbers of candidates induce intraparty competition and lead to political campaigns that are highly individualized and extremely costly (Ames 2001). As a result, most political parties in Brazil "are catch-all or cartel organizations that work primarily to ensure access to the resources they consider vital to their survival, most of which reside in the federal bureaucracy" (Da Ros 2019b: 244; Krause, Rebello, and da Silva 2015).

While elections are generally perceived to be transparent and clean, overseen by technically proficient electoral courts, the same cannot be said for the supervision of campaign finance.[13] Contributions are highly concentrated in a few donors: in the 2010 elections, the contributions of the fifteen largest donors accounted for roughly a third of all contributions (Mancuso 2015); in 2014, 33 wealthy individuals and 450 companies accounted for three-fourths of all contributions for both presidential and congressional elections (Carazza 2018: 47). Business sectors that are more oligopolistic and conduct business with the government are more likely to donate more (Taylor 2020; Carazza 2018; Mancuso 2015; Mancuso and Speck 2015). And there has been little effective action by the electoral courts to curtail off-the-books contributions by firms seeking political favors: much electoral corruption appears to be less the result of a desire to skirt official campaign donation rules (since these are in fact quite lenient), but instead an effort to make contributions using money that has been acquired illicitly.

The combination of many candidates for office with a highly concentrated set of donors leads to adverse selection: the candidates who do best in this realm either obtain access to generous contributors, or are willing to resort to illegal campaign finance, or both (Da Ros 2019a; Reis 2013; Kang 2002). Recent scandals suggest that at least as much has been spent off the books—via *caixa dois*—in electoral campaigns as has been spent on the official electoral court registers. One particularly brash corporate donor, Odebrecht, admitted to an 8:1 ratio of illicit to licit campaign spending over a decade and a half. Off-the-books financing responds to a different set of demands than on-the-books contributions; it tends to lead to more particularistic access to government services and policymakers, in a self-reinforcing cycle. Based only on on-the-books donations, Taylor C. Boas, F. Daniel Hidalgo, and Neal P. Richardson (2014) found that firms that specialized in contracts with the federal administration received at least fourteen times in contracts what they contributed to the election of winning incumbents in Congress. Perversely, access to generous donors may be pivotal for politicians' survival even in the face of corruption accusations. Scholars have found, notably, that "campaign spending attenuates the negative effect of corruption scandals on politician's electoral success," so that "over a certain threshold of campaign spending, incumbents involved in scandals can still win elections" (Jucá, Melo, and Rennó 2016: 3, 5). If campaign finance helps to overcome the possibility of electoral sanctions for wrongdoing, wrongdoers are more likely to remain in the system, heightening the challenges for an already overburdened judiciary.[14]

Although corporations were banned from making corporate campaign donations as of the 2016 elections, this is unlikely to significantly change the overall incentives in the system since individuals can still legally contribute up to 2 percent of their income each year, and little has been done to curb illegal *caixa dois* donations. Indeed, a long tradition of defective regulatory enforcement has fostered the emergence of cultures of collective deviance at major firms such as Odebrecht, institutionalizing corruption, rationalizing its use, and socializing informal rules and informal interpretations about how and when corruption could be legitimate (Valarini and Pohlmann 2019: 10). Off-the-books campaign finance is a classic example of this problem: because "everyone does it," campaign finance violations are seen as somehow less problematic than other corruption violations. Under these conditions, it seems unlikely that banning legal corporate contributions will, by itself, change the practice of funneling illegal contributions outside the formal channels.

Since 1990, the president's party has never held more than a fifth of seats in the lower house, forcing the chief executive to build a multiparty coalition to pass any legislation (Mainwaring, Power, and Bizzarro 2017). The largest party in Congress in 2019, the Workers' Party (PT), had only 53 out of the 513 available seats, slightly over 10 percent. The increasing fragmentation of the party system has forced most presidents to rely on oversized coalitions that, in many cases, are quite unstable. Even though they have increased over time, coalitions have typically incorporated nearly six parties for most of the past two decades, and have lasted, on average, approximately one year before being restructured (Carreirão 2014; Da Ros 2019b; A. dos Santos Almeida 2018). Ideology has declined as the organizing principle of the party system since the early 2000s and, therefore, as the central principle guiding the coalitions that presidents have been able to cobble together (Zucco 2009; Lucas and Samuels 2010; Carreirão 2014; Da Ros 2019b). The corollary is that, over the past decades, political parties mushroomed within an increasingly less ideological political spectrum, suggesting that most were motivated predominantly by the perks of office. Unsurprisingly, most of the massive party switching that occurred in Brazil since redemocratization was from parties that did not hold any positions in the cabinet toward those that did (C. R. Melo 2004).

The toolkit of coalitional presidentialism provides a central organizing logic to this fissiparous system, including the formal institutional powers of the presidency (e.g., decree powers) and also the powers of the purse and of appointment (Chaisty, Cheeseman, and Power 2018). It has long been the case that legislators were able to exchange legislative votes for a wide range of pork-denominated currencies in negotiations with an executive dependent on unstable and shifting coalitions (Geddes and Ribeiro Neto 1992; Chaisty, Cheeseman, and Power 2018). One way to do so has been through horse-trading over all manner of appointments in the federal bureaucracy, as well as in state-owned enterprises such as Petrobras and the Banco do Brasil. The numbers of political appointees are high by international standards, with roughly 22,000 potential appointees in the federal government, and 14,000 in the state of São Paulo alone (Portal da Transparência Estadual 2016). Of the federal slots, approximately 1,200 federal appointees are freely nominated by the president, with few required technical qualifications, and the president has great influence over the remaining appointments. Even when they are not political appointees, furthermore, senior civil servants may need *padrinhos* (political sponsors) if they are to prosper in their careers. Consequently, the distribution of positions to allies within the federal administration and the numerous state-owned enterprises plays a key role in the formation of the governing coalition (Amorim Neto 2002; Lopez, Bugarin, and Bugarin 2014; Lopez and Praça 2015). Needless to say, probity is not necessarily high on the list of priorities for many of these appointees, especially when considering how best to repay debts to their "generous" political benefactors. Meanwhile, the scope of potential budgetary resources made available by the developmental state apparatus is ample: a single Petrobras directorate involved in the *Lava Jato* case alone had a budget larger than nineteen of the twenty-seven cabinet ministries at the time (Dallagnol 2017a: 112).

Historical Cases of Grand Corruption in Brazil

Throughout the contemporary democratic era, corruption scandals have been a recurring theme of political life across all presidential administrations, without exception (Power and Taylor 2011: 2). They have been driven to a great extent by the perilous combination of weakly regulated campaign finance, the large and complex developmental state, and the extremely fragmented coalitional presidential system described in the previous section. The prominent scandals of the 1990s, 2000s, and 2010s share many attributes, including not only the same patterns but also, amazingly and infuriatingly, many of the same actors (Fleischer 1997; Carazza 2018; Praça 2011, 2013). Exemplifying this pattern during the past three decades are a variety of scandals, including the *PC Farias* scandal that led to President Fernando Collor de Mello's 1992 impeachment; the budget scandal of 1993; the reelection scandal of 1997; the *Mensalão* scandal of 2005; and the *Sanguessugas* scandal of 2006. These and other scandals involving the executive and legislative branches are described in the Appendix.

Indeed, given their steady recurrence, many of these scandals may be thought of simply as windows into one long, continuous process of state appropriation by corrupt actors. Likewise, many of the resulting accountability efforts resemble a single investigation that, over time, connects more pieces of the puzzle of grand corruption, linking various facts, individuals, organizations, and patterns of behavior. These patterns of corruption have recurred despite a multiplicity of reforms described in the next chapter. With a few exceptions, all these scandals also share another common trait: the absence of accountability before the courts (Taylor 2011; Da Ros 2019b).

Below, we analyze four major cases launched by the Federal Police before the *Lava Jato* case, with the goal of demonstrating how grand corruption functions in elite cartel fashion, the manner by which the perilous combination plays out, and how these patterns have replicated themselves over time in the absence of credible accountability. We chose these four cases—*Banestado, Mensalão, Satiagraha,* and *Castelo de Areia*[15]—for further analysis for four interrelated reasons.

First, they illustrate the multiple ties between state-owned enterprises, political elites, money launderers, and the private sector described above, highlighting that the interactions between political and economic elites revealed in *Lava Jato* were hardly unique to that case. Quite the contrary. As a matter of fact, with a few exceptions, all these cases had similar potential to lead to the sanctions eventually enforced by *Lava Jato,* even though they ultimately fell short. They are, in this sense, largely negative cases that help us understand how and why *Lava Jato* was such an exception to the rule when it began to enforce sanctions. These cases thus serve as control cases and help us avoid the problem of selecting on the dependent variable of success, while also beginning to understand the causes of *Lava Jato*'s relative initial success.

Second and related, these scandals help to illustrate the enormous hurdles to imposing legal sanctions for wrongdoing in Brazil, as well as the lessons—legal and otherwise—that accountability agencies such as the police and the federal prosecutors' office have learned over the course of the past two decades.[16]

Third, all these cases have either led to or resulted from criminal investigations. The existence of a criminal investigation provides greater detail about corruption, with more concrete details on the individuals, organizations, and practices that have structured corrupt practices. However, it may also lead to an inevitable temporal bias that readers should be aware of. As these cases and the ones in the Appendix highlight, Brazil seems to have increasingly transitioned from "political" to "police" corruption scandals over the past three decades. The locus of investigations and the sanctions imposed shifted increasingly from Congress to the criminal justice system (including the police, prosecutors' offices, and the courts). That is, scandals have resulted increasingly from the workings—quite literally—of "police patrols" and decreasingly from the efforts to set off "fire alarms" through congressional oversight. Similarly, sanctions increasingly moved to the judicial arena. This evolution of the locus of accountability draws attention to the empowerment of legal accountability agencies over the past decades in Brazil, described in Chapter 3, as well as to the decreasing control political elites seem to have had over the onset, pace, and consequences of most political scandals, at least for a time. Once pivotal in the 1980s and 1990s, congressional investigations have grown less important since the mid-2000s, and increasingly appear to be used to sidetrack the efforts of legal accountability agencies. Attempts to limit investigations have kept pace, moving away from efforts to influence Congress and, instead, toward efforts to influence the high courts and prosecutors, control the appointment of the prosecutor-general, and influence the Ministry of Justice, which oversees the Federal Police. Our case selection reflects and captures these important changes in accountability in Brazil over the past three decades.

Fourth, the cases below also embody an important, if frequently unheralded, change in the patterns of legal accountability that emerged in Brazil over the late 1990s and early 2000s. Although the patterns of political corruption have remained quite similar since the José Sarney presidency in the 1980s, the manner by which corruption has been confronted by legal actors has changed qualitatively, especially after passage of the 1998 Anti–Money Laundering Law, which generated increased institutional capacity within the judicial system, with the emergence of specialized courts, prosecutorial task forces, and investigations of financial crimes. As Chapter 3 highlights, legal accountability in Brazil evolved from tackling corruption proper to targeting the gains from corruption through the enforcement of money laundering laws. This strategy was referred to as the "financial asphyxiation" of criminal organizations (Secretaria Nacional de Justiça 2012: 20). Our first case is the *Banestado* case, which marks the first step in this significant transformation of the accountability process.

Banestado

On the face of it, the *Banestado* case was a simple case of money laundering by illegal foreign exchange traders known colloquially as *doleiros*. *Doleiros* are some of the many *malandros* (rascals or rogues) that make up the folkloric tapestry of the Brazilian underworld (DaMatta 1979), and, for many years, especially in the hyperinflationary period, they played a central and often necessary function in the economy by facilitating foreign exchange transactions. With passage of the new Anti–Money Laundering Law in 1998, many hitherto borderline activities became clearly illicit, and federal law enforcement agencies were given new tools to target *doleiros* and their offshore activities. The *Banestado* case was a first major step toward dismantling these *doleiro* networks, demonstrating the scale of their offshore activities and the degree to which seemingly reputable firms and politicians were using offshore accounts. It was also an early exemplar of the use of illicit funds and murky channels by politicians and business executives, as well as a case on which many leading law enforcement authorities first cut their teeth.

At the core of the *Banestado* case was the finding that enormous volumes of money were being sent abroad to offshore bank accounts, via a then legal channel known as the CC-5 account. The so-called CC-5 accounts were named after the Central Bank regulation that established them in 1969, Carta Circular 5 (CC-5). Reference to the massive amounts being transferred through these accounts became public as early as 1997 in a congressional committee of investigation (*CPI dos Precatórios*), but it took two other such congressional inquiries (*CPI dos Bancos* in 1999 and, ultimately, *CPI do Banestado* in 2003) for this black box to be more clearly ventilated.[17] The 2003 congressional investigation suggested that over US$130 billion had been sent through CC-5 accounts during the period 1996–2002, including US$20 billion through the Banco do Estado do Paraná (known as Banestado), which was owned until October 2000 by the Paraná state government, and then was privatized.

CC-5 accounts were created so that foreign residents of Brazil could move currency into and out of the country at a time when foreign exchange operations were highly regulated, but the government needed foreign investment.[18] More than half of the transfers from 1996 to 2002, however, may have been illegal funds resulting from money laundering or tax evasion, often processed through the accounts of unwitting third parties, known colloquially as *laranjas* (Beirangê 2015). Money sent through the CC-5 ended up in many remote locations, including Switzerland, France, Italy, the Isle of Man, and the Cayman Islands. One money launderer—Alberto Youssef—admitted in a 2004 plea bargain to having paid bribes to the director of international operations at Banestado to facilitate US$5 billion in offshore transactions (Gois 2014). Youssef would reappear in later scandals, first as a suspected facilitator of illicit payments in the *Mensalão* case, and then as a crucial piece in the giant *Lava Jato* puzzle (Justiça Federal 2014).[19]

Perhaps the most important outcome of *Banestado* was that congressional investigators forced the Central Bank to reveal more than

400,000 transactions that had been made via CC-5 accounts between 1996 and 2002, overcoming judicial protections of bank secrecy. These revelations tore back an enormous veil. Although nobody could clearly discern which transfers were legal and which involved illegal funds or illegal transfers, CC-5 account holders were found to include major media groups (TV Globo, RBS, Grupo Abril, SBT); banks (e.g., Banco Araucária, owned by a prominent political family, the Bornhausens); retailers (including Brazil's largest, Casas Bahia); and construction firms (including Odebrecht, Andrade Gutierrez, OAS, Queiroz Galvão, and Camargo Corrêa). Furthermore, the CC-5 accounts linked up to a variety of offshore accounts that police alleged were tied to more than 100 political figures, among whom the most frequently cited were Partido da Social Democracia Brasileira (PSDB) treasurer Ricardo Sérgio de Oliveira; Senators José Serra (PSDB–São Paulo), Jorge Bornhausen (Partido da Frente Liberal [PFL]–Santa Catarina), and Ney Suassuna (Movimento Democrático Brasileiro [MDB]–Paraíba); Governor Jaime Lerner (PFL-Paraná); Mayors Celso Pitta (Partido Trabalhista Brasileiro [PTB]–São Paulo) and Paulo Maluf (Partido Progressista [PP]–São Paulo); and Deputies José Janene (PP-Paraná) and Wigberto Tartuce (PP–Distrito Federal) (*Istoé Dinheiro* 2003; Justiça Federal 2014; *O Estado de S. Paulo* 2003; Silveira 2004; *Consultor Jurídico* 2004).

Of all the revelations in the course of the investigation, one of the most explosive was that Senator Bornhausen's family bank, Banco Araucária, was serving as a conduit for transferring money abroad to Banestado's offices in New York, and that Bornhausen and his brother were the offshore beneficiaries of multiple transfers from other offshore accounts. These revelations led the Central Bank to close down Banco Araucária in March 2001. Even before these allegations emerged, the relationship between Bornhausen's PFL party and President Fernando Henrique Cardoso's PSDB had begun to fray, but the Araucária revelations placed enormous additional stress on a coalition that was already in dire straits as the end of Cardoso's second term approached. The PFL, which hitherto had been a faithful supporter of Cardoso's reforms, began to block key votes in Congress. As quickly as it could, the Federal Police called back its investigators from New York, and shut down the investigation. If there was any doubt about the message that was being sent, the police forensic accountant who had done the most to investigate the CC-5 accounts was transferred to the automobile registration department, where he spent his days on the floor of the Federal Police garage, verifying the chassis numbers under the bottoms of cars (R. Valente 2013: 119–130).

The *Banestado* case is a classic example of the murkiness of scandal in a country with weak accountability institutions and a collusive elite. It produced great smoke and even some fire, but the 2003 congressional investigation at the heart of the case failed to produce a final public report due to internal discord between the committee president and the committee's rapporteur. Additionally, Rubens Valente (2013: 137) suggests that the opposition Workers' Party may also have been less active than it otherwise might have been in pushing the congressional inquiry because it threatened to expose irregularities committed by the party in the municipality of Santo André.

In the judiciary, the results were not much more promising than they had been in Congress. However, several prosecutorial innovations proved important in the case, and were emulated in later cases. In 2003, the Ministério Público Federal (MPF) founded one of the— if not *the*—very first task forces ever to be established in a grand corruption case, and one that would become an actual case study in task force manuals produced by the Brazilian federal prosecutors' office (Paludo 2011: 91–114). The task force's investigations, led by federal prosecutors Carlos Fernando Lima and Vladimir Aras (who would later become key players in *Lava Jato*), resulted in several additional investigations. These include *Operação Farol da Colina* in 2004, which arrested dozens of individuals in seven Brazilian states, and other follow-up investigations of the money trail lasting until September 2007, when the task force was dissolved (Paludo 2011: 112).[20] *Banestado* also marked the first time a plea bargain agreement was signed in a corruption investigation in Brazil. The 2004 plea was signed precisely with *doleiro* Alberto Youssef, who, as noted above, would become a recurring figure in various subsequent scandals.

The so-called CC-5 task force led to the filing of more than 680 charges, resulting in 97 convictions for money laundering offenses (MPF 2017). Still, only relatively small fish were netted, predominantly *doleiros* and other financial operators (I. Lopes 2014). Furthermore, despite the relatively large number of convictions, only thirteen individuals were actually jailed after conviction, due to the lenient rules governing the statute of limitations on money laundering crimes (Dallagnol 2017a: 24–25). Partly because of the murkiness of the facts, partly because investigators—both congressmen and prosecutors—did not push energetically for accountability, *Banestado* offered only an early hint of how the illicit links between politics and business worked in Brazil. None of the political figures alleged to have been involved in the case were ever convicted. Further, on the basis of the convictions obtained, it was impossible to make many claims about the veracity of alleged links between businessmen and politicians.

Nonetheless, because it was one of the first major demonstrations of the extent to which massive volumes of money were being moved out of the country, because some of the prosecutors and judges would later become key players in the *Lava Jato* investigations,[21] because some of the criminals netted by the operation were also netted in later scandals, and because the case demonstrated the difficulty of overcoming a bias toward impunity, *Banestado* was a significant watershed in a movement toward improved accountability. Even though the case did not lead to much engagement by the public and the media, the authorities involved learned many useful lessons, such as the importance of creating multiagency task forces in complex investigations, building institutional capacity to ensure effective cross-agency cooperation, the need for international cooperation in investigating financial crimes, and the need for improved criminal statutes such as clearer rules on plea bargaining and lengthier *prescrição de penas* (roughly, statutes of limitation) in corruption cases.

Mensalão

Although it seems quaint in retrospect, the *Mensalão* scandal was a historical milestone, irrefutably demonstrating the dark operational underbelly of coalitional presidentialism, including the transactional nature of relations between politicians and business executives in the pursuit of campaign funds. It also was important because it broke a precedent of presumed impunity for high-ranking political and business figures, twenty-five of whom were sent to jail beginning in 2013. The scandal was relatively small in terms of the numbers of federal politicians involved: fifteen, two of whom were subsequently absolved on the basis of insufficient evidence. But the convictions confirmed that long-standing rumors of scandalous political behavior were not just a figment of the public imagination. This was perhaps an underappreciated contribution in a setting where widespread allegations were seldom verified.

The case first began to emerge in March 2005, when a businessman working with the state-owned Correios postal service filmed himself paying a small bribe to a postal appointee. The appointee happened to be the political "godson" of Congressman Roberto Jefferson, president of the PTB, a recurrent junior partner in various government coalitions since 1988, including the coalition of President Luiz Inácio Lula da Silva when the scandal emerged.[22] Feeling that he had been abandoned to the baying hounds of the press corps by the administration of Luiz Inácio Lula da Silva, in early June Jefferson blew open the case in a bombastic interview to the *Folha de S. Paulo* newspaper. Jefferson admitted that several political parties (including his own) were receiving regular bribes, which he dubbed a *mensalão* (large monthly allowance), directly from PT party treasurer Delúbio Soares and businessman Marcos Valério. According to a subsequent congressional inquiry (*CPI dos Correios*[23]), the payments were made between 2003 and the beginning of 2005, and were used to pay off parties that had joined the government coalition, to bribe individual deputies who switched parties, and to buy votes on specific legislation (UOL Notícias 2012). Prosecutors would later note that, in the ten days prior to important congressional votes, large amounts of cash were withdrawn from suspect accounts (MPF 2013; Montambeault and Ducatenzeiler 2014).

The practice, however, was hardly new, nor was it a novelty introduced by the PT. Cases of direct payouts to politicians to advance important votes in Congress had been cited in the press earlier, as in the reelection scandal of 1997, when congressmen allegedly received cash to vote in favor of the constitutional amendment that allowed President Cardoso—and everyone in an executive office since then—to run for reelection. Likewise, some of the same actors who played central roles in *Mensalão* had also appeared earlier in the so-called *Mensalão Tucano,* a scandal that erupted when the governor of Minas Gerais, Eduardo Azeredo, of Cardoso's PSDB, was accused of receiving illegal campaign contributions for his reelection run in 1998. In fact, in the indictment, the prosecutor-general argued that the "*modus operandi* of the criminal facts investigated [in the *Mensalão*] had its origin in the campaign . . . for State Governor of the State of Minas Gerais in the year of 1998" (PGR 2007: 4).

The incumbent PT used the money from illicit campaign contributions to pay off debts incurred by the party and by its coalition partners. Subsequent testimony by PT campaign publicist Duda Mendonça noted that he alone had received more than R$10 million[24] in an offshore account in the Bahamas. Most damaging to the Lula administration, Jefferson—a raconteur whose colorful tales engaged the public's attention—alleged that he had spoken with Lula and several ministers about the payments. The president's chief of staff, José

Dirceu, was forced to resign, and was replaced by Dilma Rousseff, a change with lasting historical reverberations.

Prosecutors filed charges in August 2007, in what would become the landmark *Ação Penal* 470, decided by the Supreme Federal Tribunal (STF) six years later, in late 2013. Prosecutors demonstrated that the Lula administration had paid bribes to members of Congress to ensure they remained in the governing coalition. Dirceu was convicted of having worked with Marcos Valério, the owner of two advertising agencies, to launder money: businesspeople would falsely contract Valério's firms to provide services; Valério would pass these illegal contributions on to the PT, including via foreign accounts, and then he would obtain loans from the BMG, Banco Rural, and the Banco do Brasil to cover his financial tracks (Galli 2007). Most remarkably, several bigwigs in the PT—including party president José Genoíno, secretary general Sílvio Pereira, and treasurer Delúbio Soares—were found to have cosigned the fraudulent bank loan documents, contributing to their subsequent convictions on racketeering, corruption, and money laundering charges. Also convicted were several bank executives, Valério's partners and staff, and another eight members of Congress in addition to Genoíno and Dirceu.[25]

Investigations concluded that the public sector was a key source of the illegal campaign funds, which either came out of state-owned enterprises or took advantage of state shareholdings in private sector firms. Visanet, a private sector clearing system for credit cards, made payments of R$74 million at the behest of state-owned Banco do Brasil (which controlled 32 percent of Visanet's shares). Valério's firms won rich public sector contracts from the postal service and the Chamber of Deputies, the latter controlled by Chamber president João Paulo Cunha (PT-SP), who was convicted for receiving R$50,000 in bribes for his efforts. The congressional inquiry raised questions about contracts between Valério and the Labor Ministry, the Sports Ministry, the Federal University of Rio Grande do Sul, and state-owned Eletronorte and Instituto de Resseguros Brasil (IRB), but ultimately did not press forward on any further action against those state entities.[26] Investigations also found suspect private sector contracts: payments by Usiminas and Cosipa, for example; and payments of more than R$150 million by Telemig and Amazônia Celular, controlled by prominent banker Daniel Dantas's Opportunity bank (CPMI 2006: 582–751; Valente 2013: 199). The congressional inquiry recommended further investigation of Usiminas and Cosipa (CPMI 2006: 654), and that Dantas be indicted for influence trafficking, tax evasion, and corruption (CPMI 2006: 654), but prosecutors ultimately decided not to pursue either trail.[27]

The *Mensalão* case was a watershed for a number of reasons. It contributed to eroding the otherwise quite compelling image of the PT as an outsider in the political establishment. Contrary to the image it projected of itself until then, the PT had not behaved very differently from other political parties with regard to campaign finance or the management of its governing coalition (Assunção 2014). Perhaps because it seemed such a shift from the PT's original hopeful promise, the party's fall from grace was a political drama that kept the public engaged for various years, ultimately peaking in the *Lava Jato* case. The prison terms meted out to politicians and business executives, similarly, were a remarkable break from past tolerance of elite wrongdoing (Michener and Pereira 2016). Equally important was the enhanced role of the courts, and the STF in particular: televised coverage of the supreme court hearings was played daily around the country. The public was introduced to a new and complex legal vocabulary—*dosimetria da pena, embargos declaratórios, embargos infringentes*—and STF justices became more recognizable than many politicians. Although the case dragged on for an eternity, with final judgment only in late 2013, the *Mensalão* trial offered the hopeful promise of a new era of legal accountability. It also provided concrete evidence of the complex interplay within the perilous combination of coalitional presidentialism, the developmental state, and campaign finance.

Satiagraha

Operation *Satiagraha* was a natural outgrowth of the *Mensalão* scandal, as police investigators followed the trail of the money used in that case, and particularly, money from the two telephone companies—Telemig and Amazônia Celular—that had placed large contracts with Marcos Valério's firms. After four years of investigation, *Satiagraha* hit home in a big way, with the July 2008 arrests of two important businessmen, Naji Nahas and Daniel Dantas, on accusations of corruption, fraud, and tax evasion. Dantas's Opportunity bank, which controlled the two telephone companies, was alleged to have used offshore accounts to make corrupt payments, while Nahas was alleged to have laundered money out of the country.

Dantas and Nahas were major players on either side of a major business conflict that had arisen out of the privatizations of the 1990s. Dantas's Opportunity had played a big role in the privatizations, participating in the purchase of mining giant Vale, as well as energy producer CEMIG (Companhia Energética de Minas Gerais). This helped bring Dantas to the attention of Citibank, and Opportunity would later partner with Citibank, Telecom Italia, and the pension funds of various state-owned enterprises to buy Tele Centro Sul, the regional phone company that became known as Brasil Telecom. Dantas also emerged from the privatizations with partial ownership of Telemig Celular, Amazônia Celular, a sanitation company known as Sanepar, and the company administering Brazil's largest port, Santos Brasil. By 2000, however, he was in open battle with his partners in many of these ventures: Telecom Italia in Brasil Telecom, the Canadian firm TIW in Telemig Celular, and the pension funds of state-owned companies, which had holdings in all three phone companies: Brasil Telecom, Telemig, and Amazonia Celular.

Over the course of the next few years, Dantas's resentment against what he saw as the political manipulation of the pension funds against his interests led to a range of bizarre and allegedly illicit actions that spanned the public and private sectors. Brasil Telecom—which Dantas ultimately controlled through Opportunity[28]—hired Kroll, a US investigative company. Kroll allegedly tapped the phone lines of numerous executives at Telecom Italia, as well as government officials, in an operation that went public in a banner headline at the *Folha de S. Paulo* in 2004, leading to a police investigation (Operation *Chacal*) that was litigated in both US and Brazilian courts (Aith 2004). One of the targets of the wiretaps was Naji Nahas, who was hired by Telecom Italia to negotiate with Dantas. Both Dantas and Nahas were simultaneously working channels in Brasília in an effort to influence the pension funds, the Banco do Brasil, and the telecom regulatory body, Anatel. Kroll allegedly tapped the phones of the communications minister Luiz Gushiken and Banco do Brasil president Cassio Casseb, at least in part because in 2003 they had pushed the pension funds of five state-owned companies who were shareholders in Brasil Telecom to change the shareholder agreements that gave Dantas de facto control of the company (Aith 2004).[29]

In 2004, citing the reputational risks of continuing to work with Dantas, Citibank broke off its relationship with Opportunity. Yet despite a series of escalating wiretaps and hacking scandals between Brasil Telecom and Telecom Italia, in April 2005 the two companies reached an agreement, and in 2007 the state pension funds bought out Telecom Italia's shares in Brasil Telecom.

Dantas then attempted to sell Brasil Telecom to Oi,[30] which would have created a monopoly that violated much of the regulatory legislation governing the telecom market. By this point, Dantas was locked in a serious dispute with the pension funds. In an effort to influence the government on regulatory matters and in the dispute with the pension funds, Dantas hired a former PT congressman, Luiz Eduardo Greenhalgh (UOL Notícias 2009).[31] Greenhalgh, a trusted longtime lawyer for the PT, was helped along by a mysterious figure referred to by Dantas (caught on police wiretaps) as the "Architect." The Federal Police concluded this was João Vaccari Neto, PT party treasurer. By 2008, the obstacles to a deal with Oi had been overcome: President Lula issued a decree that permitted the previously prohibited purchase of one telephone company by another, Anatel withdrew its objections, and the BNDES (Banco Nacional de Desenvolvimento Econômico e Social) and Banco do Brasil provided financing for the deal. Oi paid R$5.8 billion for Brasil Telecom, creating a huge national monopoly worth R$29 billion (R. Valente 2013: 140–325).

The questionable tactics used by Dantas, Opportunity, Brasil Telecom, and its partners helped to convince police and prosecutors to deepen their investigations, and provided them with evidence later used against Dantas. In 2007, as a consequence of the *Mensalão* investigations, prosecutors received permission to search Opportunity's corporate server. Although they did not find information related to the *Mensalão,* they did find evidence of financial crimes (Michael 2008). These included the possibility that residents of Brazil were shareholders in the Opportunity Fund in the Cayman Islands, which was not permitted by law, and could lead to criminal penalties if these shareholders had participated in the privatization process. Simultaneously, word of the *Satiagraha* investigation had leaked out, and Dantas allegedly asked one of his former executives to try to neutralize the federal police investigations. The executive hired a fixer, who met with Federal Police agents and, in a sting, was recorded offering a bribe to quash the operation (R. Valente 2013: 281).

Fearing further interference in the investigation, police and prosecutors moved to arrest the alleged wrongdoers. In an unprecedented scene, former São Paulo mayor Celso Pitta was filmed as he was dragged off to jail in handcuffs and pajamas. Dantas and Nahas were each arrested at home, filmed in their handcuffs as they were thrust in the back of police SUVs.

These scenes shocked justices on the high court, members of Congress from various parties (including the opposition PSDB), and the defendants' attorneys, who complained of the "spectacularization" of crime fighting (Coelho 2013: 170). In what would become a landmark case, the chief justice of the STF, Gilmar Mendes, twice overturned decisions by trial court judge Fausto Martin De Sanctis that jailed Dantas, sparking public debate between lawyers supportive of Mendes and judges and prosecutors supportive of De Sanctis (Milício 2008). Dantas was first arrested on the morning of July 9, 2008. Mendes ordered him released from prison at 11:30 P.M. that night, and he left prison at 5:30 A.M. on July 10. At 2:30 P.M. on that day, he was arrested a second time under orders from De Sanctis, who justified his decision on the basis of new evidence that had been acquired by later search warrants. The move angered Mendes, who again ordered Dantas to be released from jail and allegedly moved to punish De Sanctis, sending copies of his decision to the Corregedoria (internal affairs) of the National Council of Justice and the regional appeals court that sat above De Sanctis's trial court, recommending an investigation into the judge's behavior for having disrespected a high court decision (Coelho 2013: 193).

Mendes's request to investigate De Sanctis sparked a wave of controversy and resulted in one of the most profound crises to date between lower and higher courts (Da Ros 2013). Over the following days, De Sanctis received public expressions of support from more than 100 of his colleagues, from judges on the regional appeals court, from federal prosecutors, and from various legal associations, many of whom explicitly criticized Mendes for having suggested inquiries into De Sanctis's behavior and for his decisions to release Dantas twice (Coelho 2013: 193–196). As senior prosecutor Douglas Fischer noted on a popular legal blog, Dantas's lawyers had requested habeas protection against the investigation and their motions had been rejected in the third regional appeals court (TRF3), in the Supreme Tribunal of Justice (STJ), and in the STF. When Dantas was placed under temporary arrest, on the basis of newly collected evidence, his lawyers jumped the judicial hierarchy and went straight to the STF with their habeas request, where the injunction of a single justice, Gilmar Mendes, saved Dantas from prison time. Fischer noted that this was reminiscent of George Orwell's *Animal Farm,* where "all animals are equal, but some animals are more equal than others" (Fischer 2008). In November 2008, justices at the STF coalesced around the chief justice's earlier decision and decided in a 9–1 vote to confirm Mendes's injunction, highlighting the alleged "disrespect" of the STF by De Sanctis's second decision to imprison Dantas (Coelho 2013: 200; R. Valente 2013: 375).

Brazilians have a slang phrase, *acabou em pizza* ("it ended up in pizza"), to describe a process that gets so gummed up that it goes nowhere. Despite having collected thirty-nine volumes of police evidence over four years, the *Satiagraha* case is perhaps the epitome of ending up in pizza, with so many dramatic story lines leading to stalemate that it is hard even to know where to assign blame (Matsuura 2009). The Federal Police concluded their final report on the case in April 2009, in no uncertain terms: "We are facing an organized criminal group . . . [whose] leader is Daniel Valente Dantas" (R. Valente 2013: 389). The Justice Ministry blocked more than US$2 billion in accounts linked to the case, primarily in the United States (*Consultor Jurídico* 2009). Yet the Federal Police agent heading the investigation, Protógenes Queiroz, was himself investigated on orders of Justice Minister Tarso Genro, and hastily transferred away from investigative work and into the police academy. Queiroz successfully ran for Congress for the Partido Comunista do Brasil (PC do B) in 2010, but then lost in 2014 and fled to Switzerland in 2015 after the STF upheld his conviction on charges of violating secrecy provisions during the *Satiagraha* case. Along the way, Queiroz lobbed accusations that Dantas had paid off the prosecutor-general, Roberto Gurgel, and his wife (Canário 2014a). Dantas responded with a libel suit; meanwhile, Dantas was charged with bribing another Federal Police agent and sentenced by De Sanctis to ten years in jail and a R$12 million fine (*Consultor Jurídico* 2008).

Dantas pushed back hard on his accusers, targeting journalists with lawsuits seeking damages, and subjecting judges to disciplinary suits. Judge Fausto De Sanctis faced twenty disciplinary hearings in the National Judicial Council (CNJ) at the request of Dantas's lawyers, and, although these hearings subsequently cleared De Sanctis of any wrongdoing, they were a costly distraction (Konchinski 2016). STF Justice Mendes was criticized for his close links to Dantas's lawyers: his wife worked in the office of one prominent Dantas lawyer, Sérgio Bermudes, and records emerged of out-of-session meetings between Mendes and Dantas's counsel (R. Valente 2013: 362–368). Adding drama, Mendes alleged that his office had been wiretapped, and, although these allegations were never substantiated, they led to histrionic headlines and several high-level meetings between Mendes and the executive branch (Beirangê 2015). Meanwhile, Mendes reached an agreement with Chamber president Michel Temer, Senate president José Sarney, and President Lula to propose legislation limiting wiretaps and the so-called abuse of authority (R. Valente 2013: 380–382).

In light of the many twists and turns in the case, it was not terribly far off plot when a panel of the STJ, Brazil's second-highest court, annulled the case in 2011. In a decision that was later upheld by the STF, a judge on the STJ, Arnaldo Esteves Lima, argued that the evidence in the case had been illegally transcribed, and therefore was inadmissible (*O Globo* 2017b). The fact that investigators had enlisted the help of members of Brazil's intelligence agency, the Agência Brasileira de Inteligência (ABIN), to assist with transcription without proper prior authorization nullified the evidence (Canário 2014b). The Federal Police admitted that seventy-five agents from the ABIN had joined the investigation over the space of four months, but because they had not participated in wiretapping or conducting police investigations, neither police nor lower court judges overseeing the case had believed there was anything untoward about their cooperation (De Sanctis 2017).[32]

There were at least four important outcomes of the case. First, it resulted in greater constraints on police operations. Perhaps because of the difficulty of obtaining any kind of judicial sanction of corruption, police had been turning to the media to publicly televise arrests, and to impose a second-best reputational sanction on alleged wrongdoers (Arantes 2011). Even though public engagement was surely not as prominent as it had been in the *Mensalão* case, it played an important role. A mounting public backlash against media coverage of police actions coincided with a series of complaints about how filming handcuffed defendants deprived them of the presumption of innocence (Coelho 2013).[33] Police overreach, such as threats to arrest members of the press and erroneous apprehensions, contributed to the backlash (*Consultor Jurídico* 2008; Coelho 2013; Marona and Barbosa 2018).

Second, the high court made it clear that it would set a high bar for prosecutors and police to effectively demonstrate money laundering, and that any prosecutions were subject to reversal by a hostile high court (*Consultor Jurídico* 2010). Even when well substantiated, allegations of bribery, such as those against Dantas—who allegedly conspired with his firm's executives to bribe federal agents—would be insufficient to justify incarceration without convincing proof of direct involvement by the defendant. Senior judges signaled that they would uphold strict evidentiary standards: for example, the high courts invalidated evidence collected on a hard drive at Opportunity's headquarters, alleging that, because the search warrant was for the third floor and the drive was found on the twenty-eighth floor, the evidence on the drive was improperly seized (L. Borges 2014). Although Judge De Sanctis issued a new warrant in that case, the high courts then found that because the ABIN had been involved in transcribing the wiretaps, the evidence was tainted, and the "fruit of the poisonous tree" argument ultimately led to the case being thrown out (De Sanctis 2017). All of the evidence collected over the course of several years was discarded; a special appeal of this decision by the prosecutor-general was rejected on procedural grounds by the STF in 2012. *Satiagraha* was a stark lesson on the limits of judicial tolerance for certain police investigatory practices, as well as the high bar set for successful prosecution of elites. As Judge De Sanctis said soon after the case concluded, "It seems that soon we will ask defendants for permission to convict them" (R. Valente 2013: 436).

Third, and more positively, the case contributed to carving out a principle of wide publicity of court decisions and legal evidence. Many elements of the case were made public, albeit with small exceptions such as evidence obtained when bank and tax secrecy provisions were temporarily lifted by a judge (Matsuura 2009). Such publicity was a significant change after decades in which the principle of judicial secrecy was often invoked by powerful defendants. Greater transparency increased public pressure on the courts. At the end of the day, though, *Satiagraha* proved yet again the difficulty of effectively tackling corruption in a capricious judicial system that seemed designed to protect political and economic elites.

Fourth, in retrospect, *Satiagraha* marked another qualitative turning point in accountability dynamics. Institutional capacity at the federal level had been steadily increasing since the late 1990s and early 2000s, particularly within the Federal Police, but its efforts had predominantly targeted state and local political elites up until *Satiagraha* (Arantes 2011). *Satiagraha* in many ways marks the end of a pattern of national scandals initiated by political elites or the media. Most scandals until then had been the by-product of a breakdown in negotiations within the governing coalition in Congress (e.g., Balán 2011). Both *Banestado* and *Mensalão,* for instance, started with congressional investigations and only subsequently moved to legal accountability agencies. *Satiagraha* was one of the first instances where accountability agencies like the Federal Police took the first shot at tackling grand corruption at the federal level. The timing, pace, and content of anticorruption efforts since *Satiagraha* have increasingly changed hands from the political elite to accountability bureaucrats. Fire alarms have been replaced by police patrols. This transition generated more uncertainty about the political dynamics of corruption scandals. It perhaps should not come as a surprise, then, that *Satiagraha* also led to significant backlash from the political, legal, and media establishments.

Castelo de Areia

The *Castelo de Areia* (Sandcastle) operation began in 2008, and by 2009 had uncovered evidence of alleged payments by executives at the Camargo Corrêa construction firm to politicians. In many ways, this case served as a direct precursor to *Lava Jato,* providing an inkling of the links between construction companies and politicians, as well as of the use of offshore firms to camouflage transactions. As *Lava Jato* prosecutor Deltan Dallagnol suggested years later, if *Castelo de Areia* had not been dismissed on procedural grounds at the high courts, the *Castelo de Areia* case might well have developed into an investigation on the scale of *Lava Jato* (W. Nunes and Bächtold 2017).

Four Camargo Corrêa executives were arrested and placed in preventive detention in March 2009. Drawing on data collected by Brazil's financial intelligence unit (Conselho de Controle de Atividades Financeiras, COAF), prosecutors led by Karen Louise Jeanette Kahn filed charges against three Camargo Corrêa executives and four *doleiros* for financial crimes and procurement fraud.[34] As in *Satiagraha,* the case was overseen by trial judge Fausto De Sanctis, in São Paulo. The investigation raised suspicions about a possible cartel among construction firms in big public works and of collusion between Camargo Corrêa and its ostensible competitor Andrade Gutierrez, although these allegations were never prosecuted (*Consultor Jurídico* 2009c). Also significant was the discovery of possible overpricing in several major construction projects, including the Abreu e Lima oil refinery—an early hint of a possible link between major construction firms and state-owned oil company Petrobras (*Consultor Jurídico* 2009b).

Prosecutors found that a Uruguayan firm was used to move money out of the country to banks in Switzerland, Germany, Israel, and the Cayman Islands (*Consultor Jurídico* 2009b). Kurt Paul Pickel, a Swiss-Brazilian businessman who had been accused by an anonymous tipster of illicit foreign exchange transactions, was overheard on police wiretaps plotting payments with Camargo Corrêa executive Pietro Giavina Bianchi. Pen drives seized from company executives listed politicians who had received bribes, using animals' names as code to hide their true identities (Justiça Federal 2009: 5; W. Nunes and Bächtold 2017).

Although the executives would admit to making contributions to some parties, and although emails were found with discussion of contributions to other parties, these contributions were never prosecuted, and it is not clear whether the contributions were made through licit or illicit channels (*O Globo* 2009).[35] Meanwhile, the Tribunal de Contas da União (the federal accounting tribunal, TCU), which should have investigated any bid rigging, came under a cloud of suspicion when the son of one of its ministers was alleged to be Camargo Corrêa's fixer in Brasília: FIESP director Luiz Henrique

Maia Bezerra, son of former senator and TCU minister Valmir Campelo Bezerra, was mentioned in the wiretaps as Camargo Corrêa's intermediary on campaign donations (Éboli 2009; Justiça Federal 2009). Further clouding the picture, a list of politicians found at the home of one Camargo Corrêa executive included members of the TCU (*Consultor Jurídico* 2009b).

Pushback against the operation was immediate. A group of senior politicians, mostly from the opposition—PSDB president Sérgio Guerra, Democratas[36] (DEM) president Rodrigo Maia, Partido Popular Socialista[37] (PPS) president Roberto Freire, and DEM Senator José Agripino Maia, whose name had emerged in the case because of campaign contributions from Camargo Corrêa—met with the president of the STJ, Cesar Asfor Rocha, to request that the Federal Police be subjected to external control. The politicians complained of the excessive "exposure" of defendants by the police, and the political nature of the investigations, echoing much of the criticism in *Satiagraha* (*Consultor Jurídico* 2009d).

The entire operation was shut down in January 2010 by an injunction from Asfor Rocha, in response to habeas corpus petitions by defense lawyer Antônio Cláudio Mariz de Oliveira (Haidar 2011). Trial court judge De Sanctis was well aware of the high court's skepticism of the evidence, and spent several pages of his decision explaining why society's freedom from organized crime and crimes against the financial system needed to be balanced against the defendants' rights to privacy. He emphasized that the techniques used by the police were in accordance with those permitted under various international treaties, as well as with previous STF jurisprudence (Justiça Federal 2009: 32–35). But after lengthy debate, a panel of judges on the second-highest court, the STJ, voted unanimously against De Sanctis's decision, arguing that he should not have authorized wiretaps on the basis of an anonymous tip. While many legal systems find similar problems with basing a case around anonymous tips, what was unique here was the decision to throw out all of the associated case materials rather than simply the tainted evidence. With that, all of the criminal cases associated with the operation were annulled (Beirangê 2015).

In 2011, trial court judge De Sanctis was promoted to the regional appeals court. At the last moment, however, he was shuffled from the court's criminal appeals chamber, where his experience would be most relevant, to the chamber dealing with pension cases (De Sanctis 2017). This upward promotion—and the surprise transfer to a pension court—was widely interpreted in legal circles as an effort to muzzle, and then punish, De Sanctis. More recently, in 2019, former STJ judge Asfor Rocha (now retired) was targeted by investigators in the *Lava Jato* case for his earlier decisions annulling *Castelo de Areia*. This investigation was driven by a plea bargain agreement signed by former finance minister Antonio Palocci, who alleged that Asfor Rocha received payments abroad for his decision (J. Marques 2019; Ortega and Macedo 2019). The investigation against Asfor Rocha was suspended in May 2021. Whether or not his decision was corrupt, *Castelo de Areia* reaffirmed the empathy of the highest courts for members of the political and economic elite. It also showed that allegations of corruption cut across the party system, as well as across all branches of government in Brasília.

Patterns of Wrongdoing in the Political Arena

The cases above demonstrate several common characteristics. As Matthew M. Taylor (2020: 150–151) notes with regard to *Lava Jato,* the cases found ample evidence of cooperation between four types of actors who, in principle, should have little legitimate reason to cooperate: politicians; prominent private sector businessmen; public employees at state-owned firms and civil servants within the federal bureaucracy; and a variety of shady external operators, who made the schemes function, whether by helping to launder payments within Brazil, by making offshore payments, or by negotiating bribes on behalf of private sector firms.

Second, punishment was almost always meted out only to the operators, *doleiros,* and fixers in the scheme. Political elites remained above the fray. The calculus about who was likely to be punished has changed over time: perhaps because of the experience of significant jail sentences for operators in the *Mensalão* case such as Marcos Valério, *doleiros* like Alberto Youssef moved to cooperate more quickly in *Lava Jato,* leading to the unprecedented arrest and incarceration of many business executives in that case. With few exceptions, however, legal accountability has not reached economic and political elites involved in these scandals.

These scandals also had many repeat actors, appearing across widely different cases, as data from Taylor (2020), further elaborated on here, demonstrates. Brazil had 1,499 discrete federal officeholders between the 2002 and 2014 elections, holding 2,349 distinct electoral slots in the Chamber, Senate, and state gubernatorial mansions, as well as ministerial postings in the presidential cabinet.[38] While the slow pace of the courts and the high degree of impunity means that data on judicial convictions is almost nonexistent, we use a proxy for criminality compiled by Taylor (2020) in legal cases that have been brought against these officeholders.[39] Figure 2.1 demonstrates this proxy measure of criminality for these nearly 1,500 officeholders, grouped by party size within the universe of officeholders.

Although false claims against politicians, of course, are possible, the proxy is a realistic if imperfect indicator of criminal behavior, in part because the relative strength of defamation provisions and the relative power of officeholders vis-à-vis police and prosecutors suggest that charges brought haphazardly would likely lead to significant costs. The criminality indicator in Figure 2.1 illustrates that of the nearly 1,500 politicians in office during this period, 28 percent faced an investigation or indictment in federal courts for any type of crime, including crimes as varied as tax evasion and homicide.[40] The corruption indicator in Figure 2.1 refers to the proportion of officials from each party who were allegedly implicated in five major corruption cases: any one of the four cases discussed in this chapter and the *Lava Jato* case. Nearly 13 percent of the politicians in the sample are being investigated or have been indicted on criminal grounds in any one of these five cases (and some were implicated in more than one of these five cases).

There are at least three implications of the data in Figure 2.1 regarding the likelihood that politicians will move to curb corruption or improve accountability.

First, the ubiquity of wrongdoing. Criminality and corruption appear to significantly affect all political parties, with roughly three of every ten politicians under suspicion, meaning that the pattern is likely not a case of a few bad apples, but rather a systemic one. Political corruption at the federal level follows a logic closely attuned to the perilous combination between loose campaign finance enforcement, coalitional presidentialism, and a developmental state with vast and diversified resources. As the epigraphs on the opening page of this chapter illustrate, democracy has not done away with avarice, but it has brought a particularly pernicious form of systemic corruption: campaign finance abuse, on a large scale and with the intention of tilting the playing field in favor of incumbents. The willingness of clean politicians to fight corruption may be undercut by the fact that intercoalitional financial transfers can be significant, so calling out wrongdoing by coalition allies may undermine a candidate's own sources of campaign finance. Worse yet, even clean politicians could end up accused of having received illegal contributions, as these are

Figure 2.1 **Federal Politicians Investigated or Indicted for Corruption or Criminality, 2002–2016 (in percent)**

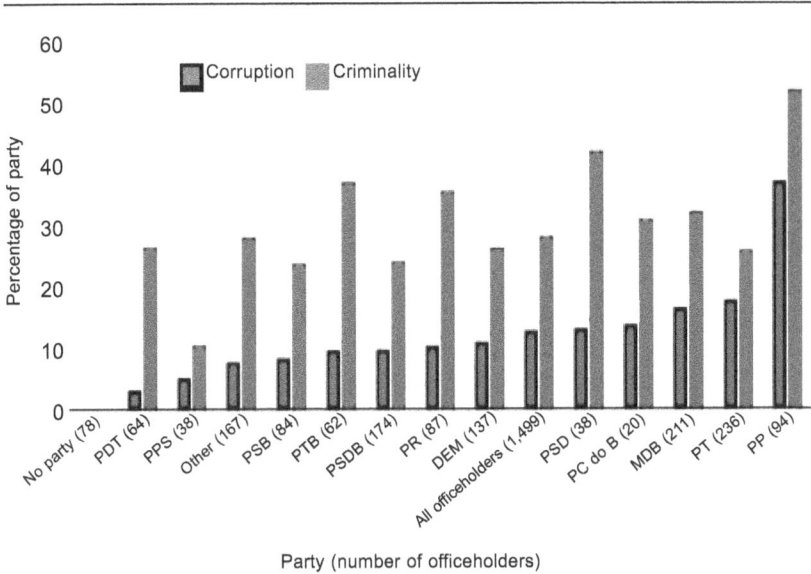

Party (number of officeholders)

Sources: Compiled by the authors; Taylor (2020: 150–151).
Notes: PR includes members of the former Liberal Party (PL) and Partido da Reedificação da Ordem Nacional (PRONA); DEM includes PFL; Partido Progressista (PP) includes Partido Progressista Brasileiro (PPB). Party is the last party identification claimed by the politician at election time, up through the 2014 elections.

frequently transferred among candidates and the party directorates within the same party or electoral coalition, further diminishing the incentives for sounding the alarm. The normalization of illegality means that there is little incentive to fight corruption, and many otherwise clean politicians adopt a passive free-rider strategy, rather than stepping into the arduous task of corralling a coalition to combat corruption. On the flip side, a rational but corrupt politician knows that acting opportunistically to break up the network would mean forgoing future returns from years of past exchanges, and that the risk of detection and punishment is minimal, in any case.

Second, the weakness of opposition parties as anticorruption enforcers. Although politicians in the incumbent Workers' Party coalition had a slightly higher propensity of being implicated, parties such as the PSDB and DEM who were in opposition for all of the years in this period, 2002–2016, also had relatively high levels of politicians implicated in corruption cases (10 and 11 percent, respectively), which may have altered their incentives to push for robust anti-corruption efforts. As the *Banestado* case illustrates, when the PT was in opposition, it may have been more passive than it otherwise might have been because it feared the investigation could reach its municipal administrations; similarly, the PSDB may have been more acquiescent during the Lula and Rousseff years because several of its most prominent members were potential targets in cases such as *Satiagraha* and *Castelo de Areia*. Likewise, because most scandals touched on political parties that served as coalition partners to *both* the PT and the PSDB, these presidential parties were possibly unwilling to dig deeper into the cases that could damage their shared allies. This weak mutual oversight often carried over into accountability institutions, such as Congress and the TCU accounting tribunal, where parties and their nominees often worked together to avoid public oversight or sanction, rather than competing to increase accountability. Said another way, politicians appear to have reached a tacit agreement to compete electorally, but collude corruptly: politicians are aware of their peers' wrongdoing, but remain mum for fear of upsetting the apple cart. This leads to an unusual form of political dominance: rather than one-party rule, à la Communist China or Mexico under the PRI, Brazil faces multiparty collusion, at least when it comes to political corruption. We return to this point in the next chapter.

Third, the incredible weakness of the accountability process for politicians further undermines the likelihood that politicians will act against their colleagues. Of the 423 officials who were under investigation or indictment, as of 2015, only 16 had been convicted, and only 8 (one-half of 1 percent of all officials) actually served jail time (Bretas 2015). These figures align with other studies: for example, Luciano Da Ros and Matthew M. Taylor (2019) found that fewer than 6 percent of criminal cases in the high court were decided against criminal defendants and fewer than 1 percent led to conviction. Somewhere between 10 and 13 percent of criminal cases heard in the STF are tossed out due to the statute of limitations; another 10 percent have led to absolution (J. Falcão et al. 2017; Gomes Neto and Carvalho 2021). The remainder of cases largely linger. Convictions, even of the most partial sort, are reached in only 3 percent of cases (Gomes Neto and Carvalho 2021). Pivotal here is the impact of the original jurisdiction of the high courts—known alternately as the *foro por prerrogativa de função, foro privilegiado,* or *foro especial*—whereby federal officeholders can be prosecuted for their crimes only before the STF. This is a form of protection from prosecution whose specific rules have carefully been recalibrated to preserve political elites, in ways discussed in the next chapter.

With this logic in mind, then, the natural next question is, What changed in the 2000s to upset the applecart? Why did so many corruption cases begin to emerge, with such destabilizing effect? The answer lies less with the democratic political process proper—elections, or checks and balances between the elected branches—than with the manner in which democracy empowered the bureaucratic agencies charged with tackling corruption. Bureaucratic capacity, in other words, expanded enormously over the past generation in Brazil. In the next chapter, we look at how the accountability system works, its flaws and shortcomings, and how improvements over a generation of reform transformed the treatment of corruption.

Notes

1. Netto (2016: 64). Here and throughout the book, all translations are by the authors.

2. *Folha de S. Paulo* 2005.

3. Johnston (2005) discusses four syndromes of corruption that encapsulate most country experiences: influence markets, common to advanced democracies, where abuses "revolve around specific outcomes" (5); elite cartels, where networks of political and economic elites are able to form "cartels" that are defended through corruption; "oligarchs and clans" in fragile states, where personal networks are more important than institutions; and "official moguls" in nondemocratic regimes, where a few individuals can act with almost complete impunity.

4. Indeed, we both have personal experience of petty corruption by police and fixers at the motor vehicles department, and there are regular tales of avarice by bureaucrats of all types.

5. The comparison is made possible by rescaling three variables from V-Dem: public sector corruption; executive corruption index; and legislature corrupt activities. The rescaled scores on a 0–1 scale are, respectively, 0.31; 0.52; and 0.94.

6. Our focus here is on the federal level. All indications are that corruption at the state and municipal levels is probably much worse (Da Ros 2014; Macaulay 2011; Senters, Weitz-Shapiro, and Winters 2019; C. Ferraz and Finan 2011). In his plea bargain in *Lava Jato,* for example, former Transpetro CEO Sérgio Machado noted that the "political cost" of bribes was 3 percent at the federal level, 5 to 10 percent at the state level, and 10 to 30 percent at the municipal level (Dallagnol 2017a: 49).

7. *Petty theft* is when "street-level bureaucrats privately pocket illegal fees"; *speed money* is payments made to speed up public services or to avoid penalties; *grand theft* is when "top officials illegally siphon public funds," "create ghost payroll," or "collude to embezzle funds"; and *access money* is when "businesses directly pay massive bribes for deals" (Y. Y. Ang 2020: 28).

8. The survey was conducted in 2017 and 2018. The fifteen countries include countries from low-income (Bangladesh, Ghana, India, Indonesia, Nigeria),

middle-income (Brazil, China, Russia, South Africa, Thailand), and high-income groups (Japan, Singapore, South Korea, Taiwan, and the United States).

9. Likewise, this does not imply that corruption did not exist prior to the return of democracy in Brazil. Quite the opposite: corruption involving construction companies abounded during the previous military regime (Campos 2014). The fundamental difference is that corruption has now come to light.

10. From a conceptual standpoint, it is worth noting that the central issue with regard to corruption is not government size, but instead the role that the government is being asked to play, and the manner by which that role can be co-opted by specific actors such as firms and business leaders.

11. The effective number of parliamentary parties is an index of party fragmentation adjusted by taking into account the number of representatives per party (Laakso and Taagepera 1979).

12. On the difficulties posed by open list proportional representation with regard to corruption see, for example, Chang (2005). As Treisman (2007: 23) notes, however, the effect of electoral systems is not yet conclusively established: "Although the effects might exist, the evidence for them is fragile."

13. Brazil does quite well in the Institute for Democracy and Electoral Assistance (IDEA) political finance regulation database (Casas-Zamora 2016). But enforcement is another matter (Sadek 1995; Fleischer and Barreto 2009; Speck 2012). It is also worth noting that although the voting process is generally quite transparent, in some districts there are still opportunities for political machines to monitor voter choices (Praça 2018: 22).

14. The system in some ways is even more perverse because election to office means that politicians are afforded the original jurisdiction of the Supreme Federal Tribunal. One indication of the reality of this perverse system is that it is not all that unusual, for example, for a senator accused of wrongdoing to drop out of the Senate race and instead run for the Chamber of Deputies, which typically requires fewer votes (e.g., Aécio Neves of the PSDB and Gleisi Hoffman of the PT in the 2018 election). Running for the Chamber rather than the Senate permits the politician to maintain a foothold in Congress and preferential treatment in the high court at a much lower cost.

15. The names of these cases are shorthand, drawn from the names used by either judicial officials, police, or the press. As such, the names often refer to investigations and indictments across a range of different courts, rather than a single case file.

16. We may be reasonably criticized for at least two reasons: for analyzing only high-profile cases, and for analyzing cases in which the absence of convictions means that no definitive truth has been established. The problem of analyzing only the cases under the proverbial lamppost is a recurring one for corruption researchers. Yet there are few convincing ways to resolve this problem, and, in the Brazilian case, the problem is further exacerbated by the fact that because of judicial inoperancy and the practical impunity it facilitates, even the cases directly under the lamppost are often only vaguely illuminated. We do not have a magic wand to wave at this problem and we therefore accept the criticism, use the cases that have been best illuminated, and move on. The problem of using cases that may never lead to conviction is also a difficult one. Failure to convict could be a consequence of false accusations or faulty evidence. But in contemporary Brazil, failure to convict is just as likely an outcome of judicial inoperancy. For this reason, we caution against drawing conclusions here about legal culpability, and we have been careful to cite only information that is already in the public record. But these corruption scandals nonetheless enable us

to paint—using a potentially incomplete and imperfect empirical database of allegations, evidence, indictments, and, in rare cases, convictions—the links between a critical mass of allegedly corrupt practices and the political system. Ultimately, it is worth remembering that prosecution and conviction rates "are as likely to reflect the zeal, competence, and integrity of the police and judiciary, or the political priority placed on fighting corruption, as they are to capture the true scale of the phenomenon" (Treisman 2007: 216).

17. A congressional investigation (*CPI dos Precatórios* of 1997) led to the discovery that nearly all illicit funds in that investigation were being funneled out of the country either through banks in Foz do Iguaçú or through CC-5 accounts (Senado Federal 1997: 159–161). Later, in 1999, an investigation into CC-5 accounts enabled a federal prosecutor, Celso Três, to obtain access to the account ownership information (Valente 2013: 119–120). Interestingly, the investigation—which took place in the city of Cascavel, state of Paraná—was overseen by Sérgio Moro in one of his first positions as a federal judge. That year, another congressional inquiry by the Brazilian Senate (*CPI dos Bancos*) revealed investigations by the Receita Federal (Federal Revenue Service) involving 413 individuals and 345 businesses concerning possible fiscal irregularities in CC-5 accounts amounting to R$14.5 billion between 1996 and 1998 (Senado Federal 1999: 520).

18. The CC-5 regulation has been regularly rewritten various times, with a general trend since the 1990s toward tightening use of such accounts. The CC-5 accounts were eventually abolished in 2005 (Wolffenbüttel 2007).

19. Youssef was believed to be the true owner of the Bônus-Banval trading company, which was used to make payments to Pedro Henry (PP-MT), Pedro Corrêa (PP-PE), and José Janene (PP-PR) in the *Mensalão* case (Gois 2014).

20. Other investigations led by the task force included *Zero Absoluto* (2004), *Ilha da Fantasia* (2005), *TNT* (2005), *Hawala* (2006), *Pôr do Sol* (2006), and *Zapata* (2006).

21. Four of the six prosecutors on *Banestado,* Judge Sérgio Moro, and some federal police officers participated in both cases (Dallagnol 2017a: 69). Federal Police officer Érika Marena worked on the CC-5 task force starting in 2006 (Paludo 2011: 112).

22. Apart from the Lula administration, the PTB was also a member of the governing coalition during the Collor, Cardoso, and Temer administrations (Amorim Neto 2019). More recently, the party allied itself with President Bolsonaro (Bragon 2020).

23. This CPI recommended the *cassação* (expulsion) of eighteen deputies, but only three were removed by Congress: Dirceu (who had returned to his legislative seat after resigning from the presidential cabinet), Jefferson (PTB-RJ), and Pedro Corrêa (PP-PE) (*R7 Notícias* 2009; BBC Brasil 2013; CPMI 2006).

24. Here and throughout, R$ refers to the Brazilian currency, the real, which has been in circulation since 1994. In the year the *Mensalão* emerged, the exchange rate oscillated between R$2.2 and R$2.75 to the US dollar.

25. Bispo Rodrigues (PL-RJ), Pedro Corrêa (PP-PE), Pedro Henry (PP-MT), Roberto Jefferson (PTB-RJ), Romeu Queiroz (PTB-MG), Valdemar Costa Neto (PR-SP), João Paulo Cunha (PT-SP), José Genoino (PT-SP), José Borba (MDB-PR), and José Dirceu (PT-SP). José Janene (PP) died before his case went to trial.

26. The inquiry was headed by Senator Delcídio Amaral, who was later jailed in the *Lava Jato* case.

27. Perhaps most remarkable from the perspective of the logistics of the corruption revealed by the *Mensalão* scandal was the fact that the Federal Police

found more than 80,000 false tax receipts at Valério's offices, including some that were used to bill services to Visanet, Eletronorte, and the Labor Ministry.

28. Officially, as R. Valente (2013: 242) points out, Dantas did not own any bank, but, through family members and trusted executives, he was the controlling figure at Opportunity.

29. The pension funds were Sistel, Telos, Funcef, Petros, and Previ.

30. Oi, a private company, was created out of the former state company Telemar.

31. Greenhalgh was suspected by police of being the link between Dantas and corrupt legislators, but they did not find enough evidence to convince a judge to authorize his arrest.

32. ABIN was headed at the time by Paulo Lacerda, who had been the director general of the Federal Police until 2006 and would be forced to resign from ABIN in 2008 following the events of *Satiagraha* (L. Souza 2008).

33. By the time of the *Lava Jato* investigation, police and judges were extremely cautious about using handcuffs. Judge Moro rebuked the Federal Police when they handcuffed former Rio governor Sérgio Cabral as he was being transferred to prison, and he issued a specific order to police prohibiting handcuffs when former president Lula was conveyed to prison.

34. *Doleiros:* Kurt Paul Pickel, Maristela Brunet, José Diney Matos, and Jadair Fernandes de Almeida. Executives: Pietro Francesco Giavina Bianchi, Dárcio Brunato, and Fernando Dias Gomes.

35. The PT, PTB, and PV were alleged to have received legal contributions, and the PSDB, DEM, PPS, PP, PSB, PDT, and MDB were alleged to have received illegal payments.

36. The PFL changed its name to Democratas in 2007.

37. In 2019, the PPS changed its name to Cidadania.

38. Because the Senate is elected on a one-third then two-thirds rotation, the database of officeholders also includes senators elected in 1998, but serving the second half of their eight-year terms as of 2002. Although they are not, strictly speaking, federal officeholders, governors frequently cycle in and out of federal office and the presidential cabinet, and play an important role in policymaking, so they are included here. *Suplentes* are not included. There is considerable movement in and out of the cabinet, which can expand and contract at the president's whim, but all ministers who served more than a provisional role are included.

39. This database was created by combing through dozens of media reports on indictments and allegations, as well as the high court website. This has a precedent in the study of corruption in the United States: databases on criminal convictions for corruption based on annual reports by the US Department of Justice, Public Integrity Section, have been widely used in research in the United States as proxies for corruption, particularly at the subnational level (Alt and Lassen 2014; Gradel and Simpson 2015). Of course, any such proxy may be imperfect and can be criticized for its aggregate and often imprecise nature (Cordis and Milyo 2016). But in the absence of more compelling data, this proxy serves as an indirect measure of the extent of the problem.

40. Although they are not formally a part of the federal court system, we include here the STJ and the STF since they serve as appeals courts above the federal trial and appeals courts.

3

The Incremental Approach to Accountability, 1985–2014

It is essential to recognize the merit of the government of former president Luiz Inácio Lula da Silva in strengthening mechanisms for the control of corruption, including prevention and repression, especially the investments made in the Federal Police during the first term, the strengthening of the Comptroller General . . . and the preservation of [prosecutorial] independence. . . . This was not solely a presidential initiative, of course, since confronting corruption is a demand that arises from the maturing of democracies, but the merit of political leadership cannot be ignored.

—Judge Sérgio Moro, sentencing statement, July 12, 2017[1]

Over the past generation, Brazil has seen enormous shifts in the prevailing patterns of accountability. Accountability in 2014, at the outset of the *Lava Jato* investigations, looked nothing like it did in 1985. In fact, *Lava Jato* itself would have been unthinkable without the intervening changes. The big push of *Lava Jato,* though, had its own effects: patterns of corruption and accountability in 2021 do not look as they did in 2014, but they also do not look like a full or even partial return to the status quo in 1985. The push and pull of reforms has entirely remade the accountability panorama.

With this shifting terrain in mind, this chapter proceeds in three stages. In the first, we lay out a heuristic model of the accountability process, which will provide a framework to evaluate accountability over time. In the second, we describe the significant, if uneven, improvements in the accountability terrain between the 1985 return to democracy and March 2014, just prior to the *Lava Jato* investigations. We analyze accountability transversally, focusing on the six elements of the accountability heuristic. In the third section, we discuss how incremental changes in the accountability equation led to shifts in the modal or archetypical grand corruption scandal between 1985 and 2014. In the conclusion, we discuss why so many anticorruption reforms were approved in Brazil during this period if incentives for corruption are indeed as pervasive as Chapter 2 suggested.

Framework of Analysis: The Accountability Approach

Stated succinctly, the problem we seek to understand and address is political corruption; the ultimate objective is a virtuous equilibrium that we label "integrity"; and the path between the two, which we can think of as a public policy response, is accountability. *Accountability* refers to the obligation of public officials to inform the public about their actions, to justify and explain them, and to answer for those actions; it is about allocating responsibility for particular actions to particular public agents, retrospectively and prospectively; and it is the process of deterring and punishing deviations from established norms so as to (re-)establish public perceptions of the validity of those norms (Schedler 1999; Grant and Keohane 2005; Fox 2006; O'Donnell 1999, 2003; Smulovitz and Peruzzotti 2003; Bovens 2007; Lindberg 2013).

How should policymakers strategize, design, prioritize, and sequence accountability policies? To answer this question, we address accountability as an outcome of rules and behaviors in six domains.[2] In this approach, accountability (A) is understood as the outcome of transparency (T), oversight (O), and sanction (S), all of which are moderated by state capacity (C) and the degree of engagement (E), tempered by the level of economic and political dominance (D):

$$A = (T + O + S) * (C + E - D)$$

In greater detail, the key components of the model are as follows:

- Transparency (T), defined in its most essential sense as public access to meetings, procedures, and information about the government's work. Transparency gives public agencies, private individuals, and nongovernmental organizations the information they need to evaluate the government's performance on whatever criteria those groups find most relevant. There are any number of ways in which transparent data can be made more useful to citizens and, at its worst, public disclosure can sometimes be no more than an elaborate ruse manipulated by bureaucrats (Bersch and Michener 2013). At its best, though, transparency assumes an inclination toward information sharing, easily accessible and timely provision of data, and the ability to verify data across sources. It may become an essential tool in building the reputation of public officials and agencies, allowing for the well-informed evaluation of their performance (Picci 2011, 2012).

- Oversight (*O*) is the susceptibility of government functions to surveillance that gives public or private agents the right to evaluate the government's performance more intensively than by simply accessing data furnished by government itself. Ideally, oversight would be almost unlimited, and all government accounts, processes, and agents would be susceptible to random or targeted audits. Oversight is likely to be most effective when it relies on the reinforcing perspectives provided by multiple overlapping accountability bodies, operating independently but conjointly. Ideally, this web of accountability agencies would be equally able to operate in fire alarm and police patrol modes, sometimes reacting to unexpected revelations, but also continuously probing vulnerabilities to unmask inadequate or inappropriate performance (Mainwaring 2003).

- Sanction (*S*): Cesare Beccaria (1764 [1986]), Jeremy Bentham (1843 [2011]), and Gary Becker (1968) all suggested that the perceived costs of committing criminal acts weigh heavily on the decision to engage in wrongdoing. But sanctions also serve a societal role: effective sanctions may ultimately be less about altering the individual calculus than about generating societal trust (Bayley 1994). Because mutual trust is so important to anticorruption, more important than punishment of a single individual is (1) demonstrating that there is a societal norm at work and restoring it to its proper place in the wake of a violation; and (2) the iterative process by which transparency, oversight, and sanction together point to underlying dynamics that may be contributing to governance failures. Sanctioning processes thereby provide clues about how best to realign institutions and incentives to deter abuses. Sanctions need not be solely restricted to criminal justice, indictment, or conviction, of course; they might include the reputational losses caused by scandal, the loss of electoral support, the administrative and civil penalties, the loss of public employment, and so forth—each with a different level of severity and probability of enforcement.

Transparency, oversight, and sanction are moderated by institutional capacity (C) and civic engagement (E), tempered by the degree of economic and political dominance (D):

- Capacity (C) refers to the features of the institutional environment where accountability takes place, particularly with regard to the state agencies responsible for enforcing it. It exerts a largely positive role on accountability and encompasses three dimensions: (1) a professionalized bureaucracy with the ability to implement policy free of undue external influence (Bersch, Praça, and Taylor 2017a: 161[3]); (2) the institutional toolkit, including relevant laws and adequate budgets; and (3) the organizational structure, including allocation of personnel to key areas and coordination within and across bureaucracies. These elements of capacity are typically built within the state, endogenously.
- Engagement (E), by contrast, relates to the exogenous pressures beyond the state for accountability, understood at its simplest as the degree in which the public is attentive to and able to participate in public decisionmaking. It plays a predominantly positive role in accountability. Engagement is a consequence of the structure of society outside the state, including the education and civic "culture" of publics, but also the role of civil society organizations as channelers of public engagement, and of the media as a force that may mobilize particular publics in response to particular issues.
- Economic and political dominance (D) refers to the degree of concentration of powers and influence of political and societal actors. High levels of dominance have a negative impact on accountability, by diminishing the incentives for transparency, active oversight, or energetic sanction. Other things equal, the more that the incumbent party or government allies dominate state agencies, the less likely these will be able to effectively fulfill their accountability function. Similarly, economic dominance may narrow the field of effective accountability, either

because of the influence economic actors wield over accountability organizations, or simply because of the disturbances
accountability might cause to an economy of the "don't upset
the applecart" or "don't kill the golden goose" variety—see, for
example, Kang 2002 on chaebols' dominance in South Korea.
Dominance, political as well as economic, is usually prejudicial
to accountability, as it generates incentives for the protection of
dominant players or even the creation of artificial rents that
accrue to those same actors. Only rarely does it lead to the Pla-
tonic guardian, a ruler in the Paul Kagame or Lee Kuan Yew
mold, and then often only because of the exceptional conditions
that brought those leaders to power.[4]

There are empirical reasons to focus on these specific components.
The trajectory of countries that have effectively achieved an equilibrium shift in their corruption levels over the past generation, such as
Georgia, Rwanda, and Japan, adhered to the basic logic of the model,
with improvements across diverse components of the model. Countries
that have not advanced or have moved backwards despite momentous
anticorruption campaigns either failed to overcome bottlenecks in a
key component such as dominance (e.g., China, Mexico), or emphasized one component while neglecting others, such as focusing solely
on judicial sanction, without broader improvements in transparency,
oversight, and effectiveness (e.g., Italy) (Taylor 2018).

This heuristic model of accountability can serve a retrospective
diagnostic function as well as a prospective, strategizing function.
Retrospectively, the model enables scholars and policymakers to
think about accountability policy in terms of its component elements,
identifying specific problems that recur over time. It provides a quick
shorthand that can guide policy diagnosis of past accountability
efforts across a range of countries, regimes, policy sectors, and levels of analysis, from municipal councils to national legislatures.

Prospectively, the heuristic model is specific enough to tailor
accountability policy responses to particular "syndromes" of corruption (Johnston 2005, 2014), to identify specific "bottlenecks" to
accountability (Hausmann, Rodrik, and Velasco 2005), and to strategically plan interventions, rather than adopt a nonstrategic, helter-
skelter, kitchen-sink approach that fails to align policy responses
with each of the component accountability elements. This point is
essential. Too often, anticorruption "strategies" are nothing more
than a list of institutions and practices that all countries with "good"

corruption control seem to currently have in place. Lists of this sort are problematic because they do "not suggest a dynamic of change—in other words, what puts what into motion—it is quite impossible to prioritize policies on its basis" (Mungiu-Pippidi 2015: 76). In the accountability approach, integrity is the overarching goal; each of the six component variables offers specific strategic objectives; and within each of the components, policymakers can think about tactics ("specific actions for carrying out the strategy"; Fox 2016: 5) that would overcome particular bottlenecks.

Breaking accountability into smaller components may provide a road map for different principals—ranging from the electorate to the directors of state agencies and middle-ranking bureaucrats—to improve accountability within different arenas and organizations. By breaking accountability into smaller component parts, reformers may also enable more effective collective action, while presenting a smaller target for counterreformers. In other words, the approach helps to bite off smaller pieces of a much larger puzzle, dicing the overwhelming policy problem of corruption into more easily digestible and politically viable targets.

But it would be misleading to conclude that the only guidance provided by the heuristic model is to break the accountability problem into smaller parts. To the contrary, one implication is that it is important for reformers to remember the big picture, since focusing on only one of the components in isolation is unlikely to bring systemic change that shifts the prevailing equilibrium. Each of these components is mutually reliant on the others, and accountability efforts that focus only on any single component to the exclusion of the others are unlikely to lead to a shift in the overall accountability equilibrium. This means, for instance, that souped-up police forces or hypermuscular transparency efforts may lead to gains but, in making those gains, new bottlenecks may emerge. The accountability approach requires constant evaluation and reevaluation of both progress and obstacles across all six components.

Mapping Accountability

To digest the evolution of accountability in Brazil, in this section we evaluate the component elements of accountability as they developed incrementally from the return to democracy in 1985 until the outset of the *Lava Jato* investigations in March 2014. We analyze each of the components of the accountability heuristic in sequence: transparency, oversight, sanction, capacity, engagement, and dominance.

Transparency

Of all the elements of the accountability equation, transparency was a bright spot for much of the period 1985–2014 in Brazil. The 1988 Constitution instituted a number of transparency guarantees, the federal bureaucracy largely complied with these norms, and the trend on transparency was upward, especially after hyperinflation was vanquished. A number of laws and policies increased the availability of and access to information of public interest that helped citizens and oversight agencies to monitor government decisions and performance.

The text of the 1988 Constitution on the public bureaucracy set out legality, *impessoalidade* (neutrality), morality, *publicidade* (publicness), and, ten years later via constitutional amendment, efficiency, as key rules for the bureaucracy.[5] While constitutional writ alone does not guarantee the transparency of public sector information, inclusion in the constitution served as an important foundation for later claims that government data needed to be made public. The battle against hyperinflation and in favor of greater rationalization of spending was also essential. Hyperinflation threw mud in citizens' eyes. Journalists and watchdog groups had enormous difficulty adjusting the constantly accelerating size of budgets and contracts to reflect their true underlying value. Meanwhile, budget information was not at all systematized at the beginning of the democratic regime: different bureaucracies had different datasets, there was little centralized budget data, and different agencies held multiple government bank accounts.

Economic policymakers worked hard to improve the situation, including by creating a National Treasury Secretariat and the Integrated System for the Financial Administration of the Federal Government (SIAFI) to monitor all federal government expenditures in the late 1980s (Nóbrega 2005; Taylor 2009, 2020). The SIAFI's creation was essential to gaining control over the fiscal accounts, but it was also significant in that it made large volumes of government data available for oversight for the first time (Sacramento and Gomes de Pinho 2016; Olivieri 2010). The success of the Real Plan of 1994 had an extraordinarily salutary effect on the transparency of public accounts, allowing citizens to better understand where, how, and at what scale public funds were being spent. The Fiscal Responsibility Law of 2000 cemented this transparency into place by requiring regular accounting for budgetary expenditures (Abrucio and Loureiro 2005; Abramo and Capobianco 2004). Improved capacity in the Receita Federal (Federal Revenue Service) around this same time allowed the government to evaluate individuals' tax declarations against the size of their financial transactions, with important repercussions for oversight of illicit financial flows (Power and Taylor 2011: 267). In parallel, a 1990 law forbade unidentified overnight financial applications, which had been previously allowed and had made potential taxpayers "invisible" to the Receita Federal. Assets amounting to US$1 billion were seized by the Central Bank in the wake of this law, which required those seeking to retrieve their money to identify themselves (Senado Federal 1997: 90).

Fiscal decisionmaking was made more transparent not only within the executive branch, but also in Congress. The rules surrounding the budgetary process underwent at least two major reforms that took place in the wake of major corruption scandals, the first having resulted from the *Anões do Orçamento* scandal of 1993, and the second from the *Sanguessugas* scandal of 2006. As a result, congressional procedures regarding the approval of annual budgetary laws have increasingly been decentralized away from a few individual power brokers, and stricter rules for decisionmaking reduced discretion and made proceedings more transparent (Praça 2011).

Economic policy also carried over into anticorruption in other ways. A 1986 law federalized crimes against the national financial system, including tax evasion and under-the-table foreign exchange transactions. The regulation of the business environment, whether through the strengthening of the competition authority Conselho Administrativo de Defesa Econômica (CADE) or laws on market competition, helped target cartels with administrative and criminal sanctions.

Public procurement was significantly reformed. First, a 1986 decree-law clarified rules inherited from the military regime and adopted stricter criteria for government contracts. Later, in the wake of a major corruption scandal, a 1993 law made rules even stricter, criminalizing behavior associated with public procurement. In the 2000s, electronic bidding procedures and a system for tracking federal transfers to subnational governments were introduced as a way of discouraging fraud in public purchasing (Fleischer 1997; Abrucio 2007; Giacomuzzi 2011; Praça and Taylor 2014; Bersch 2019: 155–167). Starting in the early 2010s, however, new modalities of public contracts with increased flexibility—initially designed to speed up the pace of the works needed for the 2014 FIFA World Cup and the 2016 Summer Olympics, following a 2011 law—were implied in a variety of fields, from health care infrastructure to science and technology, with potentially negative effects for procurement transparency.

The federal civil service was significantly reformed under the aegis of a new Ministry for Administration and State Reform and of a new statute for federal civil servants, enacted in 1990, with greater emphasis on performance and transparency (Bresser-Pereira 1996; Abrucio 2007). Asset disclosure requirements became legally required of top federal officials and candidates for public office (Martini and Soares 2016). The government increasingly hired journalists to work in the public sector, a shift that increased communication with the media, as well as building journalistic understanding of how government worked (Mick 2021).

A variety of laws enhanced data accessibility. The 1991 Archives Law made the state responsible for preserving public documents and for making them available to the public. A 2004 law required the timely reporting of spending on a government Transparency Portal. The 2009 Transparency Law expanded requirements for budget disclosure at all levels of the federation, and established new rules for compliance. The 2011 Access to Information Law included mechanisms for citizens to access government data, including a fairly broad tool for freedom of information requests.[6] While this law did not solve all problems of transparency—for example, critics note that many bureaucrats have found ways around strict compliance with the law and that the law preserves several tiers of secrecy that restrict access to some information for decades—it nonetheless set a bar for expected transparent behavior (Cunha Filho 2019; Michener, Moncau, and Velasco 2016). It guaranteed that information would be provided in user-friendly formats (which had been a major problem), and even imposed rules on state-owned enterprises. The amount of information available on government websites—particularly the federal government's Portal da Transparência—became so significant that sometimes the greater difficulty lay not in finding the data, but in making it legible to the public; that is, easily identifiable and understandable (Picci 2011, 2012; Michener 2019).

In another critical area for accountability, regulations were reformed to make campaign contributions more transparent. Following scandals in the early 1990s, two laws were enacted to make business contributions legal: one in 1993 specifically for the elections of the following year, and another in 1997 applicable to subsequent elections. Irrespective of their effects on the concentration of such contributions and of the fact that off-the-books contributions remain significant, such laws had the profound effect of shining light into an otherwise entirely opaque environment. As a result, due to the diligent work by the electoral courts, important data on campaign contributions was made public in a relatively organized and systematic fashion (C. P. R. de Souza 2013). Much of the data that demonstrates the extreme concentration of campaign contributions, for instance, was collected only due to these laws (Mancuso 2015; Mancuso and Speck 2015; Carazza 2018).

At least at the federal level, Brazil did reasonably well on measures of bureaucratic transparency. The Natural Resource Governance Institute ranked it highly in its Resource Governance Index, with a score of 71 out of 100, or sixth out of eighty-nine countries in 2017 (Natural Resource Governance Institute 2017). The protections in Brazil's Access to Information Law placed it in the second-best quintile of nations with freedom of information laws, in a 2011 evaluation (Centre for Law and Democracy 2020). Andrew Williams (2014) placed Brazil in the upper tercile for information transparency and political transparency in a thirty-year index of 191 countries. The International Budget Partnership's 2015 Open Budget Index placed Brazil's federal government in its second-best category ("provides substantial information"), just behind the United States and ahead of France, the UK, and all other Latin American nations (International Budget Partnership 2015).

Oversight

One of the most remarkable effects of the return to democracy was the growth in the number and power of oversight agencies, ranging from those in charge of monitoring financial transactions and public spending to those responsible for criminal investigations. The ability of such agencies to uncover otherwise hidden irregularities grew steadily from the late 1980s. However, oversight was not always as effective as desirable, due to the weakness of individual agencies and poor coordination among them. Likewise, this was not always a steady movement forward, but oftentimes a case of two steps forward, one step back.[7]

At the federal level, key oversight agencies within the executive branch include the Federal Police, the financial intelligence unit (Conselho de Controle de Atividades Financeiras, COAF), the Controladoria Geral da União (Federal Comptroller's Office, CGU), and the Receita Federal. On the legislative side, Congress has its own federal accounting tribunal (Tribunal de Contas da União, TCU) and can also convene occasional congressional committees of investigation (comissãos parlamentar de inquérito, CPIs). Outside of the executive and legislative branches, the Ministério Público Federal prosecutorial service, electoral courts, and judicial oversight bodies such as the National Council of the Ministério Publico (CNMP) and the National Judicial Council (CNJ) all play a role.

Within the executive branch, much of the increase in oversight during this period followed a global trend toward investigating money laundering. Perhaps nowhere is this more visible than at the COAF. The COAF is a financial intelligence unit that grew out of the Anti–Money Laundering Law of 1998, which in turn was a response to Brazil's commitments as a member of the Financial Action Task Force (FATF) and the Egmont Group. As an interagency council, the COAF has a relatively small staff, but its presence enables coordination of information flows across the federal government, as well as oversight of suspicious transaction reports (STRs).

A similar trend toward focusing on money laundering was visible in other executive branch agencies. The Federal Police have a wide range of responsibilities not entirely associated with fighting corruption such as border control and drug trafficking. After more than twenty years in which the Federal Police were understood simply as a federal security service, the 1988 Constitution made the agency a criminal investigative force for the first time. This enabled the Federal Police to develop as a central oversight agency, perhaps best reflected by the fact that without the Federal Police investigation of money laundering, in fact, and its use of authorized wiretaps and access to bank records, it is unlikely that the *Lava Jato* investigation—and most corruption investigations prior to it, described in the previous chapter—would have emerged. Largely as a result of its growing capacity (reviewed later), the number of large-scale investigations run by the Federal Police has grown dramatically, especially after the turn of the century. In 2002 there were 18 such investigations; in 2007 they reached 183, a tenfold increase in only five years. By the end of 2013, just as *Lava Jato* was about to begin, large-scale investigations by the Federal Police reached what was then a peak of 303 operations in a single year (Arantes 2015; Fagundes 2018). Importantly, most of these investigations revolved around corruption and white-collar offenses, a significant departure from the predominantly anti–drug trafficking priorities of the Federal Police during most of the 1990s (Arantes 2015; Fagundes 2018). Still, the agency has a long list of responsibilities and has been internally split among various not entirely cooperative—and frequently rival—career tracks, including *delegados* (senior investigators), *agentes* (rank-and-file investigators), and *peritos* (forensic experts). Perhaps even more damagingly, it continues to battle an old reputation for executive dominance, politicization, and corruption in its ranks.

Still on the oversight of financial transactions, the Receita Federal has played an important role in the evolution of oversight. Increasing capacity within the agency and the application of advanced information technology during this period enabled the Receita Federal to greatly increase capacity and credibly report when tax payments or bank holdings exceeded declared income. Revenue specialists have played an important role in investigations of corruption, in part because of their ability to cross data on individual and corporate tax returns and financial flows. A study by Arthur Trindade Maranhão Costa, Bruno Amaral Machado, and Cristina Zackseski (2016: 251) found that the Receita Federal is second only to the TCU as the institution that provides the most information to the Federal Police in the lead-up to criminal investigations into petty and grand corruption.

The Federal Comptroller's Office, created in 2001, emerged during the Workers' Party's years in government as a significant oversight body for monitoring outlays of federal funds by state and municipal governments. Its creation was an important breakthrough, pulling many of the previous anticorruption units out of the different ministries they oversaw and into one central agency, following a 2003 reform that structured the CGU along its current lines (Olivieri 2010; Loureiro et al. 2012; Aranha and Filgueiras 2016). The CGU undertook a series of new initiatives and laws, including a much-lauded system for random audits of subnational governments' spending on federal programs that had a highly significant symbolic and deterrent effect, and generated data that has been thoroughly examined in the corruption literature (Ferraz and Finan 2008, 2011). These audits uncovered irregularities that did not pertain solely to subnational governments, but that also tied back to members of Congress, as in the *Sanguessugas* scandal (see Appendix). The CGU also developed oversight over federal employees' asset and income declaration forms and, through its national disciplinary board, gained the ability to impose a variety of punishments on civil servants accused of disciplinary violations. The CGU also received regulatory authority to bar companies from federal contracts under federal procurement law, although it has applied that authority somewhat haphazardly (LaForge 2017).

On the legislative side of the ledger, oversight has long been deemed lackluster. The TCU accounting "tribunal"—which despite its name is not a judicial body, but rather an audit institution subordinate to Congress—has historically been quite weak. The TCU has constitutionally mandated responsibility for evaluating the annual accounts submitted by the president; judging the accounts of the public administration, including foundations and firms in which the government holds a stake; evaluating the legality of public sector hiring and retirements; undertaking inspections and audits of all branches of government; monitoring transfers to states and municipalities; advising Congress; and applying fines and sanctions against those found responsible for illegal or irregular spending. In addition to the TCU at the federal level, there are Tribunais de Contas at the state level, as well as in some municipalities (however, these subnational accounting institutions have dramatically different levels of performance; M. A. Melo and Pereira 2013; Da Ros 2018). The ultimate authorities on the TCU are nine *ministros* (justices), who are supported by a large staff of professional auditors.

Within the universe of auditing institutions and external control bodies worldwide, the TCU has many relative institutional strengths, including its large and professionalized staff and a comfortable budget, which has put it ahead of accounting bodies in other Latin American countries (Santiso 2009). It also has a variety of oversight powers such as the ability to blacklist companies from public bidding for up to five years and to ban individuals from political appointment positions. Likewise, with a few important exceptions,[8] the TCU has broad jurisdiction, covering nearly all federally funded policies and agencies. The TCU's routine monitoring of public spending has uncovered various petty corruption scandals.

With regard to grand corruption, one of the most important oversight programs developed by the TCU is Fiscobras. Since 1997, the annual budgetary law has required the TCU to inform Congress about irregularities in ongoing public works. If there is serious evidence of wrongdoing, the TCU may even suggest that funding be suspended (TCU 2016). The value of public works audited by Fiscobras increased from R$2.2 billion in 1997 to an all-time high of R$38.3 billion in 2012, a nineteenfold increase over fifteen years. However, the total number of public works audited decreased over time. Combined, these two data points suggest that the TCU increasingly focused its oversight powers on fewer public works involving large volumes of public funds, rather than dispersing them more broadly across a wide range of public works. This may be problematic because Fiscobras data shows that the share of public works with evidence of serious irregularities, which may require the suspension of public funding, has been significant over time.

Moving beyond the TCU, the most momentous form of legislative oversight has been congressional investigatory committees, a typical fire alarm mechanism (McCubbins and Schwartz 1984). Congress has used CPIs to bring in witnesses, dig into public records, and otherwise shine light on the scandal of the day. The use of CPIs was frequent during this period: one study showed an average of 3.6 a year between 1999 and 2010, resulting in actionable recommendations to executive branch agencies in 91 percent of cases (Cadah and Centurione 2011: 93). Given the strong links between congressional coalitions and the executive branch, however, CPIs were seldom created over the strident opposition of the executive. Even when they were, they often petered out in discord, as in the *Banestado* and *Mensalão* scandals. Worse yet, they sometimes were purposely used to frustrate investigations being conducted by other accountability agencies. Yet CPIs had the potential to waylay the government entirely, should the executive branch lose its governing majority, as it did during the presidency of Fernando Collor de Mello, when a CPI contributed directly to the impeachment effort. As a result, legislative oversight through CPIs served as a "spasmodic" form of accountability, intermittent and limited to a few episodes of great scandals (Pérez-Liñán 2007).

One of the most remarkable innovations since the return to democracy was the autonomy given to the public prosecutorial office, the Ministério Público Federal (MPF),[9] following a 1985 law that expanded its powers beyond the traditional criminal arena into the civil and administrative spheres. The 1988 Constitution further expanded the responsibilities of prosecutors, and the more than 11,000 state prosecutors and more than 1,000 federal prosecutors (CNMP 2015: 275) were provided with significant budgetary autonomy and career protections, on a par with those of judges (Arantes 2015: 35). The independence of the Ministério Público Federal has meant that the prosecutorial service is recognized as a "fourth branch" of government, and passing the examination as a prosecutor is considered a high honor (Mazzilli 1993; Sadek and Cavalcanti 2003; Sadek 2008; Arantes 2002; Kerche 2007). The only political appointee within the Ministério Público Federal is the prosecutor-general, who is nominated by the president to a two-year term, with Senate approval.[10]

Among the MPF's most significant oversight powers is the ability to conduct its own investigations of wrongdoing, which can take two forms. The first follows the 1985 law mentioned above, whereby *inquéritos civis* (civil investigations), particularly those leading up to the filing of civil administrative improbity cases, can be conducted exclusively by the Ministério Público Federal, with no need to involve the police. These cases enable prosecutors to solicit evidence under penalty of law (Arantes 2015). The second is the *procedimento investigatório criminal* (criminal investigative procedure), which is less frequent and also more controversial. There has been a long debate about the constitutionality of prosecutors' use of criminal investigative procedure, which was only settled in favor of the prosecutors' powers to conduct such investigations in a 2015 STF ruling. Despite their unclear constitutionality, the MPF conducted thousands of these criminal investigations over the years, a large share of which focused on corruption. Between 2012 and 2014 alone, for instance, there were 830 such procedures focused exclusively on corruption (Londero 2021). Part of the impulse toward conducting its own investigations, whether civil or criminal, came from a perception that prosecutors had been ill served by underperforming police investigators, at least until improvements in the Polícia Federal (PF). On the other end of the prosecutors' cases, the glacial pace of the courts and their overall bias in favor of powerful defendants may be extraordinarily discouraging for prosecutors who may spend five to ten years on a case, only to have it dismissed on highly technical grounds (Taylor 2017).

The electoral courts are the branch of the judiciary tasked with overseeing elections. As such, they also have oversight of campaign finance, which has long been linked to many of the most important cases of grand corruption. The electoral courts have been effective at overseeing actual polling (Fleischer and Barreto 2009: 118). But although the electoral courts do oversee huge volumes of campaign spending, and have gotten better at working with the Receita Federal and Central Bank to oversee campaign finance (Mancuso and Speck 2014: 139–140), they have not been especially proactive or effective in anything more than the most formalistic procedural oversight of campaign finance. For years, experts have regarded campaign finance reports as little better than a "piece of fiction" (Bohn, Fleischer, and Whitacker 2002: 351). There are many reasons for this inability to effectively oversee campaign spending, including the fact that the electoral courts spend much of their time adjudicating minor disputes such as the allocation of free airtime rather than investigating electoral crimes. But the most significant is that there has long been a tacit gentleman's agreement among politicians not to question each other's financing too vigorously, which has in turn contributed to weak campaign finance reporting requirements and somewhat tepid oversight by the electoral courts (Sadek 1990, 1995; Taylor 2006, 2011).

Since their creation in a 2004 constitutional amendment, quasi-judicial bodies such as the National Council of the Ministério Publico and the National Judicial Council have exercised oversight of prosecutors and judges. Among the most significant effects of these bodies has been to generate systematic data on judicial performance, tackle exceedingly high court congestion, move casework online, and streamline judicial processes. The CNJ has also been active in tackling the judiciary's worst abuses, including nepotism in the hiring of courtroom staff, particularly at the state level (Ingram 2015). But as a result of the bargains struck in creating these councils, there is not much external representation by nonjudicial actors on the councils, undermining their capacity to oversee the courts and the prosecutorial offices in a transparent and effective manner (Da Ros and Taylor 2019; Kerche, Oliveira, and Couto 2020).

Sanction

As noted earlier, the ability of Brazilian voters to punish corruption by politicians has been limited. The open list proportional representation system with large magnitude districts, associated with an extremely fragmented party system and the possibility of alliances across diverse parties during the elections and later in government, means that the direct line from voters to politicians is weak. Further distancing voters is the electoral quotient: any votes above those needed for a candidate to win office are transferred to members of the candidate's party or coalition. Parties have often employed a *puxador de voto* (vote puller) with a big name to pull in votes for less well-known or less popular candidates. Because of vote transfers, it would be remarkable if voters knew who their vote actually elected, but, in any case, almost half of voters had no recall of their intended choice just one month after casting their ballots (Bello 2017). Clarity of responsibility, as a result, has been quite reduced in Brazil (Rebello 2015; Tavits 2007). Further complicating accountability, the incumbent advantage—especially with regard to campaign finance—has traditionally been strong.

This is not to say that politicians facing credible corruption allegations have not paid an electoral price, however. Research suggests that parties will remove candidates facing corruption accusations from the party lists: after two particularly egregious scandals in 2005 and 2006, 43 percent of the eighty-eight implicated deputies either dropped out or were dropped by their parties from competing for reelection (M. Castro and Nunes 2014). This may be at least in part because scandal-ridden politicians receive fewer campaign donations (Pereira, Rennó, and Samuels 2011; Cordeiro 2014). But voters also have their say: of the fifty deputies who did run for reelection in the wake of involvement in the scandals, only nine (18 percent) were actually elected, a far lower reelection rate than the overall average (69.7 percent in 1998, and 58.8 percent in 2006) (M. Castro and Nunes 2014). In majoritarian elections, too, there is evidence that voters may have imposed costs on politicians involved in scandal by forcing them into a second round of voting: after *Mensalão,* for example, Luiz Inácio Lula da Silva was pushed into a second round in the 2006 presidential election (Rennó 2011). That said, even scandal-ridden politicians may be able to overcome voter disgust and survive in politics if they collect enough money: research by Ivan Jucá, Marcus André Melo, and Lucio R. Rennó (2016) shows that big spenders have been able to overcome the negative effect of corruption allegations on votes.

Similarly, both the executive and the legislature can sanction behavior by their own members. The president, for instance, may respond to corruption allegations by removing ministers from their cabinet (as the Appendix describes, Dilma Rousseff removed eight ministers in the early months of her first term; Araújo, Costa, and Fittipaldi 2016). In Congress, however, the cases of deputies and senators accused of corruption have only rarely led to removal from office. This is particularly troubling in light of the numerous allegations of wrongdoing involving legislative officeholders. Whereas cases of alleged misconduct have reached the hundreds over the past decades, removals have been rare, and usually occurred only after a major congressional inquiry in the wake of a large scandal. The Conselho de Ética (Ethics Committee) in the Chamber of Deputies initiated dozens of proceedings, but, between the committee's creation in 2001 and 2014, only four deputies had their mandates revoked by their peers (Hirabahasi 2017). Prior to the establishment of this committee, such decisions were also rare. Among the few congressmen who had their mandates revoked by their peers were the deputies involved in the

Anões do Orçamento scandal of 1993, and Sérgio Naya, a deputy expelled from office in 1998 after the fatal collapse of a building that his company had constructed (Damé and Madueño 1998).

Beyond political accountability, another potential source of sanction emerges from legal accountability. *Legal accountability* can be defined as the application of a punishment established in law for failing to comply with, or actively breaking, the behaviors stipulated in law (Da Ros 2019a; Bovens 2007; Karklins 2005; Lindberg 2013). As such, it is considered "the most unambiguous type of accountability, as . . . legal scrutiny will be based on detailed legal standards, prescribed by civil, penal or administrative statutes, or precedent" (Bovens 2007: 456). Legal accountability is the form of accountability most clearly associated with the judicial system more broadly, as in civil and criminal cases. However, it may also involve administrative sanctions, which are enforced by agencies outside the realm of the judiciary proper.

Legal accountability in Brazil has always been a game of privilege: only the poorest people of color have historically been held responsible for alleged wrongdoing. The cruel old saw in Brazil is that jails are for only three p's: *pobres* (the poor), *pretos* (Afro-Brazilians), and *prostitutas* (prostitutes). Notably missing is a fourth p: *políticos* (politicians), or political and economic elites more generally. For many years, there was a hopeful belief that the special protections afforded to elites were a relic of the dictatorship and that, gradually, these protections would fall by the wayside as democratic institutions began to function normally (DaMatta 1993). Yet despite the many significant improvements in transparency and oversight described in previous sections, legal accountability for political elites up until the 2010s remained more the exception than the rule.[11]

Before discussing the weakness of court-imposed sanctions, however, it is worth noting that a number of legal administrative sanctions can be imposed by agencies such as the TCU, CGU, and MPF. Even though the courts may subsequently void some of these sanctions, they do have a reputational effect and often carry a considerable administrative penalty.[12] The number of civil servants removed from their posts for malfeasance grew from 268 in 2003 to more than 500 a year between 2011 and 2016, of whom nearly two-thirds were accused of corruption (CGU 2016; Odilla 2019, 2020). Special audits, furthermore, present an administrative headache and carry potential legal jeopardy, thereby serving a dissuasive function. The CGU also has regulatory authority to bar companies from federal contracts under federal procurement laws, although it has applied that authority haphazardly (LaForge 2017).

Despite the TCU's increasing ability to detect serious irregularities in public works via audits, its willingness to enforce administrative sanctions—such as suspending funding for works with signs of wrongdoing—has long been limited. This is likely a consequence of the selection process for its ministers, who have traditionally been heavily embedded in national politics (Speck 2011; Teixeira and Alves 2011).[13] The top position at the TCU is considered a "reward for retiring politicians or a stepping stone in a political career" (OECD 2012: 81; Speck 2011). Of the eleven TCU ministers who served between 2010 and 2014, seven (63 percent) were professional politicians and two more (18 percent) were former Senate staffers. Five of the TCU ministers (45 percent), furthermore, faced allegations of improprieties. Neither has the politicization of the TCU been restricted to the ministers, and there are multiple examples of ministers using their influence to nominate relatives and friends to appointed positions within the TCU (Taylor 2019). Not surprisingly, in light of these political origins, empirical research shows political parties in the governing coalition have been significantly less likely to be targets of TCU audits than opposition parties (Fonseca 2021).

Beyond its lackluster enforcement of administrative sanctions, the TCU also ultimately has relied on other bodies to make its judgments stick, especially Congress. Congress not infrequently ignored TCU reports or punted on their recommendations. As Alejandro Bonvecchi (2015: 902) notes, "Congress only considered audit reports on budgetary execution after the terms of the presidents . . . who had executed those budgets had ended, and invariably validated their budgetary execution practices despite auditory objections." Said another way, the mechanics of coalitional presidentialism seem to carry over into ostensible oversight bodies such as the TCU. Even when Congress has acted on red flags raised by the TCU, as for example in a 2010 decision to halt funding for Petrobras's Abreu e Lima refinery, the executive branch vetoed the provisions of the budget law that halted the transfers (Taylor 2019). Not surprisingly, Brazil's worst score on the Public Expenditure and Financial Accountability assessment comes in the category "legislative scrutiny of external audits reports," where it received a "D" grade despite scoring quite well in other categories (PEFA 2009).

Alongside the CGU and TCU, the Ministério Público Federal also has been able to apply a number of administrative sanctions, including *termos de ajustamento de conduta* (behavioral adjustment agreements), which enjoin civil servants to alter their behavior. While these instruments may subsequently be contested in court, prosecutors have found them a useful second-best option, as they impose early reputational costs, and may slow the progress of illicit schemes within the bureaucracy even when courts are slow to act (Arantes 2015).

In its more traditional role of prosecuting cases, the changes in the performance of the MPF have been extraordinary since the return to democracy. A variety of institutional changes contributed to the growing autonomy and capacity of state and federal prosecutors, including constitutional provisions guaranteeing budgets and salaries, as well as the independence of prosecutors from each other and changes in the way in which the chief prosecutor is selected. The MPF became more capable of prosecuting corruption for a variety of reasons, including the growing independence of the chief prosecutor from the executive branch, the enactment of new laws, the changes in court jurisprudence, the modernization of criminal proceedings, the specialization of some courts in money laundering crimes, the increased discretion on criminal issues, the strengthening of the federal police's capacity to contribute to prosecutors' work, and the ability to create internal task forces (Londero 2021; Kerche and Marona 2018; Marona and Kerche 2021).

A stronger prosecutorial body contributed to a rising number of corruption cases, and, in fact, the increase in both criminal and civil cases filed based on corruption charges was one of the most fundamental changes in the accountability landscape in the run-up to *Lava Jato*. As Daiane Londero (2021: 73) shows, drawing on internal data from the Ministério Público Federal, the number of criminal cases filed on corruption grounds per year increased from only 6 in 1993 to 180 ten years later (2003), and then to 568 twenty years later (2013). Civil cases of administrative improbity filed by the Ministério Público Federal likewise mushroomed, from just 3 to 127 to 1,462 at each of those ten-year intervals (Londero 2021: 73). Whereas the yearly percentage of cases filed by the MPF involving corruption averaged only 0.62 of all cases from 1988 until 2002, it reached nearly 10 percent of all filings in 2013 (Londero 2021: 292). This suggests that corruption was increasingly prioritized by prosecutors, possibly as a result of a transformation in their professional ethos (Azevedo 2012).

Our analysis so far suggests that the ability and willingness to oversee, investigate, and prosecute corruption increased steadily from 1985 to 2014. At the same time, as a consequence of uncertain electoral sanctions and decreasingly credible legislative and administrative sanctions, prosecutors increasingly came to rely on civil and criminal sanctions. Courts, as a result, were elevated: if civil and criminal sanctions were to be effective, ultimately the judiciary had to enforce them. But *judicial inoperancy*—the ineffectiveness of the courts as institutions that could contribute to the definitive resolution of conflict—was nowhere more evident than in fighting corruption.

Judicial inoperancy played out in two ways. The first was a general reluctance to actually impose definitive legal sanctions. Although the number of civil servants expelled from the federal government rose remarkably, many, however, were readmitted. The chances of the court effectively imposing either a civil or criminal penalty on fired civil servants was lower than the 4.5 percent chance of the fired civil servant winning a suit requiring their readmittance into the civil ser-vice (Alencar and Gico 2011). Although the number of corruption cases rose vertiginously, these case figures started from a low base and the number of successful convictions was infinitesimally small (Levcovitz 2014, 2020; Madeira and Geliski 2019; Londero 2021). Moreover, given the unparalleled workload of Brazilian courts, corruption cases represented only a slim fraction of the cases tried. As of 2012, only 25,799 of the roughly 95 million cases in courts nationwide were primarily about corruption; similarly, only an infinitesimal percentage of prisoners nationwide—0.001 percent— were in jail on corruption charges (M. R. Machado 2015).[14] At the electoral courts, very few cases resulted in any kind of sanction, even though there were many cases where mayors had been removed from office by the electoral courts and the volume of candidates barred from running for election because of criminal charges increased following passage of the so-called Clean Slate Law (Lei da Ficha Limpa) of 2010 (Gehrke 2019).

At the federal level, meanwhile, the original jurisdiction of the high court in cases involving sitting politicians served as a literal "Get Out of Jail Free" card.[15] Under the terms of the 1988 Constitution, more than 58,000 politicians and public officials are availed of some form of original jurisdiction nationwide, widely known as the *foro especial* or *foro privilegiado* (*Folha de S. Paulo* 2018c). Although original jurisdiction at the STF covers only sitting federal officials, such as ministers and legislators, the volume of such officeholders still sums to more than 700 federal officeholders.

The cautious pace of the STF in judging these officials means that, as Chapter 2 noted, one of the most common outcomes of original jurisdiction cases was that the statute of limitations ran out (*pre-scrição; Folha de S. Paulo* 2016).[16] Data collected by Silvio Levcovitz (2020) highlights that until 2014, there was an increase over time in the number of corruption cases tried by the federal judiciary, but politically and economically relevant actors seemed to escape convictions at much higher rates than others. In fact, the first criminal conviction of a politician charged with corruption within STF's original jurisdiction only took place in 2010, just before the trial of the *Mensalão* case. This was the case of federal deputy Natan Donadon (MDB-Rondônia), and he was detained only in 2013, after all his appeals had been exhausted at the STF (M. Oliveira 2013).[17] While it could be that all of the other politician-defendants faced spurious and politically motivated charges in the high courts, this seems unlikely in light of the massive evidence of corruption that emerged in scandals and the enormous professional costs police and prosecutors paid for investigating powerful political actors.

Second, the high courts—and the STF in particular—introduced enormous uncertainty about the rules of the game. Brazilian courts play a significant role in defining the rules of the political system and the rules governing criminal procedure, as courts everywhere do. But in the Brazilian case, they did so in inconsistent and confusing ways that contributed to increasing institutional instability. In the political system, this was perhaps best exemplified by the 2006 decision that rendered the *clausula de barreira* (threshold clause) void, and thereby contributed to the proliferation of political parties.[18] In the realm of criminal procedure, this uncertainty was perhaps best exemplified by the ever changing rules on the original jurisdiction of the high court in criminal cases against sitting politicians.[19] Numerous inconsistent judicial decisions led to enormous swings in jurisdictional rules that translated into judicial impunity.

Coupled with multiple changes in the rules governing whether or not Congress needed to authorize indictments of sitting politicians, as well as numerous and frequent changes regarding imprisonment on appeal,[20] the picture that emerges is one of overall weak institutionalization and limited institutional effectiveness (Vieira 2018). If "institutionalization" is the process through which organizations acquire "value and stability" (Huntington 1968: 12), the ever changing rules governing judicial sanctions suggest that legal accountability is poorly or weakly institutionalized at a very basic level in Brazil: that of defining its rules of operation (Brinks, Levitsky, and Murillo 2020: 23).

Perversely, given the instability of many rules governing politicians, the rules on original standing have remained relatively stable, providing a clear escape route for politicians defending themselves against corruption charges. A criminal case filed against a sitting federal officeholder starts under the original jurisdiction of the STF, but if he or she leaves the federal office that grants original jurisdiction, the case is remanded to the trial courts, where the trial essentially begins again from scratch. This has been the most frequent path for criminal cases tried under the STF's original jurisdiction: according to one study, excluding pending cases, 69 percent of all cases involving federal officials that had ever been tried by the STF were moved to first instance courts before the STF reached any final decision (Gomes Neto and Carvalho 2021). Not surprisingly, politicians have used this tactic strategically, waiting until their cases are about to be decided by the STF and then resigning from office so as to avoid conviction and further draw out the trial time. Eduardo Azeredo, for example, was a federal deputy when he was charged with corruption for crimes committed while he was the PSDB state governor of Minas Gerais (in the so-called *Mensalão Tucano* scandal). He resigned from office in February 2014, just a few weeks before his case at the STF was to be decided, and the case against him was sent to trial court where it began again.

The reverse has also been true: if an individual is prosecuted for a given crime before a trial court, but is appointed or elected to a federal position, his or her case restarts in the STF. This opens space for a similar tactical exploitation of judicial rules: politicians such as Dilma Rousseff (who appointed Lula as chief of staff in early 2016) and Michel Temer (who appointed Moreira Franco to a cabinet position from 2016 to 2018) have been accused of using appointments and the original jurisdiction they confer to protect associates from legal accountability. Criminal cases thus move in and out of original jurisdiction with relative ease, leading to an extremely slow pace of judgment and little resolution of cases against senior politicians.[21]

The puzzle of judicial inoperancy in corruption cases has been all the more intriguing because many of the factors that are often called on to explain weak judicial performance in the rest of the world were absent in Brazil. The courts since 1988 have had tremendous constitutional guarantees of judicial independence. The courts' budget has been by far the largest in Latin America, and possibly among the largest anywhere, at 1.3 percent of the country's GDP (Da Ros and Taylor 2019). Judicial resources, not only for salaries, but also for special training, equipment, and buildings, are ample. The courts have undergone major constitutional reform and more targeted changes in procedure, including changes specifically designed to improve anti-corruption effectiveness.[22] A large number of new laws have been written to facilitate legal accountability in the corruption realm.

But for a variety of reasons, judicial inoperancy has remained the name of the game. Many protections granted to defendants have been justified by a pleasing rhetoric of democracy and human rights. Many procedural delays, in particular, have been seen as justifiable in the context of a newfound postauthoritarian commitment to civil rights. Institutionally, a number of factors such as high caseloads, ample avenues of appeal, and weak precedent contributed to delay and inconsistency. Courts may also have been timid in imposing sanctions on members of the other branches because they also had their own dirty laundry, and hoped not to be forced to impose heavy sanctions on their own colleagues. Certainly the judiciary has not been very good at policing itself: out of all disciplinary proceedings at the CNJ that resulted in some sanction against judges, only fifty-eight judges were dismissed for wrongdoing (of these, only two were criminally convicted) (Cury 2018). Dismissed judges have been permitted to retire with full benefits.

Furthermore, at the apex of the political system, the courts are in close contact with the elected branches, and the coalitional presidential system means that the political parties that are often presumed to provide effective supports for judicial independence—and thus for legal accountability—in fact offer a powerful counterweight. Despite strong guarantees of judicial independence, the courts have not floated autonomously above broader political structures, from whence they could impose sanctions unhindered by politics. Quite the opposite: at times courts have behaved like part of the elite cartel, playing an important role in an unspoken self-protection pact alongside members of the executive and legislative branches. Especially in the high courts, as the scandals described in Chapter 2 demonstrated, judges seem to have bent over backwards to find loopholes and ambiguities that would benefit other elites.

Whatever the root causes, the courts by 2014 had emerged as the main bottleneck to the effective legal accountability for elites. As tentative but hopeful improvements in transparency, oversight, and prosecution over the previous generation made it more likely that cases would find their way to the courts, the courts, paradoxically, appeared less and less able to resolve those cases in a manner that led to effective legal accountability. Slow judicial processes and ever changing legal interpretations provided breathing room for corrupt elites to push back against changes in accountability, preserve impunity, and sustain the informal exchanges between the economic and political spheres. While the *Mensalão* case in 2013, and its pioneering conviction of senior government officials, offered hope that the courts might somehow become more effective instruments of accountability, in many ways it was the exception that confirmed the rule that elites were subject to a distinct set of rules.

Capacity

Capacity expanded extraordinarily during the period 1985–2014, reflected in the scale of the professional bureaucracy and the breadth of the institutional toolkit. A professional bureaucracy implies the existence of a stable civil service free from undue external influence, as well as adequate wages and personnel. The institutional toolkit includes the formal powers granted by legislation, adequate resources, expertise, and coordination. Both saw important gains in the run-up to *Lava Jato,* although these changes progressed unevenly across agencies and over time.

The growth of a professional bureaucracy was a hallmark of this thirty-year period, in part due to the strong guarantees of civil service tenure and autonomy in the 1988 Constitution. Partly in consequence, Brazilian state agencies have been regarded as among the most capable in the region (Stein et al. 2006). Merit-based hires became the norm for most positions, particularly within the executive and judicial branches. This is perhaps nowhere clearer than in the judiciary and the MPF, whose generous wages[23] have attracted increasing numbers of applicants and made public examinations extremely competitive processes since the mid-1990s.[24] The MPF offers a striking example of this trend. Between 1993 and 2013, there were fifteen cycles of public examinations, which selected 984 new federal prosecutors. As a result, the number of active federal prosecutors nearly tripled from 345 in 1993 to 1,019 in 2014. Additionally, hiring of civil servant staff within the MPF increased even more quickly, skyrocketing from 1,047 to 8,797 over the same period (Londero 2021: 140). Meanwhile, the number of judgeships in *varas federais* (trial courts) jumped from slightly under 200 in 1991 to more than 700 by 2013, in turn allowing the courts to cover more territory and to specialize in different areas of jurisdiction, including money laundering and financial crimes (F. A. Rodrigues 2019: 50).

Other institutions also grew in this period. Following the return to democracy, the TCU expanded significantly, reaching a staff numbering slightly over 2,600 by 2014. Partly as a by-product of its key role in economic reforms, a similar process took place at the Receita Federal. The country advanced a long way from the situation in 2003, when the police investigation of the landmark *Banestado* case was almost stymied by inability to buy paper, hire telephone lines, rent a copying machine, or reimburse Federal Police for their travel expenditures (H. Marques 2003). As the epigraph by Judge Moro suggests, under a concerted effort spearheaded during the Lula presidency, careers within the Federal Police have been restructured and the number of officers expanded rapidly, rising from 7,000 in 2004 to 14,000 in 2017, with more than three-fifths hired since 1995 (Arantes 2015; Fagundes 2018).

Other agencies were created from scratch by importing staff from the economic policy bureaucracy: the CGU grew from nothing in the early 2000s to nearly 2,200 staff. Not surprisingly, the volume of oversight described in previous sections rose markedly, particularly after the mid-1990s. On the downside, not all agencies are equally endowed. The federal judiciary, Ministério Público Federal, and Receita Federal were extremely powerful, independent, and well funded. There is, however, evidence of ties between politicization, low capacity, and corruption in federal agencies, and many accountability agencies remained susceptible to significant political appointments (for detailed comparisons, see Bersch, Praça, and Taylor 2017b). Political appointees can impose constraints on civil servants, manipulating key agencies, such as the COAF, CGU, and Federal Police in the executive branch, and the TCU in the legislature. Further, accountability agencies suffer from a problem that afflicts the entire federal bureaucracy: budgets tend to go overwhelmingly to salaries, which means that there is little room for programmatic expansion in fiscally challenged times.

A second essential component of capacity, the institutional toolkit, changed dramatically in some ways, but remained stubbornly old-fashioned in others. At home, new laws have been passed at a rapid clip since the turn of the century (see Table 3.1). Much of this new legislation expanded the scope of illegal behaviors considered corrupt; increased the number, size, and types of penalties for corruption; and provided new tools for the investigation and prosecution of official misconduct. These included the introduction of new statutes specifically criminalizing money evasion, cartel formation, tax evasion,

Table 3.1 Key Statutory Accountability Reforms, 1985–2014

Law	Statute	General Purpose	Year	Administration
Public Civil Action Law	Lei 7.347	Introduces civil public interest actions, which can be filed by the public prosecutors' office	1985	José Sarney
Money Evasion Law	Lei 7.492	Establishes crimes against the national financial system	1986	Sarney
Public Bidding Decree-Law	DL 2.300	Establishes stricter rules for public procurement, updating a 1967 decree-law	1986	Sarney
Taxpayer Identification Law	Lei 8.021	Forbids unidentified financial accounts, previously allowed	1990	Fernando Collor de Mello
Ineligibility Law	LC 64	Establishes criteria for electability	1990	Collor
Civil Servants' Statute	Lei 8.112	Establishes administrative penalties associated to irregular behavior by civil servants	1990	Collor
Economic Crimes' Law	Lei 8.137	Establishes tax and economic crimes such as cartel formation and tax evasion	1990	Collor
Archives Law	Lei 8.159	Establishes the state's responsibility to preserve public documents and enable citizen access	1991	Collor
Administrative Improbity Law	Lei 8.429	Establishes civil sanctions for office-holders, including removal from office, fines, and ineligibility	1992	Collor
Organic Law of the Federal Audit Court	Lei 8.443	Defines the attributions and internal rules of the TCU	1992	Collor
Organic Law of the Federal Attorney General	LC 73	Defines the attributions and internal rules of the AGU as the institution responsible for legal aid to the executive branch, replacing the Consultoria-Geral da República	1993	Itamar Franco
Organic Law of the Federal Public Prosecutors' Office	LC 75	Defines the attributions and internal rules of the MPF as an institution independent from the executive branch	1993	Franco
Public Bidding Law	Lei 8.666	Establishes new procedures for public procurement, replacing the decree-law of 1986, and criminalizes behaviors associated with it, previously inexistent	1993	Franco
1994 Elections Law	Lei 8.713	Introduces campaign contributions by business limited to 2 percent of their revenue in the previous year, and by individuals limited to 10 percent of their income in the previous year	1993	Franco

continues

74

Table 3.1 Continued

Law	Statute	General Purpose	Year	Administration
Elections Law	Lei 9.504	Maintains the rules for campaign contributions established in the 1993 law, and introduces new types of electoral crimes, adding to those in a 1965 law	1997	Fernando Henrique Cardoso
Anti–Money Laundering Law	Lei 9.613	Criminalizes money laundering, establishes penalties, and creates the COAF financial intelligence body	1998	Cardoso
Vote Buying Law	Lei 9.840	Criminalizes vote buying	1999	Cardoso
Fiscal Responsibility Law	LC 101	Establishes guidelines and penalties for public sector budgeting, spending, and reporting	2000	Cardoso
Cabinet Reform Provisional Measure	MP 2143-31	Establishes the anticorruption agency CGU within the federal executive branch	2001	Cardoso
Immunity from Prosecution Constitutional Provision	EC 35	Removes the previous need for congressional authorization for federal officeholders to be indicted, except for the president	2001	Cardoso
Pregão Law	Lei 10.520	Establishes a new form of public bidding in procurement	2002	Cardoso
Cabinet Reform Law	Lei 10.683	Expands and empowers the CGU	2003	Luiz Inácio Lula da Silva
Criminal Code Reform	Lei 10.763	Increases minimal and maximum jail time for bribery (corrupção), from 1–8 years to 2–12 years, and conditions parole on restitution	2003	Lula
Reform of the Judiciary	EC 45	Establishes the CNJ and CNMP to oversee the judiciary and the public prosecutors' office	2004	Lula
Transparency Law	LC 131	Imposes new rules for budget transparency and reporting	2009	Lula
Clean Slate Law	LC 135	Disqualifies candidates for office who have been convicted on appeal, for eight years	2010	Lula
Differentiated Public Procurement Regime Law	Lei 12.462	Establishes new forms of public procurement, initially for the public works of the FIFA World Cup and the Olympic Games, but later expanded to various other works, including those of public health care and education, urban infrastructure, public safety, and science and technology	2011	Dilma Rousseff
Access to Information Law	Lei 12.527	Establishes rules for access to public sector data and information	2011	Rousseff

continues

Table 3.1 Continued

Law	Statute	General Purpose	Year	Administration
Brazilian System for Defense of Competition	Lei 12.529	Establishes administrative and criminal penalties for behaviors damaging to free enterprise	2011	Rousseff
Anti–Money Laundering Law	Lei 12.683	Updates Law 9.683 on anti–money laundering rules and penalties, stiffens sentences, facilitates the prosecution of money laundering crimes	2012	Rousseff
Conflict of Interest Law	Lei 12.813	Defines conflict of interest within the executive branch and imbues both the Comissão de Ética Pública of the presidency, established in 1999 by presidential decree, and the CGU to oversee it	2013	Rousseff
Anti-Corruption Law (or Clean Companies Law)	Lei 12.846	Establishes civil and administrative liability for corporate corruption, sets out rules for leniency agreements with firms	2013	Rousseff
Organized Crime Law	Lei 12.850	Defines organized crime, establishes criminal procedures (including plea bargaining), and details penalties for racketeering	2013	Rousseff

Notes: LC refers to a *lei complementar,* which has a higher threshold for approval than a common law; EC refers to a constitutional amendment. We have excluded from this table regulatory or infralegal provisions (such as decrees and executive orders), many of which bring domestic law into accord with international conventions on corruption signed by Brazil, or establish new institutions within the executive branch.

public procurement fraud, money laundering, and vote buying; the power of the Ministério Público Federal to bring administrative improbity cases under civil, rather than criminal, jurisdiction; the definition of administrative penalties for civil servant misconduct; the removal of the requirement for Congress to provide prior authorization for federal officeholders to be indicted (except for the sitting president); an increase in sentencing guidelines for bribery; the barring of candidates for office who have been convicted on appeal, for eight years; the removal of the need to prove other crimes to prosecute and convict money laundering charges; and the introduction of plea bargain agreements as an investigative technique. Many of these new laws increased the ability of legal accountability agencies to oversee, investigate, and sanction corrupt behavior. In addition, new laws clarified the responsibilities of key agencies, as in the 1993 laws that established the Ministério Público Federal and the Advocacia-Geral da União (AGU) as two separate legal bodies with drastically distinct responsibilities, distinguishing the independent prosecutorial responsibilities of the MPF from the AGU's role of legal counsel to the federal administration.

Another vital capacity-building measure was to increase coordination between the more than five dozen federal agencies that were involved in anticorruption work in the four branches of government (the Ministério Público Federal being the fourth branch). The institutional multiplicity that this large number of actors brought to the table created a potential logistical nightmare. Indeed, the early years of the century were marked by repeated signs of institutional incompatibility: in the *Banestado* case, for example, one conclusion of the congressional review was that there had been little communication between the Central Bank and the Receita Federal, allowing tax evaders to utilize CC-5 accounts to transfer money abroad with impunity (R. Valente and Christofolleti 2004). The formation of interagency working groups was discouraged by formal rules mandating that participants all be of the same rank; information systems and databases used by different agencies were incompatible; and there was a general "Babel" in interagency communications (LaForge 2017: 4). A recurring complaint in the run-up to the *Lava Jato* investigation was the "imperfect orthodontia" of the various agencies in the web of accountability (Taylor and Buranelli 2007: 79): the unworkability of a multiplicity of control institutions that too often were inconsistently brought to bear without any strategic integration (Olivieri et al. 2015; Prado, Carson, and Correa 2015; Aranha and Filgueiras 2016; T. M. de Oliveira 2019).

Yet institutional multiplicity offered a number of different ways of triggering corruption investigations, by permitting different agencies to tackle the same issues from different perspectives (Prado, Carson, and Correa 2015; Carson and Prado 2016). It also was a rich source of targeted ideas for addressing Brazil's ills. An interagency forum known as the Estratégia Nacional de Combate à Corrupção e à Lavagem de Dinheiro (National Strategy for Fighting Money Laundering and Corruption, ENCCLA), created in 2003, brought together as many as seventy of these agencies annually to brainstorm, propose, and benchmark reforms that would improve accountability (Cunha, Medeiros, and de Aquino 2010; Augustinis 2011; I. M. Corrêa 2011; Aranovich 2007: 128–129; Praça and Taylor 2014; LaForge 2017; Taylor 2020). Initially conceived to address money laundering, ENCCLA quickly turned its attention to corruption as well.[25] In so doing, ENCCLA gradually provided interinstitutional coordination and helped to disseminate expertise among accountability institutions. ENCCLA used a soft law approach reliant on peer pressure and consensus to move ideas forward, with skillful leadership encouraging diverse civil servants to connect and experiment with new policies (LaForge 2017: 7–9). This led to implementation of a variety of new ideas about how to improve processes, agencies, and laws, many of which are now a part of the statutory framework. As Pedro Abramovay, a former secretary of legislative affairs in the Justice Ministry, noted, bills that had achieved consensus within ENCCLA tended to face less opposition when they went before Congress, making them "pretty much guaranteed to pass" (LaForge 2017: 19; Abramovay interview 2018, in Taylor 2020).

Task forces were another response that drew on institutional cooperation to tackle wrongdoing (Hartmann and Chada 2017). As noted earlier, the *Banestado* case became a case study for the Ministério Público Federal, which replicated the practice of task forces to other cases (Paludo 2011). Standing task forces were also created to centralize information flows between otherwise separate civil and criminal cases pertaining to the same facts and thereby prevent bureaucratic competition, as in the Núcleos de Combate à Corrupção that were created in twenty-four states across the country in early 2014, following a pioneering experience in Rio Grande do Norte beginning in 2007 (Londero 2021).

Even the courts saw improved results as a result of these joint efforts. The twenty-seven specialized federal anti–money laundering courts—including the Curitiba trial court headed until 2018 by Judge Sérgio Moro, which lay at the heart of the *Lava Jato* case, and the São Paulo court headed until 2011 by Judge Fausto De Sanctis, which heard the *Satiagraha* and *Castelo de Areia* cases—were an institutional innovation that was replicated nationwide by order of the Conselho da Justiça Federal (Federal Justice Council) beginning in 2003. One of the driving causes for their creation was that the issue of financial secrecy posed an enormous roadblock to effective investigation and prosecution: to obtain bank records, investigators had to find the bank holding a suspect's account, obtain judicial authorization to access the data, and then navigate complex rules about how they could share the information with other investigators, prosecutors, and judges. The specialized courts accelerated the process of judicial authorization, as did the creation of more streamlined bank account information databases within the COAF financial intelligence unit.

From nothing, the coverage of specialized anti–money laundering courts reached roughly 6,000 cases of financial crimes annually
by 2017 (De Sanctis 2017; Bruno 2015).[26] The courts' creation
spurred further specialization in money laundering and corruption by
prosecutors and federal police assigned to work on financial crimes.
They created hubs that brought together specialists on financial
crimes from the ranks of police, prosecutors, and judges (LaForge
2017: 11–12). The Organized Crime Law of 2013 provided prosecutors and judges with clearer guidance on how to undertake plea bargains, which were largely unheard of in Brazilian courtrooms before
the turn of the century. Procedurally, too, courts innovated. After the
Mensalão case was decided in 2013, for example, the STF revised its
own procedures, moving future corruption cases out of the plenary
and into the smaller *turmas,* where a smaller number of justices
would be involved in each case. A 2007 resolution also permitted
STF justices to delegate early trial motions to lower court judges
known as *juízes de instrução,* who would coordinate witness testimony, oversee depositions, and authorize necessary criminal arrests,
among other procedural matters, thus speeding up pending corruption
cases in the STF (the auxiliary judges were based on the experience
of state supreme courts that dates back to the 1988 Constitution; Da
Ros 2014, 2018).

International pressure was also important in shaping the institutional toolkit. Brazil, like much of the rest of Latin America since the
turn of the century, built a "new normative edifice" of international
agreements alongside improved national laws and policies that gave
teeth to previously weak anticorruption bodies (Casas-Zamora and
Carter 2017). Brazil is a signatory to all of the major international
conventions against corruption, and the review mechanisms used by
the Organization of American States, Organisation for Economic Cooperation and Development (OECD), and FATF, for example, led to
significant reflections on the shortcomings in the accountability system, as well as attempts to improve existing legislation (Vaz Ferreira
and Morosini 2013; Vaz Ferreira 2016). The push and pull of these
agreements was evident, for example, in Brazil's support for the
OECD Declaration on Automatic Exchange of Information in Tax
Matters (Kar 2014). On the one hand, the Brazilian government
pushed the declaration internationally because it enables tax authorities to obtain information on taxpayers' overseas assets; on the other,
membership in these types of agreements committed the government
to certain qualitative improvements in domestic tax oversight capac-

ity. Brazil also benefited enormously from the effect of these international pressures in other jurisdictions, such as increased transparency about Swiss accounts that made possible increased cooperation with Swiss authorities in corruption cases. And of course, signing on to a variety of international agreements helped to bind the hands of future governments: although Brazil is not a member of the OECD, as a party to the OECD Convention on Combating Bribery because it ratified the convention in 2002, Brazil was subject to pressure from the OECD to update its corruption legislation to impose direct liability on companies for bribery. Brazil passed such legislation in 2013. New bureaucratic capacity frequently accompanied the signing of these treaties, as in the creation of the Justice Ministry's Department of Assets Recovery and International Legal Cooperation (DCRI) in 2004, in part a consequence of the UN Convention Against Corruption (LaForge 2017: 6). Often the increased international engagement has led to capacity-building through foreign training, the development of international contacts, and the possibility of collaboration with partner agencies such as prosecutorial bodies abroad (Engelmann and Menuzzi 2020).

On the negative side of the ledger, the institutional toolkit remained frustratingly antithetical to accountability. Rivalries between different agencies were deep, and much of the period 1985–2014 was occupied by squabbles over different agencies' prerogatives, as in the long tug-of-war between police and prosecutors about who had the constitutional right to investigate crimes (current answer: both police and prosecutors). The overlapping responsibilities of various agencies posed a huge collective action problem and, while individual agencies were sometimes effective, the frictions between agencies often led to overall systemic inefficiency (Aranha 2017; Taylor and Buranelli 2007; Speck 2002: 481; Taylor 2017). These rivalries were further complicated by the fact that although federal agencies played an active role, much anticorruption responsibility still resided with state police, state prosecutors, and state courts. These institutions responded to local political contexts and introduced state-level influences into already complicated federal accountability processes, making interinstitutional coordination and cooperation even more difficult (Macaulay 2011; Da Ros 2014).

The speed with which the statutory environment changed also led to uncertainty and friction in the application of new laws. The Anticorruption Law of 2013, in particular, generated a host of questions. In Brazil's complex federal system, for example, which authorities have the right to determine what counts as adequate compliance by firms (*The Economist* 2014)? Which authorities can negotiate leniency agreements with firms that self-report wrongdoing (Pimenta 2019, 2020; Richard 2014; V. A. de Carvalho 2020)? An effort by President Rousseff to regulate the anticorruption effort (Decreto 8.420 of 2015) was widely panned, furthermore, for diluting the harshest penalties on companies and adding additional uncertainty to the law by instituting an appeals process chaired by agency officials who might be susceptible to further corruption (Dantas 2015).

Civic Engagement

Civic engagement is an essential component of effective accountability, helping to keep up pressure on the political system for probity, reform, and effectiveness. Perhaps because of its tradition of clientelist and corporatist exchanges, civic engagement in Brazil has long been deemed anemic. That said, democracy shifted the playing field, and a combination of top-down mobilization of public participation with bottom-up grassroots efforts helped to increase "social accountability" (Peruzzotti and Smulovitz 2006; Fox 2015).

As noted earlier, however, the vertical accountability between voters and politicians is tenuous, the political system has traditionally been fairly unresponsive to electoral pressures, and reforms aimed at improving the situation have often failed or backfired. Most notably, in 1995 Congress passed a law setting minimum thresholds for party representation in Congress, a rule that was designed to be implemented only a decade later; this law was struck down by the STF after an appeal by small parties (Marchetti 2008). Again, Brazil's particular form of coalitional presidentialism—which adds to the coalitional presidential mix unprecedented levels of party fragmentation, party switching, and party rebranding, as well as federalism—played a crucial role in reducing clarity of responsibility (Powell 2000; Tavits 2007; Rebello 2015). With such a large and confusing number of elected officials to monitor, and the many challenges to effective monitoring, low interest in politics or even disengagement should not be surprising. Likewise, limited party institutionalization, including tenuous roots in society and virtually inexistent internal democratic processes, tended to push citizens away from greater involvement in the daily lives of political parties. For instance, none of the five largest parties in the state of São Paulo—including the Workers' Party, which was often cited as a party more open to public participation—held any form of primary elections to select its candidates for federal deputy (Braga 2008).

This is not to say that there were no improvements in the vertical ties among voters and politicians between 1985 and 2014. Notable changes took place, such as judicially imposed restrictions on party switching, and the Clean Slate Law of 2010, which barred politicians who had been convicted on appeal from running for office.[27] The Clean Slate Law was largely the consequence of civil society engagement, as it was put on the legislative docket through the public initiative process, which guarantees that a proposed bill is heard by Congress when it receives the signatures of 1 percent of the electorate. Similarly, passage of a law against vote buying in 1999 was made possible through a public initiative process, driven by traditional associational bodies alongside grassroots organizations.

Democracy and the rise of a broader middle class also helped to change the scope of citizen demands while providing the wherewithal for greater civic engagement. Brazilians rank highest in the region on survey questions relating to their belief in the ability of ordinary people to make a difference in the fight against corruption by reporting cases to the appropriate authorities, according to Latinobarometro (Pavão 2019: 100). And the people often mobilized in massive public protests. Although citizens' most expansive demands for anticorruption reforms were not met, Collor's impeachment was followed by a series of small and large reforms, such as the Administrative Improbity Law of 1992, and Rousseff attempted to assuage the 2013 protesters with a variety of anticorruption proposals of her own. Massive public mobilization online was central to the signature drive for the Clean Slate Law, and online mobilization helped to overcome the ingrained opposition of politicians, approximately one-third of whom stood to lose their jobs if the law passed (Beyerle 2014: 70). Politicians ignored the street at their own peril, and if Congress often responded more slowly than might be desirable, it nonetheless demonstrated an understanding that the streets demanded to be heard.

At a grassroots level, new civil society organizations emerged devoted to issues of crime, corruption, voting rights, and improved public sector performance. Among these groups, some of the most prominent in the anticorruption field were Amarribo, Articulação Brasileira Contra a Corrupção e a Impunidade (ABRACCI), Instituto Ethos de Empresas e Responsabilidade Social, Movimento de Combate à Corrupção Eleitoral (MCCE), Transparência Brasil, and Observatório Social do Brasil. Turnover among associational groups was considerable, however, and many groups emerged around specific policy issues, moved them forward, and then faded away. A weak tradition of funding for think tanks and citizen and public interest groups was an impediment to some anticorruption organizations, which were often sustained on a tight budget and by the volunteer efforts of their directors. Further, the government often—wittingly or not—absorbed the energies of these civil society groupings by appointing their leaders to advisory bodies and other consultative functions. Another tendency was to fall back on more traditional associational bodies, including the Ordem dos Advogados do Brasil (Brazilian Bar Association, OAB), the Confederation of Brazilian Bishops (CNBB), the Association of Members of the Ministério Público (CONAMP), and the Association of Brazilian Judges (AMB). This had the virtuous effect of mainstreaming reform proposals, but it also may have induced a certain stasis with regard to entrenched interests.

Academics have focused a great deal of attention on participatory forms of civil society engagement since redemocratization in Brazil. Especially under the governments of the Workers' Party, there was an explosion of multiple forms of top-down public participation such as policy councils, participatory budgeting, and policy conferences (e.g., Gurza Lavalle 2011; Isunza Vera and Gurza Lavalle 2010). But little research has been conducted on the effect of such participatory institutions on corruption, even if some do seem to have improved the conditions of citizens in municipalities that adopted them (Baiocchi, Heller, and Silva 2011). Yet if the scandals of the PT's years in federal power are any indication, it seems that participatory bodies are likely to be kept far removed from some of the most important sources of corrupt rents such as state-owned enterprises and political nominations. Even the Ministry of Cities, which was created by the PT as it took the presidency in 2003 with the aim of nationalizing some of its previous subnational participatory experiences, was allocated to the right-wing PP by 2004 in exchange for congressional support (Maricato 2011).

Between 2010 and 2012, during Rousseff's first term in office, the government undertook the only explicitly participatory anticorruption policy conference at the federal level to date, Consocial (1ª Conferência Nacional sobre Transparência e Controle Social). After a complex set of deliberations at the municipal, state, and federal levels, organized predominantly by the CGU, the conference came up with eighty distinct policy proposals across a wide range of themes. However, after that initial effort, the Consocial was never again convened. As this episode demonstrates, while participatory institutions have achieved the laudable goal of expanding participation to previously underrepresented segments of society, they have done so in highly constrained situations, often with a controlled agenda and small budgets, and mostly under rules imposed from above. To this point, Maíra Martini and Mariana Borges Soares (2016) note that during the 2000s, about half of the money given to civil society organizations came from federal and local government, 40 percent from international sources, and 10 percent from the private sector. Under such conditions, civil society organizations may easily have been compromised by government funding.

Another important motivator of civic engagement relates to the media. The free press played an important role overseeing politics and actively reporting on corruption cases. In fact, as various scandals reported in the Appendix highlight, many significant corruption scandals first erupted due to the diligent work of investigative journalists at outlets such as *Folha de S. Paulo* and *Veja,* particularly in the early years of democracy. Especially during the late 1980s and early 1990s, the media worked as a vital fire alarm that set Congress in motion.

That said, many scholars have raised serious concerns about the media's partiality. Given regional income disparities and low levels of literacy, most media consumption is via TV and radio, which are dominated by news stories reported out of the wealthier regions of the country. In the poorer regions, media ownership tends to be economically viable only in the context of a broader political strategy (Abramo 2007). Radio and TV ownership tends to be dominated in these markets by politicians and their families, which can severely limit media oversight (Ferraz and Finan 2008). Further, many of the reports published in these markets are simply a reairing of stories from the largest markets in Rio de Janeiro and São Paulo (Porto 2011). Even in the wealthiest markets, furthermore, the competitive drive for profits means that there is not as much investment in serious investigative journalism as there once was. In the poorer markets, meanwhile, it can be dangerous to report the news; threats, physical attacks, abusive judicial proceedings, and even murders have made Brazil one of the more dangerous places to be a journalist (ranked 108 out of 180 countries; Reporters Without Borders 2020). The concentration of media competition into four or five big family-owned outfits, the enormous government outlays on advertising, the fact that Brazilian media companies have often had other business interests and a pro-business mind-set, and the resulting perceptions of a bias against leftist parties, furthermore, suggest that the media's role in oversight may have been less neutral than desirable (Campello et al. 2020; Damgaard 2018a, 2018b).

Finally, one instance where engagement expanded significantly was in the provision of information about possible irregularities to accountability agencies. Here, institutional innovations such as *ouvidorias* (ombudsmen) met and stimulated latent demands from society—similar to what Jonathan Fox (2015) termed the "sandwich strategy," where opening from above meets mobilization from below. The Ministério Público Federal's anticorruption efforts, for instance, were often driven forward by information from private citizens. Information about potential corruption cases was brought to the Ministério Público Federal by private individuals in 57 percent of corruption cases, in contrast to just 11 percent in other types of cases (Londero 2021: 164–165).

Political and Economic Dominance

Since the return to democracy, Brazil has been a strange case when it comes to the dominance of the political system: with such an extreme level of party fragmentation, no single party or actor has clearly dominated the political system since the return to democracy. Yet there has also been little effective opposition to speak of, especially since 2002. The PT had been a vociferous opponent of all governments prior to Lula's election to the presidency, but, after his election to national office, most significant parties outside government played only a timid role, at least until 2014. This pattern of lackluster opposition emerged as a result of four interrelated factors: the strength of the PT coalition; the PT's governance during a period of historically unprecedented economic growth, which made opposition more costly; the so-called *peemedebização* of politics, whereby ideological malleable parties like the MDB found ways to serve presidents of all stripes; and the fact that cross-cutting allegiances weakened the opposition's willingness to hold incumbents to account.

At its broadest, the fact that no single party dominated the party system should have been positive for anticorruption purposes, by making it difficult for any single force to take command of the levers of accountability. Yet the fact that the coalitional system thrives on horse-trading and control of bureaucratic appointments (including in law enforcement institutions) has meant that accountability can be muted by coalitional bargaining within each governing coalition and over time.

If on the one hand intracoalitional squabbles have often been the source of corruption revelations (Balán 2011), on the other hand the coalition often has responded jointly against perceived external threats to the status quo such as from prosecutors or police. Importantly, the opposition was often weak as an agent of accountability, perhaps because wrongdoing cuts across all parties. Opposition parties were often compromised by their own experiences, whether as incumbents at the state and municipal levels, or by campaign donations received from the same donors accused of corrupting governing incumbents at the federal level. Similarly, because most corruption within the governing coalition cut across various parties in the cabinet, one party's current opponents could be tomorrow's allies. The consequence was that opposition parties were seldom accountability crusaders because pointing fingers at members of the current coalition might endanger one's future chances of being elected and, for presidential parties, of forming a governing coalition once elected.

Much of the literature on the party system in Brazil has emphasized the polar roles that the PT and the PSDB exerted in structuring electoral competition for the presidency since the mid-1990s (for a review, see Carreirão 2014). Indeed, not only did these two parties govern Brazil for over twenty-one years, between 1995 and 2016, but they also were the most important contenders in presidential elections during this long period. That said, it is important to look beyond the head of the executive branch, and to the governing coalition as a whole, to understand how political dominance worked.

Despite the PT and the PSDB having held the presidency for more than two decades, they were not the parties who had the greatest hand in governing democratic Brazil. Other parties were members of the governing coalition for longer—and sometimes much longer—than the thirteen and a half years of PT or the eight years of PSDB in the presidency. Four political parties, in fact, have held cabinet positions for longer time periods than either the PT or the PSDB: the MDB, the PP, the DEM, and the PTB.[28] All four of these political parties, astonishingly, were capable of holding numerous cabinet positions in *both* the PT and PSDB administrations.

The MDB perhaps best epitomizes the forces that have been greasing the wheels of governability in Brazil since redemocratization. In the thirty-five-year period from 1985 until 2020, the MDB was a member of the governing coalition in the executive branch for thirty years. With the exception of the Collor administration (from late 1990 until late 1992), the first year of Lula's presidency (2003–2004), and, at least formally, the Jair Bolsonaro administration's first two years, the MDB was always a member of the governing coalition (Amorim Neto 2019: 303–305). Regardless of the ideologies of the presidents it served, the MDB has been an integral part of the executive coalition almost 90 percent of the time since 1985. As such, it has been the leading member of a group of parties colloquially known as Centrão, or the big center, a group that is known for its malleability and willingness to serve presidents of any stripe, for a price.[29]

Nowhere is the MDB's power over the chokeholds of decision-making better illustrated than in the Brazilian Senate. Between 1985 and 2020, the MDB held the presidency of Brazil's high chamber in most years, except for the period 1997–2001 when Senator Antônio Carlos Magalhães (DEM) held the position, and 2019–2020 when Davi Alcolumbre (DEM) held the post.[30] Neither the PT nor the PSDB ever held the position of president of the Senate despite having held the Brazilian presidency for more than two decades. Additionally, the MDB held the presidency of the Câmara dos Deputados (Brazilian lower house) for seventeen of the thirty-five years ending in 2020. Finally, the MDB held the national presidency itself three times, even though it had never been directly elected to the position: an MDB vice president took office in 1985 (José Sarney), 1992 (Itamar Franco), and 2016 (Michel Temer), replacing presidents who could not take office (Tancredo Neves, who passed away before taking office) or were impeached (Collor and Rousseff). Symptomatically, the first two MDB presidents were not members of the MDB when they were vice presidents, but became members of the party as president when they needed the party's support to govern.

The fact that presidents have relied on an interwoven coalition of political parties, many of whom serve whoever is in office, has meant that the opposition's incentives to monitor and report corruption are limited, and tend to be ineffective (Kunicová and Rose-Ackerman 2005: 584). Unsurprisingly, most threats to the status quo between the return to democracy and 2014 came either from within the federal bureaucracy (e.g., Federal Police or Receita Federal) or from the independent prosecutorial service. But the bureaucracy's anticorruption drives were often successfully thwarted by the governing coalition through the skillful use of appointments, reassignments, and budgetary reallocations. The Ministério Público Federal, meanwhile, had to rely on a judiciary that was not only slow and timid in tackling elite wrongdoing, but also—especially in the two highest courts, the STF and STJ—deeply intertwined with the very political forces it was asked to control. Fully one-third of the STF's justices were party members, although that percentage decreased during the 2000s (Da Ros and Marenco 2008; Da Ros 2010, 2012). The Federal Senate, which vets appointments to the high courts, has not rejected any judicial nominations since the return to democracy, suggesting that appointees to the STF and STJ were largely perceived as unthreatening to the coalition (Llanos and Lemos 2013; Praça 2018: 94–98). Furthermore, the appointment process has been an embroglio of *padrinhos* and close friendships, almost guaranteed to preserve powerful political figures against serious judicial challenges (Recondo and Weber 2019).

The consequence of this system has been that checks and balances are weaker than desirable. Rogério B. Arantes (2015) makes the point that considerable institutional rivalries have existed between the various accountability agencies. But these were not, strictly speaking, checks and balances so much as they were turf wars; that is, jealous efforts to constrain rival bureaucratic power. While there was vigorous electoral competition and no hegemonic electoral party, once elections took place the coalitional system tended to coalesce in ways that blunted competition and led political parties into collusion with the executive branch, diminishing the incentives for opposition oversight of the government. The courts had many of the tools that, in theory, should have made them more effective, whether to fight corruption in the political system or ensure the rule of law more broadly: for example, independence, well-qualified staff, and ample budgets. But as discussed earlier, in the corruption sphere, legal accountability usually fell prey to judicial inoperancy. The judiciary—and especially the high courts—played a role more as an arbiter of conflict within the governing coalition and as a watchdog of the bureaucracy, rather than as a deterrent to grand corruption.

Further fueling dominance was the large role played by the state in the Brazilian economy. This took form in numerous ways, including the predominance of state-owned enterprises in various sectors of the economy such as energy and banking; the constant interaction of a few large private conglomerates that had business with the state in areas such as energy, heavy construction, banking, and agribusiness; the role played by the large pension funds belonging to employees of state-owned enterprises in investments and even in privatized business such as highways and telecom; and the participation of state-owned banks as shareholders in various enterprises, which fueled business concentration. Ensuring access to the rents derived from these enterprises, in turn, was often vital for both political and economic success. As such, the pattern of accommodation within the political elite also expanded to encompass economic elites dependent on state regulation. Linking together these two realms were campaign finance regulations, which, in addition to benefiting from lackluster oversight, allowed for the extreme concentration of contributions to candidates, further inducing coalitional coalescence and domination by political and economic elites (Mancuso 2015; Mancuso and Speck 2015; Carazza 2018; Taylor 2020).

The Changing Shape of Accountability, 1985–2014

Between 1985 and the outset of the *Lava Jato* investigations in 2014, the life cycle of the typical corruption scandal in Brazil changed subtly but perceptibly, in a manner that mirrors the evolution of accountability agencies. As accountability expanded through diverse improvements in the components of the accountability equation described above, the pattern by which grand corruption was treated also shifted in important ways, leading to a change in the balance between reputational, political, and legal forms of accountability.

Early scandals in the first seven years following the return to democracy in 1985 emerged from the strengthening of civic engagement and transparency mechanisms such as increased media coverage and greater citizen access to public information inherent to democracy. But the reputational sanctions that tended to be the sole form of accountability after scandal remained an unsatisfactory form of accountability because, although transparency and engagement (especially by the media) increased the visibility of corruption, it did not lead to any corresponding legal accountability for corrupt actors. Under Sarney, in particular, a variety of different scandals erupted, but then simply faded over time without any significant legal consequences for the political actors who were allegedly involved.

In the most notorious scandal of this early stage of democracy, President Collor did suffer a drastic political sanction when he was impeached for truly scandalous corruption, but the punishment he suffered was somewhat of a fluke. Collor's efforts to govern without support from the political establishment—indeed, casting himself as a savior against the establishment—meant that as soon as public outcry over the scandal reached a crescendo, Congress was happy to show him the door (Rosenn and Downes 1999). More typical of the scandals of this period, however, is that the scandal that led to impeachment emerged largely as a result of infighting within the Collor household, and was then driven forward by the media. Governmental accountability bodies had virtually no role to play in bringing Collor's wrongdoing to light, and when Collor's case reached the high court after his impeachment, it was tossed on a legal technicality, meaning that the only significant sanction he faced was political: impeachment and loss of his political rights for eight years, at the end of which he returned to Congress in a senatorial sinecure he has held since 2007. Despite clear evidence of self-enrichment and campaign finance shenanigans, no legal sanctions were enforced.

Under Franco and Cardoso, much reform took place in oversight mechanisms, especially as a consequence of the increased attention to fiscal matters that resulted from these presidents' intense focus on ending hyperinflation. The Franco and Cardoso administrations reorganized the civil service and began a salutary effort to clear the bureaucracy of deadwood. Partly as a consequence of a desire to control subnational governments and improve fiscal conditions, oversight agencies such as the Receita Federal and the Central Bank were strengthened. Oversight bodies such as the CPIs, the TCU, and the Federal Police began to test their newfound capacity and became quite capable of discomfiting wrongdoers. But major shortcomings persisted such as weak interagency coordination, statutory voids, and insufficient staff for some agencies to actively do their jobs (Taylor and Buranelli 2007).

The Franco and Cardoso administrations saw themselves engaged in a battle against long-standing spendthrift behaviors by Congress and subnational governments. They were also enormously wary of a fiercely combative opposition led by the PT. They feared the opposition might be able to capture oversight bodies through their ample presence in the civil service or, alternately, might seize control of congressional investigations in the pursuit of histrionic headlines. This was not an entirely paranoid or irrational fear, given the demonstrated prowess of the PT in both regards.

As a result, throughout the 1990s, corruption scandals at the federal level followed a similar script: they emerged less because of the work of oversight agencies than as a consequence of intracoalitional disputes that led supposed coalition allies to denounce each other's wrongdoing (Balán 2011). Equally important, the executive branch pushed its allies hard to quash CPI motions before they could move forward, including notably during the *CPI da Corrupção* in 2001. As CPIs, the opposition, and the media were the main ways of exposing corrupt deals, controlling Congress and the governing coalition was an essential defensive strategy, reinforcing the patterns of domination described in the previous section.

In the judicial realm, the Cardoso administration relied on Prosecutor-General Geraldo Brindeiro, whose opponents famously nicknamed him the Engavetador-Geral da República (which can be translated loosely as "Stasher-General of the Republic") for his ability to shunt away scandals by stashing the paperwork in the back of a drawer someplace. Four times, Cardoso named Brindeiro (the cousin of his vice president Marco Maciel) to the two-year prosecutor-general term, where he controlled which cases against sitting politicians would be filed at the STF. Some of the criticism against Brindeiro is probably unfair, given that under the rules prevailing until September 2001, sitting politicians could be indicted only with congressional authorization; without such authorization, his ability to indict them at the STF was limited. Yet whether the cause was the actor (Brindeiro) or the institution (congressional rules), the fact is that between 1995 and 2001, Brindeiro oversaw 626 *inquéritos* (investigations), mostly of political figures: 194 of federal deputies, 33 of senators, 11 of Cardoso ministers, and 4 against President Cardoso himself. By 2001, only 60 of these investigations had resulted in indictments. The remainder had either been shelved (217) or had stalled for unknown reasons (242), and another 88 had been remanded to lower courts (Gaspar 2001). The prosecutor-general began to be seen as a key bottleneck to accountability in the political realm, with an uncanny ability to keep a lid on investigations. Given that most criminal cases died before reaching the courts, nearly all of the successful legal accountability efforts in this period consisted of civil cases of administrative improbity filed by federal prosecutors in trial courts. Some of these prosecutors, in fact, became household names in the late 1990s and early 2000s, such as Luiz Francisco de Souza and Guilherme Schelb. Most of these cases, however, are still pending, with no definitive decision reached by the courts.

By the early years of the new century, however, improvements in state capacity, including the rise of a new generation of staff trained entirely during the democratic period, led to a more proactive role for oversight bodies. Corruption was increasingly unveiled by oversight (a consequence of the creation of the CGU and COAF and the strengthening of the TCU) and investigation (by the PF and MPF), with an increasing focus on administrative, civil, and even criminal forms of legal accountability (Arantes 2011, 2015). Much of this transformation took place in parallel to an important change in how legal accountability agencies approached corruption—increasingly through money laundering, not necessarily through corruption proper. Scandals now tended to emerge less in the press or from intracoalitional finger-pointing (although these remained important), and instead from state agencies that had become more politically autonomous such as the Federal Police and MPF and, to a lesser extent, the CGU and TCU. The incremental accumulation of capacity meant that, by 2005, these agencies were capable of reacting to early signs of wrongdoing, and increasingly began to proactively pursue the cases described in Chapter 2.

The first three rows of Table 3.2 summarize the complex history between 1985 and 2014 described in this chapter. As Table 3.2 illustrates, the prototypical scandal in each of these moments progressed quite differently. In the early stages, judicial responses to corruption were almost inexistent and the media, intracoalitional disputes, the opposition, and CPIs were the primary force driving accountability, a pattern that also meant that most sanctions were merely reputational. By the turn of the century, however, there was also active engagement by oversight agencies, and even prosecutorial efforts, especially at the subnational level (*Banestado*) and via civil cases (*Precatórios do DNER*). By the 2010s political scandals were actually finding their way into the courts, with powerful elites initially protected by the court system (*Satiagraha, Castelo de Areia*), but by 2012 they were in fact leading to legal accountability (*Mensalão*).

The Paradox of Accountability Reforms

Brazil's experience between 1988 and 2014 poses a seeming paradox: if elite cartel corruption was so pervasive in Brazil, why did the political elite—particularly the executive branch (Filgueiras and Araújo 2014)—enact so many accountability reforms? This question is striking because so many reforms ultimately helped to unveil and punish corruption by that same elite. Whether it was through the enactment of new laws, through the establishment or overhauling of entire agencies, or through incremental processes of learning and adaptation, this chapter has shown that much was done to improve accountability processes during the first three decades of democracy.

Table 3.2 Evolving Patterns of Federal Accountability, 1985–2021

Period	Transparency	Oversight	Sanction	Capacity	Engagement	Dominance	Representative Scandals	Accountability Response (stylized)
1985–1992	Weak	Very weak	Very weak	Very weak	Very weak	**Strong**	*Ferrovia Norte-Sul* CPI da Corrupção PC Farias (Collor impeachment)	Some reputational sanctions Low political sanctions No legal sanctions
1993–2002	Moderate	Moderate	Very weak	Weak	Weak	**Strong**	*Anões do Orçamento* Reelection *Precatórios do DNER* SUDAM Banestado	Reputational sanctions Some political Some legal, especially via civil cases
2003–2014	**Strong**	Moderate	Weak, improving	Moderate	Moderate	**Strong**	*Banestado* (cont'd) *Sanguessugas Satiagraha Castelo de Areia Mensalão*	Reputational Political Some legal, including administrative and increasing criminal sanctions
2014–2016	**Strong**	**Strong**	Moderate, improving	Moderate	Strong	Moderate to weak	*Lava Jato Greenfield Zelotes*	Reputational Political Legal, including administrative, civil, and criminal sanctions
2016–2021	Moderate, declining	Weak, declining	Weak, declining	Moderate, declining	Weak	**Strong**	*JBS Queiroz affair Covaxin*	Reputational Weak political Weak and declining legal sanctions

Notes: The shading indicates the intensity of each of the six variables (note that darker shading in the column on dominance reflects greater dominance, which is prejudicial to effective accountability). DNER, National Department of Roadways; SUDAM, Amazonian Development Superintendency; JBS, a meatpacking company.

In fact, although every presidential administration has had its fair share of scandals since 1985, each presidential administration also approved a number of reforms that improved the various components of the accountability equation.

It may ultimately be impossible to provide a definitive answer to the question posed above. And it would be presumptuous to assume that there could be any single explanation for all of the reforms described in this chapter. The large number of reforms, and the dramatically changing circumstances faced by each president mean that it is unlikely that a single motivation or rationale connects all of them. Instead, we expand on Luciano Da Ros (2019a) and classify some of the most relevant reforms that took place since 1985 into three basic types—*reactive, proactive,* and *endogenous* reforms—given the different types of circumstances that led to their enactment.

First, *reactive reforms* have been those pushed forward primarily as responses to contexts of crisis or popular pressure. Many of these reforms took place in the wake of corruption scandals or during periods of relatively intense public dissatisfaction, often in parallel to mass protests (Speck 2006). The political elite met and sought to assuage popular dissatisfaction through the enactment of new laws and accountability-enhancing reforms. Civic engagement, in other words, helped to overcome the collective action problem, leading to punctuations in an otherwise relatively stable corruption equilibrium.

Examples of reactive reforms abound, with extremely consequential results. In the wake of the *PC Farias* and *Anões do Orçamento* scandals of the early 1990s, major reforms included the Administrative Improbity Law of 1992, the Public Bidding Law of 1993, the Election Law of 1993 (which legalized corporate campaign contributions), and budgetary reforms in Congress approved in 1995. Scandals within the court system, including the *Foro Trabalhista de São Paulo* of 1999, drove forward judicial reform in 2004, against the opposition of many judges. Similarly, in the wake of the *SUDAM* scandal, the CGU was first established in 2001. The 2013 protests led to the approval of the Anti-Corruption Law (sometimes also referred to as the Clean Companies Act) and the Organized Crime Law. These would prove essential to *Lava Jato*'s early successes, as they introduced plea bargain and corporate leniency agreements (akin to deferred prosecution agreements in the United States) more clearly into Brazilian law. Finally, even though they did not result from specific scandals or protests, two important laws were approved as a result of popular initiatives: the Vote Buying Law of 1999, and the

Clean Slate Law of 2010, which banned anyone convicted on appeal of running for elected office.

In all such reforms, the agenda was largely set from the outside in. Rather than being proactively pursued by the political elite, proposals for anticorruption reform gained momentum either during or right after periods in which politicians seemed to be under pressure and needed to provide some minimally credible response to the public. Importantly, not all scandals led to reform, and most of the reforms that ultimately were enacted were not conceived during the scandals themselves. Rather, several were proposals that had already been long debated in Congress, but had not yet found their way onto the governing agenda. The exogenous events, in other words, did not seem to have shaped the reforms' basic content, but precipitated their enactment. Such reactive reforms, in fact, seem to follow the basic garbage can model of organizational choice, where new policies emerge only at a moment of temporary alignment between problems, solutions, participants, and choice opportunities in decisionmaking processes (Cohen, March, and Olsen 1972; Kingdon 1984).

Second, *proactive reforms* were those purposefully pursued by political actors, often within the federal administration. Unlike reactive reforms, proactive reforms do not seem to emerge from moments of crisis or popular pressure, but are advanced in their absence. Proactive reforms have been pushed by the government either as part of an explicit anticorruption agenda or to resolve other equally salient policy concerns. One example of the former is the expansion of the CGU in 2003, following the PT's rise to the presidency, as it sought to deliver on its anticorruption electoral promises. The latter is illustrated by transparency-enhancing measures that were in many ways by-products of economic policies, including the Taxpayer Identification Law of 1990, and the Fiscal Responsibility Law of 2000. Likewise, some reforms were developed in response to relatively clear mandates written into the 1988 Constitution, even if they took a long time coming. An example is the Access to Information Law of 2011, the enactment of which arguably resulted in large part from the personal leadership of President Rousseff (Cunha Filho 2019). Other such reforms derived from Brazil's international commitments, some of which were not directly related to the control of corruption. The Anti–Money Laundering Law of 1998 and the subsequent establishment of the COAF are important examples, as they were initially conceived as a tool to fight drug trafficking, rather than corruption. Similarly, the bill that eventually became the Anti–Money Laundering Law of 1998 was proposed by the executive branch in late 1996, justified under the 1988 UN Convention Against Illicit Traffic in Narcotic Drugs and Psychotropic Substances, as well as other international conventions on the topic within the Organization of American States (Câmara dos Deputados 1997: 3872). Some proactive reforms seemed to follow the logic of insurance theories (Ginsburg 2003; Epperly 2019), whereby political elites faced with increased political competition enact reforms that may enhance their position once in opposition. One illustration of this dynamic is the change in the constitutional provision on immunity from prosecution, enacted in late 2001, at the end of Cardoso's second term in office.

Finally, *endogenous reforms* were largely driven by the agencies responsible for the implementation of different anticorruption tasks. As such, they predominantly involved innovations at the organizational level such as training and specialization programs, initiatives for interinstitutional coordination, and the development of new technologies and processes. The establishment of ENCCLA, the proliferation of task forces, and the creation of judgeships specialized in financial crimes are clear examples of this logic of endogenous reform. Such reforms either do not depend directly on the approval of political elites or can be designed in such a way that they pass by largely unnoticed by them, "smuggled" in by policy entrepreneurs through subtle shifts in legislation, or through changes in procedure and organization (Bersch 2019; Taylor 2009, 2020).

Reactive, proactive, and endogenous reforms are not mutually exclusive. In fact, many reforms followed multiple logics simultaneously. Furthermore, some earlier reforms led to later, initially unforeseen, reforms over time. For instance, the decision by President Lula's justice minister Marcio Thomaz Bastos to strengthen the anti–money laundering capacities within his ministry—which included the creation of the DRCI and increasing professionalization at the Federal Police—piggybacked on the 1998 Anti–Money Laundering Law, which, in turn, followed from Brazil's international commitments to fight drug trafficking. The decision to focus on money laundering within the Ministry of Justice, in turn, was followed by organizational changes in the courts, the Ministério Público Federal, and the Federal Police, with specialization, task forces, and ENCCLA soon following and increasingly targeting corruption. The enactment of the 2012 law that facilitated the enforcement of the 1998 Anti–Money Laundering Law also reflected the learning process that took place among law enforcement authorities.

With proactive reforms in particular, the short-term horizons of most politicians seem to have played an important role in facilitating reform, especially because the impact of such reforms has seldom been immediate and instead took years for many of these measures to become effective. For instance, laws establishing new types of crimes may have provided new tools for prosecutors, but the political elite almost inevitably could count on judicial inoperancy to delay any significant impact from the new laws. Reforms that did directly and immediately impact political elites faced a steeper climb, leading to a fourth category, of reforms that did not happen. For example, none of the reforms described above addressed the institutional incentives that have contributed to high levels of political corruption such as the coupling of an extremely fragmented party system with concentrated campaign finance. In these cases, any reforms would have extremely concentrated costs, and political incumbents have thus been resistant to change.

The various reforms that were enacted, however, produced a significant cumulative effect over time. By the 2010s, the accumulation of reforms enhancing the institutional capacity of law enforcement agencies seemed likely to lead to an eruption of legal accountability efforts. For the attentive observer, the only questions were where and when such an eruption would take place. As it turned out, the eruption began in March 2014 in the southern city of Curitiba, and would soon be known to everyone as *Lava Jato*. The next two chapters detail this investigation's rise and fall.

Notes

1. Justiça Federal (2017: 211).
2. This approach draws from Taylor (2018), but includes an important revision to his framework, better distinguishing capacity from engagement.
3. Levi (1999: 8) notes that "a competent and relatively honest bureaucracy not only reduces the incentives for corruption and inefficient rent-seeking but also increases the probability of cooperation and compliance."
4. Capacity, engagement, and dominance correspond to three dimensions in broader political analysis: an *institutional* one, a *behavioral* one, and one related to (im)balances in the distribution of *power* itself.
5. Especially Articles 5, 37, 58, and 216.
6. Criticism of the law remains significant, especially regarding its appeals process (Martini and Soares 2016).
7. One example of this back and forth movement was the Comissão Especial de Investigações (Special Committee of Investigations, CEI). Established in 1993 within the executive branch and given relatively broad powers following

the significant scandals of the early 1990s (e.g., *PC Farias, Anões do Orça-mento)*, the CEI was ultimately extinguished in 1995, with all its pending inves-tigations transferred to the Ministry of Justice.

8. An important and disputed case here is Petrobras. Articles 67–68 of Law 9.478 led to Presidential Decree n. 2745, of 1998, and established bidding rules specific for Petrobras due to the deregulation of the oil market in Brazil, which broke Petrobras's historic monopoly on oil exploration. The presidential decree led to a long battle with the TCU at the STF over which public procurement law should be applicable to Petrobras's oversight, starting in 2006 (Peixoto 2014: 23–25). Whereas the TCU argued that the general and stricter Public Procure-ment Law of 1993 should also be applicable to Petrobras, Petrobras argued that its bidding practices could be guided exclusively by the presidential decree of 1998. The authors thank José Guilherme Giacomuzzi for his insights.

9. There are also prosecutorial bodies at the state level. Throughout this book, our focus is solely on the Ministério Público Federal (MPF). Unless oth-erwise specified, Ministério Público refers to the federal body.

10. In 2001, the Associação Nacional de Procuradores da República (ANPR) began voting among its rank and file on potential candidates for prosecutor-general, following a similar practice used in state Ministérios Públicos. This practice did not exist in the Ministério Público Federal, where the prosecutor-general only needed to be a career prosecutor, older than age thirty-five. In the first vote, in 2001, Geraldo Brindeiro came in seventh among potential candidates. Starting in 2003, the Lula presidency acknowledged the list and began a practice that continued for more than a decade: picking the highest voted among federal prosecutors. The informal norm was ignored for the first time in 2019, when President Bol-sonaro nominated Augusto Aras as prosecutor-general.

11. At the subnational level, state courts have strikingly different perfor-mances. Some state courts, such as those of Rio Grande do Sul, have criminally convicted hundreds of mayors, whereas in other states, such as Bahia, convic-tions have been even rarer than at the national level (Da Ros 2014; Bento, Da Ros, and Londero 2020).

12. Law 8.429 of 1992 permits corruption to be dealt with via the civil code, as in cases of administrative improbity, which punish corruption with a fine, sus-pension of political rights, and repayment of the damages.

13. Of the nine TCU ministers, only two must be chosen from among the technical TCU staff of auditors and prosecutors. The remaining ministers are selected by the executive branch and the legislative branch. The latter appoint-ments are often a perk for retiring politicians or for politicians who were not reelected; such appointees are seen as unlikely to battle their former coalition allies in Congress and the executive branch. As Speck (2011: 155) notes, "Politi-cians are frequently nominated to join the TCU at the height or the end of their political career in what is sometimes seen as a kind of early retirement. . . . Age and political background thus have a profound impact on ministers' connections to the political world and their commitment to their new institution."

14. The small number of prisoners in jail on corruption charges may be due in part to the leniency of sentencing. Although there are minimum sentences for crimes like corruption, the overcrowding of prisons incentivizes the cycling of prisoners to avoid even more severe overcrowding. This has led to a number of systems for early release, including pardons, progressive imprisonment, and parole. *Indultos* (pardons) are frequent. There are various forms of progressive imprisonment: closed, semiopen, and open. *Closed* is for prisoners who spend all

their time in jail; *semiopen* allows prisoners to work outside prison during the day and return for the evening; and *open* refers to prisoners who sleep in a halfway house. (Brasília has no such halfway house, so prisoners in open imprisonment are remitted to open house arrest, meaning they are free during the day and must sleep at home at night!) Most prisoners can move from closed to semiopen, or semiopen to open, after completing one-sixth of their prison term. *Liberdade condicional* (parole) is available to convicts who have completed one-third of their sentences (or half of their sentences if they are recidivists) (Barroso 2017; Taylor 2017).

15. A study of legal provisions that protect elected politicians from prosecution in ninety democracies concluded that Brazil is the country with the third-highest de jure protections (tied with Argentina), after only Paraguay and Uruguay. The authors found that, controlling for a variety of factors, these legal provisions are associated with greater corruption, and that the effect is probably causal (Reddy, Schularick, and Skreta 2020).

16. Cases of petty corruption do seem to have a slightly different fate in the courts. Alencar and Gico (2011) found that final convictions of federal civil servants expelled from office due to corruption allegations reached only 3 percent. Yet not all civil servants expelled from office in their sample had been indicted, suggesting that the basis for their expulsion from office may not have reached the standard of a criminal prosecution. Of the 441 civil servants fired from office in their sample, 224 were indicted, and in only 94 cases did the courts reach a decision on whether to acquit or convict (59 acquittals and 35 convictions). One underappreciated finding in their study is simply the enormous delays surrounding court decisions, largely due to an extremely permissive appeals system. In fact, out of 224 indictments, only 25 had been definitely resolved in the courts at the time of writing. See also Odilla (2019: 227), who found that nearly one out of every five penalties imposed on civil servants in 2009–2015 could not be effectuated because the statute of limitations had expired.

17. Donadon was the first politician to be convicted under the original jurisdiction of the STF since 1988. But although he had been convicted and arrested, his congressional peers declined to expel him from Congress. This vote led to a public outcry, which spurred the elimination of the secret vote in expulsion cases. In a public vote in February 2014, Congress finally expelled Donadon (A. Guimarães, Perlin, and Maia 2019: 43).

18. Other judicial reversals of reforms that the parties themselves undertook include reforms to the party finance fund and rules on the transparency of corporate campaign donations.

19. For a detailed account of the shifts in the rules governing original jurisdiction, see Da Ros and Taylor (2021b).

20. Up until 2009, defendants convicted in an appeals court could be sent to jail. An STF decision that year changed this rule, and established that convicted defendants should start serving jail time only after all their appeals had been exhausted (Vieira 2018). As Chapter 5 notes, another STF decision in 2016 returned to the understanding held by the court until 2009. Later, in 2019, the court again reversed its understanding of the issue, and reestablished the rule that convicted defendants could serve jail time only after all their appeals had been exhausted.

21. It is worth noting that until 2018 such cases could be entirely unrelated to the federal position itself, including charges as varied as homicide and environmental crimes. In 2018, the STF altered its stance, limiting original

jurisdiction to sitting federal officeholders and only to cases related to their exercise of public office.

22. Apart from the federal courts, numerous experiences at the subnational level have also accumulated over the decades. In fact, some have even been the inspiration for federal changes (e.g., *juízes de instrução* at the STF were inspired by a specialized panel at the Supreme Court of Rio Grande do Sul, which adopted this practice beginning in 1989). Specialized prosecutors' offices dedicated to mayoral crimes currently exist in at least six states (Rio Grande do Sul, Paraná, São Paulo, Minas Gerais, Goiás, Bahia), some dating back to the early 1990s (Da Ros 2014, 2018). However, subnational efforts at curbing corruption have been uneven. Whereas some subnational experiences serve as models to be adopted by the federal government, many subnational governments began to act more assertively only after the federal administration did so—the "boomerang effect" described by Ingram (2015: 267). And all this unevenness exists in spite of the fact that most rules (e.g., those on criminal law, criminal and civil procedure, and administrative improbity) are determined by federal statutes and are, therefore, identical throughout the national territory. In fact, a federal system, such as Brazil, that concentrates rule making at the federal level is not expected to decentralize policy implementation.

23. The starting wages for federal judges and prosecutors are the same, are more than ten times higher than per capita GDP (Da Ros and Taylor 2019), and rank among the highest of all professions in the country (Canzian 2020).

24. Within the federal judiciary, each of the five regional appellate courts hires its own magistrates. Since 1988, they have each performed between fourteen and eighteen public examination hiring processes (F. A. Rodrigues 2019: 53).

25. ENCCLA was initially called only the Estratégia Nacional de Combate à Lavagem de Dinheiro (National Strategy for Fighting Money Laundering, ENCLA); it added "and Corruption" to its name in 2006 (Secretaria Nacional de Justiça 2012: 35).

26. The idea of specialized courts came out of a 2003 study by the Conselho da Justiça Federal, which noted that one of the biggest difficulties for investigators was to break bank secrecy protections, and that there were far fewer cases of money laundering than warranted. In Brazil, bank secrecy can be lifted only by judicial order; moving cases to specialized courts helped to streamline this process for police and prosecutors.

27. In the Congress sworn in during 2003, fully 193 of 513 deputies (38 percent) switched parties. Rosenn (2014: 306–308) notes that the constitutionality of the Clean Slate Law was challenged in the STF in 2010 and, while both judicial and legislative opposition to the law was significant, public pressure helped to ensure its survival.

28. The MDB was formerly known as the Partido do Movimento Democrático Brasileiro (PMDB); the PP is an amalgam of the former parties Partido Democrático Social (PDS), Partido Progressista Reformador (PPR), and PPB; and the DEM was formerly known as the PFL. We report here the parties' time in office using their current moniker.

29. The *Centrão* is a widely used but elusive concept that refers broadly to a large group of parties within the Brazilian party system that seek to ally themselves to government, independent of who the sitting president might be. The term *Centrão* is often used pejoratively, referring to these parties' mercenary quest for appointments and budget allocations, which are exchanged for legislative support

without much attention to ideology or the content of policy. Marcos Nobre (2013: 42–43) has referred to this system of exchange as *medebismo,* in reference to one of the most iconic parties of the Centrão, the MDB. Throughout, we will use the term to refer to the ideologically malleable, often transactional parties that have provided support to governments of various ideological stripes in exchange for rewards from the executive branch (for discussions of the Centrão, see Nobre 2013; Borges 2021; Da Ros and Taylor 2021c; Vasconcellos 2021).

30. This excludes interim presidencies at the Brazilian Senate. There were two in the period 1985–2018: Edison Lobão (first of the DEM, later MDB) was interim president of the Brazilian Senate for one day in September 2001, and Tião Viana (PT) held the position for two months in late 2007 (Senado Federal 2020).

4

Lava Jato and the Big Push, 2014–2016

What needs to be fought, I repeat,
is rampant corruption. And that means
strengthening our institutions.
—Governor Aécio Neves, presidential candidate, 2014[1]

I think that [the Lava Jato *investigations] can,*
in fact, change Brazil forever. In what sense?
In the sense that they will end impunity.
—President Dilma Rousseff, 2014[2]

By the 2010s, many informed observers thought that Brazil might even be on the cusp of a transition toward a less corrupt society. Previous chapters of this book described how Brazil had made gradual improvements along the various components of the accountability equation, enabling the country to incrementally move toward a new world in which grand corruption investigations began reaching the federal courts in the first two decades of the new century. This progress along the accountability frontier facilitated the emergence of *Lava Jato*, which would have been unthinkable even a few years earlier.

In this chapter we explore how, despite Brazil's persistent bottlenecks with elite impunity and a unique form of political dominance, *Lava Jato* initially prospered in ways that suggested the country was on the cusp of a shift to a new accountability equilibrium. The chapter begins with a brief rundown of the early years of *Lava Jato,* then we describe the dual shock it caused, revealing systemic corruption in a fresh and transparent fashion while also demonstrating how judicial processes could function more efficiently. We describe the prevailing political, economic, and social conditions that influenced *Lava Jato*'s initial success, as well as the new capacity that was brought to bear and the strategic legal and political approaches that were conscientiously employed to ensure greater success, in what would become a big anticorruption push involving a wide range of anticorruption agencies, mobilizing civil society, and designing a variety of reforms to quickly shift prevailing behaviors and eliminate old players.

Lava Jato Bursts onto the Scene

The headlines surrounding Operation *Lava Jato* in the years following its eruption were any publisher's dream. "Brazil's Great Oil Swindle," the *New York Times* pronounced (Segal 2015). "The Biggest Corruption Scandal in History?" the *Guardian* asked (Watts 2017). "A Brazilian Bribery Machine," the *Financial Times* declared (Leahy 2016). Not to be surpassed, the *Wall Street Journal* concluded that Brazil "Finds Corruption Under Every Rock" (Pearson 2017).

Academics, usually a staid bunch, were just as breathless, labeling it "a massive scheme of contract fraud and enrichment" (Rotberg 2017: 6). A book coauthored by one of the founders of Transparency International argued that "the entire state of Brazil seems to have been captured by a corruption network, whereby politicians of all parties participated" (Heimann and Pieth 2017: 6). An edited volume dedicated solely to the investigation called it the "largest corruption scandal in the country's history" (Lagunes and Svejnar 2020b: 7). Two leading corruption specialists declared *Lava Jato* simply "the largest corruption scandal ever to beset a democratic nation" (Fisman and Golden 2017: 13).

Journalists and academics could be forgiven for their breathlessness. The judicial results of *Lava Jato* were truly astounding, especially in a country with long-standing elite impunity for corruption. The list of accomplishments was long: more than 360 convictions, nearly 400 plea bargains, and nearly 30 corporate leniency agreements in the seven years following the case's eruption in March 2014. High-level officials were jailed, including two former presidents, senators, congressmen, and governors. Nearly US$1 billion (at the 2020 exchange rate) was returned to the public coffers, and nearly US$3 billion in fines, penalties, and voluntary indemnities by defendants was imposed by 2020 (Ministério Público Federal 2020). Another approximately US$10 billion was being sought in pending civil cases (Jones and Pereira Neto 2020; Londero 2021). Such results were simply unprecedented.

Lava Jato washed over Brazilian politics in successive waves that battered long existing structures and swept old players out to sea. In its first year, 2014, the investigation threatened the PT's hold on the presidency. In 2016, it played a major role in the crisis that led to President Dilma Rousseff's impeachment. During 2017 and 2018, the operation threatened her successor's tenuous grip on power, with Michel Temer only narrowly holding on to the presidency for lack of a viable alternate and because much of Brazil was too exhausted by scandal to engage before the 2018 elections. In 2018, the arrest of former President Luiz Inácio Lula da Silva by order of Judge Sérgio Moro, the intrepid magistrate commanding the operation in the trial courts, upended the electoral calculus and opened the way for the election of a maverick, Jair Bolsonaro. The nomination of Moro as Bolsonaro's justice minister in 2019 was seen by some as confirmation of Moro's political intentions all along, and by others as the harbinger of serious reform; regardless, it provided Bolsonaro with a veneer of anticorruption legitimacy that helped him to overcome a lackluster backbencher's record. Moro's fiery resignation in April 2020 once again upended politics, casting doubt on Bolsonaro's political future, fueling rumors of impeachment and launching discussion of Moro's possible presidential candidacy in 2022.

Lava Jato began, like most corruption investigations, on slim pickings.[3] It was fueled at its outset by a series of lucky coincidences. The first break came when police investigating money laundering at a currency exchange store located on the second floor of a laundromat within a gas station in Brasília, just 3 kilometers from Congress, recognized the voice of Alberto Youssef on a wiretap. Youssef was a *doleiro* who had been arrested on multiple occasions and had been a key witness during the *Banestado* investigation in the early 2000s. Investigators trailing Youssef caught a second break when they found an email from Youssef to Paulo Roberto Costa, a former high-ranking executive at the state-run oil company Petrobras in Rio de Janeiro, detailing his gift of a Range Rover to Costa. This was unusual, to say the least, especially given that Youssef had a criminal background, and Costa had for decades been a senior executive at what was then the sixth-largest company in the world by market capitalization, accounting for 10 percent of the Brazilian GDP (Segal 2015).

The third break was location. The simple fact that Youssef had worked in Paraná state meant that the case came across the desks of two key figures, Deltan Dallagnol and Sérgio Moro. Dallagnol, in his mid-thirties, was a crusading prosecutor in the Ministério Público Federal, Brazil's quasi-autonomous prosecutorial body, who had specialized in anticorruption, worked closely with a team of police and investigators in past investigations, and was willing to aggressively push the boundaries of Brazilian law on plea bargains. Moro, less than a decade his senior, was the first of a generation of federal judges specialized in money laundering. He had copiously researched the Italian *Mani Pulite* case of the 1990s; had worked on a variety of anti–money laundering and corruption cases in his trial court, which happened to be in Curitiba, the capital of Paraná state and a hotbed of smuggling and money laundering; and had spent time as an auxiliary judge at Brazil's highest court, the Supreme Federal Tribunal (STF), when that court was hearing the *Mensalão* case, a corruption case that was in many ways a smaller precursor to *Lava Jato*. Both Dallagnol and Moro had long known of Youssef, having both worked on the *Banestado* case more than a decade earlier.

Finally, investigators caught a lucky break after Costa recanted an early confession. Having initially copped to the crime, in August 2014 Costa appeared before Congress and denied that there was corruption at the state-owned company. The very next day he was arrested on charges of holding more than US$26 million in Swiss accounts, but there was no sign that he would reverse his recantation. The police, however, obtained security photo images of Costa's daughters and sons-in-law collecting documents at Costa's office and were able to charge them with intent to destroy evidence. Under terrible pressure that his family might be sent away, Costa joined Youssef in signing a plea bargain. More than 100 depositions later, Costa had provided a remarkably detailed road map to the vast corruption scheme between politicians, construction firms, Petrobras, and *doleiros*. The consistency and rich detail of Costa's and Youssef's plea bargains—complete with names, bank accounts, and bribes paid and received—helped to generate considerable pressure on other suspects to cooperate (Almeida and Zagaris 2015: 89).

There were seventy-nine numbered phases to *Lava Jato* in Curitiba between 2014 and 2021 (Pontes 2021). These phases are a bit of an artificial construct: a *phase* is merely a series of coordinated actions by police and prosecutors, which may or may not lead to concrete legal actions. But the various phases of *Lava Jato* clearly evolved in pursuit of distinct targets. Like branches on a tree, they grew from the same trunk, but branched out into new spaces.

Lava Jato's first and still most fruitful branch investigated the ties between *doleiros*—the wealthy, influential, and yet ultimately illegal money exchangers that have long populated the gray world between legitimate and illegitimate business activities in Brazil—and Costa, who had been director of supply logistics between 2004 and 2012 at Petrobras, Brazil's behemoth state-controlled oil company. The *Lava Jato* task force marveled at the ties between Costa and their longtime nemesis Youssef, whose mix of a long rap sheet and numerous political connections was as unseemly as it was unlikely.

The next branch may be said to have begun with Phase 7, in November 2014, immediately following the reelection of President Rousseff. The task force turned to other Petrobras executives—Pedro Barusco, Nestor Cerveró, and Renato Duque, whose coverage on the nightly news quickly turned them into household names—and used them to leverage accusations against midsized construction firms and the *empreiteiros* (owners and executives at construction companies) at the heart of the corruption scheme.

Brazilians watched in horror as details emerged of backroom dealings to set prices at artificially high levels, gouging Petrobras and, by extension, the long-suffering Brazilian taxpayer. Pulling the pieces together, it became clear that Brazilian construction firms had built a cartel, whose executives received lists of forthcoming construction projects from corrupt Petrobras officials. The executives would meet at the Rio de Janeiro offices of the Brazilian Association of Industrial Engineering (ABEMI) to divvy up forthcoming projects, agreeing on who would bid and how much. By rigging the market even before bidding took place, companies in the cartel were able to corner all of the most significant projects, not only at Petrobras, but throughout the federal government. Seven of the cartel companies were able to capture between 55 and 75 percent of all government construction contracts between 2003 and 2014 (Valarini and Pohlmann 2019). They often proceeded to further boost their profits by having vague language inserted in the contracts to justify later amendments, overcharging for project inputs, and delaying project completion so as to force the federal and state governments into paying surcharges for additions "necessary" for project completion (Orta 2017; Praça 2018: 43–61).

By early 2015, enough evidence had accumulated so that the task force felt confident enough to take the dangerous step of moving into political terrain, charging former congressmen André Vargas (PT), Pedro Corrêa (PP), and Luiz Argolo (PP), who were no longer in office and thus could be charged in the fast-moving trial court, rather than claiming special standing under the original jurisdiction of the high court. The task force moved rapidly up the food chain from these former congressmen to the PT party treasurer, João Vaccari, allegedly the string puller at the heart of the incumbent party's campaign finance shenanigans, and from these political brokers to the major corruptors at the heart of the scheme, the large construction firms.

Phase 14, and its aptly named *Erga Omnes* operation, sought to put lie to the long-standing truism that wealthy elites face no justice in Brazil. In scenes never before seen in the history of the country, king-makers were brought down, as the chief executives of the country's three largest construction firms—Odebrecht, Andrade Gutierrez, and Camargo Corrêa—were shuttled off to jail. These men were royalty: they rode helicopters from their corporate headquarters to their palatial homes, owned private jets that ferried politicians to and fro, had their names recorded in presidential diaries, generously funded the campaigns of leading politicians at all levels of government, and were the descendants of fathers and grandfathers who had exercised influence before them over more than half a century, well before the democratic regime. No one, especially in Brasília, could imagine in a million years that one of these men would see the inside of a jail cell. The sight of princeling Marcelo Odebrecht, in particular, being escorted by heavily armed federal police in a T-shirt and handcuffs became the stuff of breathless TV news, keeping all of Brazil on tenterhooks and ensuring that *Lava Jato* was at the center of all discussion.

The details of Odebrecht's elaborate corruption practices suggested that this was less a private sector company than a criminal organization: the company had a special division dedicated solely to bribery, with a Caribbean bank, a dedicated off-the-books accounting system, and a staff that was in regular contact with politicians across the political spectrum. Odebrecht tallied record revenue of nearly R$108 billion (roughly US$40 billion at the time) in 2014 (Odebrecht 2015). It did so with no research and development (R&D) department, but a fully structured bribery sector, making it possibly the most iconic example of one of corruption's most perverse effects: corruption leads businesses to invest in rent seeking rather than in technological innovation to increase profits. During the fifteen-year time frame covered by the company's agreement with prosecutors, Odebrecht had undertaken 155 construction projects across Latin America, 110 of which were outside Brazil (Orta 2017). This would lead to a ripple effect of scandals in several other countries, implicating a host of high-ranking political figures, including all four Peruvian presidents elected after

Alberto Fujimori (Alejandro Toledo, Alán García, Ollanta Humala, and Pedro Pablo Kuczynski; Marin 2019).

From *Erga Omnes,* it was a hop, skip, and jump to the political nucleus of the Petrobras scheme. By August 2015, the task force had moved against wrongdoing at the Planning Ministry. It arrested José Dirceu, President Lula's chief of staff, already disgraced and convicted for corruption in the 2005 *Mensalão* case. It moved against other close associates of Lula, including his friend José Carlos Bumlai, political marketing gurus João Santana and Monica Moura, and former finance ministers Guido Mantega and Antonio Palocci, arrested in September 2016. Wrongdoing at Petrobras also led, in September 2018, to what was then the biggest settlement ever with US authorities under the Foreign Corrupt Practices Act (FCPA), totaling US$1.78 billion (Cassin 2018a).[4]

Separate branches of *Lava Jato* sprouted simultaneously, as the big push continued. In other times, these might have led the nightly news; in the *Lava Jato* context, they were merely sideshows, offering only further confirmation of the rot that had taken hold of Brazilian politics and business. Phase 16, in July 2015, took aim at corruption in the state-run Eletronuclear firm, disgracing the widely respected admiral, Othon Luiz Pinheiro, who headed Brazil's nuclear energy efforts (Ortega and Macedo 2020). Between March and July 2016, *Lava Jato* moved against the international operators who had made the corruption possible, reaching several businessmen abroad and showing links to the Panamanian dark world operations of Mossack Fonseca, the law firm at the heart of the Panama Papers leaks, which was alleged to have engaged in serial tax evasion and money laundering on behalf of select clients.

Along the way, *Lava Jato* contributed to sinking the Rousseff presidency. In parallel to the corruption scandal, simultaneous economic and political crises were brewing, reinforcing each other and destabilizing the coalition that sustained Rousseff. While Rousseff was never charged by *Lava Jato,* her government was battered around the head by anticorruption protests; by her long links to Petrobras, where she had served as chair of the board; by her ties to many of the PT figures implicated in the scandal; and by her unwillingness—principled, naïve, or possibly both—to stand up to protect the political world of Brasília by quashing the investigations. Failure to quash *Lava Jato* may have been the straw that led her coalition to rebel. Whatever the case, by May 2016, Rousseff had been temporarily removed from office in an unsavory impeachment drive headed by her onetime coalition allies in the MDB.

But *Lava Jato* continued to move forward, drawing on its momentum and on the reserve of public support that it had built up in its first thirty months. In October 2016, soon after the impeachment wound down, Eduardo Cunha, a practitioner of the darkest political arts and a master of the transactional politics that interwove his home state of Rio de Janeiro with federal largesse, was jailed. A month later, Rio governor Sergio Cabral and several of his state secretaries were behind bars, where they soon would be joined by state legislators, accused sequentially over the course of the next two years of wrongdoing in the 2014 World Cup reconstruction of the iconic Maracanã soccer stadium, price gouging in the Rio metro system, theft in the Rio highway system, graft in the state penitentiaries, operating a criminal organization in the transport sector, corruption in the 2016 Olympics, and price-fixing and theft in the state health sector. Rio entrepreneur Eike Batista, the flashy CEO of an oil and logistics empire, who in the heady days of the early pre-salt oil discoveries of the late 2000s had briefly been the seventh-richest man on Earth and was heralded as the beacon of a new private sector entrepreneurial spirit in Brazil, soon was shunted off to join Cabral in prison, his head shaved and his bravado, for once, dimmed.

Federally owned enterprises and federal projects continued to be a significant branch of the *Lava Jato* tree. Petrobras's efforts in shipbuilding were the focus of various phases, including the 2016 investigation of price gouging in the construction of offshore drilling platforms, the 2017 phase targeting corruption by domestic and foreign firms in Petrobras-related shipbuilding, as well as a related 2017 investigation of the Transpetro logistics subsidiary, and the 2018 phase focused on the Petroquisa subsidiary. Aldemir Bendine, a former president of Petrobras, a former president of the state-owned Banco do Brasil, and a stalwart of the Workers' Party during its time in office, was arrested in July 2017. The construction of a Petrobras headquarters in Salvador, Bahia, became the focus of Phase 56, followed closely by an investigation of Petrobras storage facilities the next month. But other federally controlled projects also were swept up by *Lava Jato*: Phase 49 in March 2018 targeted corruption in the pharaonic Belo Monte dam project; and in April investigators turned their attention to state-owned enterprises' employee pension funds, which have historically provided the federal government with leverage over private sector investment decisions through interwoven shareholding arrangements.

Along the way, other branches of the investigation brought down state governors in Minas Gerais, Tocantins, and Paraná. Mario Negromonte, a former cities minister under Rousseff, long reputed to be involved in shenanigans but nonetheless serving on the state accounting tribunal in Bahia, was felled. São Paulo state, run for more than two decades by the opposition PSDB party, became a focus of the investigation by 2018, as evidence emerged of construction-related corruption in the building of the São Paulo beltway and a variety of highway projects, in a scandal that cast a pall over the entire PSDB and demonstrated, if there was any doubt, that corruption was not solely the domain of the PT and its coalition partners (J. Marques 2020). Former PSDB presidential candidate Aécio Neves became critically entangled in the investigation of Joesley Batista's wrongdoing in 2017, in an ancillary case with links to *Lava Jato*. In February 2019, former senator and foreign minister Aloysio Nunes Ferreira, the PSDB's vice presidential candidate in the 2014 elections, was in the cross-hairs of the sixtieth phase of *Lava Jato,* suggestively named *Ad Infinitum.* PSDB senator Paulo Roberto Bauer, a member of Bolsonaro's presidential secretariat, became a target in early 2020 for taking bribes as a senator, allegedly to favor the interests of a large supermarket chain.

But perhaps the most momentous and politically fraught moments of the later years of *Lava Jato* were the six months between June 2017 and January 2018. Already, prosecutors had made it clear that this corruption scandal might rise as high as the presidential office: in September 2016, the lead prosecutor on *Lava Jato,* Deltan Dallagnol, had presented an unsubtle PowerPoint slide with fourteen arrows pointing to Lula's name, allegedly at the center of all schemes. While the slide was widely lampooned as a jumbled and incoherent case against Lula, the former president was at serious legal risk, and would ultimately face investigation or indictment in thirteen distinct cases (BBC Brasil 2019).

Now prosecutors began to move against the most senior political authorities. In June 2017, recordings of President Temer's corrupt dealings with disgraced meatpacking tycoon Joesley Batista went public, forcing Temer into a defensive crouch from which his presidency never emerged. In July, trial court judge Sérgio Moro convicted former president Lula in the first of the cases against him, sentencing him to nine years in jail. In September, new charges were filed against a host of PT heavyweights, including Palocci, Mantega, and Vaccari, former communications minister Edinho da Silva, as well as the power couple of Paulo Bernardo, a former planning minister, and Gleisi Hoffman, a senator. Soon thereafter, it was the MDB's turn, with charges filed against party luminaries, including former president José Sarney, as well as a notable collection of legislators, including Edison Lobão, Jader Barbalho, Renan Calheiros, Romero Jucá, and Valdir Raupp. In

January, the appeals court upheld Lula's conviction on the first of the charges against him and raised his sentence to twelve years.

The appeals court conviction, under the then prevailing rules, meant that Lula could be jailed immediately. Over two days, Brazilians followed the drama minute by minute to see if Lula—a beloved politician who had left office in 2010 with a stratospheric personal approval rating of 87 percent (Reuters 2010; Bonin 2010)—would voluntarily surrender to police. Supporters thronged the headquarters of the metalworkers' union in São Bernardo do Campo, where Lula had begun his career fighting the military regime as a labor leader. Supporters pledged never to surrender Lula to authorities. Finally, on a tense Saturday afternoon, Lula emerged with his lawyers, peacefully walking through the adulatory crowd to enter a police car that would drive him slowly through the crowd to a predetainment medical exam and then off to prison in Curitiba.

The Double Shock of *Lava Jato*

As the story above suggests, *Lava Jato* was a shock, bringing into glaring focus the degree to which corruption was endemic, systemic, and monumental. For anyone who took the time to read them, Paulo Roberto Costa's depositions in 2014 were a shocking dose of reality, perhaps best summarized in his first deposition (cited in the first epigraph to Chapter 2), depicting the rotten ties between the political system and the developmental state apparatus, and the central role of campaign finance in linking the two. For a country that had taken pride in its ability to conquer hyperinflation, found hope in its pre-salt oil discoveries, and delighted in its seeming emergence as a more just and equitable democracy under the back-to-back presidencies of Cardoso and Lula, this was a harsh reality check.

It is worth going back in time to reflect on the extent to which *Lava Jato* represented a shock to the system when it came to the public eye in 2014. At some level, most observers already "knew" that there was extensive corruption in Brazil. There were clearly many facilitators of corruption, both structural (e.g., inequality, authoritarian legacies) and institutional (e.g., the extremely fragmented coalitional political system, a slow and inefficient judiciary). And there were many red flags about the scale of corruption, ranging from foreign prosecution of leading politicians (e.g., São Paulo governor and former presidential candidate Paulo Maluf, convicted by Jersey authorities for stashing bribes in a Deutsche Bank account on that isle) to the domestic arrests of judges (e.g., federal judge João Carlos Rocha Mattos, convicted in 2003 for receiving bribes).

But because evidence had long been hard to find, the prevailing mind-set was that Brazil was somehow in a category of its own, distant from some of its "underdeveloped" and *caudillista* South American neighbors. Although some observers were more cognizant of the depth of corruption, many at the time had a bad apples perspective: the view that corruption in Brazil was largely an individual problem, the consequence of a few amoral bad actors taking advantage of old and perhaps lingering loopholes in the system that might soon be overcome by the increasing institutionalization of a consolidating democracy.[5] The rhetoric of scandal as it was covered in the press tended to reinforce this bad apples perspective, focusing on the "two congressmen" who allegedly were bought off to approve the constitutional amendment permitting reelection, rather than the systemic problem of vote buying not only in Congress, but in legislatures across the nation; on "Paulo Maluf" and his offshore accounts on Jersey, rather than on the fact that politicians laundered enormous amounts of money in tax havens overseas or the systemic problem that many construction projects had been designed solely for rent seeking by politicians and construction firms; or on "a dirty federal judge," such as Rocha Mattos, rather than on the systemic problem of the protections that courts afforded to corrupt elites. Under-the-table campaign finance contributions were an issue that had long been discussed (Fleischer 1997), but many observers thought of it as a flexing of economic muscle akin to the lobbying and influence peddling of wealthier democracies, rather than a correlate of, or even a direct cause of, systemic corruption. Even informed observers often conceived of corruption as the last gasps of the old order, rather than the regular modus operandi of the new democracy (DaMatta 1993).

The second jolt brought by *Lava Jato* to Brazilian perspectives on corruption was more hopeful: corrupt actors actually appeared to be wilting in the face of a judicial onslaught. Beginning in March 2014, the investigations seemed to march inexorably forward, with bombastic new allegations emerging regularly. Newspaper headlines somehow managed to top each other, week after week. Rather than going nowhere and ending up in pizza, as so many past scandals had, the investigations seemed to be leading to an unprecedented degree of accountability. In 2012 and 2013, the *Mensalão* case had jailed top aides to the president and was largely considered "a great leap forward for democracy and the rule of law," serving as a "compelling indicator that the country is learning to put its national motto, 'order and progress,' into practice under the aegis of democracy" (Michener and Pereira 2016: 25). And by the end of 2014, it was increasingly obvious that business heavyweights and other politicians implicated in *Lava Jato* would soon join them in prison.

How did this sudden acceleration in anticorruption come to pass? Summarizing grossly, the incremental changes in accountability described in Chapter 3 seemed to have built to critical mass, especially with regard to transparency, oversight, capacity, and engagement. Even the bottleneck of ineffective sanction seemed to be seeing improvement, in small pockets of the Ministério Público Federal and the judiciary. Prosecutors in the *Lava Jato* case, moreover, were moving more ably to punish wrongdoing because they had been enabled by schisms within the governing coalition, which diminished the ability of politicians to react. Dominance, in other words, was reduced, at least momentarily. Said another way, much of *Lava Jato*'s early success was made possible by the incapacity of political elites to curb the investigations, in light of severe political gridlock during the first two years of the investigation. This permitted the investigations to prosper, and even allowed prosecutors to dream big, designing a much broader anticorruption push.

In the next section, we detail the conditions that allowed *Lava Jato* to emerge, focusing particularly on the interaction between prosecutors and judges on the one hand, and the political system on the other. We begin with an overview of the general context in which *Lava Jato* unfolded, before turning to how legal authorities used new capacity and novel political and legal strategies to push forward in historically unprecedented ways.[6]

The Seismic Shock to Patterns of Dominance

It is virtually impossible to separate *Lava Jato* from the political and economic trajectory of Dilma Rousseff's presidency (2011–2016), which began triumphantly as the country roared back from the global financial crisis, and ended ignominiously in impeachment. There is no room to tell the full story here, but highlighting a few points along this trajectory will help to explain how and why *Lava Jato* prospered, starting in 2014.

Rousseff was elected in 2010, as Lula's handpicked successor. Her campaign for the presidency promised a continuation of his historic legacy of economic growth and equality-enhancing social policies. Lula's astronomic popularity at the time practically guaranteed

Rousseff's election, while his energetic campaigning and ripping GDP growth of 7.5 percent in 2010 sealed the deal. Rousseff was elected with 56 percent of the vote, against 44 percent for her opponent, former São Paulo governor José Serra. This was a significant victory, not least because Rousseff was a technocrat, had never before run for elected office, and her skill set seemed more focused on making the trains run on time than on the glad-handing that was needed to succeed in mass politics. Nonetheless she took office with 47 percent of Brazilians saying she was "good" or "excellent," higher than Lula had managed during his first year in office (*Folha de S. Paulo* 2013). This provided Rousseff with the support she needed to continue the interventionist economic policies that the Workers' Party had adopted in the wake of the 2006 discovery of the pre-salt finds.

Soon, however, there were signs of trouble. Growth in the run-up to the election had been artificially boosted by fiscal stimulus and government lending, the exchange rate was increasingly overvalued, the commodities boom of the 2000s was petering out, and many of the government's policies were made possible only by fiscal artifice (Bresser-Pereira 2009; Ban 2013; F. J. C. de Carvalho 2016). Growth began to slow on a quarterly basis beginning in the first quarter of Rousseff's term, deteriorating continuously in constant prices through her first two years in office (FRED 2020). Inflation began to rise, and the expansionary fiscal policy forced the government into increasingly complex accounting maneuvers.

At the same time, corruption scandals began to pop up within the federal government almost as soon as Rousseff was inaugurated. In May 2011, her chief of staff Antonio Palocci provided unconvincing explanations of the sources of his assets, which had grown impressively while he had served as finance minister of the Lula administration (2003–2006) and congressman (2007–2011). Lacking support within his party and from the president, he resigned from office the following month (*O Estado de S. Paulo* 2011). This episode, however, was just the beginning. In the short period between June 2011 and February 2012, numerous cabinet ministers, many of whom had been inherited from Lula's administration and whose names would later resurface as targets of *Lava Jato,* were implicated in corruption scandals. Although not all cabinet members accused of wrongdoing left the administration, seven were either dismissed or resigned from office due to such allegations, in what came to be known as *Faxina no Planalto* (Cabinet Cleaning; see the Appendix).

Symptomatically, in February 2012, it was Petrobras's turn. Even though it was not publicly explained as corruption related, Rousseff fired Petrobras president Sergio Gabrielli, who had been appointed by Lula to head the state-owned company in 2005, soon after Rousseff stepped down as minister of energy (the ministry that oversees Petrobras) to become Lula's chief of staff. Gabrielli was replaced by Maria das Graças Foster, a career employee of Petrobras with more than three decades at the company. Crucially, by April 2012 future *Lava Jato* defendants Paulo Roberto Costa, Renato Duque, and Jorge Zelada were all replaced as Petrobras's directors, leading to complaints from some parties within the governing coalition, who lamented their lost influence (D. Pereira 2012; *G1* 2012a; Oswald, Jungblut, and Ordoñez 2012; Limongi 2020).

Despite the economic slowdown and the corruption troubles, Rousseff's popularity seemed unshakable for much of her first term. At the end of her cabinet cleaning, the Rousseff administration's approval rating reached 64 percent (F. Rodrigues 2012). A year later, by March 2013, the popularity of Rousseff's administration remained above 60 percent and, perhaps most strikingly, the president's personal approval rating stood at a staggering 79 percent (Campanerut 2013). The administration had other reasons to celebrate. Under Lula, Brazil had won the coveted opportunity to host the 2014 FIFA World Cup—and its preparatory event, the 2013 FIFA Confederations Cup—as well as the 2016 Summer Olympic Games.

But the bloom soon began to fade. The deteriorating economic outlook turned what should have been celebrations into focal points of dissent. Cost overruns and white elephants, such as several expensive sporting arenas that would clearly serve no useful purpose after these mega sporting events passed, made the games seem a dispensable luxury. The Zika virus, which emerged in the run-up to the games, led athletes and tourists alike to criticize the Brazilian government. Although the games came off without a hitch, they cast a pall over the triumphalist narrative of Brazil's emergence in the new century.

Initially, there seemed to be little reason to fret, and Rousseff's popularity remained high. But in June 2013, local protests in São Paulo against bus fare increases exploded into a nationwide furor after the police violently repressed demonstrators (Winters and Weitz-Shapiro 2014; Benson and Levine 2013). What had originated as a protest by left-of-center student-led groups mutated into a centrist middle-class revolt against police brutality, the FIFA soccer confederation, and the perceived self-dealing of national politics (A. Freitas and da Silva 2019: 148; F. Nunes and Melo 2017: 282; Hagopian 2016). Although no political party benefited from the protests, the governing Workers'

Party was particularly hard-hit by the explosion of popular rage. Rousseff's popularity, according to Datafolha polls, fell precipitously from a high of 65 percent who thought she was doing a good or excellent job in March 2013 to only 30 percent in late June.

The government responded to what became a long-simmering series of protests with a variety of initiatives, including spending cuts and proposed anticorruption reforms—the most famous and consequential of which were the Anti-Corruption Law (Lei n. 12.846), which established rules for leniency agreements with companies, and the Organized Crime Law (Lei n. 12.850), which more clearly established plea bargain agreements in Brazilian law. Both would prove pivotal to *Lava Jato*'s results just a few months later. But the government's policy implementation was lethargic and its ability to control the narrative was weakened. Meanwhile, public sentiment began to shift in imperceptible ways as justices on the STF began hearing the *Mensalão* case, which had come to light in 2005 but whose legal denouement arrived at the high court only in late 2012 and 2013.

The court's unusual proactivity, and its decision to convict powerful political figures, including Lula's former chief of staff, José Dirceu, led some contemporaneous observers to conclude, reasonably, "that state institutions in Brazil are becoming more willing and better equipped to reveal, investigate and prosecute corruption" (Michener and Pereira 2016: 479).[7] The conviction of PT leaders like Dirceu also eliminated any last vestige of the PT's claim to be a "different" party, somehow more ethical than others. Polling data shows that Brazilians had believed the PT's claim to ethical exceptionalism in earlier times (Michener and Pereira 2016: 490), but now even the PT's defenders claimed that the party was simply engaging in the kinds of backroom negotiations long perfected by other parties. This was hardly a robust defense, and voters harshly punished the rank hypocrisy. Support for the PT, and membership in the party, would fall dramatically over the following years. Public sentiment increasingly adopted a "pox on all their houses" attitude, lumping the PT in with parties that had a much-longer tradition of ethical lapses. The PT lost cohesion, which was particularly damaging to a president like Rousseff who had little personal history in the party and thus could not fall back on a reservoir of goodwill to corral party members.

Rousseff's challenge became even greater as she headed into the 2014 election year. If 2013 had brought protest and *Mensalão,* 2014 brought the more formidable *Lava Jato,* which splintered her support in Congress, within her own party, and among voters, who overwhelmingly began to express a desire for change. In August 2014, two months before the election, Costa began his plea bargain; in the final week before the second round of the election, the conservative newsmagazine *Veja* published a cover story reporting on Youssef's plea bargain, with an ominous picture of Lula and Rousseff in shadow, under a quote from Youssef's testimony: "Eles Sabiam de Tudo" (They Knew About Everything) (Bonin 2014).

Rousseff won the election by the narrowest margin since the return to democracy, three percentage points. Aécio Neves, the two-time PSDB Minas Gerais governor who ran against her in the second round, had substantial flaws of his own, but he nonetheless focused his campaign around the argument that Brazilians deserved better management and less corruption. The PT had lost its halo and even Rousseff, who was believed to be personally above reproach, seemed to have lost the confidence of many middle-class Brazilians. Eventually, she was carried to reelection largely by the loyalty of the lower classes, especially in the poorer regions of the north and northeast of Brazil, who had benefited enormously from the Workers' Party's social programs.

On taking office in 2015, Rousseff thus faced three intertwined problems: economic collapse, political crisis, and corruption scandal. We will not say more on the economic collapse, except to note that the economy's slide continued more or less continuously through the end of the decade, contributing to a precipitous deterioration in the government's fiscal results, despite frantic efforts by the Rousseff administration and its successors to close the spending spigot. This decline was worrisome for Rousseff, not least because regionwide studies show that scandals' effects depend greatly on economic conditions and, without a strong economic environment, there is little to cushion the political fall (Pérez-Liñán 2007; Carlin, Love, and Martínez-Gallardo 2014). Similarly, the fact that Rousseff appointed the fiscally conservative Joaquim Levy as finance minister further alienated much of her left-leaning constituency, in part because she had promised not to tighten public spending just a few months earlier, during the 2014 campaign that led to her reelection.

The political crisis, meanwhile, became increasingly inseparable from the corruption scandal. Rousseff's challenge in her second term was to simultaneously deal with multiple constituencies and their differing reactions to the scandal, while addressing the economic and political meltdowns. *Lava Jato* forced her to manage Brazilians who were furious with corruption, many of whom, by March of 2015, engaged in *panelaços* (pot-banging) every time she appeared on TV. But simultaneously, she was facing criticism from within the governing coalition, for not doing enough to defend coalition allies against the investigations. Making things even harder, it seemed that Rousseff could not count on the support of many members of her own political party. After the massive cleanup of her first months in office and subsequent turnover in other cabinet ministries, not a single member of Lula's faction within the PT held any position in Rousseff's cabinet by early 2015. Many members of Lula's faction, furthermore, appeared likely to become targets of the emerging *Lava Jato* investigation (Limongi 2020).

Triangulating among these pressures would perhaps have been an impossible task even for the most gifted politician. It posed more of a challenge than usual in the 2010s because the increasing fragmentation of the party system—and the mutual jealousies between members of the presidential coalition—made coalition management a supremely taxing task (A. Borges 2021). Rousseff's decision to clean out her cabinet, her efforts to strengthen the new PSD party so as to sideline the MDB, and the drastic decline in congressional budget amendments that were actually paid out by the government during her time in office (Guimarães, Perlin, and Maia 2019: 35) all contributed to deepening dissatisfaction within the coalition, particularly among members of the MDB. Tensions simmered throughout Rousseff's first term. In March 2012, Rousseff replaced the longtime government leader in the Senate, MDB senator Romero Jucá, after the Senate pointedly rejected her nominee to head the transportation regulatory body, Agência Nacional de Transportes Terrestes (ANTT). Early the next year, MDB congressman Henrique Alves was elected president of the Chamber of Deputies, promising to make legislators' budget amendments obligatory, rather than subject to the executive branch's whims (by 2015, Congress had approved a constitutional amendment in this regard). A slow revolt was clearly under way, with influential factions of the MDB beginning to break away from their longtime partners in the PT (Magalhães, Guerreiro, and Iglesias 2012; Borba 2012).

Things hit a boiling point in February 2015, when the Chamber of Deputies rebelled against Rousseff's efforts to elect a PT congressman as Chamber president and, instead, overwhelmingly backed MDB deputy Eduardo Cunha, who promptly declared his independence from the administration. Cunha was a remarkably tough rival: he was a master of backroom negotiations, already renowned for his clientelism in a Congress that was hardly a paragon of ethics, and venerated by his peers for his quiet ability to squeeze whatever he needed out of the government of the day (Limongi 2015). When *Lava Jato* revealed that Cunha held secret foreign bank accounts, but the government did nothing to quash his indictment, Cunha turned from a hard-bargaining negotiator into an outright opponent of the Rousseff administration. The last straw came when the PT members of the Chamber of Deputies' Ethics Committee voted to punish Cunha. Immediately, Cunha responded by unleashing an impeachment petition against Rousseff. Within a year, Rousseff had been booted out of office, replaced by Vice President Michel Temer, a senior member of the MDB.

Temer would ultimately fare little better as president, facing protests and scandals within his cabinet, first, and then corruption troubles of his own, as his nefarious negotiations with corrupt meat-packing tycoon Joesley Batista went public. His caretaker government did what it could to push back against *Lava Jato,* as the next chapter describes, but ultimately Temer's time in office was too short and turbulent to fully revert *Lava Jato*'s effects on public opinion and the political system.

During its early years, then, *Lava Jato* was able to prosper due to the surrounding context of declining economic prospects; a weakened president, with uneven political skills and a nearly impossible set of challenges to tackle; increasing public anger over perceived malfeasance and poor governance, which coalesced into an antisystem mood; and the increasingly fractious governing coalition, whose cohesiveness declined in inverse proportion to *Lava Jato*'s success.

Expressing this in the language of our heuristic accountability model, *Lava Jato* was able to rapidly prosper, especially following events in early 2015, because political dominance had declined considerably due to the many fractures within the governing coalition, the president's party, and across branches of the government. Further, declining popular support and rising dissatisfaction contributed to a massive increase in civic engagement. Even if not all mobilizations and protests expressed a clear anticorruption tone—many were broadly antisystem or specifically anti-PT—they all temporarily aligned to set the political system on its heels. Jointly, all these factors made it increasingly difficult for political leaders to interfere with the workings of *Lava Jato*. In fact, a key driver of Rousseff's impeachment was political elites' perception that they needed to reassert political dominance to break *Lava Jato,* a point we discuss further in Chapter 5.

New National, Local, and Case-Specific Capacity

If this confounding economic, political, and social backdrop made it difficult to govern, it provided the *Lava Jato* task force with much-needed space to move forward in ways that might not have been possible in more prosperous times. As it did so, the task force was also helped by newly developed institutional capacity at the national, local, and case levels, reinforced by international pressures.

Chapter 3 already explored many of the changes—intended and unintended alike—that contributed to improving capacity at a national level during the three decades leading up to 2014. These included a variety of laws on money laundering, public sector corruption, and organized crime enacted since the 1990s, many of which have resulted from Brazil's signing of international treaty commitments; the generous resources and autonomy granted to the Federal Police, the Ministério Público Federal, the federal courts, and to other agencies and institutions over the previous generation; the creation of specialized anti–money laundering courts starting in 2003; and improvements in interinstitutional coordination among law enforcement agencies achieved via initiatives such as ENCCLA.

Innovations in federal agencies were especially critical to *Lava Jato*. Beginning in 2003, President Lula began to respect a longtime demand from prosecutors by choosing the chief federal prosecutor from a so-called *lista tríplice* (triple list) of potential nominees to head the Ministério Público Federal. By adopting this informal practice, presidents would protect themselves against charges of bias and, in the process, expand the autonomy of the prosecutor-general from the executive branch. Second, three vital new laws were approved in 2012 and 2013: (1) the reform of the 1998 Anti–Money Laundering Law; (2) the Anti-Corruption Law; and (3) the Organized Crime Law. These laws formally instituted *colaboração premiada* (roughly translated, plea bargaining), a technique that was already being used in Brazil, but without clear standards (Fernandes and Bulla 2015). They also more clearly established liability for corporate corruption, laid out rules for leniency agreements with firms, and detailed penalties for racketeering. Finally, they facilitated the prosecution of money laundering charges by removing the need to present evidence of the crimes from which the laundered money originated. A study of all the *Lava Jato* cases heard by Judge Moro showed that his trial court's convictions were made significantly more likely as a consequence of the changes in those three laws (Fontoura 2019: 65).

Locally, the fact that *Lava Jato* originated in Curitiba, in the southern state of Paraná, and performed so well by comparison to other contemporaneous operations elsewhere, was no coincidence. Law enforcement and judicial institutions in Curitiba were unmatched in their expertise and experience involving corruption and money laundering cases. Within the Federal Police, as early as 2002, nearly 56 percent of all investigations into money laundering in Brazil were headed by the Paraná directorate (Polícia Federal 2002: 127; Da Ros and Taylor 2019). In the border city of Foz do Iguaçu, for instance, three police operations (*Macuco, Cover,* and *Casa Limpa*) were responsible for 558 *inquéritos* (investigations) into corruption and money laundering that totaled an estimated R$57 billion (in 2002 reais), more than four times as much as all other money laundering investigations in Brazil that year (Polícia Federal 2002: 130–134). Possibly due to this long experience, the Delegacia de Crimes Financeiros (Financial Crimes Division) of the Federal Police in Paraná was already considered one of the most capable in the country before *Lava Jato* began (Costa, Machado, and Zackseski 2016).

Prosecutors were similarly well established in Paraná. Beginning in the late 1990s, prosecutor Celso Três had been one of the first to investigate the CC-5 accounts that had been responsible for so much money laundering in Brazil until then. Even more saliently, the *Banestado* scandal, beginning in 2003, had been one of the—if not *the*—first major cases run under a task force model. Four out of the six original prosecutors who participated in the initial *Lava Jato* task force had been on the *Banestado* task force at some moment (Dallagnol 2017a: 69; Paludo 2011). As part of that task force, they signed what may have been the first plea bargain in the country, with a much-younger Alberto Youssef (MPF 2019d; Paludo 2011).

Within the judiciary, a specialized anti–money laundering court had been operating in Curitiba since 2003, the second ever to be first established in Brazil after passage of the 1998 Anti–Money Laundering Law. It was headed by federal judge Sérgio Moro, considered one of the most prominent of a generation of young judges specialized in money laundering cases. Moro had written about the *Mani Pulite* anticorruption operation in Italy, was the trial judge on the CC-5 cases investigated by prosecutor Celso Três and the *Banestado* investigations of money launderers, and, as noted earlier, had served as *juiz de instrução* (adviser) to the STF during the *Mensalão* trial. The Tribunal Regional Federal da 4a Região (fourth regional appeals court, TRF4), which heard all of the appeals from Moro's court, including appeals of search warrants and wiretaps, was particularly well situated to hear cases, in part because it had invested heavily in moving its caseload online, which facilitated the sharing of voluminous case documents and sped up the appeals process. By virtue of its location, the TRF4 also had significant expertise in hearing money laundering and associated corruption cases.

The individual capacities of each of these bodies was complemented by their ability to cooperate, which was facilitated by the personal rapport between key players. Several of the key authorities had worked side by side in the past on *Banestado* and other investigations. In fact, to an important extent, *Lava Jato* may have been possible only because these officials already knew and trusted each other. In 2012, a member of the Federal Police investigating money laundering at a gas station in Brasília, who had worked on the *Banestado* case, recognized Youssef's voice on a wiretap (Netto 2016). With judicial authorization, the Federal Police put Youssef under surveillance. It was through that surveillance that they discovered the suspicious gift of a Range Rover from Youssef to Paulo Roberto Costa, an unlikely link between these two men that led to the exposure of the corruption scheme.

Other personal ties played a role. The Receita Federal, which has not always been smoothly integrated into corruption cases, had a man on the ground, Roberto Leonel de Oliveira Lima, who had been heading the local fiscal intelligence unit since the *Banestado* case (Rodrigues 2019: 151). He quickly became a partner in the police investigations. Similarly, Erika Mialik Marena, whose previous work experience at the Central Bank helped make her the perfect investigator on this case, had also participated in *Banestado* (Rodrigues 2019: 154). It was Marena, in fact, who gave *Lava Jato* its name, playing on the words for jet wash and jet plane (Polícia Federal 2014). Another federal police investigator, Márcio Anselmo, had held numerous appointments as an instructor at the national police academy, but also had extensive prior experience as a functionary of the federal courts in Paraná state.

Finally, as it progressed, *Lava Jato* gained its own capacity. The prosecutor-general, Rodrigo Janot, instituted new rules to ensure coordination within the MPF, including efforts to align priorities between the eleven prosecutors in Curitiba and a team of more than a dozen senior prosecutors in Brasília who were advising Janot, who had the constitutional responsibility for prosecuting sitting federal politicians before the STF.[8] Two weeks after *Lava Jato* began, furthermore, the prosecutor-general radically restructured the so-called 5ª

Câmara de Coordenação e Revisão (5ª CCR), a committee within the headquarters of the MPF explicitly tasked with combating corruption. Whereas previously corruption cases were dealt with separately, by different teams of prosecutors in their respective civil and criminal jurisdictions, the "new" 5ª CCR ensured that the criminal and civil ramifications of the same cases were assigned to the same team of prosecutors, preventing dispersion and improving information sharing. This also led to the proliferation of Núcleos de Combate à Corrupção (Nuclei to Combat Corruption, NCCs) in nearly all regional offices of the Ministério Público Federal in Brazil (Londero 2021).

Janot's team was filled with corruption experts, including prosecutors who had previously worked on cases such as *TRT de São Paulo, Anaconda, Monte Carlo,* and, inevitably, *Banestado* (Vasconcelos 2013). Similarly, as cases made their way to the TRF4 in Porto Alegre, the STJ in Brasília, and trial courts in Rio de Janeiro and São Paulo, task forces of prosecutors were formed to work before each of these courts on behalf of *Lava Jato.* Later, as the Greenfield investigation into the pension funds of state-owned companies progressed in Brasília, its task force also became responsible for *Lava Jato* cases tried before first-instance courts in the capital (F. A. Rodrigues 2019). As of 2019, fifty-nine prosecutors were involved in different task forces directly linked to *Lava Jato* throughout the country—equivalent to 5.1 percent of all active federal prosecutors in Brazil (MPF 2019b, 2019c).[9]

The fact that such a great number of prosecutors within the Ministério Público Federal worked together in *Lava Jato* did not preclude them from eventually disagreeing with each other as the investigation progressed. This included semipublic dissents about how potential targets of the investigations were prioritized, the public exposure of its participants, and the use of investigative tactics by different prosecutors. In fact, as Fernando Limongi (2020) observed in his reflection on books authored by *Lava Jato* chief prosecutor Delton Dallagnol (2017a) and former prosecutor-general Rodrigo Janot (2019), such episodes were not uncommon. Yet it would have been surprising if there was no friction since this was the first time an investigation of this scale was attempted, aligning a task force on the ground in Curitiba with the prosecutor-general in Brasília. No previous investigation in Brazil had required such "vertical" coordination within the Ministério Público Federal. Previous cases rising from first-instance prosecutors to the prosecutor-general had usually been met with bleak and lethargic responses in Brasília. Whatever friction it generated, the alignment among prosecutors was ultimately essential to *Lava Jato*'s results, helping put pressure on the first-instance courts and the STF, as detailed below.

Efforts by the Ministério Público Federal were matched by other agencies participating in *Lava Jato*. The staff of the task force grew to fifty in Curitiba by December 2015 (Dallagnol 2017a). The Federal Police assigned new members not just to the Curitiba task force, but also to an STF task force in cases involving sitting politicians, as well as to investigations in other states with branches of the *Lava Jato* case.

Within the federal courts, perhaps the most momentous change was that the docket of Judge Moro's specialized court in Curitiba was cleared of all other cases so that it could work exclusively on *Lava Jato,* a change that remained in place even after Moro left the bench to become justice minister in late 2018 (Rodrigues 2019). Under the direction of the TRF4, Moro's trial court thus shifted from being a specialized money laundering court to an exclusive *Lava Jato* court. A similar decision was applied by the TRF2 to the Rio de Janeiro court headed by Judge Marcelo Bretas, which also gained new staff to deal with the workload. The TRF1 did not follow this trend for the trial court in Brasília involved in *Lava Jato,* a decision Fabiana A. Rodrigues (2019: 194) suggests may have contributed to the relative sluggishness of that court by comparison to its peers in Curitiba and Rio (it did, however, designate an auxiliary judge to help with the case). In São Paulo, finally, cases pertaining to the *Lava Jato* investigation were split among the three trial courts specialized in money laundering, making coordination harder and possibly contributing to less robust results from the São Paulo chapter of *Lava Jato*.

Capacity was also enhanced by technological innovations developed during *Lava Jato*. One such innovation was a shared information system used by prosecutors and the revenue service to analyze bank and fiscal records. This Sislava system permitted document sharing of more than 3.5 million documents on nearly 60,000 individuals and firms cited in the investigations (Rodrigues 2019: 152). Online access to bank records, in turn, had also been expanded for criminal investigations, especially following the establishment of the Bacenjud system and its upgrades over the previous years. Also significant were the more than 500 requests for international cooperation that were made over the course of the case, involving forty-five different countries, which generated a wealth of new material from numerous overseas accounts in tax havens.

Extraterritorial enforcement of foreign laws had an important effect on how firms behave and put new pressure on the government to improve institutional effectiveness. The US Foreign Corrupt Practices Act was used in the 2010s to target a number of Brazilian firms, beginning with Embraer, which in 2016 paid more than US$200 million to settle FCPA charges. Scandals involving foreign firms acting in Brazil, such as Siemens, Alstom, and Walmart, also changed business practices.[10] In 2016, Brazil became the country with the highest number of FCPA cases. Class action lawsuits brought in the United States against Brazilian firms listed on US markets also awakened business executives to the real costs of failure to improve compliance. The consequence has been a frenzy of legal activity: a survey by Deloitte showed that the number of Brazilian firms with internal legal compliance departments doubled to 60 percent between 2013 and 2015 (Stauffer 2016); between 2015 and 2016 the companies surveyed by KPMG with compliance measures in place rose from 57 percent to 76 percent (Osborn 2017).

A Conscientious Legal-Political Strategy

The deteriorating economic and political situation was insufficient to fully protect the *Lava Jato* investigation (and, in any case, its contours were not entirely discernable to the *Lava Jato* task force at the time). To bring their new capacities to bear, then, the task force developed a clear legal-political strategy for facing two significant challenges: the unique form of political dominance generated by the coalitional presidential system, which might enable politicians to push back against anticorruption efforts, and judicial inoperancy, which would slow and could perhaps neuter the prosecution. The strategy sought to address a number of interrelated issues. First, how could they ensure that the case stayed in Curitiba? Second, how could they ensure that the investigation was not quashed, either by the inaction or the proactive efforts of higher courts? Third, and related, how could they ensure public support? And finally, how could they ensure that the efforts in this particular case were carried forward, beyond *Lava Jato* itself, in ways that would guarantee long-term change and reduce the chances of reversal? In answering these questions, the *Lava Jato* task force ultimately adopted a big push approach that went beyond legal action alone, encompassing active public outreach, a media strategy, and a broad reform initiative.

Assert Jurisdiction

From the beginning, it became clear that it would be essential to keep as much of the case as possible in Curitiba for as long as feasible, so as to avoid the disappointments of the *Banestado, Satiagraha,* and *Castelo de Areia* cases. They had ultimately accomplished little of what prosecutors expected: the first led to the conviction of only small fish, whereas the last two were dismissed on procedural grounds without any decision on the merits. There was little trust in the high courts, and prosecutors feared the loopholes defense lawyers and the high courts could exploit. Past cases had been killed by a variety of stratagems. A prominent one was fragmentation, or break-ing up the case into multiple smaller cases, with each individual defendant able to draw on numerous vicissitudes of legal argument, and with prosecutors hamstrung by the difficulty of presenting the full breadth of evidence in broad corruption schemes in a case against a single individual whose role may not have encompassed all of the broad facets of the case.

Moro made clear early, therefore, that it would be important to centralize the case at his trial court, the 13ª Vara Federal de Curitiba (Thirteenth Federal Court of Curitiba), one of the two federal judge-ships specialized in money laundering in the city with jurisdiction over all money laundering cases in the state of Paraná. When sen-tencing Youssef and three other defendants, for example, he wrote that "this inquiry . . . began with the investigation of a laundering crime consummated in Londrina, Paraná, subject therefore to the jurisdiction of this court" (Justiça Federal 2015: 24). Subsequent cases frequently reiterated this jurisdictional claim, with sentences by Judge Moro at times simply copying and pasting excerpts from his previous decisions. Perhaps most symptomatically, in many of his decisions, Moro repeatedly suggested that the cases simply followed investigations dating back to 2006 and 2009 in which Carlos Habib Chater (the owner of the gas station in Brasília) and Alberto Youssef had been defendants—mostly in the context of the *Banestado* investi-gation and its spinoffs. Moro further argued that Youssef's plea bargain agreement signed in the 2000s had been violated by the revelations about his participation in the emerging *Lava Jato* wrongdoing.

Another skillful maneuver by the task force in Curitiba was the navigation of the tricky rules on *foro privilegiado*—that is, the fact that the STF has original jurisdiction in all criminal cases involving sitting federal politicians. Particularly in the first phases of *Lava*

Jato, Moro was careful to keep any mention of sitting politicians out of his courtroom, so as to ensure that his judgments could not be overturned on jurisdictional grounds (Canário 2014b). This included even the *mention* of sitting politicians, whose mere presence in the case could move it to the high court. Prosecutors initially sought to include a clause in some plea bargains in which defendants agreed not to contest the trial court's standing, but Moro struck this down for fear that it might be seen as a violation of the right to full access to justice. As a result, the *Lava Jato* task force in Curitiba initially focused only on *doleiros,* bureaucrats, and businessmen; nonsitting politicians and party bureaucrats began to be targeted directly only in 2015, a year after the investigation had begun.[11]

Of course, this did not prevent even earlier nonpolitician defendants from attempting to move the case to the STF, leading to a tense sequence of events that could very well have disrupted the entire investigation. In May 2014, Costa's attorneys filed a petition at the STF arguing that *Lava Jato* was also investigating federal deputy André Vargas (PT), which, if true, would require the entire case to be raised to the high court. On receiving this report, the rapporteur for the case, Justice Teori Zavascki, suspended the entire *Lava Jato* investigation and released all jailed defendants, including various *doleiros* and their associates, Paulo Roberto Costa, and even a drug trafficker who had laundered money through the gas station where the investigation began. The following month, after Judge Moro requested further clarification on the scope of Zavascki's decision, Zavascki reconsidered and allowed the case to proceed in Curitiba, and ordered the various defendants back to prison (F. A. Rodrigues 2019: 189–190).

Lava Jato's jurisdiction could not remain confined to Curitiba forever, however. In time, as the original team of prosecutors and investigators accumulated significant evidence, jurisdiction over *Lava Jato* cases began to split. The first court to hear *Lava Jato* cases outside Curitiba was the STF, one year after the case had begun. Then, it was Rio de Janeiro's turn, following a decision by Justice Zavascki in October 2015 to farm out investigations pertaining to Brazil's nuclear program to Rio de Janeiro, where a task force was formed in mid-2016. *Lava Jato* arrived in São Paulo in June 2016, although the task force there was created more than a year later. Curitiba remained the main hub, but it increasingly shared jurisdiction.

It was worth emphasizing that *Lava Jato* became famous as an investigation into high-level corruption at Petrobras, but it was initially conceived of predominantly as a money laundering case (Polícia

Federal 2014). This resulted largely from the specialized jurisdiction of Moro's trial court, and it was only because of the money laundering that investigators uncovered evidence of the massive corruption at the state-owned oil company. In fact, money laundering has been the most frequent criminal charge in Moro's trial court during *Lava Jato*: of the four most frequent charges during *Lava Jato,* money laundering has been charged 242 times, followed by 102 charges of *organização criminosa* (criminal association), 95 of *corrupção ativa* (bribe-offering), and 82 of *corrupção passiva* (bribe-taking). Similarly, of all defendants sentenced by Judge Moro over the course of the investigations, *doleiros* and other financial operators are the second-most-numerous group of defendants, behind only business executives (Fontoura 2019: 48).

Corruption at Petrobras, in other words, was essentially caught by the emphasis on money laundering, an approach that had a number of benefits. The specialization of Moro's trial court in money laundering was particularly important in speeding the case along. It may also have been easier to prove that money laundering crimes took place than corruption crimes. Since a 2012 reform of the 1998 Anti–Money Laundering Law, the specific regulations on money laundering in Brazil do not require prosecutors to prove where the laundered money came from; that is, prosecutors do not need to prove that the money was illicitly obtained, only that it was illicitly concealed. Said another way, money laundering is an "autonomous" criminal charge and does not require prosecutors to demonstrate that "antecedent crimes" took place to obtain a criminal conviction. The TRF4's moves to online caseload management proved extremely important to following the trail of the laundered money, allowing Judge Moro to frequently reference evidence and decisions from one case in other cases. This led to a network of case files in which it almost seemed as if a "single" megacase was being constructed, through the virtual amalgamation and cross-linking of various cases (Fontoura 2019; F. A. Rodrigues 2019).

Trigger Domino Effect Before Reaching STF

A related concern was to ensure that the cases moved forward as much as possible before reaching the high courts. This would allow the prosecution to build up a head of steam and public support before it reached justices who shared Brasília's small community with politicians and often seemed reluctant to upset the cordial ethos of the capital's elite. Prosecutors worked aggressively. This was particularly the case in 2015 and 2016, when thirty phases of the operation—that is, one phase every twenty-four days—were conducted. Each led to numerous arrests, warrants, and depositions, which in turn led to new plea bargaining agreements, investigations, and further indictments.[12] Prosecutors engaged in the unprecedented use of techniques such as plea bargaining agreements, *conduções coercitivas* (similar to bench warrants, used 348 times), pretrial detentions (539, averaging 281 days each—with some reaching well over 800 days),[13] and search warrants (1,662) during the busiest years of the investigations, between 2014 and the end of 2018 (Rodrigues 2019: 165; MPF 2019a).

The aggressive and speedy use of these tools had a clear legal calculus. For example, as Fabiana A. Rodrigues (2019: 165) explains, *conduções coercitivas* allowed a potential defendant to be brought in for questioning without knowledge of the evidence prosecutors had already gathered against him or her. Any subsequent defense motion would need to overcome gaps between the testimony gathered during the *condução coercitiva* and other evidence, thus casting doubt on the veracity of the initial defense. Furthermore, the *condução coercitiva* helped to overcome a common problem prosecutors face in Brazil: the willingness of courts, and especially the high courts, to generously grant habeas corpus to wealthy defendants (F. A. Rodrigues 2019: 165). *Lava Jato*'s police operations often began in the dawn hours, in part because if the police struck early enough, judges would only be awake and signing habeas petitions long after the *condução coercitiva* had been concluded.

Similarly, use of pretrial or preventive detention was a clear way of inducing cooperation. While pretrial detention is common in Brazil—accounting for roughly two of every five prisoners nationwide—its use against elites was unheard of and therefore extraordinarily effective, at least initially. The mere threat of pretrial detention may have induced some potential targets of the investigation to seek out plea bargains. Other plea bargaining defendants signed their agreements only after a period in detention. This was the case, for instance, of Ricardo Pessoa, owner of UTC Engenharia and the first businessman to sign such a plea agreement: he was arrested in November 2014, was released five months later by an STF decision, and signed a plea agreement in May 2015 that implicated sixteen sitting politicians, including influential figures such as Senators Aloizio Mercadante (of the PT, who had been chief of staff and minister of education under President Rousseff), Aloysio Nunes Ferreira (of the PSDB, who had been Aécio Neves's running mate in the 2014 presidential elections), and Ciro Nogueira (president of the PP since 2013) (Balthazar 2018).

In addition to this prosecutorial repertoire, Judge Moro also innovated by demonstrating a willingness to convict in instances in which there was not a clear quid pro quo among corrupt actors, but a course of conduct over many years and a preponderance of indications of illegal exchange. This approach was clearly demonstrated in the conviction of former president Lula.[14] As noted earlier, this legal approach—referred to as *teoria do domínio do fato* in Portuguese (see note 7)—had originated during the *Mensalão* trial, a case Moro himself worked in as auxiliary judge (Michener and Pereira 2016; Arantes 2018; Prado and Machado, forthcoming, a).

Partly in consequence, Moro was far more likely to convict than many of his peers. The STF issues convictions in no more than 3 percent of cases (Falcão et al. 2017; Gomes Neto and Carvalho 2021). The rate of conviction in cases involving federal civil servants accused of corruption is around 6 percent (Alencar and Gico 2011: 96–97). A study of state-level prosecutions of mayors in the Rio Grande do Sul state court found a conviction rate of 18 percent (Bento, Da Ros, and Londero 2020: 358). The federal courts have a conviction rate of 47.5 percent in all corruption cases (Levcovitz 2020: 120). By contrast, Moro had a high conviction rate, of around 75 percent in *Lava Jato* cases, and 100 percent of the politicians who were tried in his court (Da Ros et al. 2021). Moro also moved extraordinarily quickly, with most of his sentencing decisions handed down within less than a year of indictment, a pace that was about one-quarter the national average of four years and four months from indictment to sentence (Fontoura 2019: 54; M. C. Carvalho and Nunes 2017).

Simultaneously, of course, the *Lava Jato* prosecutors and judges had to avoid any of the missteps that had been used to quash previous corruption investigations, such as the erroneous search warrant described in Chapter 2 that voided the entirety of the evidence in the *Satiagraha* case. The *Lava Jato* task force was cautious about observing past precedents established by the high courts: for example, barring the handcuffing of defendants and providing defendants with the content of other defendants' plea bargains. The task force also pushed back forcefully in the public arena against claims of overzealousness. For example, in response to defense lawyers' arguments that preventive detention was being used to extract plea bargains from defendants, prosecutors noted that of 158 plea agreements signed in Curitiba and Brasília until October 2017, only twenty-five defendants were in detention at the time the plea deal was signed, or fewer than one in six (Galvão 2017).

Although some members of the high courts did express concern about the tactics used by prosecutors, the STJ and STF largely upheld the trial court's decisions in the early years of the case. All of the habeas corpus requests that reached the STJ in the crucial first year of the investigation were declined (*Consultor Jurídico* 2014). Likewise, the STF justices tasked with oversight of *Lava Jato* largely upheld the trial court's decisions.

Together, the aggressive, but careful, use of these legal tactics contributed to a domino effect among defendants, an approach that Judge Moro had emphasized in his study of the *Mani Pulite* case as one of the causes of Italian prosecutors' success (Moro 2004). The domino effect was clearly at work in Brazil, as the investigation moved through its various phases to take down specific groups of conspirators, working its way from *doleiro* Alberto Youssef to Petrobras's bureaucrats to a variety of powerful businessmen and, finally, to political elites.

Ensure Public Support

Deltan Dallagnol, chief prosecutor on the task force, reflected in the early years of *Lava Jato* that social communication was essential to *Lava Jato*'s early success against powerful political and economic interests, and that it would help to neutralize the attacks that come from outside the judicial system (Dallagnol 2017a: 125). Data compiled by Daiane Londero (2021: 200) based on annual reports by the Ministério Público Federal show the intense efforts by the prosecutors to sustain a close relationship with the media. Prosecutors responded to more than 60,000 press inquiries between 2014 and 2018, resulting in predominantly positive coverage of their work. Social communication strategies and the *Lava Jato* case became so intertwined at the Ministério Público Federal, in fact, that measures of responses to press inquiries and positive repercussion in the media came to be included in the MPF's annual reports (Londero 2021: 200). As the most visible face of the task force, Deltan Dallagnol personally engaged heavily in social communication: having joined Twitter in January 2014, just two months before the beginning of *Lava Jato,* he had approximately 1.3 million followers six years later (Twitter 2020). Critics also noted *Lava Jato*'s less transparent forms of media outreach, including calculated leaks to favored journalists, which in some cases helped spur plea bargains and fuel the prosecution's case (Damgaard 2018b).

The *Lava Jato* task force's reliance on high public support, intense media visibility, and major reforms suggest that its members perceived anticorruption as a collective action problem that required a big push that went beyond prosecution alone. As chief prosecutor Deltan Dallagnol noted in 2017, "[*Lava Jato*] will not be judged by who it arrested or convicted. It will be judged by its capacity to mobilize society and catalyze efforts so that anticorruption reforms are completed, [so] that we can reach a more just country" (*Veja* 2017). Task force efforts were based on the assumption that political corruption was systemic in Brazil and, as such, that it could be fought only by an actor from the outside who contributed to an exogenous shock of moralization and punishment, followed by a significant institutional overhaul. Under these conditions, to cultivate massive support, *Lava Jato* had to foster media coverage and rely on a receptive public for support. As it turns out, Brazilians' patience was running particularly low when *Lava Jato* emerged in 2014. The stage was set for *Lava Jato* to arrive within a context of intense—and increasing—political engagement and polarization.

Second, the task force and Moro fell back on the strength of transparency provisions in Brazil, releasing case documents to the media and the public in a manner that was largely unprecedented: a "tidal wave of raw, unprocessed information," in the words of two journalists (Bulla and Newell 2020: 85). In doing so, they were engaged as much in legal maneuvering as in political messaging. In many cases, the release of information sought to ensure that the high court could not find a loophole that would allow it to override the trial court surreptitiously (Recondo and Weber 2019). For example, when federal deputy Luiz Argôlo (PP) was implicated in the investigations early in *Lava Jato,* Moro sent the information to the STF publicly, without any secrecy, in an effort seemingly calculated to make it difficult for the STF to find a way to protect Argôlo as they had protected powerful defendants during previous cases such as *Castelo de Areia* (F. A. Rodrigues 2019: 190–191). The MPF also adopted openness as a rule: as one prosecutor noted, "[Our] position was always to reveal everything as soon as it was no longer useful to the investigations, because the people have to know [what's going on]" (Nunes 2020). The public airing of massive amounts of detail about the case contributed to a "hyper-competitive environment that bolstered the existing culture of judicial independence," ensuring that the public was kept up-to-date on the massive and fast-moving investigations (Bulla and Newell 2020: 88).

In fact, the domino effect described in the previous section—resulting from the combined use of plea bargaining agreements, bench warrants, and pretrial detentions—produced another consequence critical for the success of *Lava Jato*: ensuring increased public support and engagement via intense media visibility. This was another one of the lessons Judge Moro had drawn from his study of the Italian *Mani Pulite* investigations.[15] The fast pace of *Lava Jato*'s progression, involving numerous important political figures, drew immense attention from the public and spurred a wave of support. Judge Moro's actions, for instance, were supported by over 60 percent of the population by early 2016 (T. M. de Oliveira 2019; Dávila 2016).

Similarly, as various massive public demonstrations led millions of Brazilians to the streets over 2015 and 2016, many protesters voiced their explicit support of the investigations (Senters, Weitz-Shapiro, and Winters 2019). Even if not all protests were explicitly anticorruption and many participants more clearly professed anti-Rousseff, anti-PT, and antiestablishment messages, the diverse protest agendas temporarily aligned for mutual benefit. The Datafolha polling institute, for instance, surveyed participants in the massive March 15, 2015, protests and asked their reasons for participating: 47 percent claimed to be protesting against corruption, 27 percent for the impeachment of President Rousseff, 20 percent against the PT, and 14 percent against politicians in general. Symptomatically, however, 82 percent declared that they had voted for defeated presidential candidate, Aécio Neves (PSDB), in the 2014 elections, and many exhibited an upper-class profile, holding college degrees and declaring relatively high income.

Although protests would continue in ensuing years, they reached their apogee in March 2016, following the release by Judge Moro of wiretapped conversations between President Rousseff and former president Lula, in which they discussed the appointment of Lula as presidential chief of staff, a proposal widely interpreted as a tactic to provide Lula with the original jurisdiction of the high court and, thereby, shield him from the investigations in Curitiba. The resulting protests drew millions to the streets, in what may have been the largest protests ever held in Brazil (*G1* 2016a). This uproar underlined the mutually beneficial alliance between anticorruption and antiestablishment messages, especially as once trusted opposition leaders such as Aécio Neves and Geraldo Alckmin were also openly criticized by protesters.[16] Simultaneously, Rousseff was losing popular support, as her approval rating had reached a historical low of 13 percent in the wake of the first round of protests (L. Ferraz 2015). In fact, as the conservative newsmagazine *Veja* acknowledged at the time, the "only character universally praised [in the demonstrations] was federal judge Sérgio Moro" (*Veja* 2016a).

Lava Jato attracted enormous coverage from the news media over the years, beginning especially in November 2014, immediately following the reelection of Rousseff to the presidency (Feres, Barbarela, and Bachini 2018: 210). Coverage of *Lava Jato* differed from previous cases, with journalists proving more supportive of investigators than in past scandals. Marjorie C. Marona and Leon Victor de Queiroz Barbosa (2018: 137) show that coverage by *O Globo* was both less intense and more critical of the *Satiagraha* investigations than it was during *Lava Jato*. Between 2008 and 2011, a total of 505 stories were published about *Satiagraha*. Various editorials criticized what they called a "spectacularization" of the case, including the allegedly arbitrary use of handcuffs during the arrests and the selective leaking of information by the investigation. From 2014 to 2016, by contrast, *O Globo* published 10,589 stories on *Lava Jato*—a twentyfold increase. Most were neutral in tone, highlighting the novelties associated with the increased use of plea bargaining agreements, pretrial detentions, and bench warrants.

The combination of massive public support and media coverage was useful for *Lava Jato* in at least two ways. First, because the STF had already been responsive to public pressure on at least one previous occasion involving a corruption case, during the long and highly visible *Mensalão* trial, prosecutors may have been aware that this newfound responsiveness of the STF to the public could be used to their advantage.[17] That is, by helping to keep the case in the media and the streets, pressure was also geared toward the STF, so that it would work more responsively to *Lava Jato* (Recondo and Weber 2019). In fact, as already noted, a number of decisions made by the STF during the course of *Lava Jato* helped—and, to a large extent, allowed—the investigation to progress.

Second, public support raised the costs of curtailing the investigation. One of the most important things the investigators learned from previous experiences was that the political system could fight back at any time. Prior to *Lava Jato,* this happened most notably during *Banestado* and *Satiagraha,* when the police officers directly responsible for the investigations were removed from the cases by their superiors. By keeping the investigations in the news, it would be possible to frame these decisions in a manner that the public understood, and to ensure that the public was aware when pushback came.

Finally, public attention to corruption reinforced the narrative that a change was needed in the political system in Brasília. This had concrete effects: the 2018 elections were marked by the election of

Jair Bolsonaro, but, just as importantly, they were marked by the most significant turnover in legislators seen in any election since the 1980s. Many new legislators, in fact, not only were new to Congress, but also were first-timers in any elected position. Partly in consequence, the number of deputies who were under investigation for any sort of crime fell from 178 (35 percent) to 93 (18 percent), and the number of senators under investigation fell from 44 (54 percent) to 25 (31 percent) (Sardinha and Calixto 2019a, 2019b). But as the next chapter shows, even if the actors themselves changed, the underlying patterns of the perilous combination that marked the political system changed only marginally.

Convince the High Court to Behave More Aggressively

Even though it was remarkably successful, *Lava Jato* could not follow its early strategy of circumventing the STF forever. To reach sitting politicians, it would need to work its way through—and not around—the STF. The central question was, How would the high court behave during *Lava Jato?* Would it be the proactive court of the *Mensalão* trial, or the passive and sometimes even defensive court of *Satiagraha* and *Castelo de Areia?*

Chronology matters here. Even though the scandal called *Mensalão* occurred prior to *Satiagraha* and *Castelo de Areia,* the *Mensalão* trial took place much later. The *Mensalão* became public in 2005, but was tried between late 2012 and early 2014—the last appeal of the case was decided in February 2014, just a month prior to the beginning of *Lava Jato* in Curitiba and only a few months before the first appeal of a *Lava Jato* trial court decision reached the STF (Arantes 2018: 382). As *Lava Jato* reached the STF in early 2015, then, there was good reason for *Lava Jato* prosecutors to expect a somewhat more punitive posture by the high court justices, more akin to their stance in *Mensalão* than in older cases, such as *Satiagraha* and *Castelo de Areia.*

The STF, however, ultimately adopted a middle-of-the-road position, even during the heyday of *Lava Jato.* It was neither as proactive as it had been in *Mensalão* nor as reactive as it had been in *Satiagraha* and *Castelo de Areia.* The STF did not put brakes on *Lava Jato,* and even indirectly encouraged it, especially in its initial and most intense years of activity, reaching two decisions that contributed directly to the prosecutors' success in Curitiba. First, in May 2015, the STF resolved a long-standing debate over the legality of prosecutors' undertaking criminal investigations—a responsibility the federal police had long argued was theirs alone—in favor of prosecutors.[18] Then, in 2016, the court altered an understanding about postappeal imprisonment it had held since 2009, in a case reported by Justice Teori Zavascki, who was the rapporteur for a majority of the *Lava Jato* cases at the STF during its first two years.[19] Until this decision, it was virtually impossible to jail a convicted defendant until every last one of his or her appeals had been exhausted (including appeals up to the high court and all interlocutory appeals of high court decisions) (STF 2017; Vieira 2018). In practice the slow pace of the courts, combined with an infinity of possible appeals, meant that even in the most egregious cases, imprisonment of wealthy elites with access to good lawyers was rare.

With the 2016 STF decision, however, it now became possible to jail convicted criminals once their first appeal failed. *Lava Jato* took place in Curitiba, and the Curitiba court was under the appellate jurisdiction of the TRF4, which had a track record of upholding the penalties imposed by Moro, and at times even increasing them (*Consultor Jurídico* 2016; Kobielski 2020).[20] Together, the STF's decision on jail on failed appeal and the affirming decisions offered by the TRF4 meant that defendants faced a real risk of prison time, which may have altered their calculus about whether or not to sign plea agreements. This had an influential effect on the investigations, which the STF at the time saw as a way to induce more potential collaborators to sign plea bargain agreements (Rodrigues and Arantes 2020).

Similarly, decisions by the STF directly related to *Lava Jato* mattered. When the government whip in the Senate, Delcídio Amaral (PT), was caught on wiretap offering to help Petrobras's services director Nestor Cerveró escape Brazil in return for his silence during the investigations, the STF—under the stewardship of Justice Zavascki—immediately ordered his arrest, under the accusation of obstruction of justice, in November 2015. This decision was backed by the majority of the Senate. It was the first time a sitting senator had been removed from office and preventively sent to prison since redemocratization. It also suggested an inflection in the STF's positions during *Lava Jato*—from supporting the trial court in Curitiba to taking action directly.[21]

Less grandiose decisions by the STF were also important for *Lava Jato*. At the beginning of the high court's involvement in *Lava Jato*, when prosecutor-general Rodrigo Janot submitted the names of forty-eight sitting politicians to be investigated at the STF in March 2015, Justice Teori Zavascki had to decide whether to keep the investigations secret or not. He followed a behavior modeled by the trial court: making them public and, thereby, ensuring enormous visibility for the case. The *Lista de Janot* (Janot's list), as it became known, was comprised of the names of some of the most influential figures in Congress, including the sitting presidents of the House and the Senate, Eduardo Cunha and Renan Calheiros (both of the MDB), as well as longtime leaders of various political parties such as Senators Romero Jucá (MDB), Gleisi Hoffman (PT, former chief of staff to Rousseff), Fernando Collor (PTB, former president of Brazil), Ciro Nogueira (president of the PP), and Antônio Anastasia (PSDB, former governor of Minas Gerais state) (Sardinha 2015). *Lava Jato,* in other words, was lucky to have supporters among the STF justices: first Teori Zavascki and then, after Zavascki's tragic death in a plane crash, Edson Fachin. As Moro commented after Justice Zavascki's death, "Without him, there would have been no Lava Jato" (*Época* 2017).

It is hard to pinpoint all the paths by which the trial court and the TRF4 were able to influence the high court. But the example of the *Lista de Janot* suggests that the lower courts had an important influence on high court behavior, pushing it in the direction of greater transparency. One legal scholar concluded that the *Lava Jato* team and Moro were able to use popular mobilization and anger about corruption to push the high court in "unorthodox" directions, as in the arrest of Amaral described above (F. de Almeida 2019: 107). Moro, as noted earlier, had already served as an auxiliary judge on the court, which may have made him savvy to the justices' personalities and their susceptibility to particular legal arguments. He had a direct line to the STF through personal contacts but, more importantly through his cases, which often spoke directly to the legal debates of the day. Indirectly, too, he was able to bat far above the weight of a typical trial court judge, through his and the task force's intensive media access.

Finally, the *Lava Jato* team appears to have been uncommonly cautious about targeting judicial elites, perhaps because it feared the high court might begin to react differently if the operation began to sully the judiciary. The task force came across allegations of judicial corruption, including on the high courts, but, in most cases, it let those leads fade rather than open yet another front in its battle against the establishment (Angelo 2021). In one case, executives at J&F mentioned three STF justices in their plea bargains, albeit without accusing them of specific crimes (*Exame* 2017). In a later case, in his plea bargain former Rio governor Sérgio Cabral accused Justice Dias Toffoli of selling a decision that benefited two mayors in Rio state who had been accused of electoral irregularities (Macedo 2021; Mattoso, with Zanini, Serapião, and Seto 2021). The Federal Police sought to investigate the allegations, but the prosecutor-general's office decided to file the case away. One reason to adopt a more cautious approach on this front might have been to elide the practical issue of original jurisdiction: senior judges can be tried only in the high courts, which would move any cases involving them out of the trial court. Defense lawyers, too, may have been reluctant to level accusations of judicial corruption for fear of retaliation, especially if they were negotiating, or had negotiated, a plea bargain. Nonetheless, *Lava Jato* indicted the state prosecutor-general in Rio de Janeiro (*Istoé Dinheiro* 2020), and ensnared one state appeals court judge and several federal prosecutors in its investigations.

Carry Reform Forward

Finally, the political strategy of the *Lava Jato* task force went well beyond what one could expect of law enforcement authorities engaged in one of the largest prosecutions in living memory. Prosecutors, Dallagnol in particular, engaged in public campaigning to enact new legislation. The number of anticorruption proposals in Congress quintupled from 165 in the years preceding *Lava Jato* to more than 1,000 in 2018 (M. R. Machado and Paschoal 2016). Particularly emblematic in this regard were the so-called 10 Medidas contra a Corrupção (10 Measures Against Corruption), officially launched in early March 2015 by the prosecutor-general (MPF 2015b). This was a package of legislative changes drafted predominantly by task force prosecutors that aimed to institute quicker and more rigorous punishment of corruption by criminalizing behaviors, establishing harsher jail times, and reducing the number of possible judicial appeals, among others (MPF n.d.). To advance the goals of enacting the package into law, prosecutors openly campaigned for the signatures needed to directly submit the package as a bill to Congress.[22] After approximately one year of intense campaigning, during which signatures were collected online and at public demonstrations, over 2 million citizen signatures for the package had been assembled, and over 1,000 organizations from Brazil and abroad (including Transparency International) had expressed their support for the initiative. This, in turn, allowed prosecutors to submit the package to Congress as a bill in March 2016 (MPF 2015c). There, however, the bill progressed erratically (see Chapter 5).

Finally, albeit not directly related to the investigations, *Lava Jato* provided the STF with an opportunity to once again revise electoral rules in pursuit of greater integrity. A case requesting a ban on corporate campaign contributions had been in the STF's docket since September 2011, filed by the Brazilian Bar Association. The court had even begun to decide the case on the merits in late 2013, but the case's final decision was suspended for further analysis by Justice Teori Zavascki on that occasion, and once again in April 2014, by Justice Gilmar Mendes, who released the case for final decision by the full court only in September 2015.[23] As overwhelming evidence accumulated over the course of the *Lava Jato* investigations on the promiscuous relationship between politicians and business firms, supported by an apparently never-ending cycle of allegations linking corruption to campaign finance, the STF banned corporate campaign contributions in September 2015. In doing so, the STF weakened—but did not eliminate—one leg of the perilous combination of coalitional presidentialism, a developmental state, and loose campaign finance.

Conclusion

Although it never framed it in those terms, the *Lava Jato* task force's strategy in many ways echoed the logic of the accountability equation described in earlier chapters, leaning heavily on those pillars of accountability that were strong, and using them to counteract weaknesses in two domains: the sanctioning power of the courts and the unique form of dominance in the Brazilian political and economic space. They were helped by the political and economic chaos we have described, which distracted Brasília and, for a time, forestalled an effective political response. They were also helped by the unique confluence of justices passing through the STF in these years, which included new thinkers such as Joaquim Barbosa, Teori Zavascki, Edson Fachin, and Luís Roberto Barroso. But most importantly, task force members adopted a conscientious strategy to address the challenges described above, leaning heavily on those pillars of accountability that were most developed—transparency, oversight, capacity, and engagement—and attempting, through public mobilization and media engagement, and by moving reform proposals forward, to engender a big push against corruption. As Brazil's unique form of political dominance reasserted itself in the wake of President Rousseff's impeachment in 2016, and in response to task force overreach, however, the investigation became more vulnerable to pushback and reversal. That is the story of the next chapter.

Notes

1. Neves (2015).
2. *G1* (2014).
3. The name *Lava Jato* is often associated with a *lava a jato* (high-pressure car wash). But ironically, the gas station where the case began had no such car wash. Instead, it had a currency exchange shop where much of the money laundering originated. The *lava* in *Lava Jato* comes from "washing" or "laundering," in reference to the money laundering that took place. The *jato* refers to a private jet, in an ironic comment about the scale of the laundering that was going on: the gas station was not just laundering volumes of money on the scale of a car wash, it was laundering volumes of money that were more indicative of expensive executive jets (Arantes 2020: xv).
4. Petrobras also agreed to pay US$2.95 billion in a class action filed by shareholders in a US court (Cassin 2018a).
5. Many scholars also believed that Petrobras was an island of excellence: "one of the few successful cases of bureaucratic insulation against political exploitation" (M. A. de Almeida and Zagaris 2015: 87).
6. Some of the arguments in this chapter reprise those found in Da Ros and Taylor (forthcoming), although we have restructured them here to fit the framework of the volume and added significant new detail. We are grateful to the editors of that volume for pushing our thinking forward.
7. Michener and Pereira (2016: 496) point to several causes of the effectiveness of the prosecution in the *Mensalão* case: procedurally, the STF allowed all the defendants to be judged together in the same court, and then bunched together the cases by subject matter, to accelerate the hearings; in terms of doctrine, the court followed Claus Roxin's *Tatherrschaft,* known in Portuguese as *teoria do domínio do fato,* which holds that a preponderance of circumstantial evidence is sufficient to convict, by contrast to the more difficult standard of direct evidence.
8. Much of this institutional commitment to fight corruption within the Ministério Público Federal appears to have resulted from the increasing prioritization of corruption cases nationwide. A survey with state and federal prosecutors in Brazil at this time ranked the fight against corruption as the number one priority for prosecutors at the federal and the state level, with 62 percent of the respondents in favor (Lemgruber et al. 2016: 30). A similar study, exclusively among federal prosecutors, by Azevedo (2012) showed a similar commitment to punishing financial crimes such as money laundering and corruption.
9. There were 1,156 active federal prosecutors as of April 2019 (MPF 2019a).
10. Allegedly, Alstom and Siemens, alongside other companies, formed a cartel and bribed officials to gain contracts with São Paulo's metro system (*G1 São Paulo* 2014). Walmart allegedly attempted to obtain access to the Brazilian market through bribes (Corkery 2019).
11. The first former politicians arrested by the *Lava Jato* task force in Curitiba were André Vargas (PT), Luiz Argôlo (Solidariedade), and Pedro Corrêa (PP), all of whom had been expelled from Congress previously—the first two in late 2014 due to facts revealed by *Lava Jato,* and the last one in 2006 following

his involvement in *Mensalão*. Albeit he was not himself a politician, João Vaccari Neto (treasurer of the PT) was also arrested in April 2015.

12. There were seven phases of *Lava Jato* in Curitiba in 2014, fourteen in 2015, sixteen in 2016, ten in 2017, ten in 2018, and three in 2019 (until April) (MPF 2019e).

13. This is the total number of arrests, not the number of individuals who have been arrested. We stress this because some individuals have been arrested more than once. Examples of long pretrial detentions include those of *doleiro* Alberto Youssef (900 days) and Renato Duque (800 days) (Canário 2017).

14. See, especially, page 869 of Lula's sentence (Justiça Federal 2017).

15. In Judge Moro's own words: "Those responsible for operation *mani pulite* made wide use of the press. . . . The publicity granted to the investigations had the positive effect of alerting the potential investigated individuals about the increases in the volume of information available to the magistrates, favoring new confessions and plea bargains. Most importantly: it ensured the support of public opinion to judicial action, preventing public figures from obstructing the investigations. The arrests, confessions and the publicity granted to the collected information generated a virtuous cycle, which is the only possible explanation for the magnitude of the results achieved by the operation *mani pulite*" (Moro 2004: 59).

16. Especially after Rousseff's impeachment, in 2017 and 2018, protests were in many cases instigated and channeled by online-based conservative-leaning movements such as Vem pra Rua, Movimento Brasil Livre, and Revoltados Online (McLean 2021).

17. The trial required more than fifty full days of deliberations at the STF in 2012 alone, when the main judgment took place, all of which were televised live from the court and watched intensely all over the country (Michener and Pereira 2016; Arantes 2018).

18. Recurso Extraordinário n. 593.727, tried on May 18, 2015. The case had been on the STF's docket since 2008, and its original rapporteur, Justice Cézar Peluso, had already retired when the case was finally decided on the merits (STF 2018).

19. A single STF justice is nominated as the rapporteur (*relator*) for most cases in the STF. The rapporteur is responsible for writing up the case report and compiling written votes that will be used to orient other justices on the court; the rapporteur may also offer so-called monocratic decisions in many circumstances.

20. Not only did the TRF4 not overturn the individual cases, but they also were supportive of decisions on judicial procedures as, for example, the use of telephone wiretaps.

21. Delcídio Amaral was arrested on November 25, 2015, after the Federal Senate corroborated the decision by the STF, in a 59–13 vote. After eighty days in custody, he was released and returned to the Senate, from which he was expelled on May 10, 2016 (Senado Notícias 2016).

22. Brazilian legislation allows bills of "public initiative" to be submitted to Congress for appreciation. The proposal must receive the signatures of 1 percent of the electorate (at least 1.5 million citizens) endorsing the initiative so as to be placed on the congressional agenda (MPF 2015a).

23. This was *Ação Direta de Inconstitucionalidade* (ADIn) 4650.

5

The Unmaking of *Lava Jato* and Its Ramifications, 2016–2021

> *This shit has to be fixed . . . the government needs to be changed so as to stanch the bleeding.*
> —Senator Romero Jucá, 2016, caught on wiretap[1]

> *I closed down* Lava Jato, *because there is no more corruption in the government.*
> —President Jair Bolsonaro, 2020[2]

The *Lava Jato* prosecutorial task force was officially closed down in 2021. Even before that happened, investigations had slowed considerably from the energetic pace of 2014–2016. The remnants of the task force had been slowly dismantled through selective retirements and reassignments. Police investigator Erika Mialik Marena, who played a vital early role, was reassigned. Judge Sérgio Moro, the trial court judge who had become one of Brazil's most well-known anticorruption figures, left the judiciary in 2018 for what turned out to be a short-lived stint as Jair Bolsonaro's justice minister. In 2020, chief prosecutor Deltan Dallagnol left the investigation, ostensibly to spend more time with his family (Baran 2020). Finally, in February 2021, the Ministério Público Federal announced that the investigations would no longer be the responsibility of an independent task force, but would instead be folded into the regular organized criΔ152 me operations of the MPF.[3]

Along with the slowing pace of the *Lava Jato* investigations came a broader slowdown—and even a reversal—of the many accountability reforms that had helped create the hopeful perception of improving accountability described in Chapters 3 and 4. The new Congress, which included more first-term incumbents than any Congress since 1990, soon reverted to past practices of coalitional deal-making, demonstrating that even as the actors changed, the informal practices of coalitional presidentialism persisted. Anticorruption reform proposals withered and an anti–*Lava Jato* coalition emerged. The executive reined in the autonomy of accountability agencies, and the judiciary reverted to an old tradition of obsequiousness toward elites. Jailed conspirators were released as they reached parole eligibility, received presidential pardons, or benefited from changes in judicial rules or appeals in high court. Many defendants with cases pending before the court returned to public life, especially those with cases before the inoperative STF. The old system seemed to have reemerged triumphant, and accountability, in many ways, reverted to an equilibrium worse than the one that prevailed at the outset of *Lava Jato* in 2014 (see last row, Table 3.2).

This chapter seeks to explain how this reversal came to pass. We begin by painting the arc of the *Lava Jato* investigations, in three moments: the "surprise" of *Lava Jato;* the response by the political system, beginning with Dilma Rousseff's impeachment; and, then, the slow strangulation of anticorruption efforts and reversion to a new and less promising equilibrium under Michel Temer and Jair Bolsonaro. Then, we detail the forces that contributed to that reversion. We focus specifically on the formal and informal institutional changes that affected the six component variables in the accountability equation: transparency, oversight, and sanction, moderated by capacity, engagement, and dominance.

Two words of caution before we proceed. First, although Chapter 4 focused on anticorruption gains, and this chapter focuses on reversals, the process of progress and reversal was not sequential. Instead, it proceeded with a few steps forward, a few steps back, and many steps sideways. In part, this is because it also was not a two-sided game between angels and demons: there were many legitimate reasons to slow anticorruption efforts, just as there were many illegitimate reasons to move forward with investigations. Although we have tried to separate the progress from the regress in framing these two chapters, in reality the two processes moved jointly and simultaneously. Second, although *Lava Jato* is now a shadow of its former self, the *Lava Jato* cases are not entirely moribund. Cases are pending in several courts, and it is possible that, with the end of the pandemic or the 2022 national elections, the cases and even some lingering investigations might receive a jolt of new energy. But the slow smothering of *Lava Jato* has been ongoing for long enough to allow us to draw some conclusions about the causes of its reversal, as well as the overall deterioration of the accountability equation in recent years.

The Arc of *Lava Jato*, 2014–2021

In retrospect, it is possible to discern three distinct political moments around *Lava Jato*. The arc of the investigation began hopefully. From March 2014 until May 2016, *Lava Jato* built up an impressive head of steam. During this period, it could be characterized as a big push, a wide-ranging anticorruption effort concentrated in space and time, with the goal of destabilizing prevailing norms and driving federal politics toward a new and more "virtuous" equilibrium. As Chapter 4 demonstrated, the surprising early successes of *Lava Jato* were made possible by the political and economic crises, which opened a window of diminished dominance that offered an opportunity for change. In a context of crisis and severe gridlock brought on by the open conflict between Rousseff and Eduardo Cunha, as well as the president's isolation from her own party and her governing coalition, accountability agencies and the judicial system faced minimal political interference and had considerable freedom of maneuver.

Although the Rousseff administration half-heartedly tried to rein in *Lava Jato* at various moments during these twenty-six months, including by twice replacing the justice minister, interest was high and the public response was quick, ensuring that the case continued to move forward with relatively limited political interference. The strongest headwinds that *Lava Jato* faced during this period therefore emerged less from the executive and legislative branches than from the slow and uneven pace of the courts, particularly in São Paulo and Brasília.

The arc began to bend downward with Rousseff's impeachment by the lower house in May 2016, culminating in her definitive removal in August. Rousseff's removal was engineered by a cabal of longtime MDB heavyweights who later would also lead a proactive effort against *Lava Jato*. While the impeachment was unsavory, and made possible mainly by an obscure technicality in the laws on fiscal responsibility, nearly 60 percent of the public supported it, perhaps because the impeachment trial was intertwined with discussion of corruption at Petrobras and the economic crisis (Dávila 2016). That is, even though impeachment was legally justified primarily by the narrow fact that the administration had engaged in "creative accounting" maneuvers to temporarily paper over excessive public borrowing, this was a thin reed. Rousseff's impeachment was ultimately possible only because of the *conjunto da obra* (whole of her oeuvre), including political mismanagement, alienation of her coalition, economic missteps, and the pervasive corruption *Lava Jato* uncovered (Lima and Bresciani 2016; Schreiber 2016; *Jornal da USP* 2016). Not all of it was Rousseff's doing, but the overall mess was laid at her feet.

The second moment began as Rousseff was replaced, first on a temporary basis, and then permanently by her vice president Michel Temer (MDB), a savvy politician with an innate talent for manipulating the coalitional incentives that moved many members of Congress. Temer's cabinet advisers included longtime MDB legislators Geddel Vieira Lima, Romero Jucá, Henrique Alves, Eliseu Padilha, and Moreira Franco. Publicly, the government paraded these power brokers' expertise in pushing legislation through Congress, which, it was argued, would help Temer push through the reforms needed to regain investor confidence and overcome the economic crisis. In his first speech to the nation as acting president, Temer suggested that digging out of the hole was his primary task, admonishing Brazilian workers: "não fale sobre crise, trabalhe" (don't talk about crisis, work) (*Época Negócios* 2016). Behind the scenes, though, many in Brasília saw the new cabinet's selection as a sign that Temer intended to slow the *Lava Jato* bloodletting, and their goals were perhaps most cogently expressed by Senator Romero Jucá's true feelings, caught in the wiretapped conversation reproduced in the first epigraph to this chapter.

The Temer government and the *Lava Jato* task force played at cat and mouse for much of 2016 and, especially, 2017. The MDB aimed at preserving whatever public support it could while simultaneously neutering the investigations. On the one hand, President Temer publicly vetoed or blocked congressional actions that might be seen as directly targeting *Lava Jato* such as a congressional amnesty on illegal campaign contributions and a congressional bill to prevent "judicial abuses." On the other, though, Temer's allies fatally mangled the anticorruption reform package proposed by the MPF, while Temer himself began nominating pliant allies to head key accountability agencies.

Prosecutors, police, and the media did not sit idly by. The short-lived Temer presidency tottered on the brink of catastrophe, not least because in late 2016, a second *lista de Janot* of politicians implicated by plea bargaining Odebrecht executives came to light. Temer's closest party confidants fared poorly: Eduardo Cunha was jailed soon after Rousseff's removal, and was later convicted on money laundering charges by Judge Moro in Curitiba; Geddel Vieira Lima was forced out of public life by a series of scandals, topped off by the discovery of an apartment stuffed full of R$51 million in unexplained cash, which would render him a criminal conviction from the STF in late 2019; Jucá resigned from the Planning Ministry soon after he was appointed, due to the release of the wiretaps of his conversation with Transpetro president Sérgio Machado; Henrique Alves resigned after news broke of his corrupt ties to Transpetro; Eliseu Padilha was indicted by the prosecutor-general; and Moreira Franco was investigated and then detained preventively in March 2019, alongside Temer.

Temer himself became a largely ineffectual president after mid-2017, when meatpacking tycoon Joesley Batista's recordings of his conversations discussing corruption at the presidential palace were released to the public. The recordings were not always easy to follow, but they made clear that, with Temer's consent and the assistance of Congressman Rodrigo da Rocha Loures, Batista intended to buy the silence of former Chamber president Eduardo Cunha. Rocha Loures was then filmed by the Federal Police receiving a bag of money from a meatpacking executive. As sitting president, Temer could not be tried by the STF without congressional approval. Twice, the president managed to corral enough legislative support to avoid that fate, but the unseemly process cost Temer any lingering legitimacy he might have had, with his popularity falling to historic lows. His administration's approval rating fell to 82 percent disapproval in May 2018, and disapproval remained well above 60 percent until the end of his term (*Folha de S. Paulo* 2018a). Likewise, the scandal severely undermined the Temer administration's ability to enact any significant public policies. For the first time in thirty years, Congress failed to pass any significant constitutional reforms in 2018: neither desperately needed economic reforms, nor anticorruption reforms.[4]

Lava Jato, of course, did not stop at Temer and his entourage. Aécio Neves, grandson of the revered Tancredo Neves (the first civilian president of the postauthoritarian period) and the PSDB's presidential candidate in 2014, was charged in June 2017 with taking bribes from the J&F meatpacking group and allegedly attempting to obstruct justice. The STF forced him to step down from his Senate seat (Freire 2019; J. Pereira 2018; Benites 2018). Later charges would allege that Aécio Neves also received more than R$65 million in bribes from Odebrecht and Andrade Gutierrez in exchange for influence peddling in the energy sector while he served as governor and senator (L. B. Teixeira 2020).

In July 2017, former president Luiz Inácio Lula da Silva was sentenced by Moro's trial court for having received a corrupt gift of a three-story beachside apartment from the OAS construction firm. In January 2018, the TRF4 upheld and extended that sentence and the country watched the drama as its former president was led off to a jail cell. In what seemed like a foreordained but longtime coming decision, in August the STF determined that, under the Clean Slate Law, Lula could not run for the presidency.

The third moment began with the 2018 election. Having investigated, indicted, convicted, or otherwise tarnished the three most consequential parties of the postauthoritarian period—MDB, PSDB, and PT—as well as many of their smaller allies, *Lava Jato* had paved the way for the arrival of new political forces during the October election. The election led to record turnover and removed many long-serving incumbents implicated in scandal. But it did little to change the underlying incentives within the coalitional presidential system, and, in fact, the expanding number of parties—thirty of which were elected to the new Congress—seemed likely to only deepen the need for coalition-building tools, whether licit or not. Meanwhile, the fact that *Lava Jato* had cut such a broad swath across the political system meant that there was little political support for the task force when support was most needed.

The election of a self-declared outsider as president promised change. However, the new president, Jair Bolsonaro, may have been a firebrand, but he was not really an outsider to the political system. He had served in Congress for a quarter-century, including as a member of one of the parties most deeply involved in corruption at Petrobras, the PP. He had long ties with state politicians in Rio de Janeiro, he had family members who were engaged in the typical shenanigans of political finance, and, partly in consequence, he would prove hostile to the law enforcement authorities of *Lava Jato*. Although Bolsonaro nominated Sérgio Moro as justice minister in a bid to give his administration a patina of anticorruption legitimacy, this conversion was short-lived. As Bolsonaro's family became more and more deeply implicated in various abuses of authority, the administration increasingly moved to curb the Federal Police, intimidate the MPF and courts, and otherwise complicate anticorruption efforts. By April 2020, only sixteen months after taking office, Moro chose to resign from Bolsonaro's cabinet rather than accept the appointment of a new head of the Federal Police handpicked by Bolsonaro.

Moro's accomplishments as justice minister were ambiguous on the corruption front, particularly in contrast to his impressive record as a judge. By Moro's own recounting, he served as a bulwark against Bolsonaro's efforts to reshape the Federal Police, which seemed designed to free Bolsonaro's sons from a variety of corruption and criminal allegations. Moro was also able to place a number of members of the *Lava Jato* investigative team in high-ranking positions in oversight agencies, helping to ensure that anti–money laundering and anticorruption were top of mind in the law enforcement community. Yet Moro also took many hits: his proposed anticrime legislation was watered down in Congress with the accord of his boss; his reputation was besmirched by association with Bolsonaro and by the disdain with which he was treated by Congress; and, in his absence, the trial court in Curitiba reverted to the slow pace of the rest of the judiciary (Hofmeister, Papini, and Seibt 2020). Various agencies were remade by Bolsonaro, meanwhile, in ways seemingly calculated to sow confusion and complicate their work, as the next section illustrates.

The Reversal of *Lava Jato*

Various factors caused *Lava Jato* to slowly lose steam: self-inflicted wounds that changed perceptions of prosecutors and judges; the failure to grow beyond Curitiba and Rio de Janeiro; the increasing controversy within the legal community on the use of new doctrines; and reforms that began to be rolled back by a new anti–*Lava Jato* coalition within the political system.

Self-Inflicted Wounds

The *Lava Jato* task force was damaged by self-inflicted wounds that fanned concern about the potential abuses and biases of the investigations. In many cases, these wounds came about precisely because of the conscientious legal-political strategy described in the previous chapter: recognizing that they were fighting a multifront battle with a vastly more powerful set of opponents, task force members overstepped their bounds, especially as they strayed from their legal forte and increasingly waded into politics. The political component of the strategy may have led prosecutors and the judge on the case to selectively release information, and even leak to the press, as well as to make calculated decisions about what case information to publish and when (Damgaard 2018a; Prado and Machado, forthcoming, a). In so doing, they fell into a trap common in many anticorruption campaigns: reformers are often depicted as fighting abuse with another form of abuse (Merriner 2004). Six episodes were particularly damaging to the *Lava Jato* team's public standing.

The first was the release of a wiretap of a conversation between former president Lula and President Rousseff in early 2016. In one of her last attempts to galvanize support in an increasingly defiant Congress, Rousseff sought to appoint Lula to the position of presidential chief of staff, so that his popularity could be deployed as a tool to induce legislative cooperation. During their conversation, the former and sitting presidents discussed the appointment of Lula, and Rousseff's intention to leave an order for that nomination signed and ready for whenever it was needed. Neither Rousseff nor Lula was aware that, at the time of their conversation, Lula's telephone was being surveilled by investigators. As it became apparent to the task force in Curitiba that the appointment of Lula to the position of chief of staff would shield him from investigation by the *Lava Jato* task force in Curitiba—the chief of staff position ranked as a cabinet ministry, meaning that its occupant could be tried only under the STF's original jurisdiction, with the practical immunity this guaranteed— Judge Moro publicly released the audio and transcripts of the wiretap of Lula and Rousseff's conversation on March 16, 2016. Two days later, STF Justice Gilmar Mendes granted an injunction to suspend Lula's appointment in a case filed by the PSDB and PPS (M. Oliveira 2016).[5]

The wiretapped conversation was understandably menacing to the *Lava Jato* team, suggesting that Lula might be nominated so that he could escape the jurisdiction of the trial court, and possibly even bring his enormous political capital to bear in an effort to clamp down on the *Lava Jato* investigation. It followed on Rousseff's troubling decisions to dismiss two ministers of justice in rapid succession, which, because of their command over the Federal Police, was also threatening to the task force. So the move to empower Lula was perceived by the task force in Curitiba, and by Judge Moro, as one more political maneuver that might cast sand in the gears of the investigations. Although the STF reprimanded Moro, perhaps because Moro had strong public support—a contemporaneous survey showed that almost 70 percent of the population approved of the wiretap's release (Dávila 2016)—he was not immediately punished, in contrast to what happened to Judge Fausto De Sanctis during *Satiagraha*.[6]

But however dangerous the Lula-Rousseff partnership may have seemed, or however popular the release might have been, the decision to release the wiretap was problematic for a host of reasons. The wiretapped conversations involved the sitting president of the country, Rousseff, who by law could be investigated only by the high court. The wiretapping authority granted by Moro, furthermore, had expired a few hours before the conversation took place, so the wiretap was technically illegal (Da Ros and Ingram 2018). The release of the wiretap to the media, furthermore, gave a strong impulse to Rousseff's impeachment, by eliminating any possibility of a Hail Mary, such as Lula's return, that could reassemble a functioning governing coalition. The following Sunday, Brazil saw one of its largest street protests in history, with millions of participants. Rousseff was temporarily removed from office two months after the episode, in May 2016, and then permanently removed in August. This sequence of interconnected legal and political events gave credence to Rousseff's and Lula's defenders' claims of a deep partisan undercurrent to *Lava Jato*.

A second episode six months later was more guileless, although its impact on public opinion was equally profound. In September 2016, lead task force prosecutor Deltan Dallagnol presented the case against Lula at a press conference. Standing before a PowerPoint slide framed by fourteen bubbles with arrows pointing to a central bubble labeled "Lula," Dallagnol presented a variety of vague reasons for why Lula should be charged (e.g., "greatest beneficiary" and, in two repeated bubbles, "close acquaintances in *Lava Jato*"). The public reaction was immediate. Dallagnol was widely trolled for the unsophisticated and vague charges laid out against the former president. For weeks, WhatsApp groups were filled with ironic PowerPoint slides of all that was wrong with the world, including the forays of soccer star Neymar da Silva Santos Jr. into songwriting and the Brazil team's traumatic 7–1 loss to Germany in the 2014 World Cup. For the public at large, Dallagnol's presentation may have devalued the credibility of evidence of Lula's corruption. The hand-waving presentation and its nebulous charges against the president raised hackles among a legal community that was already chaffing at the newfound use of the *domínio do fato* doctrine and its seemingly vague burden of proof.

A third self-inflicted wound came from wrongdoing on prosecutor-general Rodrigo Janot's team of senior prosecutors. In 2017, the meatpacking conglomerate J&F (owner of the JBS brand) was working to reach a leniency agreement with prosecutors.[7] The controlling shareholders of J&F, the brothers Joesley and Wesley Batista, were simultaneously working to reach a plea bargain (Ramalho and Oliveira 2018). These proposed agreements appear to have been incomplete and possibly inaccurate. Journalists revealed that one of the senior prosecutors on Janot's team, Marcelo Miller, was simultaneously working for the law firm that defended J&F (Salomão 2017; Truffi 2017). This scandal within a scandal deeply wounded the effort to bring J&F and the Batista brothers to justice. It also hobbled Janot and led to splits in the Ministério Público Federal that ultimately made it easier for President Temer to replace Janot, not with the top name on the MPF's *lista tríplice,* Nicolao Dino, but instead with Raquel Dodge, who would subsequently play a subtle but effective role in degrading the *Lava Jato* investigations.

Fourth was Moro's decision to join Bolsonaro's administration as justice minister only a few months after jailing Bolsonaro's main rival, former president Lula. By all accounts, Moro was exhausted by his years overseeing the never-ending case, eager to use the Justice Ministry to effect real change, and excited by Bolsonaro's declared willingness to grant him carte blanche. Emblematic of this intent, as he flew to the meeting with the president-elect to discuss joining the government, Moro pointedly carried with him a recently published book by Transparency International and the Fundação Getulio Vargas, *Novas Medidas Contra a Corrupção,* detailing seventy proposals for fighting corruption in Brazil. Yet however sincere that intention may have been, and no matter how much public support Moro carried with him into government, the decision to join Bolsonaro's cabinet cast another shadow on the political intentions of *Lava Jato.*

Fifth was a series of reports that began to be published in June 2019 by *The Intercept,* an online publication founded by Pulitzer Prize winner Glenn Greenwald, which showed ex parte communications via private text messages between Moro and Dallagnol (Greenwald, Reed, and Demori 2019). The messages, quickly nicknamed "Vaza Jato" (Jato leaks) suggested that Judge Moro coached the prosecutor on a witness who should be called and evidence that should be used, that the two discussed strategies for overcoming the roadblocks imposed by the STF, and that they discussed how best to communicate with the public. Whether or not these conversations were proper is the subject of legal debate—especially because many of the conversations took place not during the trial phase but rather during the investigations, when such conversations may be permitted as well as necessary (Stephenson 2019). Several prominent Brazilian anticorruption specialists, such as judges Eliana Calmon and Denise Frossard, argued that nothing was amiss since there is no legal impediment against ex parte conversations between judges and lawyers or judges and prosecutors. In the words of supreme court justice Luis Roberto Barroso, there was "more gossip here than relevant facts" (Nêumanne 2019). But the fact that Moro and Dallagnol were communicating via a confidential messaging app, and that they discussed a communications strategy for reaching the broader public, cast a pall over the investigation, and especially on the behavior of its two leading men, Dallagnol and Moro. The timing of the release, soon after Moro joined the Bolsonaro administration, only further darkened the picture, hinting at a deeper political calculus to the case and confirming the worst suspicions on the left of the political spectrum. Greenwald and his coauthors drew the darkest possible conclusion: "In other words, [as justice minister,] Moro now wields immense police and surveillance powers in Brazil—courtesy of a president who was elected only after Moro, while he was a judge, rendered Bolsonaro's key adversary ineligible to run against him" (Greenwald, Reed, and Demori 2019).[8]

Sixth was the perceived self-dealing of *Lava Jato* prosecutors in channeling a portion of the US$680 million settlement reached between the US Department of Justice and Petrobras to a foundation in Curitiba.[9] This use of the settlement money was agreed on between Petrobras and the MPF, and approved in trial court. However, it immediately generated immense controversy, not least because many within government felt the money should go to the National Treasury (R. T. de Souza 2020). Justice Gilmar Mendes, relishing a dig, was quoted as saying, "If [the prosecutors] studied at Harvard, they didn't learn anything. They're a bunch of cretins. . . . Who knows what they could be doing with that money?" (Martins 2019). Prosecutor-general Raquel Dodge heightened the pressure against the *Lava Jato* team by filing a suit against the foundation in high court, arguing that the money should be managed by the federal government, not a foundation, and that the task force members had gone beyond their powers within the MPF in creating the foundation (Rossi, Oliveira, and Bianchi 2019). Justice Alexandre de Moraes decided in Dodge's favor, staying Petrobras's transfers to the foundation. He further argued that the foundation was not mentioned in the nonprosecution agreement between Petrobras and the US Department of Justice, and that its creation was thus an "illegal distortion" of the agreement (Brígido 2019). In *Lava Jato*'s defense, Dallagnol argued that the United States did not wish for the money to return to the federal government since the federal government was Petrobras's controller. He further argued that the foundation would be a civil society organization, with a representative from the MPF sitting alongside another ten to twenty people on the board, following the model of settlements with Siemens and Alstom (Macedo 2019). In a subsequent decision in September 2019, Moraes backed an alternative agreement between the prosecutor-general, Congress, and the executive branch, and the case was dismissed (R. T. de Souza 2020). But the blemish remained, and subsequent discussions about using the money on coronavirus relief only threatened to reopen the controversy.

Failure to Grow Anticorruption Efforts Beyond Curitiba and Rio de Janeiro

Another cause for the anticorruption efforts' slowing momentum is that—outside Curitiba and Rio de Janeiro—there was no other jurisdiction that carried forward similar cases as effectively or efficiently. One joke current among lawyers during the investigation illustrates the extraordinary breadth of Judge Moro's claims for the jurisdiction of his trial court. A law professor asks, "If two cars crash on the main street in Brasília, where should your client sue for damages?" Her students answer, "Curitiba."[10] All kidding aside, the task force and trial court's ability to claim jurisdiction through the connection between the cases had the effect of ensuring efficiency, but, with hindsight, it may have also impeded the development of the case elsewhere. The bulk of *Lava Jato* cases was heard in these two courts (see Table 5.1). The runner-up São Paulo trial court dealt with far fewer indictments. Some offshoots of *Lava Jato* cases in the trial court in Brasília were folded into the less effective Operation Greenfield (described below). No other trial courts were involved in any significant way.

The narrowness of anticorruption efforts within the national judiciary is illustrated by two other potentially momentous corruption investigations that emerged contemporaneously with *Lava Jato,* but had vastly different outcomes. In March 2015, a year into *Lava Jato,* the Federal Police began an ancillary investigation, Operation Zealots, to look into a massive bribery scheme in an obscure tax appeals council within the Finance Ministry, the Conselho de Administração de Recursos Fiscais (CARF). Prosecutors alleged that the

Table 5.1   Indictments and Convictions in the Lava Jato Case, March 2014–November 2020

	Individuals Indicted	Individuals Convicted (in both trial and appeals court)
Curitiba trial court	553	174
Rio de Janeiro trial court	887	183
São Paulo trial court	89	6

Source: MPF (2021a).

scheme may have caused R$19 billion in tax revenue losses by incorrectly exempting large companies from past tax bills in exchange for bribes (*El País Brasil* 2015). Over the course of ten distinct phases of investigation, more than seventy companies and leading banks were implicated, and prosecutors indicted more than 100 defendants, including former finance minister Guido Mantega and former president Lula. Another former finance minister under the Workers' Party government, Antônio Palocci, further testified that Lula's son received R$5 million in bribes through auto dealerships seeking privileged tax treatment.

Of three prosecutors on the case, however, two dropped off and a third was transferred to a different state. Although an additional prosecutor was later added to the case (Bomfim 2019), the operation did not prosper. There were many reasons: the small team of prosecutors had to work on other cases simultaneously, distracting them from the complex investigation; some of the defendants fell under the original jurisdiction of the STF, thus requiring a separate prosecutorial effort; and prosecutors had little success in convincing the trial court judge to grant preventive detention orders against participants early in the case, so as to prevent communication between them (*El País Brasil* 2015). Early convictions in the trial court in 2016 were subsequently overturned in the TRF1 regional appeals court, which was not convinced by the trial court's depiction of a criminal organization needed to sustain a racketeering conviction, or by the argument that there were public servants corrupted in the scheme needed to sustain a *corrupção ativa* (bribe-offering) conviction (although the CARF is a public body, its members are not technically civil servants) (F. Valente 2020).

In the second case, in September 2016, prosecutors began looking into R$8 billion in losses from fraud and corruption in pension funds belonging to employees of state-owned enterprises. This operation, named Operation Greenfield, also grew out of *Lava Jato,* and investigated, among many things, the possibility that fraudulent investments were made by the government-controlled pension funds in an investment fund run by Sete Brasil, a company created after the pre-salt oil discoveries to build drilling equipment. The case was extraordinarily complex, involving the pension funds, state-owned banks, private banks, private companies, and a wide range of investment vehicles. It also grew to target a wide swath of powerful politicians, including President Michel Temer, as well as Eduardo Cunha and Henrique Alves (both former presidents of the Chamber of Deputies), and a variety of current and former cabinet ministers.

Yet for a variety of reasons similar to those present in Operation Zealots, Operation Greenfield had only mixed success (MPF 2021b). The prosecutor-general took a long time to nominate members of the task force and, even then, assigned many of them only part time. The Federal Police's allocation of staff was similarly anemic, perhaps reflecting the political challenge of staffing an investigation into a sitting president. But even once Temer was no longer president, support for the task force was tepid: during its last two years, Operation Greenfield was being renewed on a quarterly basis, which complicated planning; and, by the last year, there was only one full-time prosecutor assigned to the task force, and he eventually resigned in protest (J. Moura 2020). Meanwhile, portions of a number of ancillary investigations (*Cui Bono, Catilinárias, Sépsis,* and *Carne Fraca*) were folded into the task force's purview, expanding its scope and the complexity of the investigation without any compensatory increase in staffing.

The case also was set back by accusations against one of the prosecutors in the case, Ângelo Goulart Villella, who was charged with accepting bribes in exchange for providing information about the case to meatpacking tycoon Joesley Batista (*Istoé* 2019). While Greenfield was able to land 176 indictments, sign 11 plea bargains and 2 leniency agreements, and levy R$12 billion in fines and damages, it was less successful against many of its political targets. Prosecutors repeatedly appealed the low sentences many politicians received, to little effect. There was a lot of jurisdictional complexity: a case against former cabinet minister Geddel Viera Lima, for example, was moved to the STF because a co-defendant had special standing in the STF. Former president Temer was summarily absolved in the trial court in Brasília, ostensibly because the primary proof against him relied solely on a wiretapped conversation. Prosecutors appealed, arguing that several other types of evidence had been presented, but the case was emblematic of the political and legal challenges this overburdened task force confronted in the three and a half years before it was shut down.

Similarly, for a variety of reasons that may include everything from personal style and political sensibility to justices' legal opinions and beliefs about the proper role of the courts, *Lava Jato* did not proceed rapidly in the STF. Indeed, despite its early decisions subtly encouraging *Lava Jato* forward, the STF reverted to its old status quo ante, acting in a less assertive manner against sitting politicians in *Lava Jato* than it did in the *Mensalão* case. There are several possible explanations for this change of heart. The court may have adopted a more cautious posture because of the significant internal tensions that erupted during the *Mensalão* trial, which threatened to tear the court apart. The STF became even more cautious after a notable episode of noncompliance with its rulings by the president of the Senate (Vieira 2018: 205).[11] Internal changes in case management at the STF also made a difference: in June 2014, a few months after *Mensalão* ended, the STF transferred criminal cases involving sitting politicians from the full court (*plenário,* where all eleven justices of the court sit en banc) to its two panels (*turmas,* with five justices each) (STF 2014). The *turmas* are a smaller and less visible place to hear cases. If the procedural shift had the potential to speed up decisionmaking in the short term, it nonetheless slowed down the judicial process long term since it introduced the possibility that cases could be appealed *within* the STF, from the *turmas* to the *plenário*. It also introduced the possibility that the balance of justices in the *turmas* might be quite different from the full court, with cases being decided by a subset of justices that was either more or less permissive about evidentiary rules, the burden of proof, and corruption law generally.

In theory, this might lead us to a discussion of the differing legal opinions that key justices held on anticorruption law. Indeed, there were important fissures on the court, with Justice Ricardo Lewandowski seen as generally leading the more defense-friendly group and Justice Teori Zavascki and then Justice Edson Fachin leading the more prosecution-friendly group on the court during *Lava Jato* cases. There are also clear schools of thought on particular jurisprudential issues in the legal community, such as original jurisdiction, jail on appeal, and secrecy provisions, as well as more specialized debates about judicial process (see the next section).

But legal opinions can carry us only so far in explaining the shifting interpretations of the court. As Oscar Vilhena Vieira (2018) notes, one reason is that there was considerable inconstancy in some individual justices' opinions on the very same matters. For example, in two momentous decisions on habeas corpus protections in 2016 and 2018, key justices reversed the positions they had taken just two years earlier (i.e., Dias Toffoli, Rosa Weber, and Gilmar Mendes). Second, the court itself saw four of its eleven seats turn over between 2014 and the time of this writing due to misfortune (the accident that killed Teori Zavascki) and retirements (Joaquim Barbosa, Celso de Mello, and Marco Aurélio de Mello). Third, extremely fragmented decisionmaking procedures on the STF mean that much of the court's massive caseload is disposed of through *decisões monocráticas* (individualized decisionmaking), leading to what Diego Werneck Arguelhes and Leandro Molhano Ribeiro (2018) label "ministocracy," referring to the ability of individual justices (known as *ministros* in Portuguese) to alter the state of play. This means that the same case may be decided differently depending on whether the decision is made by a distinct individual justice, a distinct *turma,* or a particular composition of justices on the full plenary sessions.

The STF's performance thus was quite a mixed bag. If on the one hand the STF made several decisions that enabled lower courts to act more aggressively against corruption, particularly in the early years of *Lava Jato,* on the other hand the STF was sparing in its own efforts against powerful political actors implicated in the scandal. In fact, by 2021, seven years after *Lava Jato* began and six years after cases began arriving at the STF, more than 100 sitting politicians were still under investigation, and few *Lava Jato* cases had actually been tried. The STF took more than three years to convict a single sitting politician, former federal representative Nelson Meurer (PP), who as of this writing remains the only sitting politician to have been convicted by the high court in the *Lava Jato* case (Kadanus 2020). Many politicians' cases in the STF may only go to trial in the late 2020s, if at all.

In sum, in a variety of contemporaneous cases associated with *Lava Jato,* the judiciary as a whole performed quite differently from the Curitiba and Rio de Janeiro trial courts. There are many possible reasons, such as the differing capacity of individual investigators and prosecutors, the staffing of investigations, the political calculations of key players, and the distinct interpretations of the law. But overall, no other court seemed capable of escaping the gravitational field that recurrently sucked down anticorruption investigations and ensured impunity for economic and, especially, political elites.

Increasing Controversy Within the Legal Community

The centrality of courts to *Lava Jato* cast an unflattering light on the inoperancy of judicial institutions. The relative novelty of many of the legal tools that were being utilized by prosecutors and judges also meant that the legal community beyond the MPF and the court was following the case developments closely, not always in agreement with the legal processes and legal interpretations that were being employed, often for the first time.

The starting point for understanding the controversy probably needs to begin with three essential bottlenecks to legal accountability. First, although there have been repeated changes over the years, for the most part courts have banned the imprisonment of defendants until all appeals have been heard. This briefly was not the case in the critical years between early 2016 and 2019, when *Lava Jato* was moving full steam. But before 2016 and after 2019, the courts adopted the "totally illogical extension of the presumption of innocence" that is implied by the right of defendants to remain free until every last one of their appeals is heard (Rosenn 2014: 304–305).[12]

A second bottleneck emerged from the combination of the high court's original jurisdiction over cases in which sitting politicians are implicated and the high court's inefficiency as a trial court on the hundreds of cases pending against politicians. In no small part because it must simultaneously address tens of thousands of other, noncriminal, cases on its docket each year, the STF's original jurisdiction has long been an essential guarantor of elite impunity.

Third is the paralyzing lack of precedent, which leads to irresolvable conflicts between trial courts, appeals courts, and the high courts (Prado and Machado, forthcoming, b). The high court itself, which has considerable turnover due to the minimum retirement age, often rehears its own cases (as noted above) with new justices, or simply changes its collective mind on cases in light of new circumstances (for a broader discussion, see Da Ros and Taylor 2019).

The *Mensalão* case and the *Lava Jato* operation dropped a host of new and complex questions into this morass. As Mariana Mota Prado and Marta Rodriguez Machado (forthcoming, b) point out, it not only was "rent-seeking cronies" and their lawyers who were confused and preoccupied by these legal issues. Although defense lawyers were very good at ensuring an ample hearing for their concerns in the press, in academic debates, and in the courts, there were less instrumentally motivated concerns at work here as well. A growing number of legal scholars began to raise genuine concerns about the excessive punitiveness of *Lava Jato*'s new approach to corruption.

Excessive punitivism in *Lava Jato* cases against politicians can be exemplified by the case of former Chamber of Deputies president Eduardo Cunha. Perhaps because he is an unsympathetic character, known as a wily old school operator, the treatment of Cunha has not drawn much attention. The STF received the indictment against Cunha for corruption, money laundering, tax evasion, and electoral fraud while Cunha was still in Congress. After he was expelled from Congress by his peers, he lost standing in the STF and his case was moved to the Curitiba trial court. After the transfer, the electoral fraud charges against him (which the STF had already accepted) were dropped, perhaps because if the trial court allowed them, the appropriate jurisdiction would no longer be the trial court, and the case could be moved to the electoral court system, which is reputed to be slow and favorable to politicians. Instead, Cunha was tried by Moro, and sentenced to fifteen years in prison (*Correio Braziliense* 2019; Zamprogna 2019). As this example shows, there were legitimate questions that could be raised about the treatment dispensed to defendants, even the most unlikable among them.

Procedurally, critics questioned the widespread use of coercive questioning, whereby a defendant is seized by surprise for interrogation to prevent the destruction of evidence; pretrial detention, used in cases in which the defendant was thought to pose a threat to public order or enforcement of the law; the order in which plea bargaining witnesses were heard, relative to those implicated in those pleas; the understanding of judicial secrecy applied by *Lava Jato,* which adopted a far more proactive stance in publicizing cases and case documents than most courts; and the number of appeals that had to be heard before a defendant could be sent to jail.

In terms of legal doctrine, critics pointed to the controversial use of a variety of new interpretations on the original jurisdiction of the high court, which was often effectively sidestepped by the trial court in Curitiba, sometimes with the STF's approval; the use of evidence from plea bargaining; the reliance on *dominio do fato* arguments that allowed a defendant to be convicted without evidence of a clear quid pro quo; and the concept of "willfull blindness," which allowed prosecutors to "bypass one of the most severe obstacles to sentencing high level officials involved in corruption," the "very narrow mens rea" standard (i.e., proof of the defendant's intention) in the criminal code (Vieira 2018; Prado and Machado forthcoming, b).

In a legal system with a layering of seven constitutions dating back 200 years that is shaped by a host of external influences, including German, Portuguese, and Roman law, and whose high court decisionmaking is so convoluted that one influential constitutional scholar describes the term "STF jurisprudence" as "poetic license" (Hubner Mendes 2019), some concerns can be dismissed out of hand. Examples include a dismissal because such and such an innovation is "foreign" or somehow alien to Brazilian law, or because another is somehow not in line with the "traditions" of Brazilian law.

But as new decisions were made that pushed the envelope of communal understandings of the law, or as prominent defendants like former president Lula were subjected to shocking processes like coercive questioning, the legal community began to raise concerns. Many legal concerns were founded in reasoned debate and were justified by a desire to deepen the rule of law in a consolidating democracy with a history of civil rights abuses and authoritarian rule. Furthermore, as the self-inflicted wounds above illustrate, all too often there was evidence that in their zealousness, prosecutors may have taken shortcuts that ignored common understandings of the law, or at the least pushed the envelope in ways that were unlikely to pass muster when held up for rigorous inspection by higher courts or the legal community more broadly (Kant de Lima and Mouzinho 2016; Sá e Silva 2020; Engelmann 2020; Mészáros 2020).

That said, the roiling of legal consensus also took place against a backdrop of a dysfunctional supreme court, which flip-flopped on key decisions (Prado and Machado forthcoming, b; Da Ros and Taylor 2021b), engaged in "constitutional gamesmanship" (Glezer 2020: 31), was casuistic in its decisionmaking, and thus produced little more than a "cacophony" of arguments (Hubner Mendes 2019). Rather than resolving these many contentious legal issues, the dysfunctionality of the high court and its contradictory "precedents" only produced further confusion.

The legal controversy that grew up around *Lava Jato* in many ways demonstrated the costs of a judicially led big bang effort. As Rubens Glezer (2020) ably argues, *Lava Jato* politicized the judiciary, even if not necessarily in a partisan way; cast the conflict in black-and-white terms (either for or against the corruption effort); and personalized justice by focusing intently on Moro and Dallagnol rather than the full legal system. Further, making the courts central protagonists may have caused the side effects of demobilizing the public; reducing pressure for institutional change; and, perhaps in consequence of the complexity and turbulence of the case, enabling a rollback of key reforms.

Rollback Across the Accountability Equation

A final reason that the anticorruption big bang engendered by *Lava Jato* slowly flamed out was a growing pushback not just against *Lava Jato,* but more broadly, against accountability efforts generally. In the subsections below, we detail how various forces weakened the six elements of the accountability equation. We address the six components in a slightly different order than we followed earlier in the book, in keeping with how they tie in to the Brazilian politics of anticorruption: engagement, dominance, capacity, transparency, oversight, and sanction.

Engagement. Brazilians can be forgiven for growing exhausted by the political upheavals of the 2010s. From the 2013 street protests to the incendiary governance of Bolsonaro, politics had come to dominate all aspects of life for much of the decade, leading to division and despair. Social media and WhatsApp groups were filled with little else; otherwise close-knit families were rent by political debates.

Many public intellectuals began to question whether it was worth it. Prominent analysts questioned whether fighting corruption was more disruptive than productive in the long run. Alberto Carlos Almeida (2015), for example, argued that *Lava Jato* imposed high costs on society that would not be compensated for by the benefits from lower corruption (see also Augusto, Gabrielli, and Alonso 2021). One study estimated that the investigations had led to half a trillion reais in losses to the investigated companies, and more than R$40 billion in lost tax revenue (Pinto et al. 2021; D. Rodrigues, Pinto, and Rocha 2021). The democratic costs were also a concern: Bruno P. W. Reis (2017) argued that the punitive impetus at the heart of *Lava Jato* prematurely destabilized an incipient move toward political reform and the institutionalization of the party system.

The many twists and turns of *Lava Jato* also meant that it was hard for the public to know how and where to mobilize for change. Old parties were shunned, but new social movements were often seen as stalking horses for conservative political aspirations that were far from mainstream. While it followed procedural niceties, impeachment was a dividing line: the image of congressmen long known to be corrupt voting Rousseff out of office for a fiscal irregularity was viscerally offensive to many moderate voters. Furthermore, as time went by, the impeachment looked more and more like a sophisticated effort to throw Rousseff under the bus. In the memorable words of philosopher Marcos Nobre, Rousseff's impeachment seemed to follow the *boi de piranha* strategy: she was the cow that was thrown to the piranhas so that the rest of the herd of politicians could cross the river unscathed (L. Guimarães 2020).

The electoral calendar did little to help matters. Soon after the tight election of 2014, which suggested the PT's four-term hold on the presidency was increasingly tenuous, the 2018 election quickly became a focal point for many Brazilians. Corruption and the economic downturn that many associated with the *Lava Jato* scandal were central to the electoral calculus, heightened by the impeachment, the shellacking of the PT in the October 2016 municipal elections,[13] and the general wobbliness of Temer's administration. Lula's jailing in early 2018, and the PT's decision to keep him on the ballot until the courts made a foreordained (but excruciatingly slow) decision denying his eligibility to run, made it difficult to separate electoral politics from the politics of the prosecution. Every new revelation and every new conviction were judged in terms of their electoral impact, and *Lava Jato* members were closely watched for evidence of bias.

The PT, as the governing party when the *Lava Jato* scheme was under way, had political and legal reasons to highlight these links and cast aspersions on the independence of *Lava Jato* investigators. Prosecutors' targeting of the PT was interpreted in quite distinct ways: for defenders of the *Lava Jato* team, prosecuting the PT was a nonpartisan act and virtually inevitable, given that the PT had been the governing party for thirteen years, at the time the crimes were allegedly taking place. For supporters of the PT, much of the evidence seemed to point instead to a political vendetta and lawfare, with key investigations and arrests seemingly timed for maximum political effect, demonstrating elite vindictiveness against a party that had represented common people. Little things fed the narrative: for example, a photograph of Judge Moro smiling next to the PSDB's Aécio Neves was widely circulated as proof of a deeper political bias. More significantly, the slow pace with which corruption was being judged in São Paulo, long governed by the PSDB, also suggested a partisan bent.[14] While there is no known evidence of deeper collusion between *Lava*

Jato and opponents of the PT, Frederico de Almeida (2019: 108) expressed the sentiment of many sectors of the left when he concluded that there probably was a weak connection, in the sense of an "opportunistic and reactive alignment" between them. Perhaps in consequence, polls showed signs of a growing partisan polarization around the issue of corruption beginning in the mid-2010s (Senters, Weitz-Shapiro, and Winters 2019: 22).

Another cause of public disengagement was that the broad anticorruption push was messy and analytically difficult to interpret. It led to many distinct, if frequently Manichean and ultimately irreconcilable narratives: the PT against the right-wing elite; illiberal inquisitorial prosecutors against defenders of due process; naïve antiestablishment antipolitics against a degenerate, but stable, political system. Many Brazilians found it hard to know what side was up. The bipolar narrative of a tug-of-war between the PT and the PSDB, which had marked politics for nearly a quarter-century, no longer provided analytical purchase. The MDB, the leading coalition ally to both parties, had usurped power for themselves but destabilized the magnetic fields of politics in the process. Prosecutors, meanwhile, were shooting in all directions: by 2019, all but two of the seven presidential contenders who had made it to the second round of voting since 2002—Luiz Inácio Lula da Silva, José Serra, Geraldo Alckmin, Dilma Rousseff, Aécio Neves, Fernando Haddad, and Jair Bolsonaro—were under federal investigation, had been indicted by federal prosecutors, and, in one case, had been jailed.[15] The years-long barrage of news, culminating in the election of a president who delighted in torching the norms of democratic cohabitation, numbed many Brazilians. In this context, many Brazilians simply tuned out, uncertain if they were being manipulated or if mobilizing against the system could ever make a difference when all the players were seemingly just as culpable as the rest.

Dominance. Public disengagement opened up space for the reestablishment of long-standing patterns of political dominance. As noted earlier, although *Lava Jato* had contributed to a tidal wave that swept many old politicians from the scene, it did not significantly alter the mechanics of the political system. Even though Bolsonaro came to office promising to eschew coalitional practices, within months he had reverted to the standard coalitional playbook. The tidal wave had in some ways left a barren field, especially by weakening the poles of political dispute (the PT and PSDB) and the pivotal MDB. But although weakened, the MDB was still a force to be reckoned with, as the largest party in the Senate. The government leaders in the Senate and in Congress overall were MDB members. The surviving parcel of politicians from the transactional old Centrão parties, such as Valdemar Costa Neto's PL and Ciro Nogueira's PP, were able to make common cause with the new arrivals, such as the new right represented by the Partido Social Liberal (PSL) and Senator Flávio Bolsonaro, President Bolsonaro's son. This new alliance did not seem qualitatively all that different from the old coalition: for example, the newly elected president of the Chamber in 2021, Arthur Lira, was a member of the PP, having passed through at least four other parties over the course of his career, was a close ally of Eduardo Cunha, had been accused of illicit enrichment, was twice convicted for administrative improbity, and had been charged in *Lava Jato*. The Senate president, Rodrigo Pacheco, was a member of the Centrão, serving at the time in the DEM and previously in the MDB, where he abstained in the vote to investigate Temer. Pacheco was touted as a candidate for the Senate presidency by his predecessor, who claimed he was not someone who would create waves in the coalition, and he displayed great influence in getting the executive branch to nominate his former legislative staffer to the agency that regulates his family business (BBC Brasil 2021a).

The reestablishment of old patterns of political behavior has combined with an alliance of strange bedfellows into an informal anti–*Lava Jato* alliance in Brasília. This broad alliance has no single raison d'être, but instead draws on a variety of distinct goals: revenge (e.g., some of those targeted by *Lava Jato*), escaping current investigations (e.g., Bolsonaro and his family), returning to business as usual (e.g., the Centrão parties), and curbing prosecutorial and judicial excesses (e.g., some members of the courts, the MPF, and legal scholars). The new anti–*Lava Jato* coalition is heterogeneous, but has been able to effect enormous change, as the next subsections show.

Capacity. The strength of the broad "backlash coalition" is perhaps best demonstrated by the Chamber of Deputies' June 2021 vote to dilute the Administrative Improbity Law. Fully 80 percent of the members of the lower house approved the bill, with the lopsided vote (408 to 67) pulling together representatives from all political parties except the minority Partido Socialismo e Liberdade (PSOL) (10 deputies), Novo (8 deputies), and Podemos (11 deputies) (Medeiros and Tavarez 2021). Arguing that the old law was outdated and unreasonably bound the hands of civil servants, the "reform" drafted by Congressman Carlos Zarattini (PT) makes it harder to prosecute administrative improbity, by requiring clear proof of intent; prevents civil servants from being removed from office if they have already moved on to a new job different from the job in which the irregularity took place; and weakens the prohibitions for nepotistic appointments, allowing family members to be hired if they demonstrate technical skills for the position.

This is only the latest example in a long stream of reversals to the statutory anticorruption framework. Reforms that could be considered pro-prosecution have been stymied at every turn. The package of anticorruption reforms known as the 10 Measures Against Corruption, proposed by the MPF and pushed to Congress through popular initiative in 2015 went nowhere fast: it was watered down substantially in the Chamber and then ground to a halt in the Senate (Braga, Contrera, and Cassotta 2018; F. de Almeida 2019: 118). On taking office, Justice Minister Moro moved his own package of reforms forward, but this was ultimately so disfigured by Congress that Moro begged—unsuccessfully—for President Bolsonaro to veto portions of it. Gone from the bill were proposals to improve the plea bargain, to increase maximum jail time, and to permit jail after conviction on appeal; added was a proposal for a *juiz de garantias* (judge) to oversee the judicial process to avoid abuses (D. Carvalho and Coletta 2019).

By contrast, a number of counterreforms have been passed in the past few years: the Abuse of Authority Law (Lei n. 13.869/2019) and the introduction of the *juiz de garantias* in the new Anticrime Law, both designed to curb abuse by prosecutors and judges (Lei n. 13.964/2019), as well as the expansion of the scope of the crime of *denunciação caluniosa* (roughly, libelous charges) in an effort to limit the reputational effects of prosecution (Lei n. 14.110/2020). Each of these laws emerges from a mix of reasonable motivations—reducing the abuse of power—and less well-intentioned goals aimed at curtailing the autonomy of prosecutors.

Less well-intentioned reforms have also been underway. A proposal for reform of the Anti–Money Laundering Law, which would weaken one of the key causes of the newfound success of anticorruption prosecutions during *Lava Jato,* has been percolating in Congress (although the special committee to discuss the proposal was dissolved in May 2021). Law 13.655, approved in 2018, explicitly limits the scope of administrative oversight, with clear effects on the ability of accounting tribunals to do their job. Enforcement of electoral laws has also been targeted, and Congress is now discussing a "new electoral code" that introduces, among other things, the possibility that political parties may be permitted to hire private auditing companies to oversee their expenditures, which would reduce the role of the electoral courts (Bragon and Brant 2021; Brant and Bragon 2021).[16]

Meanwhile, a number of changes have been undertaken that complicate the work of anticorruption bodies. Most notably, Bolsonaro's choice of prosecutor-general, Augusto Aras, resolved to dissolve all task forces within the Ministério Público Federal and move their prosecutors into Special Groups for the Repression of Crime (GAECOs) at the state level that have traditionally been used against organized crime and drug trafficking, and never before against corruption and money laundering. While the use of GAECOs does not necessarily spell the end of anticorruption prosecutions, it will take time for their members to develop expertise and coordination, and their members may not be assigned exclusively to anticorruption efforts. As the subsections below demonstrate, under Presidents Temer and Bolsonaro, the executive branch has also gone to great lengths to weaken the capacity of the "web" of anticorruption agencies by reassigning senior staff, while shifting internal rules and procedures. The combination of executive pushback and an anti–*Lava Jato* animus in Congress, furthermore, has also opened space for counterreformers in the courts.

Transparency. There have been areas of modest improvement in transparency since 2016. As in past presidential administrations, sometimes economic policy demands led to transparency gains: for example, in 2020 Economics Minister Paulo Guedes determined that the opaque "Sistema S" of corporate and labor contributions should be subjected to the same federal transparency statutes that govern the rest of the federal government (Michener and Mohallem 2020). Similarly, a new law governing state-owned enterprises, passed by President Michel Temer in 2016, was touted as a transparency improvement, although its effects remain limited (Praça 2018: 126). Another transparency reform whose effects are still uncertain is the new Public Procurement Law of 2021.

These hopeful green shoots notwithstanding, there have been significant and more clear-cut reversals in transparency. In researching this book, we repeatedly found that data reports that had once been made available by executive branch offices were no longer being updated: the tally of financial activity reports available from the COAF, for example, has not been updated since 2019. As Marcio Cunha Filho, Gregory Michener, and Bernardo Schwaitzer (2021) show, drawing on data from the FGV's Public Transparency Program, bureaucracies seem to have learned a stonewalling approach: forcing citizens to file appeals of Freedom of Information Act (FOIA) requests, in the apparent hope that they will desist from the lengthy and burdensome process, but then granting those requests on final appeal so as to avoid being accused of noncompliance. The Bolsonaro government has actively sought to diminish transparency, by increasing the government's ability to classify information as secret (a proposal overturned by Congress) and by failing to report data on Covid-19 deaths (a practice barred by an injunction from STF Justice Alexandre de Moraes) (Michener and Mohallem 2020; Mohallem and Michener 2020; Leali 2020; Da Ros and Taylor 2021a).

Perhaps the most momentous—and potentially damaging—shift in transparency, however, has been the reversion to old patterns of judicial secrecy. One 2019 case exemplifies the shift: when prosecutor-general Raquel Dodge (2017–2019) finally submitted one construction firm executive's plea testimony to the STF, after months of delay, she asked that portions of the testimony be stricken from the record. In the stricken portions the head of OAS, Léo Pinheiro, allegedly levelled charges against STF Justice José Antonio Dias Toffoli's brother (a former mayor of Marília, São Paulo) and against the president of the Chamber of Deputies at the time, Rodrigo Maia. The fact that both Maia and Toffoli had been publicly pushing for Dodge's reappointment raised eyebrows. In response to the prosecutor-general's request to withhold these controversial elements from the public, the six prosecutors serving on the *Lava Jato* task force in the prosecutor-general's office jointly resigned (Talento 2019).

Oversight. A number of reversals have weakened key oversight bodies. Central to the effort has been the replacement of senior personnel. Temer replaced the head of the Federal Comptroller's Office (CGU) and most of the top officials in the Justice Ministry. Bolsonaro, as noted earlier, broke with his justice minister by seeking the replacement of the head of the Federal Police in Rio and, when that plan was foiled by Moro, replaced the director general of police, triggering Moro's resignation. Other officials, such as top officials in the Receita Federal and the COAF, were also sidelined after they criticized the high court or seemed unwilling to quash investigations of Bolsonaro family members. The new attorney general was fired in 2016, after only four months on the job, for taking steps against firms and politicians involved in *Lava Jato*. Both presidents reassigned key police investigators away from *Lava Jato*, in some cases following a time-honored tradition of removal by promotion. Federal Police agent Erika Marena, who is often credited with breaking open *Lava Jato* by requesting the wiretap of the gas station that gave the operation its name and who later became the supervisory agent for the Federal Police's financial crimes unit in Paraná (Netto 2016: 28), was transferred to Florianópolis in early 2017. The official line—that this was a promotion—was rejected out of hand by the head of the National Association of Senior Federal Police Agents (ADPF) (*NSC Total* 2017).

Politicians have also weakened oversight bodies by altering their roles and procedures. In a move that superficially seemed designed to increase its powers, for example, the CGU was transformed into the Transparency Ministry by Temer. While this did nothing to alter the oversight powers of the body, the move may have made the new ministry subject to greater presidential control. After his first transparency minister was caught up in wiretaps between Senator Renan Calheiros and former Transpetro president Sérgio Machado, and his second moved on to head the Justice Ministry, Temer appointed a civil servant without much of a reputation as a leader in the fight against corruption to head the body. The number of audits carried out by the body declined, as did the number of civil servants removed from their jobs after investigation, a problem that the minister chalked up to the fiscal crisis (*Carta Capital* 2017). On taking office, Bolsonaro kept Temer's appointee in place.

The financial intelligence unit COAF suffered for much of 2019–2020, as it was shunted around the federal government. Originally, Bolsonaro transferred the COAF into Moro's Justice Ministry, but, in a fit of pique with Moro, Congress mandated that it be returned to the Finance Ministry fold. Finally, in January 2020 Congress and Bolsonaro agreed to move it to the Central Bank, which some hoped might increase its autonomy and that of the Central Bank (Uribe 2020). But the repeated moves and the clear political subordination of the already lean COAF staff greatly undermined the agency.

It was further hobbled when, in July 2019, Justice Toffoli temporarily blocked all investigations from utilizing COAF data. Toffoli was responding to a request from the president's son, Senator Flávio Bolsonaro, after a financial intelligence report showed that one of the senator's advisers had received large volumes of undeclared deposits.

Toffoli's decision froze roughly 700 federal investigations into corruption, money laundering, and tax evasion, a decision the head of the COAF criticized, leading to his prompt defenestration. In December 2019, the full STF reversed Toffoli's decision and allowed the sharing of financial intelligence collected by the COAF and Receita Federal with the Federal Police and prosecutors, but imposed stringent bureaucratic rules on how that sharing should take place (D'Agostino and Oliveira 2019). The number of financial intelligence reports fell from a monthly average of 741 in the first half of 2019 to 160 in the ensuing three months (Fabrini and Mattoso 2019). Meanwhile, the COAF budget was cut by more than three-quarters for the 2020 fiscal year, ensuring that it did not have the resources to carry out its work. The agency simply stopped reporting data, for example, on the number of financial intelligence reports it conducts.

The Temer administration remade the Federal Police's contribution to the task force. In May 2017, the number of *delegados* dedicated to *Lava Jato* was cut from nine to four. In July the administration went a step further, deciding that police agents would no longer participate exclusively in the *Lava Jato* task force, but instead would report directly to the anticorruption directorate within the regional police headquarters. While the administration claimed that this would increase overall anticorruption efforts, it clearly altered those police officers' ability to directly address *Lava Jato* cases, withdrawing the dedicated support that police had provided to prosecutors in the case (*Folha de Pernambuco* 2017a, 2017b). Under Bolsonaro, there were three new directors general of the Federal Police. Many senior leaders in the police were replaced by friends of the president or his sons, shifting the agency's priorities. Perhaps as a consequence, from 2018 to 2020 corruption investigations by the Federal Police fell by more than 40 percent while money laundering investigations fell by 80 percent (Bramatti and Godoy 2021).

Legislative oversight has never been particularly strong, in part because of the perverse incentives of the coalitional presidential system. As noted in Chapter 4, the legislative oversight body known as the Tribunal de Contas da União is neither a court—despite the name "tribunal"—nor a particularly muscular oversight body. Although the TCU was one of the first bodies to uncover evidence of overpricing at Petrobras, this did not translate into effective accountability because the TCU audits were sidelined by a combination of pressures from its ministers, from legislators, from courts, and from the executive branch. At the same time, as Chapter 3 also highlighted, the number of audits at the Fiscobras program on public works has reached historic lows, and the TCU no longer reports the amount of money it audits. The share of public works for which the TCU has recommended suspension has also decreased sharply, from a peak of 42 percent in 2001, to an average of 10 percent between 2015 and 2019. While this might be an indication of improving probity, critically the 2018–2019 period saw the lowest number of public works audited since recordkeeping began in the mid-1990s. Something appears to have tempered the TCU's willingness to audit, to carry forward and enforce administrative sanctions, and to suggest legislative sanctions.

A second form of legislative oversight has been from congressional committees of inquiry, but they have proven susceptible to corrupt influences that often mean they can muddy the waters far more than they provide clarity. In the *Lava Jato* case, the *CPI da Petrobras* may have been particularly venal. Paulo Roberto Costa's initial June 2014 testimony to the CPI seemed almost intended to confuse matters, and, over the course of questioning, Costa repeatedly perjured himself. The CPI wrapped up its investigations in December 2014, only nine months after the case became public. Despite a host of allegations by witnesses, including a claim by Costa—who had now entered a plea— that he had authorized a transfer of R$2 million to Rousseff's campaign, the CPI implicated only fifty-two individuals, none of whom were sitting politicians. In retrospect, it appears as though the CPI was essentially an effort to regain control of the narrative before a new legislature took office in February 2015. The new legislature, in turn, created a new CPI, which initially implicated various figures, including the new president of the Chamber, Eduardo Cunha, but concluded in October 2015 without leveling charges against any sitting politicians. More damaging still, the CPI was manipulated by Cunha and his allies to intimidate anyone who had testified against him in *Lava Jato,* including Alberto Youssef and his lawyer, who fled the country (Limongi 2015). This is not to say that CPIs are never effective oversight bodies: a CPI into the pandemic in 2021 effectively dug into irregularities of vaccine provision. But they are an imperfect tool, susceptible to the alignment of political forces.

In late 2019, Congress passed and Bolsonaro signed a Law on the Abuse of Authority, which expanded the number of potential abuses that were subject to punishment and broadened their application from the executive branch to the MPF and the judiciary. Although a similar proposal had been defeated by public pushback in previous years, the new version was sufficiently diluted and public opinion sufficiently divided to enable passage. The new law may also have been given fresh momentum by *The Intercept*'s publication of the Vaza Jato hacks (Cerioni 2020). Prosecutors' and judges' associations criticized the law's chilling effect, complaining that while the law itself has many positive and seemingly well-intentioned aspects (e.g., prohibiting authorities from misrepresenting themselves to defendants), it also has many facets that are so vaguely worded that they seem designed to intimidate law enforcement authorities from doing their jobs (e.g., prohibiting the release of any recording that hurts the honor or the image of an investigated person or indicted defendant, and preventing authorities from freezing funds that are "far in excess" of what would be needed to satisfy the defendant's debt).

Partly in consequence of the confluence of Toffoli's ruling against the COAF and the questionable intentions behind this new law, the OECD Working Group on Bribery decided to "urgently" send a high-level mission to Brasília in November 2019. Following the visit, the working group expressed its grave concern about "backsliding on progress achieved, that could seriously jeopardize Brazil's ability to meet its obligations under the Anti-Bribery Convention." Working group chair Drago Kos warned, "We are quite alarmed that what Brazil had managed to achieve in recent years in the fight against corruption may now be seriously jeopardised. Brazil must strive toward reinforcing its framework and legal tools to fight foreign bribery, not weaken them" (OECD 2019).

Sanction. A number of changes took place, some formal and others informal, that weakened anticorruption sanctions. These were exacerbated by the meddling of politicians in criminal investigations and accountability agencies.

With regard to the MPF, the informal norm known as the *lista tríplice* governing the appointment of the head of the MPF (by which the president chose the top person from the list of three nominees elected by prosecutors) was weakened by Temer, who chose the second candidate on the triple list, Raquel Dodge. The entire list was then ignored by Bolsonaro when selecting Augusto Aras (2019–2021) as prosecutor-general. Under both Dodge and Aras, furthermore, delays in delivering plea bargains to the STF for approval may have led defendants who would have provided information to prosecutors to instead give up on cooperating. A total of 110 plea bargains were submitted to the STF for *homologação* (approval) between 2015 and August 2019, of which only one was submitted by Dodge (Rossi, Oliveira, and Bianchi 2019).

Prosecutors were also rocked by Temer's December 2017 Christmas *indulto* (pardon) that reduced the sentences of prisoners accused of corruption, influence trafficking, money laundering, and a few other nonviolent crimes, and directly impacted more than twenty prisoners in the *Lava Jato* case. Justice Barroso suspended much of Temer's decree soon after it was issued, but in May 2019 the full STF decided in a 7–4 vote that the president had the constitutional right to grant such pardons.[17] By the terms of the decree, anyone who had already served one-fifth of their sentence for those crimes in December 2017 could apply for release; the judge overseeing their case would then be able to release them, other things equal. As prosecutor Deltan Dallagnol complained, this decision would make plea bargains unviable. If the president gives prisoners the well-founded expectation of "an 80% discount in prison terms, what benefits would make anyone plea? . . . While some countries are fiscal or financial paradises, the *indulto* confirms Brazil as a paradise of impunity for white collar [criminals]" (Dallagnol 2017b).

Plea bargains were already facing many debilitating pressures. The STF's collective ability to confuse the rules of the game was one of the biggest challenges. Notably, Justices Zavascki and Fachin approved more than 100 pleas negotiated by the MPF, but in 2017 Justice Lewandowski overturned a plea bargain in a case of campaign-related wrongdoing, arguing that by offering benefits and establishing maximum sentencing times, the MPF was usurping judges' powers (M. C. Carvalho and Nunes 2017).

Brasília was also purposely slow to resolve the competition between various bodies for administrative control over plea bargains for individuals and *acordos de leniência* (leniency agreements) for firms. The resulting ambiguity played into the hands of defense lawyers. In the case of plea bargains, the MPF and the Federal Police both are accorded the possibility of signing agreements. A race to the bottom had emerged as these agencies competed to sign plea agreements (T. M. Oliveira 2019). In leniency agreements, there are even more agencies that claim the right to sign such deals: within the executive, the CGU and AGU; the legislative TCU; and the semiautonomous CADE and MPF.[18] Each of these bodies answers to different principals and different objectives, meaning that failure to arbitrate these issues permitted a certain amount of venue shopping by defendants, as well as variance in the treatment they were accorded (Pimenta 2019, 2020). Leniency agreements were further weakened by another move during the Temer administration that on the face of it seemed to represent a strengthening of accountability, but may in fact have been designed precisely to undermine the capacity of prosecutors: the government began to impose fines that were so high that no reasonable corporate executive could accede to the demands without bankrupting their firm. As one defense lawyer noted, the governing MDB seemed to be sending a message: *é uma fria* (reaching an agreement is a waste of time; Carvalho and Nunes 2018).

There was increasing political pressure by 2017 against the top court, the STF. There had been considerable public pressure in support of *Mensalão* and *Lava Jato,* of course, but since Temer's presidency strong countercurrents had emerged. *The Intercept*'s Vaza Jato reporting suggested that there had been excesses in *Lava Jato* that needed to be addressed. Defendants' lawyers, as noted earlier, were raising many questions about the legitimacy of preventive detentions, plea bargains, bench warrants, and the like. The number of impeachment petitions against high court justices grew, affecting the majority of justices (Bogéa and Da Ros 2020). Proposals began to circulate for a "Lava Toga" operation—cheekily named after the robes worn by justices—or a CPI to investigate the judiciary. Less democratic pressures also began to percolate around the 2018 campaign, exemplified by Eduardo Bolsonaro's belligerent boast that all it would take to shut down the STF would be "a corporal and a private." It is hard to say exactly how the court was affected by these pressures, but, especially from 2017 onward, the STF moved in a direction that significantly complicated the prospects for future corruption prosecutions:[19]

- In December 2017, Justice Gilmar Mendes suspended the use of the *condução coercitiva* (bench warrant). Mendes's decision was soon upheld by the full court (F. A. Rodrigues 2019: 165).[20]
- In April 2018, the second chamber of the STF moved two of the cases against former president Lula from Paraná to São Paulo, arguing that prosecutors had failed to clearly demonstrate a connection to Petrobras corruption and thus the natural jurisdiction was São Paulo, where the alleged crimes had taken place. The decision seemed justifiable on the face of it, but it was perplexing because this was the fifth time in one year that the second chamber had ruled on the issue, and it overturned its previous four determinations (Schwartsman 2018).
- The STF, in March 2019, moved jurisdiction for money laundering crimes associated with political campaigns out of criminal courts and into the electoral court system. While the STF had moved in a more stringent direction in 2016, blocking cor-

porate donations in future elections, this March 2019 decision significantly weakened the likelihood of effective prosecution of future campaign finance crimes. Many factors make the electoral courts even less effective than the federal criminal court system, among them the fact that the judges deciding most cases are rotated in from the regular courts for only temporary, part-time stints. Further, the move will require electoral courts to develop expertise and procedures that took decades to develop in the MPF and the federal courts. Unless there are significant institutional changes in the electoral courts, based on past performance this decision will make it nigh impossible to effectively prosecute illicit campaign finance, one of the central crimes uncovered by *Lava Jato* in its investigation of the ties between Petrobras, construction firms, and political parties (Schreiber 2020).

- In November 2019, a tight 6–5 majority of the STF changed the rules on prison on appeal, for the third time since the return to democracy.[21] Reversing a decision that had been made only three years earlier, the STF decided that defendants could be jailed only after all appeals in all courts had been declined. This decision led to the release of prominent *Lava Jato* defendants, including Lula and José Dirceu. More importantly, it signaled a reversion to the old status quo, which meant that punishment, if it ever came, would often be at least a decade away. This significantly undermined the leverage of prosecutors seeking plea bargains, and thus weakened the likely success of the overall domino strategy in corruption cases.

The STF has always been a problematic player in the accountability game, serving in most cases as a guarantor of elite impunity. But especially as *Lava Jato* weakened, the STF's performance became extraordinarily generous to defendants, with many of its decisions since 2017 favoring the dominant political coalition. The Supreme Electoral Tribunal (TSE) reached a momentous decision that year in favor of the Rousseff-Temer campaign, which had been charged with electoral crimes by its opponents. Although Rousseff was no longer president, a negative decision would have led to the removal of the sitting president, Michel Temer. STF Justice Gilmar Mendes, sitting on the TSE for a two-year rotation, broke the 3–3 tie between the electoral judges in a highly controversial decision that seemed to signal that the courts were no longer eager to challenge the political system.

After that momentous decision, the STF systematically decided against *Lava Jato*. The STF has already filed away or remanded to the trial courts more than half of the investigations launched by Marcelo Odebrecht's massive plea bargain, which triggered eighty-three investigations at the STF. The STF reversed course on its earlier decision to move forward on the indictment of Chamber president Arthur Lira and other members of the PP. The court overturned cases against Michel Temer, freed Eduardo Cunha, and released Lula. At the end of the day, the defendants who seem to have suffered the most were those who entered plea bargains since they confessed to a crime, served time, often paid fines, and lost the support of their peers. Those who held out in the hopes of fighting another day either went to jail and were quickly released, or never went to jail at all. The incentives this sets in place are perverse, to say the least.

Conclusion

As this chapter has shown, there were many reasons why the *Lava Jato* task force could be questioned on a variety of legal, political, and ethical grounds. These concerns reached a crescendo with the arrest of former president Lula in April 2018. Fully 35 percent of the population agreed with the opinion that Lula was treated worse than other defendants by *Lava Jato* (A. Oliveira 2019). While support for the task force remained high, with polls showing somewhere between three-fifths and four-fifths of the population voicing support for *Lava Jato,* the increasing doubts about the case and about the costs of accountability opened space for a reversal not only of *Lava Jato*'s gains, but also of accountability improvements more broadly (Datafolha 2019; Bächtold 2018). The Centrão parties that have played such a foundational role in preserving patterns of political coalition making—and, along with it, corruption—partnered with the Temer and the Bolsonaro governments in alliance against *Lava Jato,* as well as the broader accountability effort (D. Carvalho, Chaib, and Uribe 2020; R. M. Moura and Weterman 2020; Traumann 2020). Curbing *Lava Jato*'s "excesses" served as a veil under which various attempts to complicate anticorruption efforts, which would have been unthinkable and indefensible in 2014, suddenly began to seem justifiable.

The trajectory we described in this chapter suggests that a big push like *Lava Jato* has the potential to generate such a strong reaction that the reaction swamps previous incremental changes that took years to develop. Some of the backlash was directly targeted at the *Lava Jato* team such as *The Intercept*'s Vaza Jato reporting and the reassignment of key task force members. But some backlash, while motivated by the *Lava Jato* investigations, had broader consequences that will reverberate far beyond that specific case, such as the abuse of authority law and the shifting of campaign finance cases out of federal criminal courts. These changes will generate permanent consequences that seem likely to complicate anticorruption efforts for decades to come. As Chapter 3 noted, however, the backlash will not lead Brazil back to its pre–*Lava Jato* status quo. Instead, the country seems to have arrived at a new equilibrium that, in some ways, is even more severely unfavorable to accountability.

Notes

1. "Tem que resolver essa porra. . . . Tem que mudar o governo pra poder estancar essa sangria" (R. Valente 2016). Jucá was speaking with former Senator Sérgio Machado, a former president of Transpetro.

2. "Eu acabei com a Lava Jato, porque não tem mais corrupção no governo" (Della Coletta, Carvalho, and Uribe 2020).

3. The press release announcing the end of the *Lava Jato* task force highlighted its accomplishments over nearly seven years, including 130 accusations against 533 defendants, resulting in 174 convictions, 209 plea bargains, 17 leniency agreements, and negotiations for the return of R$15 billion (US$2.75 billion at February 2021 exchange rate) to the National Treasury (Pontes 2021).

4. Making things worse, the pathway to enact major policies was permanently shut for the remainder of his term, as a result of Temer's declaration of federal intervention in the state of Rio de Janeiro. Under the 1988 Constitution, any case of federal intervention halts all consideration of constitutional reforms. The Temer administration alleged that the rise in crime in Rio de Janeiro in early 2018 required federal action, but the move was widely seen as cover for the lame duck government's inability to pull together a legislative coalition before the 2018 elections.

5. According to the most senior member of the task force, the idea of publicly releasing the wiretaps was not Moro's, but the prosecutors' (Brandt and Macedo 2019).

6. As discussed in Chapter 4, De Sanctis faced numerous disciplinary hearings as a result of his decisions.

7. Leniency agreements are akin to deferred prosecution agreements in the United States. In most leniency agreements, firms admit wrongdoing and accept a fine in exchange for the possibility of participating in public bidding and reduced sanctions. The concept of the leniency agreement was introduced by the 2013 Anti-Corruption Law in Brazil.

8. A few years later, the trial judge at the heart of the Rio de Janeiro investigations, Marcelo Bretas, was caught up in similar allegations. A lawyer in Rio signed a plea bargain with the prosecutor-general, in which he accused Bretas

of unduly pushing a businessman toward a plea bargain during a conversation between himself, Bretas, and the chief *Lava Jato* prosecutor in Rio. If these allegations are confirmed, they suggest highly improper contact between the judge and the parties to the case, which might even be considered illegal because the businessman's defense counsel was excluded. The MPF contests the allegations, though, and points to the fact that the lawyer leveling the accusations was under investigation by prosecutors not affiliated with *Lava Jato* (Borges 2021).

9. "Because Petrobras issued securities in the U.S., and because U.S. law imposes criminal liability on a corporation for the conduct of the corporation's employees, Petrobras was potentially liable under the U.S. Foreign Corrupt Practices Act (FCPA), because Petrobras officers had facilitated corruption abroad (that is, in Brazil). In September 2018, Petrobras signed a non-prosecution agreement (NPA) with the United States Department of Justice, according to which the company would pay over US$850 million in penalties. But, crucially, only 20% of that penalty would be paid to the United States; the remaining 80%, according to the terms of the NPA, was to be paid by Petrobras 'to Brazil'" (R. T. de Souza 2020).

10. We are grateful to Maria Paula Bertran for the good humor and the helpful comments.

11. Responding to a suit by a political party, Justice Marco Aurélio de Mello determined that Senator Renan Calheiros should surrender the Senate presidency because he was facing charges of hiding financial payments to the mother of his illegitimate child. Failure to comply could theoretically be punished with jail time, yet Calheiros simply ignored the ruling, forcing the full STF into a humiliating reversal during an en banc hearing on the matter (Vieira 2018: 205; D'Agostino 2016). Perhaps as a consequence, when the court had to decide whether or not to imprison Aécio Neves, it argued that it would need Senate permission, something it had not asked for in the previous actions against Senators Delcídio Amaral and Renan Calheiros.

12. This was further exacerbated in the case of political elites who fell under the original jurisdiction of the STF by its decision in the *Mensalão* case to grant a rehearing in all cases in which the defendant was convicted by a margin of four justices' votes or less. As Rosenn (2014: 313) notes, "In a rationally functioning legal system, persons convicted by the highest court in the land sitting en banc should not be able to request a rehearing en banc."

13. The PT was harshly punished in these elections: none of its mayors would govern a city of more than 250,000 inhabitants after the election.

14. To exemplify: Emilio Odebrecht's plea bargain levied accusations against former president Fernando Henrique Cardoso—the only successful presidential candidate from the PSDB—for campaign finance irregularities in the 1994 and 1998 elections. These did not trigger an investigation, because any crimes would have already run out the statute of limitations. Minas governor Eduardo Azeredo, also of the PSDB, was charged in a state-level scandal similar to *Mensalão* in 2007, but due to his lawyers' maneuvers claiming and then relinquishing the original jurisdiction of the STF, his final appeals were not quashed until 2018 (*Folha de S. Paulo* 2018b). Aécio Neves, the PSDB presidential standard-bearer in 2014, was investigated for a variety of crimes in that election, but they led to no judicial action until 2019, when he was subjected to an asset freeze. Neves, meanwhile, resigned his Senate seat to run for a far-safer post in the Chamber, where he continues to benefit from the original jurisdiction of the high court.

15. Fernando Haddad was convicted in 2019 by a São Paulo trial court for illegal campaign finance in his 2012 campaign for São Paulo mayor, but he has not been targeted by federal prosecutors.

16. As of September 2021, Congress was considering at least four major reforms to electoral law and procedure: a law imposing a printed ballot, to replace Brazil's long-standing electronic polling system; a broad political reform that includes proposals eliminating the probation on electoral alliances between parties (*coligações*) and freeing existing parties of judicial baggage by allowing them to reincorporate; a near tripling in public campaign funding, from R$2 billion to R$5.7 billion; and a new electoral code, which among other changes, threatens to weaken the oversight and sanctioning powers of the electoral courts.

17. In favor: Alexandre de Moraes, Rosa Weber, Ricardo Lewandowski, Marco Aurélio Mello, Gilmar Mendes, Celso de Mello, Dias Toffoli. Against: Luís Roberto Barroso, Edson Fachin, Luiz Fux, Carmén Lúcia.

18. As Praça (2018: 112–121) notes, the CGU can negotiate a reduction in administrative penalties against a firm; the MPF can negotiate the reduction in criminal penalties. So, in theory, the CGU could negotiate a leniency agreement, only to have the MPF subsequently swoop in with criminal indictments. Such friction means that leniency agreements are still more promise than practice, and their use has dropped off significantly after an initial burst (Pimenta 2019, 2020).

19. Some other decisions had negative impacts on *Lava Jato* specifically, but they are not mentioned here because they are unlikely to significantly alter corruption prosecutions going forward. One example is the STF's October 2019 decision to annul some convictions because the defense witnesses testified before plea bargaining witnesses, and therefore had not had an opportunity for ample defense. The rules on the order of witnesses have now changed, so such decisions are no longer as relevant.

20. Court decisions in *Arguição de Descumprimento de Preceito Fundamental* (Claim of Noncompliance with Fundamental Precept, ADPF) case nos. 395 and 444.

21. In favor: Marco Aurélio Mello, Rosa Weber, Ricardo Lewandowski, Gilmar Mendes, Celso de Mello, Dias Toffoli. Against: Alexandre de Moraes, Edson Fachin, Luís Roberto Barroso, Luiz Fux, Carmén Lúcia. Until 2009, the STF had never been questioned about the constitutionality of jail time before all appeals were exhausted. In practice, this meant that each individual judge could determine the rule based on the 1988 Constitution, which states that "nobody will be considered guilty until the 'trânsito em julgado' of the criminal conviction." This phrase, *trânsito em julgado,* is usually understood as "completing the judgment process," which meant that most judges did not jail defendants until all appeals were exhausted. But the STF has changed its understanding of these rules repeatedly since the return to democracy.

6

Judicial Big Pushes in Large Democracies

Lava Jato brings a hope, creates a virtuous cycle.
—Deltan Dallagnol, chief federal prosecutor
of the *Lava Jato* task force, 2015[1]

I still very much doubt our institutional capacity to clean up Congress. The best would be for Congress to clean itself up, but that doesn't seem to be on the horizon.
—Sérgio Moro, federal judge responsible
for *Lava Jato* cases in Curitiba trial court, 2016[2]

A few broad comparative lessons can be drawn from *Lava Jato*'s seven years of investigation, prosecution, convictions, and reform efforts. In this chapter, we return to three conceptual discussions initially advanced in the introductory chapter to this book. First, we examine the dichotomy between big pushes and incremental approaches, and the equilibrium shifts that we might anticipate from each in terms of corruption and accountability. Second, we discuss the roles of judicial policy entrepreneurs and their ability to mobilize collective action in big push anticorruption efforts, which may have unintended negative consequences. Third, we conclude with a discussion of the challenges of engendering an equilibrium shift in large nations, and of the unintended consequences of doing so in large democracies.

Big Push Reform

Lava Jato was an attempt at a big bang, or big push, that failed to achieve its intended results. Like other big push efforts, it was

concentrated in time and space. Over time, the operation grew in ambi-
tion, to a point where its leaders, echoing Deltan Dallagnol in the first
epigraph to this chapter, saw their role as creating a virtuous cycle that
would move the country from a low-accountability equilibrium to a
high-accountability equilibrium, through an effort that combined
unprec-edented cooperation across various agencies in the accountability network; the investigation, prosecution, and conviction of high-level
officials; significant public relations outreach and popular mobilization;
and a series of overlapping reform efforts, in formal laws and procedures, as well as in informal understandings of law and process.
Although there have been isolated victories, the evidence in Chapter 5
suggests that the big push did not yield a shift to a sustained virtuous
cycle and, in fact, may have engendered significant pushback that led to
a regression. Indeed, one of *Lava Jato*'s unanticipated consequences is
that it may have worsened matters in various elements of the accountability equation, pushing the overall equilibrium to a new status quo
that in many ways is worse than what existed prior to *Lava Jato*.

Figures 6.1 and 6.2 provide graphical representations of this evolution, converting the content of Table 3.2 into simple quantitative
depictions of the functioning of accountability processes between
1985 and 2020. Figure 6.1 assigns a numerical value from 1 to 4 to
the qualitative evaluations of each of the components of accountability in each of the five historical periods (1 = very weak; 4 = strong[3])
and shows the sum of all six variables in each of the five periods. But
the attentive reader may recall that the accountability equation is
premised on the idea that the first three variables (transparency, oversight, and sanction) are moderated in some way by the latter three
(capacity, engagement, and dominance). With this in mind, Figure
6.2 shows the simple product of the two sets of variables

$$[(T + O + S) * (C + E - D)].$$

We do not wish to suggest that these are highly exact point estimates, that they can accurately capture all of the complex interactions between the accountability variables, or that the moderation by
capacity, engagement, and dominance necessarily yields a uniform
increase in the magnitude of transparency, oversight, and sanction.
But these figures do offer a visual complement to the overall trends
described in Chapter 3, which had been quite hopeful up until 2014
but have turned downward in the most recent period, with deterioration in the individual accountability components, as well as in the
aggregate pattern of accountability.

Figure 6.1 Sum of Accountability Components

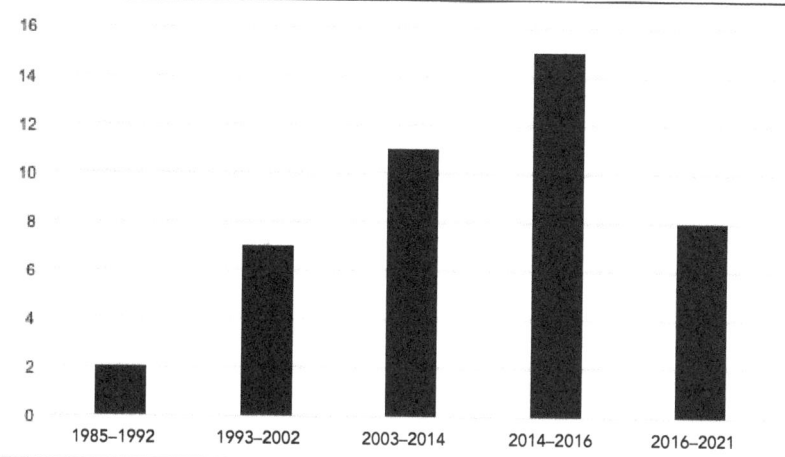

Note: This figure shows the sum of the values for each accountability component in Table 3.1 (transparency, oversight, sanction, capacity, engagement, and dominance). For each variable, "very weak" was scored as 1, "weak" as 2, "moderate" as 3, and "strong" as 4. The variable "dominance" is subtracted, since strong dominance weakens accountability. By way of example, in the first period (1985–1992), the scores were
$$T(2) + O(1) + S(1) + C(1) + E(1) - D(4) = 2.$$

Figure 6.2 Product of Accountability Components

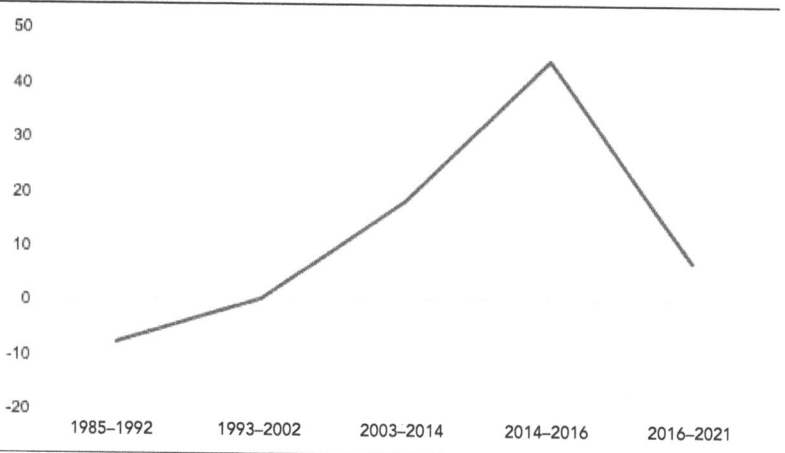

Note: This figure shows the product of the accountability equation, drawing on the values for each accountability component in Table 3.1 (transparency, oversight, sanction, capacity, engagement, and dominance). For each variable, "very weak" was scored as 1, "weak" as 2, "moderate" as 3, and "strong" as 4. The variable dominance has a negative sign, since strong dominance weakens accountability. The equation reflects that transparency, oversight, and sanction are moderated by capacity, engagement, and dominance, as described in Chapter 3. By way of example, the equation for the first period (1985–1992) is
$$[T(2) + O(1) + S(1)] * [C(1) + E(1) - D(4)] = 4 * -2 = -8.$$

Neither the qualitative depiction in earlier chapters nor the simple quantitative rendition here provides much evidence to support the contention that *Lava Jato* improved the overall accountability picture in Brazil. At best, its record was mixed, leading to some important legal victories and to the feeling that better accountability is possible, but also contributing to significant regression in aspects of the accountability equation. Rather than becoming one of the anticorruption literature's case studies of success, *Lava Jato* instead provides us with a chance to learn from the consequences when big push reforms that seek a massive systemic shift fail. It is also theoretically interesting because *Lava Jato* is a particular class of anticorruption push: one in which anticorruption leaders gave up on a long-standing incremental approach and, instead, accelerated toward a big push approach to anticorruption.

Judicial Policy Entrepreneurship and Anticorruption Big Pushes

As Chapter 1 noted, big bangs or big pushes that eventually succeed in moving countries from low- to high-accountability equilibria are not only rare, but also ill defined. Their length, scope, and relevant actors are unclear in most of the literature. As a result, we do not possess any ex ante metrics to infer precisely—or even approximately— how long a big push should last and what exactly should be done—or prioritized—while it lasts.

Similarly, there is uncertainty as to which actors should lead such ambitious reforms. For the most part, successful big bangs elsewhere around the world seem to have either been pushed forward by elected leaders who, at moments of great upheaval, channeled massive anticorruption collective action into corresponding public policy reforms, as in Georgia in the aftermath of the Rose Revolution, or by colonial powers or autocrats who assume the unlikely role of guardians, as in the famous success cases of Hong Kong and Singapore in the 1970s and Rwanda over the past two decades. In all of those cases, *political* actors were the primary driving forces behind the few successful big bangs the literature has been able to identify and examine at greater length.

In contrast, two striking features of *Lava Jato* were that the big push was led predominantly by legal authorities and that few relevant actors in the political establishment offered significant explicit support for its ambitious anticorruption goals. As a result, *legal* actors were the main—and, quite often, the sole—driving forces behind this big push. As Chapter 4 demonstrated, *Lava Jato*'s key protagonists aimed to shape hearts and minds via a conscientious strategy that sought to foster intense media coverage and encourage public engagement. The team also kept constant legal pressure on the forces of the status quo, leading to a domino effect that kept most political actors either in a defensive crouch, or even induced them—whether because of sincere motivations or merely strategic calculations—to cooperate minimally with the *Lava Jato* team, including by introducing new legislative reform proposals.

In other words, *Lava Jato* serves as a case of judicial policy entrepreneurship in a big push against corruption. We define *judicial policy entrepreneurship* as an instance where the judicial system spearheads change on a complex set of social or political issues, acting proactively to alter established norms and policies. Judicial policy entrepreneurship need not encompass only the courts proper, but can—as in Brazil—also incorporate the broader judicial system, including prosecutors and the police. Within the realm of public sector corruption, judicial policy entrepreneurship manifests itself when legal actors take it on themselves to bring corruption under control and undertake reforms that will enhance accountability for the entire society.

The concept of judicial policy entrepreneurship bears some resemblance to others in the literature. These include the concept of "role substitution" advanced by Alessandro Pizzorno (1992) and Donatella della Porta (2001), "where magistrates, faced with evident collusion of the political system, consider it necessary for 'another institution to fill the void and restore the threat of punishment for those indulging in corrupt practices'" (della Porta 2001: 4); that of "norm entrepreneurship" by Cass R. Sunstein (1996) and Ari Adut (2004, 2008), where the work of judicial actors "revolves around legal or social norms that are already established . . . but underenforced" (Adut 2008: 130–131); and that of "voluntarism" by Rogério B. Arantes (1999, 2002), whereby independent legal actors are fueled by a "belief that civil society is hyposufficient, that the political powers are degenerate, and that someone needs to do something" (Arantes 1999: 98). Ultimately, all of these perspectives pay tribute to the concept of "judicial guardianship" proposed by Donald L. Horowitz (1977a, 1977b), where the courts "play a more prominent and less interstitial role in defining and protecting the public interest, often against agencies accused of neglecting it" (1977a: 149).

Judicial policy entrepreneurship highlights the fact that various actors within the judicial system are not simply reacting to other institutions' initiatives, but ultimately are seeking to act purposefully to coordinate and lead transformational societal changes that reform the political system as a whole. Judicial policy entrepreneurship thus differs from notions of "judicial entrepreneurship," which refer predominantly to efforts within the courts proper to reform themselves (e.g., Crowe 2007, 2012; Ryder and Hardy 2019). Judicial policy entrepreneurship, by contrast, has a strong and ambitious outward focus. Judicial policy entrepreneurship by its very nature marks a shift from the predominantly passive and sober roles expected of (if not always followed by) prosecutors and the courts in a democratic society, and also marks a significant departure from the usually passive and reactive attitude of the judicial system toward corruption.

Judicial systems may approach corruption in a number of ways. Much depends on the extent of de jure and de facto independence of the courts. Indeed, many policy recommendations to improve judicial independence since the 1990s have been premised on the connection between independence and effective anticorruption efforts.[4]

But independence alone has not been a sufficient condition to explain prosecutors' and courts' accountability roles. In fact, even when independence is guaranteed, nothing ensures that judicial actors will become more active against corruption. Courts and prosecutors may behave diffidently, failing to punish most illegal behavior by political elites, for a variety of reasons having to do with histories of judicial deference, a desire to elevate civil rights above punitive goals, or an effort to preserve the institution from political conflict, among others (Popova 2012). Lisa Hilbink (2012) describes this judicial diffidence as "negative" judicial independence, whereby the judicial system formally possesses strong independence, but nonetheless fails to uphold the rule of law in an assertive, timely, and egalitarian fashion. Indeed, following strict rules of procedure often serves largely as a justification for judicial actors not to enforce the sanctions established in the legislation. Impunity for corruption before the judiciary is its most visible consequence. In such cases, judicial systems become key bottlenecks to effective accountability, and may even use their enhanced independence to shield themselves from external oversight, which in turn may foster judicial corruption (Ríos-Figueroa 2006, 2012). Previous chapters' diagnosis of judicial inoperancy in Brazil until the 2010s suggests that it neatly fits into the category of judicial diffidence during this period.

A more hopeful possibility is something approaching judicial equanimity, where the judicial system punishes wrongdoers assertively, in a timely manner; clears the names of those unjustly accused; and establishes clear and stable parameters for the behavior of other accountability agencies based on established laws and precedent. Designed to be a last line of defense against abuse, the judicial system adequately follows procedure and remains at the rearguard of complex processes of policy change. This is consistent with incremental approaches to anticorruption, with equanimity gradually spreading across the judicial system as a whole so that all its actors and institutions behave similarly in sanctioning corrupt behavior. The work of courts in most well-established democracies, whereby they encourage prudence on the part of political elites (rather than confronting them directly), illustrates this dynamic (Staton et al. 2018).

The phenomenon we call "judicial policy entrepreneurship" differs from diffidence and equanimity in important ways. Like the others, it presupposes judicial independence, without which it could not prosper.[5] Like judicial equanimity, it assumes courts are assertive rather than passive in the face of rule breaking. But unlike judicial equanimity, judicial policy entrepreneurship reflects an effort by a small faction of entrepreneurs within the judicial system to attack complex problems such as public sector corruption.[6] In part because they represent a small cohort, within the judiciary and within the broader political system, these actors will need to innovate to depart from the status quo, to engage in strategies that circumvent internal opposition, and to reach out for support to actors outside the judicial system so as to carry their intended reforms beyond the courts. Acting almost as a revolutionary vanguard, they may aggressively vie for a massive overhaul that pushes toward a new accountability equilibrium.

Policy entrepreneurship has much to be praised. It requires many characteristics that modern societies value: boldness, institutional innovation, robust action. But *judicial* policy entrepreneurship may fit democracy poorly. It relies on unelected bodies, which lack institutionalized forms of popular legitimation, to lead large-scale reform. In so doing, it reproduces the powering mentality of reformers and reforms that have succeeded in only a few small nondemocratic nations such as Hong Kong, Singapore, and Rwanda (Quah 2010; Mungiu-Pippidi and Johnston 2017). Adopting a powering mentality to the regular workings of a *democracy,* inherently defined by separation of powers and multiple political leaderships, is an uneasy task. It is also a task that is ultimately unlikely to succeed in achieving the goals of reducing corruption and improving accountability—and that may even put at risk other values important to democracy along the way. As Sandra Botero, Daniel Brinks, and Ezequiel Gonzalez-Ocantos (forthcoming) note with regard to *Lava Jato*'s effects across Latin America, "When empowered prosecution services and courts train their eyes on systemic corruption, they sometimes risk undermining the rule of law they claim to promote. Perhaps more fundamentally, they also risk unleashing unproductive clashes with the political establishment that compromise judicial integrity and, on occasion, fuel anti-political sentiments and backlash against fundamental rights."

Assessing the effectiveness of judicial policy entrepreneurship on corruption, however, is difficult. There are few well-documented instances of anticorruption judicial policy entrepreneurship in the literature, in part because judicial actors rarely engage in such efforts. Three cases of anticorruption judicial policy entrepreneurship stand out in this relatively small universe: the *Mani Pulite* investigations in 1990s Italy, the numerous investigations by low-ranking magistrates throughout the 1990s in France, and the role of the Indonesian specialized anticorruption court (known as Pengadilan Tipikor) since the early 2000s.[7]

Adding *Lava Jato* to this list allows us to see the implications of judicial policy entrepreneurship in broader perspective, and to assess some of the earlier findings of the comparative scholarship. Even though many of these records are to some extent still evolving, none of these cases seems to either have led to significant declines in corruption in their respective countries or, more to the point, to have initiated long-term virtuous cycles. There is not space here to provide the full stories in detail, but, drawing on previous studies, we attempt to summarize the cross-national experience succinctly.[8] At the inevitable risk of oversimplification, this summary allows us to demonstrate some of the recurring patterns of judicial policy entrepreneurship in anticorruption that were also present in *Lava Jato*.

The Italian and French cases follow a relatively similar plotline, although the first is more famous and has been examined at significantly greater length. In both instances, predominantly young, low-ranking judges and prosecutors, who had been empowered by judicial reforms and new laws enacted in preceding years, launched investigations in the early 1990s that began as small operations but quickly expanded to encompass a vast swath of each country's political elite. Appealing directly to the public and media with a moralizing rhetoric, working through various international collaborative networks, and at times addressing the cases with legal techniques that were considered unusually aggressive, they faced little immediate systematic opposition from political forces, in part because their efforts coincided with periods of increased political instability in both countries—episodes of cohabitation in France during the 1990s, and the realignment of the Italian party system that resulted from the end of the Cold War. After a few years of heightened public interest that resulted in numerous flashy arrests and sensational prosecutions of members of each country's governing elite, a massive but incomplete renewal of the political elite took place, as voters punished alleged wrongdoers electorally and various outsiders either took office or became politically competitive. In the wake of these episodes, however, political forces coalesced to limit the investigations, altering legislation on criminal procedure, accusing judges and prosecutors of abuse and bias, and demoting the topic of anticorruption on the public agenda.

The French and Italian cases are not identical, of course. While both predate the most common comparative measures of corruption based on expert surveys, such as the World Governance Indicators' Control of Corruption measure (CoC), it seems fair to say that at the time the scandals erupted in the 1990s, politics in Italy was more susceptible to corruption than in France. France had already begun to bring much of its corruption under control before the investigations started (Mungiu-Pippidi 2015). Partially as consequence, judicial policy entrepreneurship with regard to corruption and the ensuing political backlash were more drastic in Italy than in France. The *Mani Pulite* investigations were coordinated by a relatively small group of legal authorities working from Milan, and reached higher into governmental politics than their French counterpart. *Mani Pulite* was also temporally more concentrated, lasting only a few years. The various political scandals of the 1990s in France, by contrast, were heard in a more dispersed manner across various judicial actors and over time, did not reach as many high-ranking political authorities, and lasted longer, for almost a decade. The Italian case seems to have engendered a clearer and more aggressive backlash, epitomized by various reforms that hollowed out the criminal sanctions that had been enforced by the courts, and by the election and subsequent reelections of media tycoon Silvio Berlusconi, who had been involved in numerous shenanigans and was a recurring target of investigation. In France, while new laws were approved, including a new reform of the code of criminal procedure that reinforced presumption of innocence, those laws were not so directly targeted at curbing judicial policy entrepreneurship and rolling back anticorruption progress as in Italy. Nonetheless, even in France, a large number of acquittals in high-profile cases followed. Similarly, while the investigations may have contributed to the rise of Jean Marie Le Pen's far-right National

Front, which was the runner-up in the 2002 presidential elections, this extreme swing of the pendulum seems to have been relatively short-lived, and the National Front's share of the vote diminished over subsequent years.

The Indonesian case is less known to Western scholars and follows a somewhat different script than the European examples above, as judicial policy entrepreneurship coincided with the establishment of an autonomous anticorruption agency, the Indonesian Corruption Eradication Commission, known as Komisi Pemberantasan Korupsi (KPK). After the Asian financial crisis of the late 1990s and the end in 1998 of Suharto's three-decade-long grip on power, various reforms that aimed at increasing transparency and integrity in the public sector were enacted at the national level. Following a period of intense instability that witnessed the impeachment of the first president elected after Suharto in 2001, a law enacted in the next year established Pengadilan Tipikor, a new centralized chamber within a district court in Jakarta that had exclusive jurisdiction to try cases investigated and prosecuted by the independent KPK. The KPK was established by the same 2002 law, with broad and controversial powers such as the ability to conduct wiretaps without judicial warrants. Most high-profile corruption cases were removed from the hands of the regular police and prosecution service, and handed to the KPK, leading to a long-standing turf war with both (but especially the police).

Pengadilan Tipikor began its work in 2004, as a five-member panel comprised of two regular judges and three ad hoc judges—predominantly legal experts who did not belong to the regular judicial corps, hired on a temporary basis by the supreme court, and thought to be less susceptible to corruption than members of the regular judiciary. The Pengadilan Tipikor behaved aggressively and, in its early years, had a near 100 percent conviction rate across nearly 200 cases, which were tried following the strict and fast guidelines for trials and appeals established in the 2002 original law. This record of success brought popular support for anticorruption bodies, especially for the KPK, which quickly became one of Indonesia's most-trusted agencies.

That said, the proactivity of the new bodies led to controversy. Corruption cases that were prosecuted outside these new bodies by conventional nonspecialized prosecutors, and tried by the regular court system, led to lower conviction rates. Responding to a petition by defendants who had been convicted by the Pengadilan Tipikor, in 2006 the Constitutional Court declared the dual jurisdiction in corruption cases unconstitutional, arguing that it entailed unequal treatment before the law. In 2009, the legislature aimed to resolve the issue by expanding the specialized jurisdiction, so that all corruption cases would be heard by specialized courts, even if they had been investigated by the ordinary police and brought by prosecutors who were not members of the KPK. The reform decentralized the previously centralized court to all thirty-four Indonesian provinces, and expanded the time lines for trials and appeals, creating various new ad hoc positions for judges, many of which came to be filled by regular, nonspecialized judges. With decentralization completed in late 2011 and the filing of various cases that had not been investigated or prosecuted by the KPK, the conviction rate fell, and the jail times for those sentenced for corruption averaged only half that of the preceding period. Allegations of judicial impropriety soon followed as well, with judges from the specialized courts—ad hoc and regular—becoming involved in scandal themselves. Still, as the specialized courts came to cover all Indonesian provinces, various high-ranking officials were convicted, including ministers of the federal administration, members of parliament, provincial governors, and mayors.

Over the subsequent years, however, conflicts between the KPK and the country's national police escalated, including investigations, arrests, and attacks by one side against the other. On more than one occasion, for instance, the police arrested members of the KPK as a way to force the anticorruption agency to drop its investigation of senior police officials. In 2014, the KPK's chairman was forced to resign after the police charged him with various offenses, based on dubious evidence. Conflicts between the KPK and members of the national legislature also intensified in the 2010s. After numerous threats to cut its budget and powers, the parliament launched an inquiry into the KPK in 2017, and a subsequent ruling by the supreme court established that the KPK must comply with the parliamentary investigation, arguing that the KPK should be considered part of the executive branch.

In 2019, after closed-door deliberations and at record speed, the legislature approved a new law curtailing many of the KPK's powers and reducing its independence. The new measures determined that the agency's members must abide by the same rules of the regular civil service; limited its autonomy with regard to hiring and promoting personnel; established shorter time limits for investigations to be concluded, making it more difficult to address more complex cases; and created an oversight body that, among others, will be able to decide whether or not the agency can carry out wiretaps. The concrete consequences of these measures remain to be seen, but have generally been decried by analysts, activists, and the media as damaging to the agency's overall anticorruption mission (Da Costa and Widianto 2019; *Jakarta Post* 2019; Buehler 2019).

While inevitably marked by their unique singularities, the Italian, French, and Indonesian cases briefly described above, as well as *Lava Jato* in Brazil, all fit our definition of judicial policy entrepreneurship in anticorruption. They share several consequences, too. In all of them, the rise of an aggressive judicial effort aimed at purging public sector corruption did not come from the judiciary as a whole, but mostly from a narrow and younger faction within the judicial system that appealed directly to the public for support. These groups did so, moreover, during periods of intense political instability, so that the established political forces were initially unable to fight back against judicial efforts. In all four cases, the dynamics of judicial policy entrepreneurship fit the accountability heuristic: as dominance decreased, judicial actors who had benefited from significant gains in capacity over the preceding years instrumentalized engagement as a way to reduce dominance and increase the capacity of their agencies even further; in doing so, they pushed for a massive shift in oversight and sanction.

In all such cases, it is unclear if overall levels of corruption were reduced at all. Specific cases may have led to convictions while judicial policy entrepreneurship lasted. But the overall equilibrium did not seem to shift. We are aware that this is possibly a controversial statement, given the absence of precise metrics to assess the impact of such initiatives. As noted earlier, metrics of corruption perceptions by the World Governance Indicators' Control of Corruption (CoC) index are missing for Italy in the period prior to the episode of judicial policy entrepreneurship, precluding any comparison (pre- and post-treatment) over time. Most scholars conclude, however, that *Mani Pulite* did not significantly reduce corruption and weakened accountability agencies at the national level (e.g., Vannucci 2009; della Porta and Vannucci 2007).[9] In France, where we do have some indicators to rely on, because the scandals unraveled over a longer period of time in the 1990s the CoC indicator does not exhibit any significant changes outside the margin of error over time (most measures of corruption perceptions do not permit longitudinal comparison, but, according to its designers, the CoC does, provided margins of error are considered; Kaufmann, Kraay, and Mastruzzi 2010).

In Indonesia, CoC measures are available for the pre- and post-judicial policy entrepreneurship periods. The CoC percentile rank for the country improved from 9.6 in 2002, when the law establishing the specialized court and anticorruption agency was enacted, to 46.15 in 2018, a significant gain. It is not possible to discern if these changes resulted from the efforts by judicial policy entrepreneurs or from other factors, such as general improvements in the economy, which can exert a significant impact on perception measures of corruption (Treisman 2000, 2007; Mungiu-Pippidi 2015).[10] Yet the backlash also appears to have had an effect, even in the short time since the new law curtailing the KPK's powers was approved in late 2019. The country percentile rank fell 21 percent (beyond the margin of error) from its 2017 peak to 2019 (the last data point available), suggesting that judicial policy entrepreneurship may have led to a net curtailment of anticorruption capacity.

These cases suggest that the fact that *Lava Jato*—as massive as it was—ultimately failed in moving Brazil toward a virtuous cycle should not be all that surprising. There do not seem to be any known cases of judicial policy entrepreneurship in the literature that have succeeded in moving countries toward high-accountability, low-corruption equilibria. In Brazil, that is even more true because the move from judicial diffidence to judicial policy entrepreneurship in anticorruption was possibly too radical a shift to be sustained over time, to expand from the entrepreneurial actors to other courts, or to elicit the breadth of political response that would be needed to undertake reforms and expand on earlier accountability gains.

The frustrations that lie behind judicial policy entrepreneurship are not hard to comprehend. It is difficult not to share young prosecutors' and judges' irritation with the fact that the rising numbers of corruption cases detected by various accountability agencies in Brazil, investigated by the Federal Police, and prosecuted by the Ministério Público Federal were uniformly met with a bleak reluctance by courts to enforce legal sanctions, particularly if the cases touched on the political elite. The late years of the 2000s decade were illustrative: in 2008, the *Satiagraha* investigation was annulled by the high courts; in 2009, the *Castelo de Areia* case had the same destiny; and, also in 2009, the STF reversed a decades-long understanding and established that convicted defendants could be jailed only after a final unappealable decision had been reached by the judiciary, disproportionally benefiting defendants with ample resources, good lawyers, and access to the high courts. Judicial policy entrepreneurship by the *Lava Jato* team sought to force a reckoning with the long-standing judicial diffidence of the courts. But good intentions notwithstanding, it did not have the intended effect.

The costs of sanctioning corrupt behavior, which are by definition already high, became nearly prohibitive after *Lava Jato's* burst of anticorruption zeal, given the temporal concentration of the corruption cases, which seemed to overwhelm the high court; the relatively limited number of judges enforcing sanctions, at the trial court and appeals court levels; and the sheer number of high-profile targets of *Lava Jato,* which encompassed a significant plurality of federal politicians. Had Brazil's judicial system gradually evolved to more regularly punish political corruption in a timely and assertive fashion, such challenges might have been more dispersed over time and across targets. This, in turn, might have increased the acceptability of, and compliance with, judicial decisions by the country's political elite. Said another way, had judicial diffidence been gradually replaced by the spread of judicial equanimity in Brazil, the costs of enforcing legal sanctions might have been made more bearable to everyone, fostering their sustainability over time and providing a more fertile terrain for further incremental changes to bear fruit.[11] The behavior of the courts as an institution might have been matched, and reinforced, by the overall preferences of society, including its political and economic elites. Instead, preferences and behavior became misaligned, with the consequence that, after a period of significant turbulence, matters appear to have returned to something weaker than the previous accountability equilibrium.[12]

Perverse Effects of Judicial Policy Entrepreneurship

Instead of pushing countries into virtuous cycles, some of the most visible consequences of judicial policy entrepreneurship in Italy, France, and Indonesia seem to have been detrimental to anticorruption itself. Episodes of judicial policy entrepreneurship led to perverse effects, recalling Albert O. Hirschman's (1991) admonition that, too often, reforms aiming to improve political, social, or economic conditions result in the opposite of what was intended.

This tends to be the case because judicial policy entrepreneurship can lead to a massive renewal of the political elite's stock, but without influencing underlying incentives and practices. Judicial policy entrepreneurship creates a window of opportunity for otherwise fringe actors to ascend politically, but—especially in countries where the prevailing corruption syndrome privileges elite corruption—ultimately fails to address most of the originating incentives that drive corrupt political behavior in the first place. In the Italian, French, and Indonesian experiences, a similar pattern arose: although judicial policy entrepreneurship emerged in the midst of periods of increased political instability, political forces eventually coalesced in subsequent years to constrain the newly emergent judicial actors, often with the aid of other factions within the legal community.

The results of such political pushback are amply detailed in the literature. They include the enactment of new laws that weaken legal accountability, as well as damage to the image of impartiality and sobriety that judges and prosecutors usually seek to cultivate. These consequences of judicial policy entrepreneurship are seemingly inevitable, particularly in a democracy, where the judicial system inevitably faces separation of powers dynamics. The separation of powers in a democracy, indeed, suggests two primary reasons why one should not expect judicial policy entrepreneurship to effectively drive forward grandiose accountability transformations. The first has to do with the position from which the judicial systems tackle the problem of grand political corruption, predominantly focused on *legal* accountability. The second has to do with the political backlash that such efforts engender.

First, although a few entrepreneurs within the judicial system may be able to expand their efforts beyond their traditional confines and lead massive anticorruption reform efforts, they will invariably concentrate their efforts around oversight and enforcement of criminal and civil sanctions. This, after all, is exactly judicial actors' forte: their jobs revolve around investigating, prosecuting, and imposing civil and criminal sanctions. Other elements of the accountability equation (transparency, capacity, engagement, and dominance, as well as forms of oversight and sanction that do not lead to criminal and civil penalties) are largely absent from the efforts of judicial entrepreneurs. Furthermore, the reforms that would be needed to address underlying systemic corruption incentives tend to fall by the wayside, in part because the very legislators whose support is needed for reform may be vulnerable targets of the judicial effort. As a result, even working at the best of its ability, the judicial system can address only a limited portion of the broader reform program that is needed to effectively shift the corruption equilibrium.

In attempting to go beyond their traditional confines, furthermore, judicial actors reproduce the focus and mentality of their own work. For instance, as legal actors engage the public to propose anticorruption reforms, they may ultimately settle on solutions to the issue that resolve the bottlenecks to accountability in their narrow judicial bailiwick. The so-called 10 Measures Against Corruption proposed by the MPF during *Lava Jato*'s heyday are a good example. Measures on how to improve transparency (including, but not limited to, political finance and public procurement), strengthen oversight and sanctions by administrative agencies, enhance the autonomy and capacity of governmental agencies systemically afflicted by corruption (including, but not limited to, Petrobras), and foster minimally coherent political and economic competition (preventing cartel formation, for instance, or reforming the coalitional system), among others, are simply missing from the proposal. For the most part, the proposed measures seem intended mainly to further empower the judicial system.

Second, as much as judicial independence has been a hallmark of anticorruption reform, decades of research by judicial politics scholars have consistently shown that courts are particularly ill equipped to protect themselves against political attacks. The judiciary has long been seen as the "least dangerous branch" (Bickel [1962] 1986; *Federalist* no. 78, in Hamilton, Jay, and Madison 1961). This follows from the fact that the judiciary is inevitably dependent on the political branches even in well-established democracies (Larkins 1996). The judicial system concretely depends on the other branches of government: its jurisdiction, powers, and budget are defined in legislation, and therefore susceptible to changes by the legislature; it does not enforce its own decisions, relying especially on the executive to that end; it lacks any direct form of democratic (electoral) legitimacy; and its senior-most members are selected with the consent of the other branches (Rosenberg 1992; Ferejohn 1998; Burbank and Friedman 2002; Vanberg 2015; Staton et al. 2018).

Given these constraints, it should not come as a surprise that judicial policy entrepreneurship often emerges, at least in our limited sample, in times when political instability is high. That is, it emerges when some of the limitations mentioned above are temporarily lifted. This is in keeping with a large body of research in the field of judicial politics, showing that political fragmentation and judicial empowerment frequently go hand in hand (Maor 2004; Ingram 2015; Castagnola 2018; Hilbink and Ingram 2019). Yet judicial policy entrepreneurship often goes a step further, with legal authorities attempting to push the boundaries of judicial action, appealing directly to the public and media—including appearing on television, giving interviews to various media outlets, writing best-selling books, holding press conferences, and conducting televised high-profile raids and arrests—as a way to keep the political system on its back foot for as long as possible, in ways that advance judicial actors' ambitious goals. Along the way, unsurprisingly, the judicial system is often accused of bias, overreach, and even illegal behavior. As Horowitz (1977a: 298) noted more than four decades ago, "The danger is that courts, in developing capacity to improve on the work of other institutions, may become altogether too much like them."

In behaving politically, judicial policy entrepreneurship ends up being targeted as political behavior. That is, by going beyond conventional understandings of the proper role of courts, legal actors expose a broad (and weak) flank to political maneuvering and political attack. Once political instability ends or authority is transferred to newly elected officials, political actors are in a position to reestablish stricter controls on the judicial branch. The repertoire of political responses to judicial policy entrepreneurship is broad and diverse: it emerges precisely from the various ways in which the judicial system is dependent on the elected branches of government in a democracy. Many of these forms of mutual dependence have been extensively mapped by judicial politics scholars, but are not often considered by most anticorruption scholars.

The vast repertoire of political tools available to minimally skillful political actors with sufficient popular support range from purely discursive tactics to typical separation of powers hardball, and includes action (nominations, new legislation, budgetary adjustments) and inaction (noncompliance with judicial rulings, failure to reform). Once again returning to the heuristic accountability equation, these dynamics can be somewhat simplistically summarized: as dominance minimally reasserts itself, it targets the sources of judicial policy entrepreneurship—that is, the capacity of legal institutions and the engagement of the public and media. Along the way, political actors aim to reduce transparency, as well as oversight and the sanctions resulting from judicial efforts. Note the asymmetry here: although judicial policy entrepreneurs are usually incapable of expanding their efforts beyond oversight and sanction, by contrast political actors, in their responses, may be able to address the entire span of the accountability equation.

In the wake of a major anticorruption judicial big push, the cases analyzed here suggest elected leaders may aim to disengage the public or to shift its perceptions of judicial actors, using at least three discursive tactics. The first consists in alleging *abuse,* that is, suggesting that investigators, prosecutors, and judges went beyond their mandates and did not adequately follow procedure (Merriner 2004). Prosecutorial and judicial roles often overlap during episodes of judicial policy entrepreneurship. This means that the accusation of abuse, or at the very least, of judicial actors behaving in ways that break with convention, often has some basis in fact, and judicial policy entrepreneurship can thus be labeled as illiberal or in some way prejudicial to defendants' rights (Sá e Silva 2020). A second tactic is to allege *bias*. Once investigated or prosecuted for corruption, politicians everywhere complain that they have been victims of politically motivated persecution; their opponents, in turn, invariably stress that the investigations are independent, and that legal actors are merely doing their jobs. Judicial policy entrepreneurs are caught in the cross fire. If efforts by legal actors have been disproportionally allocated to some targets over others—and they almost inevitably are because of the necessarily limited, and therefore targeted, efforts of prosecutors and judges—these allegations may gain greater credence and contribute to delegitimizing their work, at least among some portion of the population (Maravall 2003). A third tactic politicians frequently use is simply to *shift the focus* to other issues, especially if the public has grown tired of endless investigations that do not seem to fix the country's problems and that ultimately show that corrupt actors may be the only viable option within the political landscape (Pavão 2018, 2019). These discursive tactics aim to force the judiciary to censor itself. They may either force the judicial actors to adopt less aggressive measures or, more likely, induce other legal bodies—such as high courts—to restrict the actions of judicial policy entrepreneurs. Such discursive tactics may also pave the way for legislative and executive measures that constrain the anticorruption efforts of legal actors. Here, the four experiences of judicial policy entrepreneurship explored above suggest that political actors often specifically target judicial institutional capacity.

This repertoire of reaction is replete with measures that have long been examined by the literature on court curbing (Nagel 1964; Rosenberg 1992; Clark 2009; Geyh 2009; Castagnola 2012), but also includes others that are specific to corruption cases. One tactic is to *reduce legal sanctions* for either past or new cases, or both. These could include measures such as reducing jail times for corruption-related crimes in ways that benefit defendants prospectively and retroactively, expanding the statute of limitations, granting immunities from prosecution, and handing out full-fledged pardons. Less directly, a common measure is to *alter jurisdictions*. Usually, this aims at removing specific cases from the hands of certain courts or prosecutors, often by changing the legislation on criminal and civil procedure. Such changes tend to be detrimental to accumulating experience in corruption cases, as they usually entail taking the cases away from judicial actors who have built up corruption expertise and passing them along to generalists. Similarly, another way to alter jurisdiction is to add more appeals to court proceedings, so that cases are reviewed by less rigorous judges, or cases become more likely to play out the clock to the statute of limitations. In this sense, another goal of altering jurisdictions may simply be to delay judicial decisions endlessly. One way to accomplish this is simply to change the judicial venue, which in the Brazilian case can be accomplished by assuming or resigning an office that provides the defendant with access to the original jurisdiction of the high court. Similarly, there are indirect legislative and executive measures that *impose budget constraints* on legal accountability agencies. In addition to directly affecting the capacity of the judicial system, such measures also have an indirect signaling effect to legal actors, suggesting that they tone down their efforts. Another common measure is to *remove threatening officials* from specific positions, which may be achieved by reassigning a particularly aggressive prosecutor or police investigator, or appointing them to a higher office. Similarly, political actors may *appoint protectors* to positions in which they may oversee cases of interest, dismiss or stall cases, or change administrative rules in ways that negatively alter the performance of accountability agencies under their supervision. Finally, political actors may *fail to comply* with legal decisions, a radical measure that exposes the dependence of the courts when enforcing and implementing its own rulings. Here, actors may refuse to be subpoenaed, fail to attend court proceedings, and so forth.

Political actors, of course, need not adopt such measures to limit judicial policy entrepreneurship. At times, the simple threat of such measures will induce legal actors to change their behavior, as in various strategic accounts of judicial behavior, particularly so-called separation-of-powers games (Eskridge 1991; Epstein and Knight 1998; Maltzman, Spriggs, and Wahlbeck 1999; Clark 2009). Similarly, the existence of so many discursive tactics and legislative and executive measures allows political actors to combine and deploy them either in isolation or jointly, adjusting them to their specific judicial targets over time.

The judicial politics literature suggests a variety of lessons for anticorruption scholars about judicial policy entrepreneurship. The first is that judicial policy entrepreneurship in anticorruption looks unlikely to succeed from the get-go because the judicial system simply does not offer a credible exogenous threat to corrupt actors. The judicial system is inevitably part of the political system, and the high courts, in particular, are "inevitably a part of the dominant national alliance" (Dahl 1957: 293). As independent as it may seem, then, the judicial system is never outside or above the government; it operates with different degrees of autonomy and discretion, but necessarily within its confines. As a result, it is difficult for judicial policy entrepreneurship to persist long enough to achieve a successful anticorruption big bang.

At the same time, because a political backlash against judicial policy entrepreneurship is almost inevitable, judicial policy entrepreneurship often ends up weakening the accountability system as a whole, by engendering political blowback. The most perverse effect of judicial policy entrepreneurship is that the political reactions to anticorruption seldom stop at limiting the powers of the legal actors who led the big push. Once political actors regain the upper hand, they may go even further and seek to undermine other courts, reform efforts, or agencies that are not directly related to the initial judicial threat. Judicial policy entrepreneurship thus not only may fail as a big bang on its own terms, but also may threaten other accountability reforms that took years—and, at times, decades—to be nurtured and fine-tuned incrementally.

In Brazil, the story of the CGU is illustrative. Established in 2001 and empowered in the subsequent year with the purpose of overseeing federal civil servants and monitoring the implementation of federal programs by municipalities nationwide in areas such as education and health care, the agency contributed only indirectly to *Lava Jato*. Yet every new governing coalition that took office after former president Dilma Rousseff was impeached in 2016, including coalitions under the Michel Temer and Jair Bolsonaro administrations, has worked to effectively diminish the CGU's status. Similar efforts have been under way in a variety of other agencies, including the Federal Police, the financial intelligence unit COAF, and the TCU accounting tribunal.

When Ray Fisman and Miriam A. Golden (2017: 803) argued that "anticorruption efforts must minimize unintended effects," they were referring to anticorruption measures within the limits of a single narrow program or policy. The same lesson applies to grandiose investigations such as *Lava Jato,* perhaps to an even greater degree. As the discussion above suggests, given the magnitude of such large operations, the unintended effects may be more comprehensive and widespread, rippling across numerous agencies and actors, with detrimental consequences for the overall control of corruption, perhaps for years to come.

The Challenge of Engineering an Equilibrium Shift in a Large Democracy

Another challenge that Brazil faced during *Lava Jato* has to do with the challenge of scale. Ultimately, size matters. Most countries that have successfully managed to reduce corruption are small, and oftentimes extremely small. This is a fundamental, but often overlooked, lesson that arises from closer inspection of success stories of corruption reduction.[13]

So-called contemporary achievers (Mungiu-Pippidi 2015; Mungiu-Pippidi and Johnston 2017) and most improved nations (Rotberg 2017) are almost entirely small countries. The authors of these studies do not entirely agree on which countries should be considered success cases over the past generation (their lists overlap only twice, in Georgia and Rwanda). But of the fourteen countries identified by these authors, ten nations have fewer than 5 million inhabitants and twelve are under 20 million. Only one nation of this group is a big country, with a population greater than the mean country population of 40 million people:[14] South Korea, which currently has 52 million inhabitants.

Various other historical success stories are also small nations. They include the former British territories of Hong Kong and Singapore in the 1970s (Klitgaard 1988; Manion 2004; Quah 2010), as well as Nordic nations such as Denmark, Sweden, and Finland in the nineteenth century (Rothstein 2011; Johnston 2013; Salminen 2013; Rothstein and Teorell 2015; Teorell and Rothstein 2015). Suggestively, none of these nations had more than 10 million inhabitants at the end of the twentieth century.[15] In fact, summing the current population of all nineteen countries cited in this section so far, their total populations are still some 40 million people shy of Brazil's present-day population.

There are, of course, more small countries in the world than large ones, so the skew in any sample from this universe of cases would be toward countries with smaller populations. Yet success stories are drawn almost exclusively from small nations. As noted in Chapter 1, focusing on cases of success is also misleading for another reason: in so doing, researchers and policy analysts tend to overestimate the impact of measures that seem relevant to the observed outcomes. This is a basic inferential problem of research design (King, Keohane, and Verba 1994; Geddes 2003). Yet focusing on cases of success that predominantly share small size is even more problematic since it suggests that corruption scholars have not been taking the scale dimension rigorously into account in thinking through processes of equilibrium change.

In fact, the recent history of larger countries that have adopted anticorruption measures is rife with failure, including China, India, Mexico, Italy, Nigeria, Kenya, and Indonesia. In some of these cases, such as Mexico, Kenya, and Nigeria, failure has been quite spectacular, following a well-known script: a winning candidate in the presidential elections promises a sweeping anticorruption reform; once the new government takes office, a maverick is appointed to a governmental position to oversee accountability efforts; over time, as realpolitik kicks in and the administration needs to focus on its immediate political survival, the maverick reformers are dismissed and their efforts dismantled (Morris 2009; Lawson 2009; Ocheje 2018). (In many ways, this is also the story of the dynamics surrounding the appointment and resignation of former *Lava Jato* judge Sérgio Moro as justice minister in President Bolsonaro's cabinet.) In some cases, as in China, anticorruption measures seem to have only a temporary and largely inconsequential effect on systemic corruption proper, even if they sent a few corrupt actors to jail (instead, they seem to have achieved other goals such as targeting political opponents or centralizing power) (Manion 2004; Popova 2006, 2017; Zhu and Zhang 2017; Pei 2018; Wang 2018). In other cases, such as India, anticorruption simply never picks up anything but a lackluster pace, despite reforms adopted decades ago (Quah 2008). In yet other cases, judicial policy entrepreneurship was the road taken, with all of the consequences examined in the previous two sections. Regardless, none of these cases of anticorruption reforms in large nations seem to have reduced corruption by significant levels over the past generation.

Critically, cases of large nations that have managed to reduce corruption have only been scarcely mapped in the literature, in part because such experiences are rare, especially in recent history. In fact, apart from the recent case of South Korea, the US Progressive Era from the late nineteenth to the early twentieth century, the gradual transition toward more impartial administration in the United Kingdom over the nineteenth century, the long and erratic trajectory of France over the past two centuries, and Japan over the past decades are among the few documented cases of relative success in polities with large populations (Mungiu-Pippidi 2015; Mungiu-Pippidi and Johnston 2017; Taylor 2018). Although we are not aware of historical accounts describing how their relatively positive equilibrium came to pass, some other populous nations currently exhibit cleaner records than any of the cases above (e.g., Germany, Spain), suggesting that at some point in time they also managed to establish systems to curb corruption.

This suggests that a key element policymakers must keep in mind when devising accountability measures to reduce corruption is the country's size or population. Expecting narrow measures that have worked to reduce corruption in small nations, such as Georgia, Hong Kong, Singapore, Uruguay, Estonia, Slovenia, Denmark, Sweden, and Finland, to work in the same fashion and with same degree of success in large nations, such as China, India, the United States, Brazil, Indonesia, Nigeria, and Mexico, is possibly unrealistic. That is because small countries exhibit a range of properties that make them qualitatively different from more populous and territorially vast countries for the successful adoption of anticorruption measures (as for most public policies, as a matter of fact). In short, size matters because it affects the following:

1. *Collective action:* If corruption is characterized as a "collective action problem" (Persson, Rothstein, and Teorell 2013), it follows that more populous and territorially vast countries face a harder time generating collective action, either at the mass or elite level. The sheer number of individuals who must be involved to produce a credible threat to the country's political elite or to generate an ambitious and credible anticorruption bargain that is sustainable over time is likely to be higher in large countries. As a consequence, collective action is more likely and more sustainable at the elite and mass levels in smaller countries than in larger ones.

2. *Veto players:* As a result of their dimensions, large and more populous countries often exhibit some form of either de jure or de facto territorial decentralization, so that political authority is more divided not only vertically (given federalism or semifederal arrangements), but also horizontally (often including an upper house with powers symmetrical to the lower one, but dispersed regionally). Power, as a result, is less centralized and more dispersed across a range of political actors, including members of the upper house and subnational authorities, in addition to the separation of powers arrangements typical of most democracies. The effects of such institutional frameworks are well known: by increasing the number of actors whose consent is needed to enact new policy, they diminish clarity of responsibility (Tavits 2007) and make grandiose departures from the status quo less likely (Tsebelis 2002); federalism, in turn, is known to produce joint decision traps (Scharpf 1988). Anticorruption reforms, as a result, tend to be more piecemeal than abrupt; when such countries take their chances at a big bang reform push, it often results from some temporary period of political instability or renewal that, when reversed, tends to endanger reform.

3. *Heterogeneity of corruption:* Large and populous countries often are more internally heterogeneous than smaller ones, including with regard to corruption, so that the prevailing syndromes and levels may vary at the national and subnational levels. The literature suggests that capacity and corruption vary significantly across national or federal agencies (Bersch, Praça, and Taylor 2017a; Prasad, da Silva, and Nickow 2019). At the subnational level, it is possible that multiple syndromes of corruption coexist within a single country—just as multiple political regimes coexist as, for example, in cases of subnational authoritarianism (Gibson 2005). At least in part, such heterogeneity is a function of the country's size and population. This suggests that the issue of grand corruption is not a single phenomenon in large nations, but rather a bundle of numerous multidimensional issues that require a plethora of different remedies. This means that there is no silver bullet. At the same time, going after the type of corruption that is most prevalent at the national level may open the door for other types of corruption that are prevalent at the subnational level to percolate to the national arena, especially if some subnational accountability regimes perform less effectively than national ones (Macaulay 2011; Da Ros 2014).

4. *Perception of vulnerability to external shocks:* "Vulnerability in large states produces a different politics than in small ones" (Katzenstein 2003: 27, 1985). Given their relative vulnerability, most small countries simply cannot avoid, preempt, or ignore economic and political challenges that they face. This may lead political elites in smaller countries to be more able to adjust and compromise to survive: this vulnerability, in other words, provides an incentive toward collective action. If exogenous threats are important catalysts that lead countries into virtuous cycles, they are more likely to be credible and engender a reaction in smaller nations than in larger ones. In other words, the resolute political will often associated with small nations' anticorruption success may, in fact, derive less from particularly high-minded moral or ethical leadership, and instead from the cold calculus imposed by vulnerability.

These four effects should be considered jointly. Smaller countries that have managed to reduce corruption at significant levels have exhibited many of the previous characteristics jointly: political leaders, pressed between deteriorating conditions coming from abroad and increased mobilization at home, have managed to tackle corruption up front with a series of aggressive measures enacted with relative ease by the nation as a whole. Large countries do not have such an "easy" time. There, the pressure for reform in the face of exogenous shocks is less severe. Endogenous shocks, such as protests at home, also are dissipated over a larger territory and populace. Corruption is, in many ways, a more multidimensional problem in large countries since it spreads horizontally and vertically, down various administrative levels. Solutions are therefore more complex: they require greater consensus across relevant political actors, and, as a consequence, may necessitate extensive negotiation prior to enactment and during implementation.

The distinct politics of large countries shape the context in which corruption reforms take place. While the conditions necessary for big pushes to work already are rare in small countries, they can seem almost unachievable in large nations. Not surprisingly, successful moves from low- to high-accountability equilibria in big countries have taken a long time in all instances where they have been reported. Moving toward virtuous cycles in large countries has not been a revolutionary process; rather, it has been an evolutionary, incremental process extending over long periods of time. It is similar in other policy arenas, beyond anticorruption: this is the story of the large societies we know of that have managed to engage in successful democratization, state building, and economic modernization, all policy reforms that often consume more than a generation. What successful large societies seem to have managed is the complex task of moving forward for long periods of time, engaging in constant small change, instead of rapid accelerations or big pushes punctuated by pauses or even reversion. Along the way, they also seem to have avoided the temptation to take shortcuts.

The issue, therefore, is not simply to assemble a massive coalition that tackles corruption up front and attempts to change the country overnight. Instead, with an eye toward assembling longer-term coalitions, reforms must be broken down into smaller and more digestible pieces, with attention paid in every case to whose interests are met by reform, and how to weaken the reaction of potential counterreformers. The goal is to seek collective action, and to find political support for improvements in the accountability equation that may have nothing at all to do with anticorruption per se. This helps build larger coalitions for the enactment, development, and ultimate protection of policy gains over time. A paramount example, here, is the transparency reforms enacted in Brazil in the late 1990s within the realm of economic policy. Because they were anchored in both the economic and the anticorruption realms, they found broader support, led to increasing gains over time, and proved relatively resilient to reversal.

Finally, in a consolidating democracy, it is worth remembering that the failure of big push reforms risks opening space not only for political outsiders, but also for antiestablishment and even antidemocratic politics. In hindsight, *Lava Jato*'s anticorruption big push not only helped to breed antipolitics, but also cultivated a long latent authoritarian sentiment in Brazil. As with many of the unexpected results of *Lava Jato,* there is no reason to believe that this was the intent of the prosecutors, investigators, and judges involved in the case. But the warning signs were visible as early as 2015, when a few vocal protesters began to openly call for military intervention. Helcimara de Souza Telles (2015), for instance, found in a survey collected in the city of Belo Horizonte during one of the first demonstrations of 2015 that 14.5 percent of the respondents considered a military intervention the best solution to the crisis, and that 50.5 percent agreed that in situations of too much disorder, the military should be called on to seize power.

In fact, anticorruption values have been identified as part of the package that led to Brazil's current illiberal backlash, with far-right president Bolsonaro's core voters reportedly considering corruption to be the country's worst problem (Amaral 2020; Fuks, Ribeiro, and Borba 2021; Hunter and Power 2019; Nicolau 2020; Rennó 2020). After decades when he seemed like nothing more than a burlesque caricature of a long-gone era of military rule, Jair Bolsonaro's star rose precisely as the Brazilian public was hit by revelation after revelation of corruption accusations against democratically elected politicians of all stripes. Bolsonaro's long history of egregious opinions on a variety of topics did not seem to matter to many, so long as he presented himself as something different from the status quo. The fact that he openly supported torture, expressed nostalgic feelings for the most repressive years of military regime, and was racist and misogynist, in fact, helped Bolsonaro present himself as an "authentic" person, in contrast to the cunning and duplicitous politicians unmasked by *Lava Jato.*

During the early years of the Bolsonaro administration, the president turned to military personnel to help him govern, in the cabinet and as mid-ranking appointees within the bureaucracy (Barrucho 2020; Lis 2020). Bolsonaro courted the military: significantly expanding the defense budget and carving out exceptions in the pension reform privileging the military (*Valor* 2020). Then, as the Covid-19 pandemic loomed large, killing thousands of Brazilians, he openly flirted with antidemocratic actions by attending protests that asked for a military intervention that, among other things, would have replaced all STF justices. One of the president's sons, Federal Deputy Eduardo Bolsonaro, argued that it was no longer a matter of "if," but "when" a "moment of rupture" would happen (Gugliano 2020). By July 2020, only a few months after Sérgio Moro left the Ministry of Justice, the new justice minister was accused of monitoring 579 individuals—including civil servants and police officers within the federal and state governments—identified as opponents of the Bolsonaro administration (Camporez 2020).

Whether they represented a mere flight of rhetoric or a serious move against the democratic regime, the Bolsonaro administration's antidemocratic discourse and practice qualitatively changed political dynamics in the country. Once a case of relative success, Brazil now ranks among the five countries where autocratic practices have advanced the most in the past decade, alongside Hungary, Poland, India, and Turkey (V-Dem Institute 2020). The fact that Brazil saw a sharp drop on V-Dem's Liberal Democracy Index score beginning especially in 2016, furthermore, suggests that this trend was not exclusively of Bolsonaro's making. The possibility that *Lava Jato* may have unintentionally contributed to unleashing antidemocratic sentiment in Brazil in recent years is tragically ironic, suggesting that the judicial big push may have helped to shake the very foundations of the democratic regime that allowed independent investigations to flourish in the first place.

Notes

1. Alessi (2015).
2. "Ainda desconfio muito de nossa capacidade institucional de limpar o congresso. O melhor seria o congresso se autolimpar mas isso não está no horizonte" (*The Intercept Brasil* 2019).
3. In the case of dominance, values are multiplied by –1.
4. In the anticorruption policy community, suggestions for increased judicial independence have been made by a variety of players over the years, including Transparency International, the World Bank, and the World Justice Project. In academia, the role of independent prosecutors and courts has been advocated to reduce corruption, for instance, in works by Colazingari and Rose-Ackerman (1998) based on an analysis of the *Mani Pulite* investigations in Italy, by Vogl (2012: 137–138) in an examination of Peru following the prosecution of former president Alberto Fujimori, and by Behrend (2006: 228) within a study of the Cabezas case in Argentina.
5. Note that our definition of *judicial policy entrepreneurship* does not presuppose a partisan bent to the prosecution. This is distinct from a portion of the literature that examines partisan prosecutions (e.g., M. Ang 2017; S. Gordon 2009; Popova and Post 2018).
6. Judicial policy entrepreneurship should not be confused with just any instance of anticorruption specialization, which exists in various countries and even at the subnational level in countries such as Brazil (Da Ros 2014). The

206 Brazilian Politics on Trial

Sandiganbayan court of the Philippines, for instance, has had special jurisdiction over corruption cases since the 1970s. Still, its erratic record does not allow us to classify it as a case of judicial policy entrepreneurship (Pangalangan 2010; Stephenson 2016).

7. Of course, there may be other cases of judicial policy entrepreneurship. One such case involved the efforts in holding Alberto Fujimori, Vladimiro Montesinos, and other political authorities accountable before the courts in Peru in the 2000s (Vogl 2012). But there, judicial efforts followed—rather than led—media and political accountability measures. By the time Montesinos was convicted, in late 2001, the so-called Vladi-videos had already been aired by independent media and Fujimori had been impeached (McMillan and Zoido 2004). Fujimori was only sentenced in 2009 for embezzlement. Another possible case of judicial policy entrepreneurship is Romania, but the experience there is so recent that it is difficult to evaluate and, thus, is not included here. That said, Romania seems to fit a similar sequence to Brazil, with rising capacity, increasing public engagement, and declining dominance leading to some initial success, but then a backlash emerged with allegations of excess and the arrival of populist newcomers, who threatened the continuity of the anticorruption push (Mendelski 2021; Mungiu-Pippidi 2018; Pârvulescu 2021).

8. We summarized the Italian and French cases based on the following sources: Roussel (1998, 2002, 2003); della Porta and Vannucci (1999, 2007, 2016); della Porta (2001); Hodgson (2002); Adut (2004, 2008); Vannucci (2009, 2016); Sims (2011); Ceron and Mainent (2015); Fisman and Golden (2017); Asquer, Golden, and Hamel (2020); Manzi (2021). For the Indonesian case, we based our summary on Slater (2004); Tahyar (2010); Schütte and Butt (2013); Butt and Schütte (2014); Rodan and Hughes (2014); Schütte (2016a, 2016b); Schütte and Stephenson (2016); Wibowo (2018); Butt (2019); Madeira and Geliski (2021).

9. A recent study suggested that corruption was somewhat reduced at the municipal level over the long run, conditional on increased political competition and reduced party switching (Daniele, Galletta, and Geys 2020).

10. In this same period, for instance, the country's GDP per capita more than quadrupled, jumping from US$900 in 2002 to US$3,893 in 2018.

11. While there had been incremental improvements to the accountability role of the courts in Brazil following ENCCLA, and *Lava Jato* itself benefited enormously from them, *Lava Jato* can be interpreted as an astounding departure from the ethos of ENCCLA: ENCCLA prioritized low-key, consensus-building reforms that accumulated over years, whereas *Lava Jato* was a massive attempt to tackle high-level corruption up front.

12. Brazil's measure on the CoC peaked at 63.03 in 2011, and fell beyond the margin of error, by nearly 33 percent, to 42.31 in 2019.

13. Among the few authors who have advanced this hypothesis are Quah (2010) in his comparison of Asian anticorruption agencies, and Escresa and Picci (2020) using novel data on cross-border corruption.

14. Calculated from a global population estimate of 7.8 billion, spread across 194 countries.

15. As a general criterion, we have included here only countries that have minimally changed their corruption levels over time. As such, countries that have exhibited low corruption levels almost uninterruptedly since their independence, such as New Zealand (Gregory 2006), have been excluded from our list.

7

Learning from the Brazilian Experience

É devagar!	*It's slow!*
É devagar!	*It's slow!*
É devagar, é devagar	*It's slow, it's slow*
Devagarinho	*Very slowly*
Sempre me deram a fama	*I always had the reputation*
De ser muito devagar	*Of being very slow*
E desse jeito	*And in that way*
Vou driblando os espinhos	*I go dribbling around thorns*
Vou seguindo o meu caminho	*I go following my path*
Sei aonde vou chegar	*I know where I am going*

—Martinho da Vila, musician, 1995

On May 13, 1987, a remarkable journalistic coup was consummated. The *Folha de S. Paulo* newspaper published a front-page story under the headline "Competition for the North-South Railway Was a Farce," alleging that bidding for construction of the massive railroad project had been fixed (Freitas 1987). As proof, the newspaper reprinted on its front page a classified advertisement that its reporters had published five days earlier, correctly listing in code the winners of the bid and the segments of the railway that each of the eighteen winning companies would take home. The headline was a blockbuster, and threw Brasília into a tizzy. President José Sarney (1985–1990) ordered a Federal Police investigation. Transportation Minister José Reinaldo Tavares named an investigatory commission. The bidding process was annulled. But then, progress ground to a halt. Neither the police nor the Transportation Ministry found any wrongdoing, and the Ministério Público Federal filed away the case without bringing charges (Seidl 1998; *O Globo* 2015b).

Fast-forward twenty years, to 2007. Only 200 of the 4,800 kilometers of planned rail had been built (Furlan 2017; *Veja* 2016b). As President Luiz Inácio Lula da Silva moved to put together a Growth Acceleration Program to boost infrastructure spending nationwide, and an associated National Plan for Logistics and Transport, his administration seized on the massive Ferrovia Norte-Sul (North-South Railway) project to link the north and the south of the country from Maranhão to Rio Grande do Sul. The project advanced quickly and in 2010, Lula and Sarney, who had grown close in the 2000s when Sarney was an influential senator and Lula was president, came together to inaugurate a new segment of the railway in Tocantins. In seven years, by May 2014, the Lula and Dilma Rousseff administrations had jointly completed nearly 2,000 new kilometers of railway (R. A. Machado 2018: 124).

Yet a dark cloud hung over the renewed project. Audits began in 2008 and, by July 2009, the TCU accounting tribunal reported grave irregularities in nearly US$400 million of project expenditures, recommending that payments to contractors be suspended. Repeating the experience of the 1980s, TCU audits found high budget estimates in the government's initial bidding documents, which were further elevated by alleged bid rigging among the private sector firms that bid for the project, and then, by corrupt postbidding contract enhancements authorized by Valec, the agency tasked with overseeing the railroad construction. By September 2009, Ulisses Assad, head of engineering at Valec, was forced to resign in the face of Federal Police allegations of corruption against him and Fernando Sarney, the former president's son (H. Corrêa 2009). Yet President Lula pushed back against the allegations, suggesting that reports of irregularities were just overreach by an overly punctilious accounting tribunal: Valec directors would have "to make 50 trips to Brasília," he argued, "to convince the ministers of the [TCU] that the project is right and the price is right" (H. Corrêa 2009). In 2011, further allegations toppled the transportation minister and the president of Valec, José Francisco das Neves (known as Juquinha das Neves). But no convictions were forthcoming in the courts.

Then, the *Lava Jato* operation began to envelop the Norte-Sul rail project. The Federal Police undertook at least three major investigations of the railway project between 2012 and 2018, concluding that at least R$500 million had been surreptitiously sidelined. Plea bargains in 2016 by former Camargo Corrêa president Dalton Avancini and his counterparts at Andrade Gutierrez alleged bribes were paid to Valec personnel, including Juquinha das Neves, who was accused of receiving bribes even after stepping down from the Valec presidency (*G1* 2016b). Two executives from the Odebrecht construction firm confessed in 2017 plea bargains that they paid bribes during the 2007 bidding. They specifically mentioned two groups of corrupt appointees in Valec: one headed by Congressman Valdemar da Costa Neto (PL), who had already been convicted in the *Mensalão* scandal, and a second led by Ulisses Assad who, they charged, represented the interests of the MDB in the state of Maranhão, former president Sarney's electoral bailiwick (*O Globo* 2015a). According to these allegations, politicians received 4 percent of revenues from the project, with 3 percent going to Costa Neto and the remainder to the Maranhão group (*Istoé* 2012; *G1* 2016b; *O Globo* 2015a, 2017a).

By 2016, it was believed that the federal government had spent nearly US$8 billion on the railroad, more than three times the initial 1987 budget of US$2.4 billion. Some of the workmanship was shoddy, with erosion and the absence of necessary rail sidings meaning that the railway was not completely operative, decades after work began. Portions of the railway came in 80 percent above budget. There were still forty open investigations in the TCU accounting tribunal, twenty-three of which demanded recovery for the National Treasury (Furlan 2017).

Several participants in the corruption scheme were punished, especially among the scheme's operators. Juquinha das Neves and his son Jader Ferreira das Neves were sentenced in 2017 to ten and seven years of jail time, respectively, for corruption and money laundering. Several homes, two airplanes, and financial assets believed to belong to the Neves family were seized. The construction firms' executives were convicted and signed plea bargains. The largest of the construction firms signed leniency agreements and moved forward with compliance programs intended to block corruption in the future: as part of a broader agreement, Camargo Corrêa agreed to pay R$700 million to the National Treasury, of which R$75 million was to recoup Valec's losses (*G1* 2016b). But politicians, so far, have been given a pass. Sarney has retired from politics; Lula is a leading contender for the 2022 election; Sarney's son Fernando has escaped prosecution; and Valdemar Costa Neto, symptomatically, has returned to politics as a top ally of the Bolsonaro government. Costa Neto, who was convicted in *Mensalão* and appears to have played an important role in the second Norte-Sul scheme, has been reinstated as president of the Liberal Party (PL), and a congresswoman in his party—Flávia Arruda, the wife of former senator and governor José Roberto Arruda, himself involved a variety of corruption scandals—was nominated in 2021 to head Bolsonaro's Secretariat of the Presidency, giving the party enormous influence over government-wide budgetary amendments and political appointments.

A Shift in the Accountability Equilibrium?

What do the bookends of the Norte-Sul railway case, 1987 and 2017, say about the questions raised in this book? At their most basic, they demonstrate the constancy of scandal over time. They suggest, too, that although some gains have been made in transparency, oversight, capacity, and effectiveness, at least two important bottlenecks stand in the way of effective accountability: achieving effective sanction, especially for political big shots, and shifting the unique patterns of political dominance present in the coalitional presidential system, well represented by players from the Centrão such as Valdemar Costa Neto.

It is important not to be too pessimistic: the paired railroad scandals, after all, do show some important accountability gains. But the path has been tortuous and nonlinear, and early gains have been reversed. Progress has been shallow and narrow: shallow in the sense that it is not clear that the underlying institutional incentives have changed or accumulated as significantly as would be needed to generate an equilibrium shift; and narrow in the sense that many of the most concrete wins of recent years emerged from the *Lava Jato* case, and not from a widespread shift in the effectiveness of police, prosecutors, and judges in other contemporary cases. But as previous chapters illustrated, Brazil's accountability equilibrium has clearly shifted over a generation of democratic reforms, in a somewhat—albeit not unidirectionally—positive direction.

To the extent that we can provide evidence of this shift, it is largely through observational data pointing to changes in the dominant incentives within the system. Chapter 2 pointed to the enduring syndrome of corruption in Brazil, marked by an elite cartel engaging in grand corruption, facilitated by the perilous combination of coalitional presidentialism in a hyperfragmented party system, a large developmental state, and a loose campaign finance system. This combination of complementary institutions has provided, and continues to provide, motive and means for corruption. For many years, poorly functioning accountability institutions further exacerbated the problem, as exemplified by the narrow miss in the 1987 Norte-Sul railway case: had it not been for the intrepid, careful reporting of Jânio de Freitas, the reporter at the *Folha de S. Paulo,* even the weak accountability in that case probably would not have been forthcoming. In 1987, accountability agencies like the Federal Police and Ministério Público were too timid or too politically compromised to do much, even after Freitas's report surfaced. Not for nothing, Brazilians developed a phrase, "acabou em pizza" (it ended up in pizza) to describe the complete absence of accountability, even in the face of compelling evidence of wrongdoing, that has been common to major scandals.

At the federal level, the years between the return to democracy and 2014 brought a slow and incremental progression of accountability reforms, with gains across the distinct components of the accountability equation. While there was much room for continued improvement, there were fortuitous and strategically planned improvements that increased the likelihood of corruption being uncovered, investigated, and punished.

These improvements in many ways came to a climax in the *Lava Jato* operation. Agents of accountability had learned a great deal through the trials and errors of the previous three decades, and law enforcement authorities shared a general consensus about the importance of multiagency cooperation through task forces in complex investigations, international cooperation to investigate financial crimes, the application of improved criminal statutes, the principle of publicity, and public awareness and support. Of course, consensus is no panacea, and there was also realism about the ongoing difficulties of curbing corruption, including a court system whose inefficiency and uncertainty provided protection for elites, as well as a self-protecting political class that stymied further progress on anticorruption reform. Together, judicial inoperancy and political self-protection greatly undermined checks and balances, and continued to generate incentives for politicians to prioritize self-protection above accountability.

If *Lava Jato* showed anything, it was how much collusion there was in the political system. Dirty politicians had little to gain from dismantling the corruption networks that sustained their campaigns and their political networks, or those of their opponents. Even politicians who were not egregiously corrupt faced disincentives to exposing wrongdoing: intercoalitional financial transfers could be significant, so calling out wrongdoing by coalition allies potentially undermined a candidate's own sources of campaign finance; the constant realignment of the political system meant that today's rival could be tomorrow's ally; campaign finance was concentrated, meaning that calling out another party's wrongdoers might boomerang on one's own benefactors; and cooperating with the executive branch offered a source of patronage and privilege, even for members of the opposition. The result was a vicious equilibrium: politicians had few incentives to criticize incumbents for wrongdoing, anticorruption reforms were seen as destabilizing the incumbent advantage, and, in consequence, checks and balances were weak. Most pressures for accountability came from outside the political system, from bureaucratic agencies such as the Federal Police, from autonomous bodies such as the Ministério Público, or from civil society and the media.

But even these positive accountability forces faced a challenge in dealing with the intertwining of the branches of government. Police and prosecutors relied on a judiciary that not only was slow and timid in tackling elite wrongdoing, but also—especially in the two highest courts, the STF and STJ—was deeply intertwined with the very political forces it was being asked to control. As noted in Chapter 2, fully 28 percent of federal politicians since the turn of the century faced investigation or indictment in federal court, but the number who were in fact punished with jail time was infinitesimal. One lesson a rational politician might take away was that there was little gain to be had from sticking one's neck out to call out wrongdoing since there was minimal chance that corrupt players would be permanently removed from the system. Another, possibly more troubling, lesson a seasoned criminal offender could learn from this state of affairs is that entering politics might be a savvy way to gain protection.

If this is a bit dispiriting, it is perhaps worth remembering the origins of *Lava Jato:* over the long haul, the accountability equilibrium had been moving, slowly and nonlinearly, in a positive direction. After the return to democracy there were many cases like Ferrovia Norte-Sul, with the flash of bright lights and media attention, but precious little active oversight and absolutely no judicial response. Throughout the 1990s, there was improvement in oversight, with the media, a uniquely vehement opposition party (the PT), and congressional committees of inquiry drawing attention to alleged wrongdoing (e.g., the 1993 *CPI dos Anões do Orçamento*), but oversight bodies remained deeply politicized and the scandal led to little or no subsequent judicial action. In the 2000s there was a movement toward more institutionalized oversight, which contributed to more effective investigation and prosecution, especially in lower court criminal trials (e.g., *Banestado, Satiagraha, Castelo de Areia*) and civil cases (e.g., *Precatórios do DNER*), albeit with repeated override by the high courts on procedural grounds and enormous delays. Finally, beginning in the 2010s, a few trials actually began to lead to effective punishment for powerful elites, as in the *Mensalão* and *Lava Jato* cases. It was an imperfect trajectory, and one that often proved susceptible to reversal, but over time there had been a shrinking of the institutional protections for political elites, with oversight bodies growing more autonomous of political interference.

Lava Jato emerged in this context, finding space and gaining momentum in the uncertain economic and political terrain surrounding the 2014 election. The investigations initially surfed this wave masterfully, taking advantage of an unstable environment to push forward accountability efforts in the courts, and to flex the accountability system's newfound capacity. In so doing, however, *Lava Jato* became the spearhead of a big push of judicial policy entrepreneurship, spreading beyond its limited origins in the prosecutorial system and the judiciary to destabilize politics, engage in a conscientious public mobilization strategy, and push forward ambitious anticorruption reforms.

The immediate result was to put political and economic elites into a defensive crouch, upending the Rousseff and Temer administrations. Massive anticorruption efforts contributed to immense political upheaval. The intertwined economic, political, and legal crises ongoing in Brazil since 2013 shook the foundations of the democratic regime. The 2018 elections led to the most significant renovation of the political class since the return to democracy: old pro-democracy parties such as the MDB, PSDB, and PT were decimated, while a host new politicians were elected to Congress under unwieldy party labels such as the PSL. The unlikely election of a conservative firebrand with an unconventional political style as president further upset the relationship between the executive and legislative branches.

But over time, *Lava Jato* became a victim of its own success. Public exhaustion, self-inflicted wounds, failure to expand more broadly across the judicial system, increasing controversy, and the growing opposition of judicial, political, and economic elites began to slow the progress of anticorruption efforts. Despite the 2018 election of Jair Bolsonaro and a wave of new legislators, many of the incentives of the political system remained in place, leading a new crop of politicians to turn to the tried-and-true patterns of the old coalitional system. Under a variety of different presidents, furthermore, the period 2016–2021 was marked by increasing efforts to reassert the supremacy of the elected branches over the judiciary and over the broader web of accountability institutions.

Meanwhile, the decision by actors at the heart of *Lava Jato* to enter the political fray made it easier for critics to paint the anticorruption effort as a partisan crusade. Judge Sérgio Moro's decision to join the Bolsonaro administration as justice minister was seen by supporters as a patriotic decision to sacrifice his judicial career in the hopes of pushing forward anticorruption reforms. Among his detractors, and even the undecided, however, it also cast some of his earlier decisions—especially questionable decisions about pretrial detention and a wiretap of two presidents—in a harsher light. Murky dealings within the prosecutor-general's office in the JBS matter raised questions about the probity of some prosecutors and the self-serving nature of judicial elites. The arrest of former president Lula, and his party's cries of *golpismo* and lawfare, tainted anticorruption efforts with perceptions of politicization and even political malice, at least among a sizable segment of the left and center-left. Failure to convict many politicians from the other side of the political spectrum contributed to the narrative that the prosecutions were biased.

These forays into the political realm had real-world consequences. They permitted the STF to realign in defense of defendants' rights, after a short interregnum during which public pressure for accountability pushed the court to hold politicians responsible for corruption. They permitted President Temer, and Bolsonaro after him, to decrease the budgets available to inconvenient oversight agencies, and to destabilize the bureaucracy by appointing unsympathetic directors to key agencies. They permitted Congress to stymie reforms, including first the anticorruption legislative initiative pushed forward by prosecutors and then Justice Minister Moro's own package of anticorruption reforms, which was watered down and even spiked with poison pills. Most of all, they may have sapped public support and engagement, which are essential to ensuring ongoing improvements along the whole of the accountability equation.

Where does this leave Brazil? For the time being, high-level reforms to improve the accountability equation seem likely to remain a secondary priority, and perhaps may even regress under the onslaught of political crisis and elite backlash. In fact, there is reason to believe the enormous backlash against *Lava Jato*—and against accountability more broadly—is still underway. As noted in Chapter 5, the Law of Administrative Improbity (which served as the legal basis for 62 percent of the 28,000 corruption cases brought by the Ministério Público Federal between 1993 and 2018; Londero 2021: 72) was rewritten by the Congress in ways that deeply diluted its effectiveness and was signed into law by President Bolsonaro in 2021. The 1998 Anti–Money Laundering Law that was so essential to *Lava Jato* is under attack. Although no reform has been approved so far, momentum seems to be building within Congress to dilute the law and a proposal is being discussed in closed legislative session. In sum, the antiaccountability counterreform is still very much under way as we conclude this book.

That said, it may be unduly Pollyannaish of us, but we see a potential silver lining in the gradual slowdown of the anticorruption pace: the possibility of returning Brazil to its prior, somewhat slower, and more incremental pace of reform. One of the unintended consequences of *Lava Jato* was to greatly accelerate the pace of accountability efforts in Brazil. Previous legislative reforms had required years to implement because accountability agencies had to learn and adapt to the new frameworks. The Anti–Money Laundering Law of 1998, for example, took more than a decade to implement, as various accountability bureaucracies sought to understand the law and put in place the necessary processes and staff to make it functional. These very bureaucracies, drawing on the lessons they had learned from applying the law in practice, spearheaded the rewriting of the law in 2012 to enhance its applicability. But beginning in 2013, the pace of reform shifted. A number of significant new laws were passed (e.g., the Anti-Corruption Law and the Criminal Organizations Law), which were rapidly implemented almost as soon as they had been approved, without time for organizational learning and adaptation. For example, the Criminal Organizations Law of 2013 formalized the plea bargain and, within the next three years, 266 plea bargains had been signed, largely in *Lava Jato* cases (Londero 2021: 108). Each of these plea agreements is a universe unto itself, with implications across the entire criminal justice system. The agreements require monitoring and oversight, to ensure that relevant information has not been omitted and that defendants are living up to their side of the bargain. Given the haste with which these plea bargains came into effect, there was not time to establish common rules and procedures, which were put into place only in

2018 (with the MPF's *Orientação Conjunta* No. 1). Some of the backlash against plea bargains—which were often criticized as a foreign, abusive prosecutorial tool—might have been attenuated had there been a more steady and measured rollout.

In sum, the 2010s brought an important acceleration in the pace of change. From a long and incremental process of small, marginal improvements along various dimensions of the accountability equation, the country suddenly went into overdrive with a massive anticorruption push. This big push initially had salutary effects like holding political elites with dubious reputations, such as José Dirceu and Eduardo Cunha, accountable. It also drew intense public attention to the depth and salience of the corruption issue. But, of course, it also engendered a backlash that was perhaps unavoidable in a political system with so many powerful veto players. This backlash throttled reform.

Perhaps the slowing down of the anticorruption crusade will allow actors in the web of accountability to return to a more thoughtful and calculated pace of reform that is more strategic, engenders less pushback, resumes forward progress, and patiently plans its next steps to ensure that they are effective and politically sustainable. The real risk, here, is that they will need to accomplish this while still running their respective agencies within an increasingly complex and still quite uncertain political environment.

Four interrelated areas seem ripe for incremental reform in years to come, aligning roughly with the three legs of the perilous combination of coalitional presidentialism, loose campaign finance, and the developmental state described in Chapter 1. The first would be to revise the incentives within coalitional presidentialism that drive the political system into its collusive, vicious equilibrium of collective coalitional dominance. Already reforms are under discussion, such as a new performance threshold for smaller parties, which went into effect in 2018 and limits the possibility of subnational electoral alliances in proportional elections (first adopted in the 2020 municipal elections). These may be hopeful starting points for a broader reform that would strengthen political parties, so that they would become less transactional, more beholden to voters, and thus more committed to particular policy postures and ideological positions. Together, such increased clarity of responsibility might enhance the party system's role in accountability processes. Party system institutionalization is widely believed to have a positive effect on electoral accountability and, through that, on corruption (Schleiter and Voznaya 2018).

A second, and related, point concerns campaign finance. Given Brazil's extremely concentrated campaign contributions, one idea is to develop ways to ensure multiple campaign finance streams. Already, the 2010s brought a prohibition on corporate campaign contributions (which were banned beginning in the 2016 election). With this in mind, it may now be worth establishing clearer caps for individual contributions, so that they represent specific amounts, rather than proportions of an individual's income. Other, perhaps more challenging ideas, are to think about ways to attract more contributors into the political arena, so as to increase the breadth of political financing, as well as reduce the expense of campaigns, which are expensive by international standards (Taylor 2020: 139). More also needs to be done to enhance the policing of campaign finance, in ways that finally break the gentlemen's agreement between parties that has tacitly accepted and promoted the illegal funding of politics. Now that many corruption cases have been moved into the electoral courts, this will require a combination of capacity-building and rigorous oversight. Combined, these ideas would begin to level the playing field for parties and contributors, and enhance the coherence of parties.

The third, and perhaps thornier, set of reforms would target the judicial system and particularly its role in punishing elite corruption. As glaring exceptions to the rule that impunity reigns supreme for Brazilian elites, the *Mensalão* and *Lava Jato* scandals highlighted the inoperancy of the judicial system as a central bottleneck within the broader accountability framework. If nothing else, the exceptional success of these two cases proved how high the cost-to-benefit ratio of the federal courts has been with regard to corruption. Reforms that reduce some of the egregious privileges that are provided to political actors, such as access to the original jurisdiction of the high court, have already been hesitantly moving forward over the past two decades, as Chapter 3 detailed. The 2018 decision by the STF to limit cases with original jurisdiction only to crimes related to the official jobs of their respective public officials is a case in point. But more needs to be done to improve accountability in the courts, including by moving grand corruption cases out of a high court that is institutionally poorly designed to deal with criminal cases and, perhaps more importantly, too deeply intertwined with the political forces it is asked to control.

A fourth, and associated, set of reforms would focus on improving control and oversight of the expansive developmental state apparatus, which includes government bureaucracies, massive state-owned firms and banks, a variety of semiautonomous autarkies, and a web of semi-private but state-controlled entities, such as the pension funds belonging to employees of state-owned enterprises. Improvements in the state's own instruments of control might include more emphasis on strategic planning and review of personnel hiring practices, as well as punitive measures such as more effective bans on misbehaving companies seeking public contracts and loans, and closer monitoring of the unexplained income of civil servants and political appointees.

These recommendations are necessarily vague. The key reason for this is that, as we have emphasized throughout the book, the perilous combination is perilous precisely because it is a combination. As a consequence, any reform to a single leg of the combination will have impacts that affect the other legs. One example might be reforms that institutionalize the party system, which might have positive repercussions in the developmental state by reducing demand for political appointees. A less positive example might be the effects of an increased number of campaign contributors, which could have the negative side effect of further fragmenting the party system. A related reason for our vague prescriptions is that policy practitioners have a more informed understanding of the nuance and detail within their areas of specialty, and thus have a better sense of how to balance incremental gains within the broader system. In sum, because these reforms have impacts that reverberate across the three legs of the perilous combination, we believe the most promising path forward is an iterative process of policy learning, marked by incremental and modest changes, as well as reflection and review on their intended and unintended consequences.

The mere fact that we believe that reforms along the lines described above would improve probity, of course, does not mean that Brazil's political system will go along. Indeed, as Chapter 5 demonstrated, a number of measures being considered in Congress seem to run counter to our prescriptions. Overall, the impression we are left with is that the political system in 2021 seems to be doing everything in its power to hit the reset button, forcing accountability agencies to start over, learn new rules, and adopt new processes, in a radically altered statutory environment, with dramatically changing judicial interpretations, and amidst an almost apocalyptic pandemic. One effect of this reshuffling of the rules is that individual politicians implicated in wrongdoing have won the time needed to run out the statute of limitations clock, and the political system has slowly regained its footing. Politicians no longer need to confront oversight institutions directly: they appear to have learned that if they simply shift the rules and processes occasionally, so as to force the web of accountability agencies to learn a new game, they can buy all the time in the world.

Brazil's Lessons for the World

In light of the mixed—if not downright pessimistic—perspective laid out in this book, readers may be surprised that we think that Brazil has lessons to offer the world. Brazil's failures and its successes have consequences for anticorruption efforts elsewhere, especially in the large and complex democracies that are so seldom cited as anticorruption success stories. We believe that there are three important lessons of relevance to emerge from this book: (1) the benefits of incrementalism over big bang approaches, especially when these big pushes are driven by the judicial system; (2) the gains from thinking about accountability as a process more than an outcome; and (3) the insight that collective action can be shrunk, by focusing on smaller-bore reforms to each of the components of our accountability equation.

The first lesson is from *Lava Jato,* now that the shine is off that investigation. With hindsight, the *Lava Jato* investigation perhaps moved too quickly for its own good, sowing the seeds of its own destruction by breaking down the political coalitions that structured politics while, simultaneously, building up resistance from elites. Like *Mani Pulite* before it, *Lava Jato* burned down the old structures of politics, but did not leave much in its wake to replace them: the result was to generate a widespread reaction among politicians, who moved to reassert their commitment to old norms and behaviors. Newcomers who were allowed to move from the margins to the center of the political system, against minimal opposition, showed little interest in altering the conditions that had empowered and enriched the previous political elite.

In Italy, *Mani Pulite* led to the rise of Silvio Berlusconi and a coalition that gutted laws intended to build good governance: statutes of limitations were shortened in corruption cases, the new government sought to reduce the allegedly arbitrary powers of judges, and public support for anticorruption efforts was sapped by exhaustion and exasperation with the inability of elites to effectively drive forward change.

Lava Jato has not been as different from the Italian case as its protagonists hoped. As the previous chapter concluded, *Lava Jato* may have unwittingly demonstrated the benefits to an incremental approach, especially in large, complex federal systems with multiple powerful veto players. There has never really been good historical evidence for big bang approaches to corruption, especially because most big bangs in the literature were, in fact, generation-long efforts and, even under such lengthy time lines, required massive crises such as war or the threat of invasion as motivators. They generally resulted from credible existential threats that the entire political system—the regime, even the country itself—might be at risk. Judicial policy entrepreneurship provides no motivation of that sort, instead threatening only the political elite. Although there was certainly a period of heady triumphalism at the peak of *Lava Jato,* between 2014 and 2016, this perhaps led to a sense that *Lava Jato* was the end-all and be-all, that this was Brazil's chance to finally overcome centuries of corruption, and that the further Brazil could move now, the less likely there would be a reversion to the old status quo ante. Many of these hopes of abrupt and rapid change—big bang change—have been dashed by *Lava Jato*'s loss of forward momentum, and even regression.

Neither is there much evidence from Brazil that judicial policy entrepreneurship, reform leadership driven by prosecutors and judges, is a particularly effective way of pushing forward change, especially broad reforms. The judiciary is the weakest branch, its sources of legitimation are more tenuous than other branches in democracies, and its members' ability to engage in retail politics is limited. Furthermore, the judiciary is itself a deeply factionalized organization, and it was probably utopian to assume that changes driven forward by the trial courts would always be welcomed or applauded by high court justices with close ties to the political establishment.

Incrementalism, by contrast, has many potential benefits in anticorruption reform. We have pointed to several of its benefits, of which we will reiterate only the most relevant here. Incrementalism does not require the ex ante construction of a broad anticorruption coalition; incrementalism may be the only viable political strategy in a polity marked by multiple powerful veto players; and incrementalism permits cumulative sequencing, enabling policymakers to proceed from one bottleneck to another in ways that adapt reforms to local contexts and consider the intended and unintended effects of previous reforms. Incrementalism in anticorruption requires humility, patience, and, most of all, political savvy in light of the fact that reform may always activate defenders of the status quo. As the previous chapter noted, large democracies like Brazil face a particularly challenging task of overcoming the collective action problem that lies behind corruption and weak accountability, and, in the face of large numbers of potential veto players, incrementalism may be the only viable option.

Indeed, the second lesson emerges from the progress that Brazil made at the federal level in the pre–*Lava Jato* period. Although civil servants and policymakers never expressed it in these terms, they intuitively developed an approach to corruption that was centered on incremental improvements in the elements of the overall accountability equation that they could directly control: transparency, oversight, sanction, and capacity. By focusing on accountability, and its components, rather than on corruption per se, they were able to make progress in small bites: building out a transparency law, improving audits, passing laws governing corporate behavior, and improving bureaucratic coordination, for example. These small gains did not pose a direct threat to dominant political and economic elites, as they ran in a direction orthogonal to those elites' interests. By focusing reforms on accountability as a process, rather than as an outcome, they thereby blunted opposition, and managed to slowly build out a robust structure of new agencies, agents, statutes, and procedures that contributed to the slow equilibrium shift that was under way until 2014.

Third, the Brazilian case demonstrates that collective action can be shrunk. The prevailing consensus in academia is that corruption is a collective action problem. This is an important insight, but one that can be daunting: If it is a collective action problem, what is the best way to mobilize diverse constituents for whom the costs of action in the short term may outweigh any dubious long-term gains from a cleaner system? And how can this be done in large countries where collective action could involve millions of actors and interests, just at the federal level? By proceeding incrementally against smaller objectives within the accountability equation, rather than against the broader goal of tackling corruption, Brazilian authorities were able to garner the necessary collective action for transparency, for a stronger oversight agency, for prosecutorial independence, for better anti–money laundering laws, and so forth. The oblique, indirect angle with which accountability policies tackled the sources of the vicious corruption equilibrium provided political cover, while the narrow focus of individual accountability reforms incrementally accumulated over time into a promising equilibrium-shifting effect.

Brazil is in a difficult place. But a longer-term view is warranted. The country has been in challenging situations before, and, although progress has not always been unilinear, today's equilibrium offers far better opportunities for change than the equilibrium of a generation ago. The lessons of the past generation provide a useful road map for the next. *Devagar, devagarinho, vamos driblando os espinhos.*

Appendix

Brazil's Major Federal Corruption Scandals, 1985–2021

The goal of this Appendix is to situate major corruption scandals in historical context since 1985. As a general criterion, we considered as "major federal political corruption scandals" those scandals that allegedly involved wrongdoing by members of Congress or the executive branch, or both, and that received significant attention from the national media. We excluded corruption scandals that, based on currently available information, were predominantly confined to the following:

1. State and local governments (e.g., *Escândalo dos Precatórios* of 1997, *Mensalão Tucano* of 2005, *Mensalão do DEM* of 2009, and *Operação Mar de Lama* of 2016);
2. The judiciary (e.g., *Operação Anaconda* of 2003 and *Operação Têmis* of 2007); or
3. Low-ranking officials (e.g., *Escândalo do INSS* of 1991).

These cases of subnational, judicial, or petty corruption scandals were excluded even though many involved significant amounts of money and important subnational policymakers. We also excluded scandals that did not revolve around corruption (e.g., the accusation that former congressman Hildebrando Pascoal ran a death squad).

The table in this Appendix provides the following information:

1. In the Scandal column, we identify the most common name or nickname associated with the scandal and how its timing aligned with each presidential administration since 1985. The year in parentheses after the name of the scandal refers to the date

when the scandal became public or started to receive systematic attention in the national media, not when the corrupt practices themselves took place. Often the year of discovery was several years after the alleged corruption took place. We are guided by Ari Adut's definition of *scandal* as "an event of varying duration that *starts with the publicization* of a real, apparent, or alleged transgression to a negatively oriented audience" (2008: 11, emphasis added).

2. In the Description column, we provide a short summary of the scandal itself, including a brief report on who was involved and their alleged corrupt practices. We also indicate the actors, institutions, or organizations associated with the public revelation of the scandal (the media, oversight bodies, law enforcement agencies, etc.).

3. In the Perilous Combination column, we identify whether or not the scandal fits the general pattern of interplay between coalitional presidentialism, developmental state, and campaign finance described in Chapter 2. We adopted a threefold classification: "Yes" refers to cases when all three elements of the perilous combination were evident; "Partially" refers to cases when some, but not all, elements of the perilous combination appeared in the scandal; and "No" refers to cases when none of the elements of the perilous combination were evident.

4. In the Locus of Investigation column, we identify the name of the accountability bodies that were primarily responsible for shedding light on the scandals in the first place, and that subsequently were responsible for their investigation.

5. In the Accountability column, we include information regarding the sanctions that resulted from the scandal, particularly those of a political (impeachment, resignation from office), administrative (fines, suspensions), civil (restitutions), or criminal (jail) nature.

Scandal	Description	Perilous Combination	Locus of Investigation	Accountability
José Sarney administration (1985–1990)				
1. *Ferrovia Norte-Sul* (North-South Railway, 1987)	A newspaper uncovered evidence of bid rigging by major construction companies in a railroad project worth an estimated US$2.5 billion at the time. After revelations, the bidding process was cancelled (see Chapter 7).	Yes	Congress, Federal Police	No wrongdoing found in either investigation; no charges filed.
2. *CPI da Corrupção*, (Congressional Inquiry on Corruption, 1988)	A congressional inquiry was launched following news reports on the allegedly irregular disbursement of federal funds by the Planning Ministry to municipalities governed by mayors who supported the president. Some of these transfers were allegedly intermediated by family members such as the president's son-in-law.	Yes	Congress	Impeachment charges were filed against the president and five ministers. The president of the Chamber of Deputies shelved the case in early 1989.
Fernando Collor de Mello administration (1990–1992)				
3. *Esquema PC Farias* (PC Farias Scheme, 1992)	A newsmagazine published an interview with President Collor's brother, who accused Collor's campaign treasurer, PC Farias, of a kickback and influence peddling scheme that involved various ministries and state-owned enterprises. A congressional inquiry found that many of the president's personal expenses had been paid either by PC Farias or his associates.	Yes	Congress	Impeachment charges were filed and approved in the Chamber of Deputies; the Senate found Collor guilty and barred him from political office for eight years. Collor was later acquitted by the STF, which sentenced PC Farias to seven years in jail. PC Farias was pardoned by President Cardoso. In 1996 he was killed alongside his girlfriend in a nebulous murder-suicide.

continues

Scandal	Description	Perilous Combination	Locus of Investigation	Accountability
Itamar Franco administration (1992–1994)				
4. *Anões do Orçamento* (Budget Dwarves, 1993)	A newsmagazine published an interview with a congressional aide who worked on the budget committee in Congress, accusing congressmen of writing amendments that benefited construction companies in exchange for bribes. A congressional inquiry investigated thirty-seven congressmen from various political parties (see Chapter 1).	Yes	Congress	The congressional inquiry suggested that eighteen congressmen should have their mandates revoked. Of these, eight remained in office, four resigned, and six had their mandates revoked, including the president of the Chamber of Deputies, Ibsen Pinheiro, who was later acquitted in the courts, and was returned to Congress by voters in 2006.
Fernando Henrique Cardoso administration (1995–2002)				
5. *Reelection* (1997)	A newspaper uncovered recordings suggesting that five deputies had allegedly received cash payments in exchange for their votes on the constitutional amendment allowing reelection. The scandal also cited the involvement of three other congressmen, one state governor, and the minister of communications, who allegedly helped to organize payments to the congressmen.	Partially	Congress	Two congressmen caught on the recordings resigned from office. One of them ran again, successfully, in 1998. The three other congressmen were cited in the case were all cleared in a probe by a congressional committee and remained in Congress.
6. *Marka-FonteCindam* (1999)	A newsmagazine reported that the owner of the small bank, Marka, allegedly received insider information about the Central Bank's decision to devalue the Brazilian currency, and was allowed to buy currency at below-market rates, a privilege later extended to another small bank, FonteCindam. The transactions allegedly resulted in losses of approximately R$1.5 billion to the National Treasury. The scheme allegedly involved the owners of both banks, the president of the Central Bank, and a few Central Bank employees.	No	Congress	A congressional inquiry in 1999 suggested that civil and criminal charges should be pressed against the bankers and Central Bank staff. They all received criminal sentences in 2005. Appeals remained pending before the high courts from 2007 until 2013, when the case reached the statute of limitations, and charges were dismissed in 2016. The owner of the Marka bank was jailed for three years, before receiving a presidential pardon. All those involved received civil penalties for administrative improbity in 2012, which required restitution of the amounts involved in the case, but this decision is under appeal.

continues

continues

continued: Fernando Henrique Cardoso administration (1995–2002)

Scandal	Description	Perilous Combination	Locus of Investigation	Accountability
7. *Foro Trabalhista de São Paulo* (São Paulo Labor Court, 1999)	Irregularities in the construction of a federal labor courthouse in São Paulo had been detected by the TCU as early as 1992, and in 1998 the MPF suggested that the cost of the building was overpriced. The scandal, however, was only set off after a 1999 congressional inquiry (*CPI do Judiciário*) revealed that out of the R$223 million budgeted for construction, approximately R$169 million had been siphoned off by a judge, a senator, and the owners of a construction firm.	No	Congress MPF	The judge and the senator were both suspended from office in 2000. In 2006, they were convicted alongside the businessmen involved, in a decision that was upheld in 2013. In 2016, after the last of his thirty-six appeals was rejected, the senator was finally sent to jail. The judge in the case was sent to jail briefly, but allowed to serve most of his jail time under house arrest, due to his age.
8. *Precatórios do DNER* (Judicial Debts of DNER, 1999)	Payments of judicial debts amounting to more than R$120 million by the now defunct National Department of Roadways (DNER) allegedly were reprioritized in exchange for bribes to civil servants at DNER. The scheme allegedly involved the minister of transportation and the secretary of the presidency.	Yes	MPF	Following the scandal and the privatization of various roadways, DNER was replaced by a new agency, National Department of Transport Infrastructure, in 2001. A civil administrative improbity case was brought against all those involved in 2003. The trial proceedings began in 2003. No court decision has been handed down as of this writing.
9. *SUDAM* (2001)	The president of the Senate was accused of undue influence over the allocation of R$2 billion in funds controlled by the Amazonian Development Superintendency (SUDAM), a major regional development program currently located within the Ministry of Regional Development.	Yes	MPF	The scandal led to the extinction of SUDAM in 2001, but it was reinstated in 2003. The president of the Senate resigned from office in 2001, but was elected to the Chamber of Deputies in 2002, and then to the Senate again in 2010, a position he holds as of this writing. A civil administrative improbity suit was filed against him and various other individuals in 2006. They were convicted in 2013, but all were acquitted on appeal in 2019. Two criminal cases were filed before the STF, one in 2003 and another in 2014; the former resulted in acquittal and the latter was shelved.

Scandal	Description	Perilous Combination	Locus of Investigation	Accountability
continued: Fernando Henrique Cardoso administration (1995–2002)				
10. *Banestado* (2002)	The scandal revolved around a massive money laundering scheme totaling billions of dollars between 1996 and 2002. Various high-profile politicians and businesses were cited over the years following various congressional inquiries and investigations by the Federal Police. Even though these investigations started in the late 1990s, the case rose to national prominence only in 2002, when the Federal Police transferred a parcel of the investigation from Paraná to Brasília (see Chapter 2).	Partially	Congress, Federal Police, MPF, federal courts	No conclusive report resulted from the congressional inquiry. Criminal charges were filed against dozens of individuals and a few were eventually convicted, predominantly small financial operators such as *doleiros*.
Luiz Inácio Lula da Silva administration (2003–2010)				
11. *Mensalão* (Big Monthly Allowance, 2005)	A congressman alleged in a newspaper interview that the PT, including the president's chief of staff, participated in a scheme that paid R$30,000 monthly to congressmen to ensure their support. The investigations also revealed that bribes had been paid in overpriced governmental purchases and the resulting cash was used to finance electoral campaigns and congressional support (see Chapter 2).	Yes	Congress, prosecutor-general, STF	Both the congressman and the president's chief of staff were removed from office. Criminal charges were filed at the STF in 2007, resulting in the 2013 criminal convictions of various political figures from the PT, PTB, PP, and PL.

continues

continues

continued: Luiz Inácio Lula da Silva administration (2003–2010)

Scandal	Description	Perilous Combination	Locus of Investigation	Accountability
12. *Sanguessugas* (Leeches, 2006)	In 2004, the CGU unveiled evidence of over-pricing in the purchase of ambulances by the Ministry of Health, leading to an investigation by the Federal Police. Allegedly, a company paid bribes to federal deputies in exchange for congressional amendments to the annual budget so that ambulances and hospital material could be bought at above-market prices by several municipalities. The scheme totaled approximately R$110 million and involved dozens of deputies from ten different political parties represented in Congress, with the bulk coming from the PL, PTB, PP, and MDB.	Yes	CGU, Federal Police	Following the Federal Police investigation in 2006, a congressional inquiry looked into ninety congressmen and recommended the expulsion of seventy-two. None were removed from office by Congress, although a number were not reelected later that year. Hundreds of indictments were brought against businessmen, congressional aides, mayors, and federal deputies. A 2012 survey of criminal cases from the scandal revealed that only sixty-six cases had been tried, resulting in thirty-nine convictions. Of these, five involved former deputies, all with pending appeals.
13. *Satiagraha* (2008)	An investigation by the Federal Police following the *Mensalão* scandal led to the arrests of two high-profile businessmen on accusations of corruption, money laundering, and fraud. The case quickly led to a massive reaction by political actors within the national executive and legislative branches, and by STF justices, who accused the investigators of various excesses (see Chapter 2).	Yes	Federal Police, MPF, federal courts	After being convicted by the trial court, the defendants were freed by the high court and the case was eventually dismissed because of tainted evidence. The chief police investigator and judge overseeing the case have been subjected to various disciplinary proceedings.
14. *Castelo de Areia* (Sandcastle, 2009)	An investigation by the Federal Police suggested a massive kickback and money laundering scheme by a construction company, potentially involving federal officials from various political parties (see Chapter 2).	Yes	Federal Police, MPF, federal courts	Criminal charges were filed against business executives at the construction company in early 2010, but an injunction by the STJ halted the case soon after. The following year, the entire case was dismissed because a portion of the evidence had been collected on the basis of an anonymous tip.

Scandal	Description	Perilous Combination	Locus of Investigation	Accountability
Dilma Rousseff administration (2011–2016)				
15. *Faxina no Planalto* (Cabinet Cleaning, 2011)	This was not a single scandal, but rather a series of unrelated events that led to the dismissal of eight ministers in President Rousseff's cabinet early in her first term. From June 2011 to February 2012, eight ministers—many of whom had served in Lula's administration—were allegedly involved in apparently unconnected corruption scandals, including wrongdoing within the Ministries of Transportation, Agriculture, Tourism, Sports, Labor, Development, and Cities, as well as the chief of staff, who previously had served as minister of finance (see Chapter 4).	Yes	Various	Of the eight ministers, seven either resigned from office or were fired by the president. All eight ministers later faced inquiries or were indicted; these cases are still pending. The names of six of these eight former ministers would later resurface during the *Lava Jato* case and various spinoff investigations.
16. *Lava Jato* (Car Wash, 2014)	Executives of the state-owned oil company, Petrobras, received kickbacks from construction companies in exchange for overpriced contracts. The resulting money was later laundered by *doleiros* and distributed to business executives and the politicians who sponsored the Petrobras executives' appointments (see Chapter 4).	Yes	Federal Police, MPF, federal courts	Numerous criminal cases followed the investigations, leading to the conviction of various influential politicians and executives at major construction companies. Cases regarding dozens of other senior officials are still pending, especially at the STF, as of this writing.
17. *Zelotes* (Zealots, 2015)	Political appointees serving on the CARF, which reviews decisions by the Receita Federal, allegedly received kickbacks in exchange for annulling or reducing the tax debts of major business companies and banks, amounting to R$19 billion. Accusations reached a former minister of finance, a former secretary of the presidency, and former president Lula, who were accused of having issued laws favoring the automobile industry in exchange for bribes.	Partially	Federal Police, MPF, federal courts	Criminal charges have been brought against various lobbyists and CARF employees, as well as against a former minister of finance, the minister at the Secretariat of the Presidency, and former president Lula. In early 2020, an appeals court acquitted many of the lobbyists and CARF personnel that had been convicted in trial court. In 2021, the former minister of finance, former secretary of the presidency, and former president Lula were acquitted.

continues

Scandal	Description	Perilous Combination	Locus of Investigation	Accountability
Michel Temer administration (2016–2018)				
18. *Greenfield* (2016)	Bribes allegedly influenced more than R$8 billion in investment by the directors of the employee pension funds at four large state-owned enterprises. A spinoff from *Lava Jato* (called *Operação Cui Bono*) led the Greenfield task force to level accusations that R$3 billion in irregular lending was carried out by the state-owned bank Caixa Economica Federal, allegedly under the guidance of a former congressman, minister, and then bank director, his brother (a congressman), as well as two former presidents of the Chamber of Deputies.	Yes	Federal Police, MPF, federal courts	Criminal charges have been brought against numerous directors of the pension funds, but most cases are still pending. In 2017, one of the congressmen involved was arrested after the Federal Police found R$51 million in cash in an apartment with his fingerprints. He and his brother were convicted by the STF in late 2019.
19. *JBS* (2017)	In a spinoff of the *Lava Jato* case, the Federal Police recorded a conversation between the owner of meatpacking giant JBS and President Temer at the presidential palace. The conversation suggested that the businessman would pay for the silence of a former Chamber president arrested during *Lava Jato*, with Temer's consent and the aid of another congressman, who was filmed receiving money from a JBS director. Later, another recording suggested that the businessman had bribed a former PSDB party president and presidential candidate. Ultimately, his plea bargain agreement implicated 167 members of Congress from nineteen different political parties, as well as numerous state governors and hundreds of candidates for political offices nationwide.	Yes	Federal Police, MPF, federal courts	Temer became the first sitting Brazilian president to face criminal charges before the STF. He was twice indicted by the prosecutor-general, but Congress did not authorize the cases to proceed while he was in office. Once out of office, he was arrested in early 2019, but soon set free. Criminal charges have been filed against the former president of PSDB before the STF, but the case has not been tried as of this writing. He declined to run for reelection to the Senate, and instead ran successfully for the Chamber of Deputies in 2018. Inquiries involving numerous officials implicated in the plea bargain agreement are still pending in the courts.

continues

continues

Jair Bolsonaro administration (2019–)

Scandal	Description	Perilous Combination	Locus of Investigation	Accountability
20. *Caso Queiroz* (Queiroz Affair, 2019)	This is an ongoing criminal investigation into Fabrício Queiroz, a retired police officer who worked for years as an aide to Senator Flávio Bolsonaro, the eldest son of President Jair Bolsonaro, who was at the time a state legislator in Rio de Janeiro. The COAF financial intelligence unit identified suspicious financial transactions amounting to R$1.2 million in the accounts of Queiroz, suggesting that he collected a portion of the staff wages at Flávio Bolsonaro's political offices for his own benefit. Later evidence suggested that similar practices happened in Jair Bolsonaro's offices while he was a congressman. In 2020, Queiroz was arrested at the country home of Frederick Wassef, Flávio Bolsonaro's attorney and allegedly a close associate of President Jair Bolsonaro.	Partially	Ministério Público of Rio de Janeiro (MPRJ)	Pending; ongoing inquiries as of this writing. Justice Minister Sérgio Moro resigned from the Bolsonaro administration in early 2020, announcing that his decision followed attempts by the president to interfere politically with the Federal Police, including replacing its director general and a few regional directors such as in Rio de Janeiro. Moro alleged that this interference was an effort by the president to obtain information on ongoing investigations, allegedly to protect himself and his family in various pending cases against them, including the Queiroz Affair.
21. *Laranjal do PSL* (PSL Orange Grove, 2019)	This case involves the PSL political party that Jair Bolsonaro joined in 2018 to run for president (Bolsonaro had been a member of eight t political parties prior to joining the PSL). The PSL is accused of having received federal funds to support women candidates, which it subsequently diverted to men candidates. The women candidates were *laranjas* (unwitting accomplices) in the scandal. The scandal implicated the minister of tourism, who was elected to Congress by the PSL in Minas Gerais in 2018, and a former president of the party.	Partially	Federal Police, Ministério Público of Minas Gerais (MPMG), Ministério Público of Pernambuco (MPPE), electoral courts	Pending; ongoing inquiries as of this writing. The scandal led to the resignation of the secretary of the presidency in the Bolsonaro administration, who was a former president of PSL. Criminal charges were filed against the minister of tourism in the electoral courts, but he continued to serve until late 2020. The investigation of another former president of PSL is still ongoing. In 2019, President Bolsonaro left the PSL.

continued: Jair Bolsonaro administration (2019–)

Scandal	Description	Perilous Combination	Locus of Investigation	Accountability
22. *Orçamento secreto* (Secret Budget, 2021)	A newspaper uncovered evidence suggesting that the federal administration had been operating a "secret budget" of more than US$560 million since 2020, disproportionately allocating resources to politicians allied with the government through opaque procedures that contravened budgetary rules in place since the 1990s. Initially concerned with the overpriced purchase of agricultural equipment within the Ministry of Regional Development, later evidence suggested that the practice also took place within the Ministries of Health, Defense, Agriculture, and Justice, amounting to more than US$400 million, particularly through the disbursement of federal funds to numerous municipalities throughout the country (see Chapter 1).	Yes	TCU, prosecutor-general	Pending; ongoing inquiries as of this writing. Once exposed, the government changed the budgetary rules so they returned to previous practices.

Sources: Abbud (2020); Alecrim (2016); Amorim (2019); BBC Brasil (2021); Bertim (2020); Bomfim (2017, 2018); Bramatti (1997); Brandão (2019); Brasiliense (2005); Breve (2006); Brigido (2014); Canofre, Mattoso, and Bragon (2019); J. R. Castro (2017); *Correio Braziliense* (2008, 2009, 2011, 2016); Cosso (2003); Damé (1997); *Deutsche Welle* (2021); Fabrini and Casado (2018); M. Falcão and Rodrigues (2021); Favero (2013); *Folha de S. Paulo* (1994, 1997a, 1997b, 1997c, 1999, 2000a, 2000b, 2001, 2002a, 2002b, 2002c, 2003a, 2003b, 2004, 2011a, 2011b, 2019, 2020a, 2020b, 2021a, 2021b); *G1* (2006, 2007, 2011a, 2011b, 2011c, 2011d, 2012b, 2020); *G1 Jornal Nacional* (2019); *G1 Pará* (2013); *G1 Pernambuco* (2019); *G1 Rio* (2016); Germano (2006); Henrique (2020); Lages and Paes (2019); Lo Prete (1999); N. Lopes (2019); Manfrini (2002); L. Marques (2011); Martins (2020a, 2020b); Matos et al. (2020); Mattoso, Bragon, and Suarez (2019); Mazieiro (2020); *Migalhas* (2019); MPF (2019d); Monteiro and Moura (2011); Moreno (2015); *O Estado de S. Paulo* (2021); *continues*

continued: Jair Bolsonaro administration (2019–)

Scandal	Description	Perilous Combination	Locus of Investigation	Accountability
23. Covaxin scandal (2021)	In 2021, irregularities emerged in the acquisition of various Covid-19 vaccines. In all cases, a Brazilian company managed the proposed importation of the vaccines, and it appears that the Brazilian intermediary raised the overall cost of the vaccine acquisition significantly, and in some cases, requested bribes to close the deal. In the best-known case, of the Covaxin vaccine, the dealings have led to allegations against the government whip in the Chamber and the president's sons. One congressman's brother, who works in the Ministry of Health, early in 2021 leveled accusations that the federal government was aware of the overpriced Covid-19 vaccines. He claimed to have personally warned President Bolsonaro. To date, there has been no indication that the president ordered an investigation into any alleged wrongdoing.	Yes	Congress	Pending; ongoing inquiries as of this writing. Once exposed, the government did not conclude the purchase of the vaccines.

Sources continued: O Globo (2015c, 2017a, 2019); M. Oliveira (2015); M. Oliveira and D'Agostino (2019); D. Pereira and Luz (2020); Pimentel (2019); Pires (2021a, 2021b); Pires and Shalders (2021); Pitombo and Mattoso (2017); Richter (2016); Fernando Rodrigues (2014); A. Rodrigues, Aquino, and Richter (2017); Lino Rodrigues, D'Ercole, and Melo (2012); Lorenna Rodrigues and Pires (2021); Sardinha (2012); Senado Federal (1988); Serapião and Fabrini (2017); Shores and Mendes (2021); Soares (2001); R. Souza (2019); STF (2020); Taylor and Buranelli (2007); L. B. Teixeira (2020); Tortato (2003); Tribunal Regional Federal da 1ª Região (2020); Tribunal Regional Federal da 2ª Região (2020); UOL Notícias (2012); F. Valente (2020); Vassallo (2019); *Veja* (2011, 2012).

References

Abbud, Bruno. 2020. "Frederick Wassef, o anjo problema." *Época*, June 26.

Abramo, Cláudio Weber. 2007. "A Portrait of Disparities." *Brazilian Journalism Research* 3: 93–107.

Abramo, Cláudio Weber, and Eduardo Ribeiro Capobianco. 2004. "Licitaciones y contratos públicos: el caso de Brasil." *Nueva Sociedad* 194: 69–90.

Abranches, Sérgio. 1988. "Presidencialismo de coalizão: O dilema institucional brasileiro." *Dados* 31: 5–38.

Abranches, Sérgio. 2018. *Presidencialismo de coalizão: Raízes e evolução do modelo político brasileiro*. São Paulo: Companhia das Letras.

Abrucio, Fernando Luiz. 2007. "Trajetória recente da gestão pública brasileira: um balanço crítico e a renovação da agenda de reformas." *Revista de Administração Pública*, Edição Especial Comemorativa: 67–86.

Abrucio, Fernando Luiz, and Maria Rita Loureiro. 2005. "Finanças Públicas Democracia e Accountability." In Ciro Biderman and Paulo Arvate, eds. *Economia do Setor Público no Brasil*, 75–102. São Paulo: Elsevier Editora Ltda.

Adut, Ari. 2004. "Scandal as Norm Entrepreneurship Strategy: Corruption and the French Investigating Magistrates." *Theory and Society* 33 (5): 529–578.

Adut, Ari. 2008. *On Scandal: Moral Disturbances in Society, Politics, and Art*. New York: Cambridge University Press.

Aidt, Toke. 2003. "Economic Analysis of Corruption: A Survey." *Economic Journal* 133: F632–F652.

Aith, Marcio. 2004. "Empresa privada espiona o governo." *Folha de S. Paulo*. July 22.

Akerlof, Robert. 2016. "Anger and Enforcement." *Journal of Economic Behavior and Organization* 126: 110–124.

Alecrim, Michel. 2016. "O recomeço de Cacciola." *Istoé*, January 21.

Alencar, Carlos Higino Ribeiro de, and Ivo Gico Jr. 2011. "Corrupção e Judiciário: a (in) eficácia do sistema judicial no combate à corrupção." *Revista Direito GV* 7: 75–98.

Alessi, Gil. 2015. "Deltan Dallagnol: 'A Lava Jato traz uma esperança, cria um círculo virtuoso.'" *El País*, August 13.

Almeida, Acir dos Santos. 2018. "Governo presidencial condicionado: Delegação e participação legislativa na Câmara dos Deputados." PhD diss., Universidade do Estado do Rio de Janeiro.

235

Almeida, Alberto Carlos. 2015. "Um limite para a Lava-Jato." *Valor Econômico*, December 23.

Almeida, Frederico de. 2019. "Os juristas e a crise: a Operação Lava Jato e a conjuntura política brasileira (2014–2016)." *Plural, Revista do Programa de Pós-Graduação em Sociologia da USP* 26: 96–128.

Almeida, Mônica Arruda de, and Bruce Zagaris. 2015. "Political Capture in the Petrobras Scandal: The Sad Tale of an Oil Giant." *Fletcher Forum of World Affairs* 39: 87–99.

Alt, James E., and David Dreyer Lassen. 2014. "Enforcement and Public Corruption: Evidence from the American States." *Journal of Law, Economics and Organization* 30: 306–338.

Amaral, Oswaldo E. 2020. "The Victory of Jair Bolsonaro According to the Brazilian Electoral Study of 2018." *Brazilian Political Science Review* 14 (1): 1–13.

Ames, Barry. 1995. "Electoral Strategy Under Open-List Proportional Representation." *American Journal of Political Science* 39: 406–433.

Ames, Barry. 2001. *The Deadlock of Democracy in Brazil*. Ann Arbor: University of Michigan Press.

Ames, Barry, Andy Baker, and Lucio R. Rennó. 2008. "Split-Ticket Voting as a Rule: Voters and Permanent Divided Government in Brazil." *Electoral Studies* 30: 1–13.

Amorim, Felipe. 2019. "STF condena Geddel e Lúcio Vieira Lima por R$ 51 milhões em apartamento." *UOL*, October 22.

Amorim Neto, Octavio. 2002. "Presidential Cabinets, Electoral Cycles, and Coalition Discipline in Brazil." In Scott Morgenstern and Benito Nacif, eds. *Legislative Politics in Latin America*, 48–78. Cambridge: Cambridge University Press.

Amorim Neto, Octavio. 2019. "Cabinets and Coalitional Presidentialism." In Barry Ames, ed. *Routledge Handbook of Brazilian Politics*, 293–312. New York: Routledge.

Ang, Milena. 2017. "Corrupting Accountability: Elite Control and Corruption Prosecution in Comparative Perspective." PhD diss., University of Chicago.

Ang, Yuen Yuen. 2020. *China's Gilded Age*. Cambridge: Cambridge University Press.

Angelo, Tiago. 2021. "Processo 'invisível' pode conter grampos ilegais, suspeitam advogados." *Consultor Jurídico*, March 15.

Aranha, Ana Luiza Melo. 2017. "Accountability, Corruption and Local Government: Mapping the Control Steps." *Brazilian Political Science Review* 11 (20).

Aranha, Ana Luiza, and Fernando Filgueiras. 2016. "Instituições de Accountability no Brasil: Mudança institucional, incrementalismo e ecologia processual." *Cadernos ENAP*, 51. Brasília: ENAP.

Aranovich, Tatiana de Campos. 2007. "Estratégia Nacional de Combate à Corrupção e à Lavagem de Dinheiro: o Estado organizado contra o crime organizado." *Revista de Políticas Públicas e Gestão Governamental* 6: 117–145.

Arantes, Rogério B. 1999. "Direito e política: o Ministério Público e a defesa dos direitos coletivos." *Revista Brasileira de Ciências Sociais* 14 (39): 83–102.

Arantes, Rogério B. 2002. *Ministério Público e política no Brasil*. São Paulo: EDUC.

Arantes, Rogério B. 2011. "The Federal Police and the Ministério Público." In Timothy J. Power and Matthew M. Taylor, eds. *Corruption and Democracy in Brazil: The Struggle for Accountability*, 184–217. Notre Dame, IN: University of Notre Dame Press.

Arantes, Rogério B. 2015. "Rendición de cuentas y pluralismo estatal en Brasil: Ministério Público y Policía Federal." *Desacatos* 49: 28–47.

Arantes, Rogério B. 2018. "Mensalão: um crime sem autor?" In Marjorie Marona and Andrés Del Río, eds. *Justiça no Brasil: às margens da Democracia*, 338–389. Belo Horizonte: Arraes.

Arantes, Rogério. 2020. "Prefácio." In Fabiana A. Rodrigues, ed. *Lava Jato: aprendizado institucional e ação estratégica na Justiça*, xv–xxii. São Paulo: WMF.

Araújo, Cletiane Medeiros, Saulo Felipe Costa, and Ítalo Fittipaldi. 2016. "Boa noite, e boa sorte: determinantes da demissão de ministros envolvidos em escândalos de corrupção no primeiro governo Dilma Rousseff." *Opinião Pública* 22: 93–117.

Arguelhes, Diego Werneck, and Leandro Molhano Ribeiro. 2018. "Ministrocracia: o Supremo Tribunal individual e o processo democrático brasileiro." *Novos Estudos CEBRAP* 37: 13–32.

Asquer, Raffaele, Miriam A. Golden, and Brian T. Hamel. 2020. "Corruption, Party Leaders, and Candidate Selection: Evidence from Italy." *Legislative Studies Quarterly* 45 (2): 291–325.

Assunção, Moacir. 2014. "Bandeira da ética que o PT ostentava está perdida." Interview with Cláudio Couto. *O Estado de S. Paulo*, September 7.

Augustinis, Viviane Franco de. 2011. "Gestão em redes para a construção de políticas públicas: um estudo sobre as atividades de prevenção e repressão à lavagem de dinheiro no Brasil." PhD diss., Fundação Getulio Vargas-RJ.

Augusto, Fausto, Jr., José Sérgio Gabrielli, and Antonion Alonso Jr., eds. 2021. *Operação Lava Jato: Crime, Devastação Econômica e Perseguição Política*. São Paulo: Expressão Popular.

Azevedo, Rodrigo Ghiringhelli de. 2012. "Perfil socioprofissional e concepções de política criminal do Ministério Público Federal." Brasília: Escola Superior do Ministério Público da União.

Bächtold, Felipe. 2018. "Para 84% dos brasileiros, Lava Jato deve continuar; 12% defendem término." *Folha de S. Paulo*, April 17.

Baiocchi, Gianpaolo, Patrick Heller, and Marcelo Silva. 2011. *Bootstrapping Democracy: Transforming Local Governance and Civil Society in Brazil*. Stanford: Stanford University Press.

Balán, Manuel. 2011. "Competition by Denunciation: The Political Dynamics of Corruption Scandals in Argentina and Chile." *Comparative Politics* 43: 459–478.

Balthazar, Ricardo. 2018. "Falta de provas livra políticos delatados por Ricardo Pessoa." *Valor Econômico*, July 8.

Ban, Cornel. 2013. "Brazil's Liberal Neo-Developmentalism: New Paradigm or Edited Orthodoxy?" *Review of International Political Economy* 20: 298–331.

Baran, Katna. 2020. "Sob pressão, Deltan Dallagnol deixará comando da força-tarefa da Lava Jato de Curitiba." *Folha de S. Paulo*, September 1.

Bardhan, Pranab. 2006. "The Economist's Approach to the Problem of Corruption." *World Development* 34: 341–348.

Barroso, Roberto. 2017. "Indulto José Dirceu: Reflexão crítica sobre o sistema penal brasileiro." Questão de Ordem na Execução Penal 2 Distrito Federal. Brasília: Supremo Tribunal Federal. https://www.migalhas.com.br/arquivos/2017/12/art 20171229-03.pdf.

Barrucho, Luis. 2020. "Brasil de Bolsonaro tem maior proporção de militares como ministros do que Venezuela; especialistas veem riscos." BBC Brasil, February 26.

Bayley, David H. 1994. *Police for the Future*. New York: Oxford University Press.

BBC Brasil. 2013. "Entenda alguns pontos do julgamento do mensalão." November 16.

BBC Brasil. 2019. "Entenda em que pé estão os processos e acusações contra ex-presidente Lula. November 27. https://www.bbc.com/portuguese/brasil-49647499.

BBC Brasil. 2021a. "Quem é Rodrigo Pacheco, o novo presidente do Senado." February 1.

BBC Brasil. 2021b. "CPI da Covid: Quem é quem no escândalo Covaxin." June 29.

Beccaria, Cesare. 1764 [1986]. *On Crimes and Punishments*. Translation by David Young. Indianapolis: Hackett Publishing.

Becker, Gary S. 1968. "Crime and Punishment: An Economic Approach." *Journal of Political Economy* 76: 169–217.

Behrend, Jacqueline. 2006. "Mobilization and Accountability: A Study of Societal Control in the Cabezas Case in Argentina." In Catalina Smulovitz and Enrique

Peruzzotti, eds. *Enforcing the Rule of Law: Social Accountability in the New Latin American Democracies*. Pittsburgh: University of Pittsburgh Press.

Beirangê, Henrique. 2015. "A semente dos escândalos." *Carta Capital*, November 3.

Bello. 2017. "Upgrading Brazil's Political Class: A Scandal-Ridden Congress Must Reform Itself." *The Economist*, March 30.

Benites, Afonso. 2018. "Aécio Neves, réu na Lava Jato e um fardo incontornável para o PSDB." *El País Brasil*, April 17.

Benson, Todd, and Asher Levine. 2013. "Biggest Protests in 20 Years Sweep Brazil." Reuters, June 17.

Bentham, Jeremy. 1843 [2011]. *The Works of Jeremy Bentham*, vol. 1 (Principles of Morals and Legislation, Fragment on Government, Civil Code, Penal Law). Indianapolis: Liberty Fund. http://files.libertyfund.org/files/2009/Bentham_0872-01_EBk_v6.0.pdf.

Bento, Juliane S., Luciano Da Ros, and Bruno A. Londero. 2020. "Condenando políticos corruptos? Análise quantitativa dos julgamentos de prefeitos municipais pelo Tribunal de Justiça do Rio Grande do Sul (1992–2016)." *Civitas—Revista de Ciências Sociais* 20 (3): 348–376.

Bersch, Katherine. 2019. *When Democracies Deliver: Governance Reform in Latin America*. New York: Cambridge University Press.

Bersch, Katherine, and Gregory Michener. 2013. "Identifying Transparency." *Information Polity* 18: 233–242.

Bersch, Katherine, Sérgio Praça, and Matthew M. Taylor. 2017a. "State Capacity and Bureaucratic Autonomy Within National States: Mapping the Archipelago of Excellence in Brazil." In Miguel Angel Centeno, Atul Kohli, and Deborah Yashar, eds. *State Building in the Developing World*, 157–183. Cambridge: Cambridge University Press.

Bersch, Katherine, Sérgio Praça, and Matthew M. Taylor. 2017b. "State Capacity, Bureaucratic Politicization, and Corruption in the Brazilian State." *Governance* 30 (1): 105–124.

Bertim, Felipe. 2020. "Wassef, o fiel advogado que virou uma bomba prestes a explodir." *El País Brasil*, June 24.

Beyerle, Shaazka. 2014. *Curtailing Corruption: People Power for Accountability and Justice*. Boulder, CO: Lynne Rienner Publishers.

Bickel, Alexander. 1986 [1962]. *The Least Dangerous Branch: The Supreme Court at the Bar of Politics*. New Haven: Yale University Press.

Boas, Taylor C., F. Daniel Hidalgo, and Marcus André Melo. 2019. "Norms Versus Action: Why Voters Fail to Sanction Malfeasance in Brazil." *American Journal of Political Science* 63 (2): 385–400.

Boas, Taylor C., F. Daniel Hidalgo, and Neal P. Richardson. 2014. "The Spoils of Victory: Campaign Donations and Government Contracts in Brazil." *Journal of Politics* 76: 415–429.

Bogéa, Daniel, and Luciano Da Ros. 2020. "Limitando supremas cortes: perspectivas analíticas sobre *Court Curbing* e pedidos de impeachment de ministros do Supremo Tribunal Federal." Paper presented at the 12th meeting of the Brazilian Political Science Association.

Bohn, Simone Rodrigues da Silva, David Fleischer, and Francisco Whitacker. 2002. "A Fiscalização Das Eleições." In Bruno Wilhelm Speck, ed. *Caminhos Da Transparência*, 335–354. São Paulo: Editora da Universidade Estadual de Campinas.

Bomfim, Camila. 2017. "Geddel Vieira Lima vira réu por obstrução de Justiça." *G1*, August 22.

Bomfim, Camila. 2018. "Geddel, Cunha, Henrique Alves e mais 15 viram réus na Operação Cui Bono." *G1*, November 14.

Bomfim, Camila. 2019. "Saída de procurador coloca em risco Operação Zelotes, afirma Ministério Público Federal do DF." *G1*, July 23.

Bonin, Robson. 2010. "Popularidade de Lula bate recorde e chega a 87%, diz Ibope." *G1*, December 16.

Bonin, Robson. 2014. "Dilma e Lula sabiam de tudo, diz Alberto Youssef à PF." *Veja*, October 23.

Bonvecchi, Alejandro. 2015. "Review: 'Melo and Pereira, Making Brazil Work.'" *Perspectives on Politics* 13: 901–902.

Borba, Julia. 2012. "'Governo vive momento tenso,' diz Carvalho sobre base aliada." *Folha de S. Paulo*, March 8.

Borges, André. 2021. "The Illusion of Electoral Stability: From Party System Erosion to Right-Wing Populism in Brazil." *Journal of Politics in Latin America* 13 (2): 166–191.

Borges, Laryssa. 2014. "STF anula provas apreendidas em HD da Opportunity." *Veja*, December 16.

Borges, Laryssa. 2021. "Bretas é acusado de negociar penas, orientar advogados e combinar com o MP." *Veja*, June 4.

Botero, Sandra, Daniel Brinks, and Ezequiel Gonzalez-Ocantos, eds. Forthcoming. *The Limits of Judicialization: Progress and Backlash in Latin American Politics.* Cambridge: Cambridge University Press.

Bovens, Mark. 2007. "Analyzing and Assessing Accountability: A Conceptual Framework." *European Law Journal* 13: 447–468.

Braga, Maria do Socorro Sousa. 2008. "Organizações partidárias e seleção de candidatos no estado de São Paulo." *Opinião Pública* 14 (2): 454–485.

Braga, Maria do Socorro Sousa, Flávio Contrera, and Priscilla Leine Cassotta. 2018. "O Ministério Público na Operação Lava Jato: como eles chegaram até aqui?" In Fábio Kerche and João Feres Jr., eds. *Operação Lava Jato e a democracia brasileira*, 137–198. São Paulo: Contracorrente.

Bragon, Ranier. 2020. "Novo aliado, Jefferson posta foto com arma e pede que Bolsonaro 'demita' ministros do STF." *Folha de S. Paulo*, May 9.

Bragon, Ranier, and Danielle Brant. 2021. "Reforma política na Câmara recicla propostas e quer frear TSE e poupar fichas-sujas." *Folha de S. Paulo*, May 22.

Bramatti, Daniel. 1997. "Presidente de comissão diz que só CPI poderá chegar aos corruptores." *Folha de S. Paulo*, May 18.

Bramatti, Daniel, and Marcelo Godoy. 2021. "Sob Bolsonaro, PF prende e apura menos." *O Estado de S. Paulo*, April 23.

Brandão, Marcelo. 2019. "Temer vira réu por corrupção no caso da mala, envolvendo Rocha Loures." *Agência Brasil*, March 28.

Brandt, Ricardo, and Fausto Macedo. 2019. "Decano da Lava Jato se aposenta do MPF e vai dar consultoria anticorrupção para empresas." *O Estado de S. Paulo*, March 18.

Brant, Danielle, and Ranier Bragon. 2021. "Proposta na Câmara esvazia fiscalização sobre contas dos partidos, que usam R$ 1 bi por ano em verba pública." *Folha de S. Paulo*, June 25.

Brasília Assombrada. 2017. "Anões do Orçamento: o pivô do escândalo já está solto." *Jornal de Brasília*, August 1. https://jornaldebrasilia.com.br/blogs-e-colunas/brasilia-assombrada/anoes-do-orcamento-o-pivo-do-escandalo-ja-esta-solto/.

Brasiliense, Ronaldo. 2005. "Escândalo da Sudam: todos ricos, todos soltos!" *Congresso em Foco*, December 16.

Bresser-Pereira, Luiz Carlos. 1996. "Da administração pública burocrática à gerencial." *Revista de Serviço Público* 47: 7–39.

Bresser-Pereira, Luiz Carlos. 2009. "From Old to New Developmentalism in Latin America." In José Antonio Ocampo, ed. *Handbook of Latin American Economics*. Oxford: Oxford University Press.

Bretas, Valéria. 2015. "Em 3 décadas, STF só condenou 16 políticos por corrupção." *Revista Exame*, September 22.

Breve, Nelson. 2006. "Quem se lembra do caso da máfia dos precatórios do DNER?" *Carta Maior*, October 26.

Brígido, Carolina. 2014. "STF abre processo contra Jader Barbalho pelo desvio de R$ 22,8 milhões da Sudam." *O Globo*, October 8.

Brígido, Carolina. 2019. "Ministro do STF suspende fundação da Lava Jato para gerir até 25 bilhões da Petrobras." *O Globo*, March 15.

Brinks, Daniel M., Steven Levitsky, and Maria Victoria Murillo. 2020. "The Political Origins of Institutional Weakness." In Daniel M. Brinks, Steven Levitsky, and Maria Victoria Murillo, eds. *The Politics of Institutional Weakness in Latin America*, 1–40. Cambridge: Cambridge University Press.

Bruno, Cássio. 2015. "Brasil tem quase 6 mil processos relativos a crimes financeiros; Justiça tem 27 varas específicas para esses casos." *O Globo*, July 27.

Buehler, Michael. 2019. "Indonesia Takes a Wrong Turn in Crusade Against Corruption." *Financial Times*, October 2.

Bulla, Beatriz, and Cortney Newell. 2020. "Sunlight Is the Best Disinfectant: Investigative Journalism in the Age of Lava Jato." In Paul F. Lagunes and Jan Svejnar, eds. *Corruption and the Lava Jato Scandal in Latin America*, 82–93. New York: Routledge.

Burbank, Stephen B., and Barry Friedman. 2002. "Reconsidering Judicial Independence." In Stephen B. Burbank and Barry Friedman, eds. *Judicial Independence at the Crossroads: An Interdisciplinary Approach*. Thousand Oaks: Sage.

Butt, Simon. 2019. "Indonesia's Anti-Corruption Courts and the Persistence of Judicial Culture." In Melissa Crouch, ed. *The Politics of Court Reform: Judicial Change and Legal Culture in Indonesia*. Cambridge: Cambridge University Press.

Butt, Simon, and Sofie A. Schütte. 2014. "Assessing Judicial Performance in Indonesia: The Court for Corruption Crimes." *Crime, Law and Social Change* 62 (5): 603–619.

Cadah, Lucas Queija, and Danilo de Pádua Centurione. 2011. "As CPIs acabam em pizza? Uma resposta sobre o desempenho das Comissões Parlamentares de Inquérito no presidencialismo de coalizão." In Álvaro Moisés, ed. *O papel do Congresso Nacional no presidencialismo de coalizão*, 91–97. Rio de Janeiro: Konrad-Adenauer-Stiftung.

Câmara dos Deputados. 1997. "Projeto de Lei n. 2.688/1996." http://imagem.camara.gov.br/Imagem/d/pdf/DCD06FEV1997.pdf#page=97.

Câmara dos Deputados. 2017. "Projeto de Lei n. 6.814/2017." https://www.camara.leg.br/proposicoesWeb/fichadetramitacao?idProposicao=2122766.

Campanerut, Camila. 2013. "Dilma é aprovada por 79% e supera Lula e FHC." *UOL*, March 19.

Campello, Daniela, Anya Schiffrin, Karine Belarmino, and Debora Thome. 2020. "Captured Media? Examining Brazilian Coverage of Lava Jato." In Paul F. Lagunes and Jan Svejnar, eds. *Corruption and the Lava Jato Scandal in Latin America*. New York: Routledge.

Camporez, Patrik. 2020. "Sob Mendonça, órgão federal que investiga crime organizado e pedofilia passa a monitorar opositores." *O Estado de S. Paulo*, July 25.

Campos, Pedro Henrique Pedreira. 2014. *Estranhas Catedrais: As Empreiteiras Brasileiras E a Ditadura Civil-Militar, 1964–1988*. Niterói: Editora da UFF.

Canário, Pedro. 2014a. "Outra queixa crime de Daniel Dantas contra Protógenes chega ao STF." *Consultor Jurídico*, October 17.

Canário, Pedro. 2014b. "Procuradores da "lava jato" estão preocupados com nulidades processuais." *Consultor Jurídico*, December 6.

Canário, Pedro. 2017. "Criticadas por Gilmar, preventivas da 'lava jato' duram em media 9,3 meses." *Consultor Jurídico*, February 7.

Canofre, Fernanda, Camila Mattoso, and Ranier Bragon. 2019. "Ministro do Turismo é denunciado pelo Ministério Público no caso dos laranjas do PSL." *Folha de S. Paulo*, October 4.

Canzian, Fernando. 2020. "Servidores do Brasil concentram 6 das 10 ocupações mais bem pagas." *Folha de S. Paulo*, August 24.

Carazza, Bruno. 2018. *Dinheiro, eleições e poder: as engrenagens do sistema político brasileiro*. São Paulo: Companhia das Letras.

Carlin, Ryan E., Gregory J. Love, and Cecilia Martínez-Gallardo. 2014. "Cushioning the Fall: Scandals, Economic Conditions, and Executive Approval." *Political Behavior* 37 (1): 109–130.

Carrança, Thais. 2021. "'Tratoraço': entenda o suposto 'orçamento secreto' de Bolsonaro, que deverá ser investigado pelo TCU." BBC Brasil, May 12.

Carreirão, Yan de Souza. 2007. "Identificação Ideológica, Partidos E Voto Na Eleição Presidencial De 2006." *Opinião Pública* 13: 307–339.

Carreirão, Yan de Souza. 2014. "O sistema partidário brasileiro: um debate com a literatura recente." *Revista Brasileira de Ciência Política* 14: 255–295.

Carson, Lindsey D., and Mariana Mota Prado. 2016. "Using Institutional Multiplicity to Address Corruption as a Collective Action Problem: Lessons from the Brazilian Case." *The Quarterly Review of Economics and Finance* 62: 56–65.

Carta Capital. 2017. "Como o governo Temer desidratou o Ministério da Transparência." *Carta Capital*, June 30.

Carvalho, Daniel, Julia Chaib, and Gustavo Uribe. 2020. "Bolsonaro quer turbinar centrão com cargos para se blindar após agravamento do caso Queiroz." *Folha de S. Paulo*, June 20.

Carvalho, Daniel, and Ricardo Della Coletta. 2019. "Senado aprova versão desidratada de pacote anticrime de Moro." *Folha de S. Paulo*, December 11.

Carvalho, Fernando J. Cardim de. 2016. "Looking into the Abyss? Brazil at the Mid-2010s." *Journal of Post Keynesian Economics* 39: 93–114.

Carvalho, Mario Cesar, and Wálter Nunes. 2017. "Lava Jato acelerou processos, mas 'direito penal de Curitiba' é criticado." *Folha de S. Paulo*, November 11.

Carvalho, Mario Cesar, and Wálter Nunes. 2018. "Dinheiro recuperado na Operação Lava Jato cai 90%." *Folha de S. Paulo*, January 3.

Carvalho, Victor Aguiar de. 2020. "The Shortcomings of the Leniency Agreement Provisions of Brazil's Clean Company Act." *Global Anticorruption Blog*, February 3. https://globalanticorruptionblog.com.

Casas-Zamora, Kevin. 2016. "The State of Political Finance Regulations in Latin America." IDEA Discussion Paper No. 12/2016.

Casas-Zamora, Kevin, and Miguel Carter. 2017. "Beyond the Scandals: The Changing Context of Corruption in Latin America." Inter-American Dialogue Report.

Cassin, Richard L. 2018a. "Petrobras Reaches $1.78 Billion FCPA Resolution." *The FCPA Blog*, September 27. https://fcpablog.com/2018/09/27/petrobras-reaches-178-billion-fcpa-resolution/.

Cassin, Richard L. 2018b. "Petrobras Smashes the Top Ten List (and We Explain Why)." *The FCPA Blog*, September 28. https://fcpablog.com/2018/09/28/petrobras-smashes-the-top-ten-list-and-we-explain-why/.

Castagnola, Andrea. 2012. "I Want It All, and I Want It Now: The Political Manipulation of Argentina's Provincial High Courts." *Journal of Politics in Latin America* 4 (2): 39–62.

Castagnola, Andrea. 2018. *Manipulating Courts in New Democracies: Forcing Judges off the Bench in Argentina*. New York: Routledge.

Castro, José Roberto. 2017. "A cronologia do caso JBS: pressão, delação e questionamentos." *Nexo*, September 5.

Castro, Monica, and Felipe Nunes. 2014. "Candidatos corruptos são punidos? *Accountability* na eleição brasileira de 2006." *Opinião Pública* 20 (1): 26–48.

Centre for Law and Democracy. 2020. "Global Right to Information Rating [conducted in 2011]." https://www.rti-rating.org/country-data/.

Cerioni, Clara. 2020. "Entenda a Lei de Abuso de Autoridade, que começa a valer hoje." *Exame*, January 3.

Ceron, Andrea, and Marco Mainent. 2015. "Toga Party: The Political Basis of Judicial Investigations Against MPs in Italy (1983–2013)." *South European Society & Politics* 20 (2): 223–242.

Chaisty, Paul, Nic Cheeseman, and Timothy J. Power. 2018. *Coalitional Presidentialism in Comparative Perspective: Minority Presidents in Multiparty Systems.* Oxford: Oxford University Press.

Chang, Eric C. C. 2005. "Electoral Incentives for Political Corruption Under Open-List Proportional Representation." *Journal of Politics* 67: 716–730.

Clark, Tom S. 2009. "The Separation of Powers, Court Curbing, and Judicial Legitimacy." *American Journal of Political Science* 53 (4): 971–989.

Coelho, Marja Pfeifer. 2013. "O acontecimento público Satiagraha, entre Estado e mídia." PhD diss., Graduate Program in Communication and Information, Universidade Federal do Rio Grande do Sul.

Cohen, Michael D., James G. March, and Johan P. Olsen. 1972. "A Garbage Can Model of Organizational Choice." *Administrative Science Quarterly* 17 (1): 1–25.

Colazingari, Silvia, and Susan Rose-Ackerman. 1998. "Corruption in a Paternalistic Democracy: Lessons from Italy for Latin America." *Political Science Quarterly* 113 (3): 447–470.

Collier, Paul. 2006. "African Growth: Why a 'Big Push'?" *Journal of African Economies* 15: 188–211.

Conselho Nacional do Ministério Público (CNMP). 2015. "Ministério Público: Um retrato, dados de 2014, volume IV." Brasília: CNMP.

Consultor Jurídico. 2004. "Relatório da CPI do Banestado aponta evasão de R$150 bilhões." December 14.

Consultor Jurídico. 2008. "Daniel Dantas é condenado a 10 anos de prisão por corrupção ativa." December 2.

Consultor Jurídico. 2009a. "Ministério da Justiça bloqueia US$ 2 bilhões relacionados à Satiagraha." January 22.

Consultor Jurídico. 2009b. "Corrêa é acusada de desfalque de R$71 milhões à União." March 26.

Consultor Jurídico. 2009c. "Investigados na Castelo de Areia são presos ao tentar sacar dinheiro." June 23.

Consultor Jurídico. 2009d. "Parlamentares vão ao STJ pedir controle externo da Polícia Federal." April 6.

Consultor Jurídico. 2010. "Relatório aponta que Brasil não consegue combater lavagem de dinheiro." February 15.

Consultor Jurídico. 2014. "Em 2014, casos do STJ foram da Copa do Mundo à operação 'Lava Jato.'" December 14.

Consultor Jurídico. 2016. "Lava jato não precisa seguir regras de casos comuns, decide TRF-4." September 23, 2016.

Controladoría Geral da União (CGU). 2016. "Relatório de acompanhamento das punições expulsivas aplicadas a estatutários no âmbito da administração pública federal." December. http://www.cgu.gov.br/assuntos/atividade-disciplinar/relatorios-de-punicoes-expulsivas/arquivos/consolidado-por-ano-2003-a-2016.pdf.

Coppedge, Michael, John Gerring, Carl Henrik Knutsen, Staffan I. Lindberg, Jan Teorell, David Altman, Michael Bernhard, et al. 2020. "V-Dem [Country-Year/Country-Date] Dataset v10." Varieties of Democracy (V-Dem) Project. https://doi.org/10.23696/vdemds20.

Cordeiro, Nathalia Rodrigues. 2014. "Accountability e reputação: financiamento de campanhas e reeleição de deputados envolvidos em escândalos de corrupção (2002–2006)." PhD diss., Programa de Pós-Graduação em Políticas Públicas, Estratégias e Desenvolvimento, UFRJ.

Cordis, Adriana S., and Jeffrey Milyo. 2016. "Measuring Public Corruption in the United States: Evidence from Administrative Records of Federal Prosecutions." *Public Integrity* 18 (2): 127–148.

Corkery, Michael. 2019. "A 'Sorceress' in Brazil, a 'Wink' in India: Walmart Pleads Guilty After a Decade of Bribes." *New York Times*, June 20.

Corrêa, Hudson. 2009. "Estatal afasta acusado no caso Sarney." *Folha de S.Paulo,* September 5.

Corrêa, Izabela Moreira. 2011. "Sistema de integridade: avanços e agenda de ação para a administração pública federal." In Leonardo Avritzer and Fernando Filgueiras, eds. *Corrupção e sistema político no Brasil,* 163–190. Rio de Janeiro: Editora Civilização Brasileira.

Correio Braziliense. 2008. "Dantas manda 'recados' em depoimento à CPI dos grampos." August 13.

Correio Braziliense. 2009. "Jader Barbalho é denunciado por desvios na Sudam." October 16. https://www.correiobraziliense.com.br/app/noticia/politica/2009/10 /16/interna_politica,148872/jader-barbalho-e-denunciado-por-desvios-na -sudam.shtml.

Correio Braziliense. 2011. "Caso Sudam completa 10 anos e R$ 4 milhões desviados não foram devolvidos." March 27. https://www.correiobraziliense.com.br /app/noticia/politica/2011/03/27/interna_politica,244788/caso-sudam-completa-dez -anos-e-r-4-milhoes-desviados-nao-foram-devolvidos.shtml.

Correio Braziliense. 2016. "Operação Greenfield prende empresários e Justiça bloqueia R$ 8 bilhões." September 5. https://www.correiobraziliense.com.br/app /noticia/economia/2016/09/05/internas_economia,547376/operacao-greenfield -prende-empresarios-e-justica-bloqueia-r-8-bilhoes.shtml.

Correio Braziliense. 2019. "Raquel Dodge se opõe a anular condenação de Eduardo Cunha na Lava Jato." May 27. https://www.correiobraziliense.com.br/app/noticia /politica/2019/05/27/interna_politica,757822/raquel-dodge-se-opoe-a-anular -condenacao-de-cunha-na-lava-jato.shtml.

Cosso, Roberto. 2003. "Esquema nos EUA 'lavou' US$ 30 bilhões." *Folha de S. Paulo,* February 3.

Costa, Arthur Trindade Maranhão, Bruno Amaral Machado, and Cristina Zackseski. 2016. *A investigação e a persecução penal da corrupção e dos delitos econômicos: uma pesquisa empírica no sistema de justiça federal.* Brasília: Escola Superior do Ministério Público da União.

CPMI (Comissão Parlamentar Mista de Inquérito "Dos Correios"). 2006. *Relatório Final dos trabalhos da CPMI "dos Correios."* Brasília: Congresso Nacional.

Crowe, Justin. 2007. "The Forging of Judicial Autonomy: Political Entrepreneurship and the Reforms of William Howard Taft." *Journal of Politics* 69 (1): 73–87.

Crowe, Justin. 2012. *Building the Judiciary: Law, Courts, and the Politics of Institutional Development.* Princeton: Princeton University Press.

Cunha, Alexandre dos Santos, Bernardo Abreu de Medeiros, and Luseni Maria C. de Aquino. 2010. "Corrupção e controles democráticos no Brasil." In Alexandre dos Santos Cunha, Bernardo Abreu de Medeiros, and Luseni Maria C. de Aquino, eds. *Estado, instituições e democracia: República.* Brasília: IPEA.

Cunha Filho, Marcio Camargo. 2019. "A construção da transparência pública no Brasil: análise da elaboração e implementação da Lei de Acesso à Informação no Executivo Federal (2003–2018)." PhD diss., University of Brasília.

Cunha Filho, Marcio, Gregory Michener, and Bernardo Schwaitzer. 2021. "Conspicuous Noncompliance in Transparency Regimes: Lessons from Brazil." Paper presented at the 26th International Political Science Association World Congress.

Cury, Teo. 2018. "Processos contra juízes travam na esfera criminal." *O Estado de S. Paulo,* July 16.

Da Costa, Agustinis Beo, and Stanley Widianto. 2019. "Indonesia Revises Law to Put Checks on Anti-Graft Agency, Sparks Protests." Reuters, September 17.

D'Agostino, Rosanne. 2016. "O que dizem advogados sobre Renan não cumprir decisão do STF." *G1,* December 6.

D'Agostino, Rosanne, and Marian Oliveira. 2019. "Por 10 votos a 1, STF define regra para que Coaf, Receita e MP compartilhem dados sigilosos." *G1,* December 4.

Dahl, Robert A. 1957. "Decision-Making in a Democracy: The Supreme Court as a National Policy-Maker." *Journal of Public Law* 6: 279–295.

Dallagnol, Deltan Martinazzo. 2017a. *A luta contra a corrupção: a Lava Jato e o futuro de um país marcado pela impunidade*. São Paulo: Primeira Pessoa.

Dallagnol, Deltan Martinazzo. 2017b. "Artigo: Um indulto sob medida para estancar a sangria." *UOL*, December 24.

DaMatta, Roberto. 1979. *Carnavais, malandros e heróis: para uma sociologia do dilema brasileiro*. Rio de Janeiro: Zahar Editores.

DaMatta, Roberto. 1993. "Is Brazil Hopelessly Corrupt?" *New York Times*. Reprinted in Robert M. Levine and John J. Crocitti, eds. 1999. *The Brazil Reader: History, Culture, Politics*, 295–297. Durham: Duke University Press.

Damé, Luiza. 1997. "CCJ absolve deputados acusados de apoiar reeleição por R$ 200 mil." *Folha de S. Paulo*, October 9.

Damé, Luiza, and Denise Madueño. 1998. "Naya é cassado por margem de 20 votos." *Folha de S. Paulo*, April 16.

Damgaard, Mads B. 2018a. *Media Leaks and Corruption in Brazil: The Infostorm of Impeachment and the Lava-Jato Scandal*. New York: Routledge.

Damgaard, Mads. 2018b. "Cascading Corruption News: Explaining the Bias of Media Attention to Brazil's Political Scandals." *Opinião Pública* 24: 114–143.

Daniele, Giancarlo, Sergio Galletta, and Benny Geys. 2020. "Abandon Ship? Party Brands and Politicians' Responses to a Political Scandal." *Journal of Public Economics* 184: 1–13.

Dantas, Tiago. 2015. "'Como pode colocar um político para julgar empreiteiras?' questiona Modesto Carvalhosa." *O Globo*, March 23.

Da Ros, Luciano. 2010. "Judges in the Formation of the Nation-State: Professional Experiences, Academic Background and Geographic Circulation of Members of the Supreme Courts of Brazil and the United States." *Brazilian Political Science Review* 4 (1): 102–130.

Da Ros, Luciano. 2012. "Juízes profissionais? Padrões de carreira dos integrantes das Supremas Cortes de Brasil (1829–2008) e Estados Unidos (1789–2008)." *Revista de Sociologia e Política* 20 (41): 149–169.

Da Ros, Luciano. 2013. "Difícil hierarquia: a avaliação do Supremo Tribunal Federal pelos magistrados da base do Poder Judiciário no Brasil." *Revista Direito GV* 9 (1): 47–64.

Da Ros, Luciano. 2014. "Mayors in the Dock: Judicial Responses to Local Corruption in Brazil." PhD diss., University of Illinois at Chicago.

Da Ros, Luciano. 2015. "O custo da justiça no Brasil: uma abordagem comparativa exploratória." *Newsletter do Observatório de Elites Políticas e Sociais do Brasil* 2 (9): 1–15.

Da Ros, Luciano. 2018. "As instituições estaduais de controle externo das prefeituras municipais no Brasil." In André Marenco and Maria Izabel Noll, eds. *A política, as políticas e os controles: como são governadas as cidades brasileiras*. Porto Alegre: Tomo Editorial.

Da Ros, Luciano. 2019a. "Accountability Legal e Corrupção." *Revista da CGU* 11 (20): 1251–1275.

Da Ros, Luciano. 2019b. "Korruption des öffentlichen Sektors in Brasilien: Eine Übersicht." In Katrin Möltgen-Sicking, Henrique Ricardo Otten, Malte Schophaus, and Soraya Vargas Côrtes, eds. *Öffentliche Verwaltung in Brasilien und Deutschland*, 233–265. Wiesbaden: Springer.

Da Ros, Luciano, and André Marenco. 2008. "Caminhos que levam à Corte: carreiras e padrões de recrutamento dos ministros dos órgãos da cúpula do poder judiciário brasileiro (1829–2006)." *Revista de Sociologia e Política* 16: 131–149.

Da Ros, Luciano, Luísa Z. Fontoura, Sérgio Simoni Jr., and Matthew M. Taylor. 2021. "Moro's Opinions: A Quantitative Assessment of Sentences in the Carwash Operation." Working paper.

Da Ros, Luciano, and Matthew C. Ingram. 2018. "Law, Courts, and Judicial Politics." In Barry Ames, ed. *Routledge Handbook of Brazilian Politics*, 339–357. New York: Routledge.

Da Ros, Luciano, and Matthew M. Taylor. 2019. "Juízes eficientes, judiciário ineficiente no Brasil pós-1988." *Revista Brasileira de Informações Bibliográficas em Ciências Sociais* 89: 1–31.

Da Ros, Luciano, and Matthew M. Taylor. 2021a. "*Accountability* na Era Bolsonaro: continuidades e mudanças." In Leonardo Avritzer, Fábio Kerche, and Marjorie Marjona, eds. *Governo Bolsonaro: retrocesso democrático e degradação política*, 187–204. São Paulo: Autêntica.

Da Ros, Luciano, and Matthew M. Taylor. 2021b. "O Supremo Tribunal Criminal: Entre Primeira e Última Instância da Elite Política." Working paper.

Da Ros, Luciano, and Matthew M. Taylor. 2021c. "Checks and Balances: The Concept and Its Implications for Corruption." *Revista Direito GV* 17 (2): 1–30.

Da Ros, Luciano, and Matthew M. Taylor. Forthcoming. "Kickbacks, Crackdown, and Backlash: Legal Accountability in the Lava Jato Investigation." In Sandra Botero, Daniel M. Brinks, and Ezequiel González-Ocantos, eds. *The Limits of Judicialization: Progress and Backlash in Latin American Politics*. Cambridge: Cambridge University Press.

Datafolha. 2019. "Lava Jato." April 5. Results of poll by *Folha de S. Paulo* and Datafolha. http://media.folha.uol.com.br/datafolha/2019/04/15/e4dffffcgsd52vfa68d5a 60e89b35922lj.pdf.

Dávila, Sérgio. 2016. "A opinião pública e os grandes casos criminais: perspectivas no Brasil." http://www.cnmp.mp.br/portal/images/PGR_jun2016_Sergio_Davila .pdf.

Davis, Kevin E. Forthcoming. "Anticorruption Law and Systemic Corruption: The Role of Direct Responses." *Revista Direito GV*.

Della Coletta, Ricardo, Daniel Carvalho, and Gustavo Uribe. 2020. "Eu acabei com a Lava Jato porque não tem mais corrupção no governo, diz Bolsonaro." *Folha de S. Paulo*, October 7.

Della Porta, Donatella. 2001. "A Judges' Revolution? Political Corruption and the Judiciary in Italy." *European Journal of Political Research* 39 (1): 1–21.

Della Porta, Donatella, and Alberto Vannucci. 1997. "The 'Perverse Effects' of Political Corruption." *Political Studies* 45 (3): 516–538.

Della Porta, Donatella, and Alberto Vannucci. 1999. *Corrupt Exchanges: Actors, Resources, and Mechanisms of Political Corruption*. Piscataway, NJ: Transaction Publishers.

Della Porta, Donatella, and Alberto Vannucci. 2007. "Corruption and Anti-Corruption: The Political Defeat of 'Clean Hands' in Italy." *West European Politics* 30 (4): 830–853.

Della Porta, Donatella, and Alberto Vannucci. 2016. *The Hidden Order of Corruption: An Institutional Approach*. New York: Routledge.

De Sanctis, Fausto. 2017. Matthew Taylor interview with Judge Fausto De Sanctis. September 25.

Deutsche Welle. 2021. "Como compras de vacina enredaram Bolsonaro em escândalos." July 6.

Dewatripont, Mathias, and Gérard Roland. 1995. "The Design of Reform Packages Under Uncertainty." *American Economic Review* 85 (December): 1207–1223.

Éboli, Evandro. 2009. "Castelo de Areia e TCU." *O Globo*, March 28.

Economist. 2014. "Hard to Read: The New Anti-Bribery Law Is No Panacea." January 29.

Economist Intelligence Unit. 2018. *Democracy Index 2017: Free Speech Under Attack*. London: Economist Intelligence Unit Limited.

El País Brasil. 2015. "Operação Zelotes esbarra em falta de equipe e apoio do Judiciário." April 10.

Engelmann, Fabiano. 2020. "The 'Fight Against Corruption' in Brazil from the 2000s: A Political Crusade Through Judicial Activism." *Journal of Law and Society* 47 (S1): S74–S89.

Engelmann, Fabiano, and Eduardo M. Menuzzi. 2020. "The Internationalization of the Brazilian Public Prosecutor's Office: Anti-Corruption and Corporate Investments in the 2000s." *Brazilian Political Science Review* 14 (1): 1–35.

Época. 2017. "Moro: 'sem Teori, não teria havido Operação Lava Jato.'" January 19.

Época Negócios. 2016. "Michel Temer faz seu primeiro discurso: 'Não fale em crise, trabalhe.'" May 12. https://epocanegocios.globo.com/Brasil/noticia/2016/05/michel-temer-faz-seu-primeiro-discurso-e-ministros-tomam-posse.html.

Epperly, Brad. 2019. *The Political Foundations of Judicial Supremacy in Dictatorship and Democracy.* Oxford: Oxford University Press.

Epstein, Lee, and Jack Knight. 1998. *The Choices Justices Make.* Washington, DC: Congressional Quarterly Press.

Escresa, Laarni, and Lucio Picci. 2020. "The Determinants of Cross-Border Corruption." *Public Choice* 184: 351–378.

Eskridge, William N., Jr. 1991. "Overriding Supreme Court Statutory Interpretation Decisions." *Yale Law Journal* 101: 331–455.

Exame. 2017. "Em gravação, delatores da JBS citam três ministros do STF." September 5.

Extra. 2013. "Ranking da corrupção: entrevistados em pesquisa acham que policiais fazem vista grossa a colegas corruptos." April 4.

Fabrini, Fábio, and Camila Mattoso. 2019. "Decisão de Toffoli sobre Coaf trava ao menos 700 investigações na Justiça." *Folha de S. Paulo*, October 26.

Fabrini, Fábio, and Letícia Casado. 2018. "Ex-ministro Mantega vira réu na Operação Zelotes." *Folha de S. Paulo*, March 12.

Fagundes, Andréa Lucas. 2018. "Inteligência, estratégia e ação: o desenvolvimento institucional da Polícia Federal no combate à corrupção (1988–2018)." Mimeo, Universidade Federal do Rio Grande do Sul.

Falcão, Joaquim, et al. 2017. *V Relatório Supremo em Números: O Foro Privilegiado e o Supremo.* Rio de Janeiro: Escola de Direito do Rio de Janeiro da Fundação Getúlio Vargas.

Falcão, Márcio, and Mateus Rodrigues. 2021. "Justiça Federal absolve Lula e Gilberto Carvalho em ação por corrupção passiva na Zelotes." *G1*, June 21.

Favero, Daniel. 2013. "Lembre do escândalo dos Anões do Orçamento que completa 20 anos." *Terra*, November 18.

Ferejohn, John. 1998. "Independent Judges, Dependent Judiciary: Explaining Judicial Independence." *Southern California Law Review* 72: 353–384.

Feres, João, Jr., Eduardo Barbarela, and Natasha Bachini. 2018. "A Lava Jato e a mídia." In Fábio Kerche and João Feres Jr., eds. *Operação Lava Jato e a democracia brasileira*, 199–228. São Paulo: Contracorrente.

Fernandes, Talita, and Beatriz Bulla. 2015. "O caminho da Lava Jato até o Supremo." *O Estado de S. Paulo*, March 6.

Ferraz, Claudio, and Frederico Finan. 2008. "Exposing Corrupt Politicians: The Effect of Brazil's Anti-Corruption Program on Electoral Outcomes." *Quarterly Journal of Economics* 123: 703–745.

Ferraz, Claudio, and Frederico Finan. 2011. "Electoral Accountability and Corruption: Evidence from the Audits of Local Governments." *American Economic Review* 101: 1274–1311.

Ferraz, Lucas. 2015. "Maioria foi às ruas contra corrupção, diz Datafolha." *Folha de S. Paulo*, March 17.

FIESP. 2010. "Relatório—Corrupção: custos econômicos e propostas de combate." March. www.fiesp.com.br/arquivo-download/?id=2021.

Filgueiras, Fernando, and Mateus M. Araújo. 2014. "A política anticorrupção e o marco legal No Brasil." In Isabel Ferin Cunha and Estrela Serrano, eds. *Cober-*

tura jornalística da corrupção: Sistemas políticos, sistemas midiáticos e enqua-dramentos legais, 36–71. Lisbon: Alêtheia Editores.

Financial Action Task Force (FATF-GAFI). 2010. "Mutual Evaluation Report of the Federative Republic of Brazil—Executive Summary: Anti-Money Laundering and Combating the Financing of Terrorism." June 25. https://www.fatf-gafi .org/media/fatf/documents/reports/mer/MER%20Brazil%20ES.pdf.

Fischer, Douglas. 2008. "Satiagraha, Gandhi, and George Orwell." *Interesse público* (blog). July. http://blogdofred.folha.blog.uol.com.br/arch2008-07-06_2008-07 -12.html. Accessed April 2015.

Fisman, Ray, and Miriam A. Golden. 2017. *Corruption: What Everyone Needs to Know*. Oxford: Oxford University Press.

Fleischer, David. 1997. "Political Corruption in Brazil: The Delicate Connection with Campaign Finance." *Crime, Law, and Social Change* 25: 297–321.

Fleischer, David, and Leonardo Barreto. 2009. "El impacto de la justicia electoral sobre el sistema político brasileño." *América Latina Hoy* 51: 117–138.

Folha de Pernambuco. 2017a. "Fim de força-tarefa da PF é retrocesso, dizem procu-radores da Lava Jato." July 6.

Folha de Pernambuco. 2017b. "Polícia Federal encerra grupo da Lava Jato em Curitiba." July 6.

Folha de S. Paulo. 1994. "Denúncia motivou CPI em 1988." November 20.

Folha de S. Paulo. 1997a. "Cúpula do PFL expulsa Ronivon Santiago e João Maia do partido." May 15.

Folha de S. Paulo. 1997b. "Saiba como foi feita a compra." May 18.

Folha de S. Paulo. 1997c. "Trechos das fitas são explícitos sobre Motta." May 21.

Folha de S. Paulo. 1999. "Precatórios: Padilha afasta envolvidos em fraude." Novem-ber 4.

Folha de S. Paulo. 2000a. "Justiça cassa bens de dez acusados de desviar dinheiro do Banestado." August 8.

Folha de S. Paulo. 2000b. "Saiba quem é Francisco Lopes." June 8.

Folha de S. Paulo. 2001. "Advogados contestam acusação de desvio de dinheiro." March 18.

Folha de S. Paulo. 2002a. "Entenda o escândalo das obras do TRT-SP." June 28.

Folha de S. Paulo. 2002b. "PF transfere ao DF caso que envolve pefelista." June 18.

Folha de S. Paulo. 2002c. "Transporte: DNER leva FHC e ACM a trocarem 'farpas." February 18.

Folha de S. Paulo. 2003a. "Banestado em NY 'lava' dinheiro de corrupção." February 5.

Folha de S. Paulo. 2003b. "PF vai apurar em NY remessa ilegal a banco." February 4.

Folha de S. Paulo. 2004. "Entenda o caso Banestado." January 13.

Folha de S. Paulo. 2005. "Lula diz que caixa dois é "intolerável" e critica Delúbio." November 7.

Folha de S. Paulo. 2011a. "Dilma demite Palocci e muda governo após cinco meses." June 8.

Folha de S. Paulo. 2011b. "Veja as suspeitas que levaram à demissão de Wagner Rossi." August 17.

Folha de S. Paulo. 2013. "A popularidade dos presidentes." August 19.

Folha de S. Paulo. 2016. "Ineficiência privilegiada." November 15.

Folha de S. Paulo. 2018a. "Após reprovação recorde, Temer encerra governo com rejeição em queda, mostra Datafolha." December 27.

Folha de S. Paulo. 2018b. "Condenação do tucano Eduardo Azeredo é mantida pela Justiça de Minas." April 24.

Folha de S. Paulo. 2018c. "Foro em cascata." April 25.

Folha de S. Paulo. 2019. "Entenda as evidências e as versões dos envolvidos em esquema de laranjas do PSL." October 22.

Folha de S. Paulo. 2020a. "Descobertas de caso Queiroz levantam suspeita sobre relação de Wassef com miliciano." July 1.

Folha de S. Paulo. 2020b. "FHC foi beneficiado por PEC da reeleição após compra de votos no congresso." February 27.

Folha de São Paulo. 2021a. "Entenda em cinco pontos as suspeitas na compra de vacinas que pressionam Bolsonaro." July 2.

Folha de São Paulo. 2021b. "Quebra de sigilos do caso Flávio revela indícios de 'rachadinha' em gabinetes de Jair e Carlos Bolsonaro." March 15.

Fonseca, Thiago N. 2021. "Custos e interesses: o viés político de instituições anti-corrupção independentes." PhD diss., University of São Paulo.

Fontoura, Luísa Zanini da. 2019. "A Justiça de Curitiba em números: uma análise quantitative das sentenças proferidas pela Operação Lava Jato no Paraná (2014–2018)." Master's thesis, Universidade Federal do Rio Grande do Sul.

Fox, Jonathan. 2006. "Sociedad civil y políticas de rendición de cuentas." *Perfiles Latinoamericanos* 27: 33–68.

Fox, Jonathan. 2015. "Social Accountability: What Does the Evidence Really Say?" *World Development* 72: 346–361.

Fox, Jonathan. 2016. "Scaling Accountability Through Vertically Integrated Civil Society Policy Monitoring and Advocacy." Washington, DC: Accountability Research Center and Institute of Development Studies Working Paper.

FRED (Federal Reserve Economic Data). 2020. "Constant Price Gross Domestic Product in Brazil." Federal Reserve Bank of St. Louis. https://fred.stlouisfed .org/series/BRAGDPRQPSMEI.

Freire, Sabrina. 2019. "Justiça Federal torna Aécio Neves réu em caso da Lava Jato." *Poder360*, July 5.

Freitas, Andréa, and Glauco Peres da Silva. 2019. "Das manifestações de 2013 à elei-ção de 2018 no Brasil: buscando uma abordagem institucional." *Novos Estudos Cebrap* 38: 1, 137–155.

Freitas, Jânio de. 1987. "Concorrência da ferrovia Norte-Sul foi uma farsa." *Folha de S. Paulo*, May 13.

Fuks, Mario, Ednaldo Ribeiro, and Julian Borba. 2021. "From Antipetismo to Gen-eralized Antipartisanship: The Impact of Rejection of Political Parties on the 2018 Vote for Bolsonaro." *Brazilian Political Science Review* 15 (1): 1–28.

Furlan, Flávia. 2017. "Corrupção e má gestão marcam a história da ferrovia Norte-Sul." *Revista Exame*, August 10.

G1. 2006. "Entenda a CPI dos Sanguessugas." August 21. http://g1.globo.com/Noticias /Politica/0,,AA1251927–5601,00.html.

G1. 2007. "Relembre o caso do Banco Marka." December 6. http://g1.globo.com /Noticias/Economia_Negocios/0,,MUL207283-9356,00-RELEMBRE+O+CASO +DO+BANCO+MARKA.html.

G1. 2011a. "Após denúncias, Alfredo Nascimento deixa Ministério dos Transportes." July 7. http://g1.globo.com/politica/noticia/2011/07/apos-denuncias-alfredo-nascimento -deixa-ministerio-dos-transportes.html.

G1. 2011b. "Entenda o que levou à saída de Carlos Lupi do governo." December 5. http://g1.globo.com/politica/noticia/2011/12/entenda-o-que-levou-saida-de-carlos -lupi-do-governo.html.

G1. 2011c. "Ministro do Turismo Pedro Novais pede demissão." September 14. http://g1.globo.com/politica/noticia/2011/09/apos-serie-de-denuncias-ministro-do -turismo-pedro-novais-pede-demissao.html.

G1. 2011d. "Saiba por que Orlando Silva deixou o Ministério do Esporte." October 26. http://g1.globo.com/politica/noticia/2011/10/saiba-por-que-orlando-silva-deixou -o-ministerio-do-esporte.html.

G1. 2012a. "Graça Foster assume presidência da Petrobras e promete continuidade." February 13. http://g1.globo.com/economia/negocios/noticia/2012/02/graca-foster -assume-presidencia-da-petrobras-e-promete-continuidade.html.

G1. 2012b. "Mário Negromonte deixa o cargo de ministro das Cidades." February 2. http://g1.globo.com/politica/noticia/2012/02/mario-negromonte-deixa-o-cargo -de-ministro-das-cidades.html.

G1. 2014. "Dilma diz que investigações da Lava Jato podem mudar país para sempre." November 16.

G1. 2016a. "A maior manifestação da história brasileira." March 13. http://g1 .globo.com/politica/blog/cristiana-lobo/post/maior-manifestacao-da-historia -brasileira.html.

G1. 2016b. "Juquinha das Neves recebeu propina mesmo afastado da VALEC, diz MPF." February 26.

G1. 2020. "Em reunião ministerial, Bolsonaro diz: 'Eu não vou esperar foder a minha família toda.'" May 22. https://g1.globo.com/politica/noticia/2020/05/22/em-reuniao -ministerial-bolsonaro-diz-eu-nao-vou-esperar-foder-a-minha-familia-toda -assista.ghtml.

G1 Jornal Nacional. 2019. "Troca de comando da PF do Rio provoca reação de Bolsonaro." August 16. https://g1.globo.com/jornal-nacional/noticia/2019/08/16/troca -de-comando-na-pf-do-rio-provoca-reacao-de-bolsonaro.ghtml.

G1 Pará. 2013. "Entenda a condenação de Jader Barbalho por desvio da Sudam." July 11. http://g1.globo.com/pa/para/noticia/2013/07/entenda-condenacao-de-jader -barbalho-por-desvio-da-sudam.html.

G1 Pernambuco. 2019. "Luciano Bivar e três candidatas investigadas em esquemas de laranjas do PSL são indiciados pela PF." November 29. https://g1.globo.com /pe/pernambuco/noticia/2019/11/29/luciano-bivar-e-tres-candidatas-investigadas -em-esquema-de-laranjas-do-psl-sao-indiciados-pela-pf.ghtml.

G1 Rio. 2016. "Caso Marka-FonteCindam é encerrado após prescrição, sem condenações." October 11. http://g1.globo.com/rio-de-janeiro/noticia/2016/10/caso-marka -fontecidam-e-encerrado-apos-prescricao-sem-condenacoes.html.

G1 São Paulo. 2014. "PF conclui inquérito do cartel dos trens em SP e indicia 33 pessoas." December 5. http://g1.globo.com/sao-paulo/noticia/2014/12/pf-conclui -inquerito-do-cartel-dos-trens-e-indicia-33-pessoas.html.

Gallagher, Michael. 2017. "Election indices." https://www.tcd.ie/Political_Science /people/michael_gallagher/ElSystems/Docts/ElectionIndices.pdf.

Galli, Ana Paula. 2007. "Entenda o escândalo do mensalão." *Revista Época* 483 (August 8).

Galvão, Paulo Roberto. 2017. Author email correspondence with Galvão. October 17.

Garri, Roberta, Stefano Peternostro, and Jamele Rigolini. 2003. "Individual Attitudes Toward Corruption: Do Social Effects Matter?" Policy Research Working Paper 3122. Washington, DC: World Bank.

Gaspar, Malu. 2001. "Quase Parando." *Veja*, July 6, 125–126.

Geddes, Barbara. 2003. *Paradigms and Sand Castles: Theory Building and Research Design in Comparative Politics*. Ann Arbor: University of Michigan Press.

Geddes, Barbara, and Artur Ribeiro Neto. 1992. "Institutional Sources of Corruption in Brazil." *Third World Quarterly* 13: 641–661.

Gehrke, Manoel. 2019. *How Politicians React to Anti-Corruption Investigations and Enforcement: Evidence from Brazilian Municipalities*. PhD diss., University of California at Los Angeles.

Germano, Áureo. 2006. "CPI dos Sanguessugas denuncia 72 parlamentares e inocenta 18." *UOL*, August 10.

Gerring, John, and Strom C. Thacker. 2005. "Do Neoliberal Policies Deter Political Corruption?" *International Organization* 59: 233–254.

Geyh, Charles G. 2009. *When Courts and Congress Collide: The Struggle for Control of America's Judicial System*. Ann Arbor: University of Michigan Press.

Giacomuzzi, José Guilherme. 2011. *Estado e Contrato*. São Paulo: Malheiros.

Gibson, Edward L. 2005. "Boundary Control: Subnational Authoritarianism in Democratic Countries." *World Politics* 58 (1): 101–132.

Ginsburg, Tom. 2003. *Judicial Review in New Democracies: Constitutional Courts in Asian Cases*. Cambridge: Cambridge University Press.

Giraudy, Agustina, Eduardo Moncada, and Richard Snyder, eds. 2019. *Inside Countries: Subnational Research in Comparative Politics*. Cambridge: Cambridge University Press.

Glezer, Rubens. 2020. "A ilusão da Lava Jato." *Revista piauí* 162: 28–31.

Gois, Chico de. 2014. "Do Banestado ao mensalão, a longa ficha corrida de Youssef." *O Globo*, April 8.

Gomes Neto, José Mario W., and Ernani Carvalho. 2021. "Pretores Condenando a Casta? A Atuação do Supremo Tribunal Federal no Julgamento do Foro Privilegiado." *Revista de Estudos Empíricos em Direito* 8.

Gordon, Sanford C. 2009. "Assessing Partisan Bias in Federal Public Corruption Prosecutions." *American Political Science Review* 103 (4): 534–554.

Gradel, Thomas J., and Dick Simpson. 2015. *Corrupt Illinois: Patronage, Cronyism, and Criminality*. Urbana: University of Illinois Press.

Grant, Ruth W., and Robert O. Keohane. 2005. "Accountability and Abuses of Power in World Politics." *American Political Science Review* 99: 29–43.

Greenwald, Glenn, Betsy Reed, and Leandro Demori. 2019. "Como e por que o Intercept está publicando chats privados sobre a Lava Jato e Sergio Moro." *The Intercept Brasil*, June 9.

Gregory, Robert. 2006. "Governmental Corruption and Social Change in New Zealand: Using Scenarios, 1950–2020." *Asian Journal of Political Science* 14 (2): 117–139.

Gregory, Robert, and Daniel Zirker. 2013. "Clean and Green with Deepening Shadows? A Non-Complacent View of Corruption in New Zealand." In Jon S. T. Quah, ed. *Different Paths to Curbing Corruption: Lessons from Denmark, Finland, Hong Kong, New Zealand, and Singapore*, 109–136. Bingley: Emerald Publishing.

Gugliano, Monica. 2020. "Vou intervir! O dia em que Bolsonaro decidiu mandar tropas para o Supremo." *Revista piauí* 167 (August).

Guimarães, André, Giovana Perlin, and Lincon Maia. 2019. "Do presidencialismo de coalizão ao parlamentarismo de ocasião: análise das relações entre Executivo e Legislativo no governo Dilma Rousseff." In Giovana Perlin and Manoel Leonardo Santos, eds. *Presidencialismo de Coalizão em Movimento*. Brasília: Câmara dos Deputados.

Guimarães, Ligia. 2020. "Abertura precoce de impeachment sem frente ampla vai piorar situação do Brasil." Interview with Marcos Nobre. BBC Brasil, June 6.

Gurza Lavalle, Adrián. 2011. "Após a Participação: Nota Introdutória." *Lua Nova* 84: 13–23.

Haggard, Stephan. 2018. *Developmental States*. Cambridge: Cambridge University Press.

Hagopian, Frances. 2016. "Brazil's Accountability Paradox." *Journal of Democracy* 27: 119–128.

Haidar, Rodrigo. 2011. "Castelo de Areia foi regular, afirma ministro do STJ." *Consultor Jurídico*, March 15.

Hamilton, Alexander, John Jay, and James Madison. 1961. *The Federalist Papers*. New York: New American Library.

Hartmann, Ivar A., and Daniel Chada. 2017. "A razão sem condições de qualidade." In Oscar Vilhena Vieira and Rubens Glezer, eds. *A razão e o voto: diálogos constitucionais com Luís Roberto Barroso*, 169–198. Rio de Janeiro: FGV.

Hausmann, Ricardo, Dani Rodrik, and Andrés Velasco. 2005. "Growth Diagnostics." John F. Kennedy School of Government, Harvard University.

Heimann, Fritz, and Mark Pieth. 2017. *Confronting Corruption: Past Concerns, Present Challenges, and Future Strategies*. Oxford: Oxford University Press.

Henrique, Guilherme. 2020. "Quem investiga e quem decide no caso Queiroz." *Nexo*, June 19.

Hilbink, Lisa. 2012. "The Origins of Positive Judicial Independence." *World Politics* 64 (4): 587–621.

Hilbink, Lisa, and Matthew C. Ingram. 2019. "Courts and Rule of Law in Developing Countries." In *Oxford Research Encyclopedia of Politics*. Oxford: Oxford University Press.

Hirabahasi, Gabriel. 2017. "Apenas 7 deputados foram cassados pela Câmara desde 2002." *Poder360*, March 3.

Hirschman, Albert O. 1991. *The Rhetoric of Reaction: Perversity, Futility, Jeopardy.* Cambridge: Harvard University Press.

Hodgson, Jacqueline. 2002. "Suspects, Defendants and Victims in the French Criminal Process: The Context of Recent Reform." *International and Comparative Law Quarterly* 51 (4): 781–815.

Hofmeister, Naira, Pedro Papini, and Taís Seibt. 2020. "Sentenças de Sergio Moro na Lava Jato foram mais rápidas antes do impeachment de Dilma." *Publica: Agência de Jornalismo Investigativo*. February 17. https://apublica.org/2020/02/sentencas-de-sergio-moro-na-lava-jato-foram-mais-rapidas-antes-do-impeachment-de-dilma/.

Horowitz, Donald L. 1977a. *The Courts and Social Policy.* Washington, DC: Brookings Institution.

Horowitz, Donald L. 1977b. "The Courts as Guardians of the Public Interest." *Public Administration Review* 37 (2): 148–154.

Hubner Mendes, Conrado. 2019. "Uma proposta com dez medidas elementares de ética para o STF." *Folha de S. Paulo*, February 9.

Hunter, Wendy, and Timothy J. Power. 2019. "Bolsonaro and Brazil's Illiberal Backlash." *Journal of Democracy* 30 (1): 68–82.

Huntington, Samuel. 1968. *Political Order in Changing Societies.* New Haven: Yale University Press.

Ingram, Matthew C. 2015. *Crafting Courts in New Democracies: The Politics of Subnational Judicial Reform in Brazil and Mexico.* Cambridge: Cambridge University Press.

The Intercept Brasil. 2019. "Leia os diálogos de Sergio Moro e Deltan Dallagnol que embasaram a reportagem do Intercept." June 12. https://theintercept.com/2019/06/12/chat-sergio-moro-deltan-dallagnol-lavajato/.

International Budget Partnership. 2015. *Open Budget Survey: Open Budgets. Transform Lives.* https://www.internationalbudget.org/wp-content/uploads/OBS2015-Report-English.pdf.

Ipsos. 2017. "Brasileiros são a favor da criação de regras firmes contra políticos corruptos." August 14. https://www.ipsos.com/pt-br/brasileiros-sao-favor-da-criacao-de-regras-firmes-contra-politicos-corruptos.

Istoé. 2012. "A ferrovia da corrupção." July 20.

Istoé. 2019. "Procurador vira réu por vazar informações da Greenfield para Joesley." December 6.

Istoé Dinheiro. 2003. "Os nomes e as provas do dossiê da PF." July 2.

Istoé Dinheiro. 2020. "Desembargador do RJ é denunciado." July 17.

Isunza Vera, Ernesto, and Adrián Gurza Lavalle. 2010. *La innovación democrática en América Latina: tramas y nudos de la representación, la participación y el control social.* Mexico, DF: Centro de Investigaciones y Estudios Superiores en Antropología Social (CIESAS).

Jakarta Post. 2019. "Legislative Assault on KPK." September 18.

Janot, Rodrigo. 2019. *Nada menos que tudo: bastidores da operação que colocou o sistema político em xeque.* São Paulo: Planeta.

Johnston, Michael. 2005. *Syndromes of Corruption: Wealth, Power, and Democracy.* New York: Cambridge University Press.

Johnston, Michael. 2013. "The Great Danes: Success and Subtleties of Corruption Control in Denmark." In Jon S. T. Quah, ed. *Different Paths to Curbing Corruption: Lessons from Denmark, Finland, Hong Kong, New Zealand, and Singapore*, 23–56. Bingley, UK: Emerald Publishing.

Johnston, Michael. 2014. *Corruption, Contention, and Reform: The Power of Deep Democratization*. Cambridge: Cambridge University Press.

Johnston, Michael, and Scott A. Fritzen. 2021. *The Conundrum of Corruption: Reform for Social Justice*. New York: Routledge.

Jones, Alison, and Cario Mario da Silva Pereira Neto. 2020. "Anatomy of Operation Car Wash: Challenges to Combatting Corruption and Collusion in Brazil." Paper presented at the Law and Systemic Corruption Conference, FGV São Paulo, August 5–7.

Jornal da USP. 2016. "Para analistas, Dilma 'cai pelo conjunto da obra'—e democracia segue seu rumo." https://jornal.usp.br/atualidades/o-funcionamento-da-democracia-e-o-processo-de-impeachment/.

Jucá, Ivan, Marcus André Melo, and Lucio R. Rennó. 2016. "The Political Cost of Corruption: Scandals, Campaign Finance, and Reelection in the Brazilian Chamber of Deputies." *Journal of Politics in Latin America* 8: 3–36.

Justiça Federal. 2009. Sexta Vara Federal Especializada em Crimes Financeiros e em Lavagem de Dinheiro, Vistos em Decisão, Autos no. 2009.61.81.003210-0.

Justiça Federal. 2014. Sentença da Ação Penal n. 5035707-53.2014.404.7000/PR .13a. Vara Federal Criminal de Curitiba, September 17.

Justiça Federal. 2015. Sentença da Ação Penal n. 5083258-29.2014.4.04.7000/PR .13a. Vara Federal Criminal de Curitiba, July 20.

Justiça Federal. 2017. Sentença da Ação Penal n. 5046512-94.2016.4.04.7000/PR .13a. Vara Federal Criminal de Curitiba, July 12.

Kadanus, Kelli. 2020. "STF só julgou quatro processos da Lava Jato contra politicos desde 2015." *Gazeta do Povo*, July 30.

Kang, David C. 2002. *Crony Capitalism: Corruption and Development in South Korea and the Philippines*. Cambridge: Cambridge University Press.

Kant de Lima, Roberto, and Gláucia M. P. Mouzinho. 2016. "Produção e reprodução da tradição inquisitorial no Brasil: Entre delações e confissões premiadas." *Dilemas* 9 (3): 505–529.

Kar, Dev. 2014. "Brazil: Capital Flight, Illicit Flows, and Macroeconomic Crises, 1960–2012." Washington, DC: Global Financial Integrity.

Karklins, Rasma. 2005. *The System Made Me Do It: Corruption in Post-Communist Societies*. Armonk, NY: M. E. Sharpe.

Katzenstein, Peter J. 1985. *Small States in World Markets: Industrial Policy in Europe*. Ithaca, NY: Cornell University Press.

Katzenstein, Peter J. 2003. "*Small States* and Small States Revisited." *New Political Economy* 8 (1): 9–30.

Kaufmann, Daniel, Aart Kraay, and Massimo Mastruzzi. 2010. "The Worldwide Governance Indicators: Methodology and Analytical Issues." Draft Policy Research Working Paper. Washington, DC: World Bank.

Kerche, Fábio. 2007. "Autonomia e discricionaridade do Ministério Público no Brasil." *Dados—Revista de Ciências Sociais* 50: 259–279.

Kerche, Fábio, and Marjorie Marona. 2018. "O Ministério Público Na Operação Lava Jato: Como Eles Chegaram Até Aqui?" In Fábio Kerche and João Feres Jr., eds. *Operação Lava Jato e a democracia brasileira*, 69–100. São Paulo: Contracorrente.

Kerche, Fábio, Vanessa Elias de Oliveira, and Cláudio Gonçalves Couto. 2020. "Os Conselhos Nacionais de Justiça e do Ministério Público no Brasil: instrumentos de accountability?" *Revista de Administração Pública* 54: 1334–1360.

King, Gary, Robert O. Keohane, and Sidney Verba. 1994. *Designing Social Inquiry: Scientific Inference in Qualitative Research*. Princeton: Princeton University Press.

Kingdon, John W. 1984. *Agendas, Alternatives, and Public Policies*. Boston: Little, Brown.

Kingston, Christopher. 2008. "Social Structure and Cultures of Corruption." *Journal of Economic Behavior and Organization* 67: 90–102.

Klitgaard, Robert. 1988. *Controlling Corruption*. Berkeley: University of California Press.

Klitgaard, Robert. 1998. "International Cooperation Against Corruption." *Finance and Development* 35: 3–6.

Kobielski, Marina Balestrin. 2020. "Poder Judiciário e Combate à Corrupção: Atuação e Discursos do Tribunal Regional Federal da 4ª Região." Unpublished master's thesis, Graduate Program in Criminal Sciences, Pontifícia Universidade Católica do Rio Grande do Sul.

Konchinski, Vinicius. 2016. "Um juiz não pode simplesmente atender a vontade da sociedade, diz De Sanctis, da Satiagraha." Interview with Judge Fausto De Sanctis. UOL Notícias, April 3.

Krause, Silvana, Mauricio Michel Rebello, and Josimar Gonçalves da Silva. 2015. "O perfil do financiamento dos partidos brasileiros (2006–2012): o que as tipologias dizem?" *Revista Brasileira de Ciência Política* 16: 247–272.

Kunicová, Jana, and Susan Rose-Ackerman. 2005. "Electoral Rules and Constitutional Structures as Constraints on Corruption." *British Journal of Political Science* 35: 573–606.

Laakso, Markku, and Rein Taagepera. 1979. "'Effective' Number of Parties: A Measure with Application to West Europe." *Comparative Political Studies* 12 (1): 3–27.

LaForge, Gordon. 2017. "The Sum of Its Parts: Coordinating Brazil's Fight Against Corruption, 2003–2016." Innovations for Successful Societies, Princeton University. https://successfulsocieties.princeton.edu/publications/sum-its-parts-coordinating -brazil-fight-against-corruption.

Lages, Flávia, and Paes, Cintia. 2019. "Ministro do turismo é denunciado pelo Ministério Público de MG por candidaturas-laranja do PSL." *G1 Minas Gerais*, October 4.

Lagunes, Paul F., and Jan Svejnar, eds. 2020a. *Corruption and the Lava Jato Scandal in Latin America*. New York: Routledge.

Lagunes, Paul F., and Jan Svejnar. 2020b. "Introduction." In Paul F. Lagunes and Jan Svejnar, eds. *Corruption and the Lava Jato Scandal in Latin America*. New York: Routledge.

Larkins, Christopher M. 1996. "Judicial Independence and Democratization: A Theoretical and Conceptual Analysis." *American Journal of Comparative Law* 44: 605–626.

Lawson, Letitia. 2009. "The Politics of Anti-Corruption Reform in Africa." *Journal of Modern African Studies* 47 (1): 73–100.

Lazzarini, Sérgio G. 2010. *Capitalismo de Laços*. São Paulo: Elsevier.

Leahy, Joe. 2016. "A Brazilian Bribery Machine." *Financial Times*, December 29.

Leali, Francisco. 2020. "Governo impõe sigio a pareceres para o Planato." *O Globo*, June 8.

Lemgruber, Julita, Ludmila Ribeiro, Leonarda Musumeci, and Thais Duarte. 2016. "Ministério Público: guardião da democracia brasileira?" Rio de Janeiro: CESEC, Universidade Candido Mendes.

Levcovitz, Silvio. 2014. "A corrupção e a atuação do Judiciário federal: 1991–2010." Unpublished master's thesis, Universidade Federal de São Carlos.

Levcovitz, Silvio. 2020. "A Corrupção e a Atuação da Justiça Federal no Brasil, 1991–2014." Unpublished PhD dissertation, State University of Campinas (Unicamp).

Levi, Margaret. 1999. "Trust and Governance." In Valerie Braithwaite and Margaret Levi, eds. *A State of Trust*, 77–101. New York: Russell Sage Foundation.

Lima, Maria, and Eduardo Bresciani. 2016. "Jurista argumenta que Dilma está sendo afastada pelo conjunto da obra." *O Globo*, June 10.

Limongi, Fernando. 2015. "O passaporte de Cunha e o impeachment: a crônica de uma tragédia anunciada." *Novos Estudos CEBRAP* 103 (November): 99–112.

Limongi, Fernando. 2020. "The Car Wash Operation: A Critical Assessment." Paper presented at the Law and Systemic Corruption Conference, FGV São Paulo, August 5–7.

Limongi, Fernando, and Angelina Cheibub Figueiredo. 2017. "A crise atual." *Novos Estudos CEBRAP* 36: 79–97.

Lindberg, Staffan I. 2013. "Mapping Accountability: Core Concepts and Subtypes." *International Review of Administrative Sciences* 79: 202–226.

Lindblom, Charles E. 1959. "The Science of 'Muddling Through.'" *Public Administration Review* 19 (2): 79–88.

Lipton, David, and Jeffrey Sachs. 1990. "Creating a Market Economy in Eastern Europe: The Case of Poland." Brookings Papers on Economic Activity (1): 75–133.

Lis, Laís. 2020. "Governo Bolsonaro mais que dobra número de militares em cargos civis, aponta TCU." *G1*, July 17.

Llanos, Mariana, and Leany Barreiro Lemos. 2013. "Presidential Preferences? The Supreme Federal Tribunal Nominations in Democratic Brazil." *Latin American Politics and Society* 55: 77–105.

Londero, Daiane. 2021. "O Desenvolvimento Institucional do Ministério Público Federal no Combate à Corrupção, 1988–2018." PhD diss., Federal University of Rio Grande do Sul.

Lopes, Iriny. 2014. "O Caso Banestado, a Petrobras e o feitiço do tempo." *Carta Maior*, November 19.

Lopes, Nathan. 2019. "'Laranjal' derrubou ministro, indicou outro e pode gerar debandada do PSL." *UOL*, October 9.

Lopez, Felix Garcia, Maurício Bugarin, and Karina Bugarin. 2014. "Rotatitividade nos cargos de confiança da Administração Federal Brasileira (1999–2013)." *Revista do Serviço Público* 65: 439–461.

Lopez, Felix Garcia, and Sérgio Praça. 2015. "Cargos de confiança, partidos políticos e burocracia federal." *Revista Iberoamericana de Estudos Legislativos* 1: 33–42.

Lo Prete, Renata. 1999. "Histórias mal contadas." *Folha de S. Paulo*, April 18.

Loureiro, Maria Rita, Fernando Abrucio, Cecília Olivieri, and Marco Antonio Carvalho Teixeira. 2012. "Do controle interno ao controle social: A múltipla atuação da CGU na democracia brasileira." *Cadernos Gestão Pública e Cidadania* 17: 54–67.

Lucas, Kevin, and David Samuels. 2010. "The Ideological 'Coherence' of the Brazilian Party System, 1990–2009." *Journal of Politics in Latin America* 2: 39–69.

Macaulay, Fiona. 2011. "Federalism and State Criminal Justice Systems." In Timothy J. Power and Matthew M. Taylor, eds. *Corruption and Democracy in Brazil: The Struggle for Accountability*, 218–249. Notre Dame, IN: University of Notre Dame Press.

Macedo, Fausto. 2019. "Deltan afirma que fundação bilionária 'não é da Lava Jato nem do Ministério Público.'" *O Estado de S. Paulo*, April 1.

Macedo, Fausto. 2021. "STF vê retaliação, e PGR deve defender arquivamento de pedido para investigar Toffoli." *O Estado de S. Paulo*, May 12.

Machado, Maíra Rocha. 2015. "Crime e/ou Improbidade? Notas sobre a performance do sistema de Justiça em casos de corrupção." *Revista Brasileira de Ciências Criminais* 112: 189–211.

Machado, Maíra Rocha, and Bruno Paschoal. 2016. "Monitorar, investigar, responsabilizar e sancionar: a multiplicidade institutional em casos de corrupção." *Novos Estudos CEBRAP* 104: 11–36.

Machado, Raphael Amorim. 2018. "O Estado de volta para as ferrovias: a controversa atuação da VALEC na política ferroviária brasileira a partir de 2008." *Boletim de Análise Político-Institucional* 15 (July–December).

Madeira, Lígia M., and Leonardo Geliski. 2019. "O combate a crimes de corrupção pela Justiça Federal da Região Sul do Brasil." *Revista de Administração Pública* 53 (6): 987–1010.

Madeira, Lígia M., and Leonardo Geliski. 2021. "An Analytical Model of the Institutional Design of Specialized Anti-Corruption Courts in the Global South: Brazil and Indonesia in Comparative Perspective." *Dados* 64 (3): 1–33.

Magalhães, Vera, Gabriela Guerreiro, and Simone Iglesias. 2012. "Romero Jucá deixa liderança do governo no Senado." *Folha de S. Paulo*, March 12.

Mainwaring, Scott. 2003. "Introduction: Democratic Accountability in Latin America." In Scott Mainwaring and Christopher Welna, eds. *Democratic Accountability in Latin America*, 3–34. Oxford: Oxford University Press.

Mainwaring, Scott, Timothy J. Power, and Fernando Bizzarro. 2017. "The Uneven Institutionalization of a Party System: Brazil." In Scott Mainwaring, ed. *Party Systems in Latin America: Institutionalization, Erosion, and Collapse*. Cambridge: Cambridge University Press.

Maltzman, Forrest, James F. Spriggs II, and Paul J. Wahlbeck. 1999. "Strategy and Judicial Choice: New Institutionalist Approaches to Supreme Court Decision-Making." In Howard Gillman and Cornell Clayton, eds. *Supreme Court Decision-Making: New Institutionalist Approaches*. Chicago: University of Chicago Press.

Mancuso, Wagner Pralon. 2015. "Investimento eleitoral no Brasil: balanço da literatura (2001–2012) e agenda de pesquisa." *Revista Sociologia e Política* 23: 155–183.

Mancuso, Wagner Pralon, and Bruno Wilhelm Speck. 2014. "Financiamento de campanhas e prestação de contas." *Cadernos Adenauer* 15: 134–150.

Mancuso, Wagner Pralon, and Bruno Wilhelm Speck. 2015. "Financiamento empresarial na eleição para deputado federal (2002–2010): determinantes e consequências." *Teoria & Sociedade* 23: 1–23.

Manfrini, Sandra. 2002. "Receita identifica sonegação em remessas ao exterior de R\$ 724 mi." *Folha de S. Paulo*, June 5.

Manion, Melanie. 2004. *Corruption by Design: Building Clean Government in Mainland China and Hong Kong*. Cambridge, MA: Harvard University Press.

Manzi, Lucia. 2021. "Prosecutorial Gatekeeping and Its Effects on Criminal Accountability: The Roman Prosecutor's Office and Corruption Investigations in Italy, 1975–1994." Working paper.

Maor, Moshe. 2004. "Feeling the Heat? Anticorruption Mechanisms in Comparative Perspective." *Governance* 17 (1): 1–28.

Maravall, José Maria. 2003. "The Rule of Law as a Political Weapon." In Adam Przeworski and José Maria Maravall, eds. *Democracy and the Rule of Law*. Cambridge: Cambridge University Press.

Marchetti, Vitor. 2008. "Poder Judiciário e competição política no Brasil: Uma análise das decisões do TSE e do STF sobre as regras eleitorais." PhD diss., Pontifícia Universidade Católica de São Paulo.

Marchetti, Vitor, and Rafael Cortez. 2009. "A judicialização da competição política: O TSE e as coligações eleitorais." *Opinião Pública* 15: 422–450.

Maricato, Erminia. 2011. *O impasse na política urbana no Brasil*. São Paulo: Vozes.

Marin, Denise Chrispim. 2019. "Lava Jato peruana fisgou quatro ex-presidentes subornados pela Petrobras." *Veja*, April 17.

Marona, Marjorie, and Fábio Kerche. 2021. "From the Banestado Case to Operation Car Wash: Building an Anti-Corruption Institutional Framework in Brazil." *Dados* 64 (3): 1–37.

Marona, Marjorie C., and Leon Victor de Queiroz Barbosa. 2018. "Protagonismo judicial no Brasil: de que estamos falando?" In Marjorie C. Marona and Andrés Del Río, eds. *Justiça no Brasil: às margens da democracia*, 133–155. Belo Horizonte: Arraes.

Marques, Hugo. 2003. "Banestado: Investigacao sem recursos." *Jornal do Brasil*, June 20.

Marques, José. 2019. "Lava Jato cumpre busca e apreensão em fase que mira ex-presidente do STJ." *Folha de S. Paulo*, November 29.

Marques, José. 2020. "Serra é denunciado pela Lava Jato de SP sob acusação de lavagem de dinheiro." *Folha de S. Paulo*, July 3.

Marques, Luciana. 2011. "Dilma: caso Pimentel nada tem a ver com o meu governo." *Veja*, December 16.

Martini, Maíra, and Mariana Borges Soares. 2016. "Brazil: Overview of Corruption and Anti-Corruption." *Anti-Corruption Helpdesk*, Transparency International, June 22.

Martins, Luísa. 2019. "Gilmar Mendes chama procuradores da Lava-Jato de 'cretinos.'" *Valor Econômico*, March 14.

Martins, Luísa. 2020a. "Defesa de Lula reforça pedido de absolvição na Zelotes." *Valor*, May 11.

Martins, Luísa. 2020b. "Ministério Público teme por prosseguimento da Zelotes." *Valor*, April 30.

Matos, Vitor, Luiz Felipe Barbiéri, Guilherme Mazui, and Rosanne D'Agostino. 2020. "Ex-juiz Sérgio Moro anuncia demissão do Ministério da Justiça e deixa o governo Bolsonaro." *G1*, April 24.

Matsuura, Lilian. 2009. "Leia decisão em que De Sanctis critica publicidade restrita dos autos." *Consultor Jurídico*, July 21.

Mattoso, Camila, with Fábio Zanini, Fabio Serapião, and Guilherme Seto. 2021. "Painel: Toffoli mudou voto e salvou prefeito em caso levado à PF sobre suspeita de venda de decisão." *Folha de S. Paulo*, May 12.

Mattoso, Camila, Ranier Bragon, and Joana Suarez. 2019. "Partido de Bolsonaro criou candidata laranja para usar verba pública de R$ 400 mil." *Folha de S. Paulo*, February 10.

Mauro, Paolo. 2004. "The Persistence of Corruption and Slow Economic Growth." *IMF Staff Papers* 51 (1): 1–18.

Mazieiro, Guilherme. 2020. "Moro sai e acusa Bolsonaro de interferência política e ignorar carta branca." *UOL*, April 24.

Mazzilli, Hugo Nigro. 1993. *Regime jurídico do Ministério Público*. São Paulo: Saraiva.

McCubbins, Mathew D., and Thomas Schwartz. 1984. "Congressional Oversight Overlooked: Police Patrols Versus Fire Alarms." *American Journal of Political Science* 18: 165–179.

McLean, Nicole. 2021. "Street Movements as Media Vehicles of the Brazilian New Right." PhD diss., joint from University of Melbourne and University of São Paulo.

McMann, Kelly M., Brigitte Seim, Jan Teorell, and Staffan Lindberg. 2020. "Why Low Levels of Democracy Promote Corruption and High Levels Diminish It." *Political Research Quarterly* 73 (4): 893–907.

McMillan, John, and Pablo Zoido. 2004. "How to Subvert Democracy: Montesinos in Peru." *Journal of Economic Perspectives* 18 (4): 69–92.

Medeiros, Israel, and João Vitor Tavarez. 2021. "Deputados afrouxam a Lei de Improbidade Administrativa." *Correio Braziliense*, June 17.

Melo, Carlos R. 2004. *Retirando as cadeiras do lugar: Migração partidária na Câmara dos Deputados, 1985–2002*. Belo Horizonte: Ed. UFMG.

Melo, Marcus André. 2016. "Crisis and Integrity in Brazil." *Journal of Democracy* 27 (2): 50–65.

Melo, Marcus André, and Carlos Pereira. 2013. *Making Brazil Work: Checking the President in a Multiparty System*. New York: Palgrave Macmillan.

Mendelski, Martin. 2021. "15 years of Anti-Corruption in Romania: Augmentation, Aberration And Acceleration." *European Politics and Society* 22 (2): 237–258.

Merriner, James L. 2004. *Grafters and Goo Goos: Corruption and Reform in Chicago.* Carbondale: Southern Illinois University Press.

Mészáros, George. 2020. "Caught in an Authoritarian Trap of Its Own Making? Brazil's Lava Jato Anti-Corruption Investigation and the Politics of Prosecutorial Overreach." *Journal of Law and Society* 47 (S1): S54–S73.

Michael, Andréa. 2008. "Dantas é alvo de outra investigação da PF." *Folha de S. Paulo*, April 26.

Michener, Gregory. 2019. Brazil's Information Ecosystem: What Is Transparency's Impact? *Revista da CGU* 11 (20): 1299–1310.

Michener, Gregory, and Carlos Pereira. 2016. "A Great Leap Forward for Democracy *and* the Rule of Law? Brazil's Mensalão Trial." *Journal of Latin American Studies* 48 (3): 477–507.

Michener, Gregory, Luiz Fernando Moncau, and Rafael Braem Velasco. 2016. "The Brazilian State and Transparency: Evaluating Compliance with Freedom of Information." Paper presented at the National Evaluation on Governmental Transparency.

Michener, Gregory, and Michael Freitas Mohallem. 2020. "A transparência piorou no governo Bolsonaro?" *Folha de S. Paulo*, March 1.

Mick, Jacques. 2021. *Accountability e Governança do Trabalho Jornalístico: como a cooperação entre jornalistas no setor público aprimora a prestação de contas do Executivo Federal.* Brasília: Cadernos ENAP.

Migalhas. 2019. "Condenação de PC Farias por esquema de corrupção completa 25 anos." May 20. https://www.migalhas.com.br/quentes/302364/condenacao-de-pc -farias-por-esquema-de-corrupcao-completa–25-anos.

Milício, Gláucia. 2008. "Ministros do STF apóiam decisões de Gilmar Mendes." *Consultor Jurídico*, August 1.

Ministério Público Federal (MPF). 2013. "Com término do julgamento do mensalão, MPF obtém condenação de 25 réus." https://mpf.jusbrasil.com.br/noticias/10025 1220/com-termino-do-julgamento-do-mensalao-mpf-obtem-condenacao-de-25-reus.

Ministério Público Federal (MPF). 2015a. "MPF coleta assinaturas para apoio a medidas de combate à corrupção e à impunidade." July 27. http://www.mpf.mp .br/pgr/noticias-pgr/mpf-coleta-assinaturas-para-apoio-a-medidas-de-combate-a -corrupcao-e-a-impunidade.

Ministério Público Federal (MPF). 2015b. "MPF lança dez medidas para combater a corrupção e a impunidade." March 20. http://www.mpf.mp.br/pgr/noticias-pgr /mpf-lanca-dez-medidas-para-combater-a-corrupcao-e-a-impunidade.

Ministério Público Federal (MPF). 2015c. "10 Medidas: MPF conclui primeira fase da campanha com a entrega de mais de dois milhões de assinaturas à sociedade." March 29. http://www.mpf.mp.br/pgr/noticias-pgr/mpf-conclui-primeira-fase-da -campanha-10-medidas-com-entrega-de-mais-de-dois-milhoes-de-assinaturas-a -sociedade-1.

Ministério Público Federal (MPF). 2017. "Atuação do MPF: Casos Emblemáticos." http://combateacorrupcao.mpf.mp.br/atuacao-do-mpf.

Ministério Público Federal (MPF). 2019a. "Caso Lava Jato, Atuação na 1ª Instancia." September 18. http://www.mpf.mp.br/grandes-casos/caso-lava-jato.

Ministério Público Federal (MPF). 2019b. "Equipe no MPF." http://www.mpf.mp .br/para-o-cidadao/caso-lava-jato/equipe-no-mpf.

Ministério Público Federal (MPF). 2019c. "Quadro de membros." http://www .transparencia.mpf.mp.br/conteudo/gestao-de-pessoas/quadro-de-membros.

Ministério Público Federal (MPF). 2019d. "Relação com o caso Banestado." http://www.mpf.mp.br/para-o-cidadao/caso-lava-jato/atuacao-na-1a-instancia /investigacao/relacao-com-o-caso-banestado.

Ministério Público Federal (MPF). 2019e. "Relatório de Atividades e de Execução de Plano de Ação da Força-Tarefa Greenfield." September 18. http://www.mpf .mp.br/df/sala-de-imprensa/docs/relatorio-ft-greenfield.

Ministério Público Federal (MPF). 2020. "Operação Lava Jato." http://www.mpf .mp.br/grandes-casos/lava-jato.

Ministério Público Federal (MPF). 2021a. "Caso Lava Jato: Resultados." August. http://www.mpf.mp.br/grandes-casos/lava-jato/resultados.

Ministério Público Federal (MPF). 2021b. "Relatório final de atividades e de execução de plano de ação da Força-Tarefa Greenfield, junho 2016 a novembro 2020." January. http://www.mpf.mp.br/df/sala-de-imprensa/docs/PRDF00001389.2021.pdf.

Ministério Público Federal (MPF). No date. "Conheça as medidas." http://www .dezmedidas.mpf.mp.br/apresentacao/conheca-as-medidas. Accessed May 24, 2019.

Mohallem, Michael Freitas, and Gregory Michener. 2020. "O governo contra transparência." *Folha de S. Paulo*, June 9.

Montambeault, Françoise, and Graciela Ducatenzeiler. 2014. "Lula's Brazil and Beyond: An Introduction." *Journal of Politics in Latin America* 6: 3–14.

Monteiro, Tânia, and Rafael Moraes Moura. 2011. "Tolerância com corrupção é zero, afirma Dilma." *O Estado de S. Paulo*, December 16.

Montero, Alfred P. 2014. *Brazil: Reversal of Fortune*. Cambridge: Polity Press.

Moreno, Jorge Bastos. 2015. "A incômoda companhia dos escândalos: casos de corrupção estouraram em todos os governos." *O Globo*, March 15.

Moro, Sérgio Fernando. 2004. "Considerações Sobre a Operação Mani Pulite." *Revista Centro de Estudos Judiciários* 26: 56–62.

Morris, Stephen D. 2009. *Political Corruption in Mexico: The Impact of Democratization*. Boulder, CO: Lynne Rienner Publishers.

Moura, Jéssica. 2020. "Procurador que coordenava operação Greenfield deixa força-tarefa e critica desmonte de estrutura pela PGR." *O Globo*, September 4.

Moura, Rafael Moraes, and Daniel Weterman. 2020. "Medo de Sérgio Moro levou Centrão a apoiar Bolsonaro." *O Estado de S. Paulo*, July 20.

Mungiu-Pippidi, Alina. 2013. "Becoming Denmark: Historical Designs of Corruption Control." *Social Research: An International Quarterly* 80 (4): 1259–1286.

Mungiu-Pippidi, Alina. 2015. *The Quest for Good Governance: How Societies Develop Control of Corruption*. Cambridge: Cambridge University Press.

Mungiu-Pippidi, Alina. 2018. "Romania's Italian-Style Anticorruption Populism." *Journal of Democracy* 29 (3): 104–116.

Mungiu-Pippidi, Alina, and Michael Johnston, eds. 2017. *Transitions to Good Governance: Creating Virtuous Circles of Anti-Corruption*. Cheltenham, UK: Edward Elgar.

Musacchio, Aldo, and Sérgio G. Lazzarini. 2014. *Reinventing State Capitalism: Leviathan in Business, Brazil and Beyond*. Cambridge: Harvard University Press.

Nagel, Stuart S. 1964. "Court-Curbing Periods in American History." *Vanderbilt Law Review* 18 (3): 925–944.

Natural Resource Governance Institute. 2017. "2017 Resource Governance Index." https://api.resourcegovernanceindex.org/system/documents/documents/000 /000/046/original/2017_Resource_Governance_Index.pdf?1498599435.

Netto, Vladimir. 2016. *Lava Jato: O Juiz Sergio Moro e os bastidores da operação que abalou o Brasil*. Rio de Janeiro: Primeira Pessoa.

Nêumanne, José. 2019. "Desafios ao conta-gotas de Verdevaldo." *O Estado de S. Paulo*, December 9.

Neves, Aécio. 2015. "Entrevista sobre o governo Dilma e a corrupção." July 1. aecioneves.com.br.

Nicolau, Jairo. 2020. *O Brasil dobrou à direita: uma radiografia da eleição de Bolsonaro em 2018*. Rio de Janeiro: Zahar.

Nobre, Marcos. 2013. *Imobilismo em movimento: da abertura democrática ao governo Dilma.* São Paulo: Companhia das Letras.

Nóbrega, Mailson da. 2005. *O futuro chegou: instituições e desenvolvimento no Brasil.* São Paulo: Editora Globo.

North, Douglass C., John Joseph Wallis, and Barry R. Weingast. 2009. *Violence and Social Orders: A Conceptual Framework for Interpreting Recorded Human History.* Cambridge: Cambridge University Press.

NSC Total. 2017. "Ex-coordenadora da Lava-Jato é transferida para a PF em SC." February 25.

Nunes, Felipe, and Carlos Ranulfo Melo. 2017. "Impeachment, Political Crisis and Democracy in Brazil." *Revista de Ciencia Política* 37: 281–304.

Nunes, Wálter. 2020. "Ida de Moro a ministério de Bolsonaro contaminou Lava Jato, diz ex-procurador da força tarefa." *Folha de S. Paulo*, June 7.

Nunes, Wálter, and Felipe Bächtold. 2017. "Anulada, Operação Castelo de Areia antecipou características da Lava Jato." *Folha de S. Paulo*, March 1.

Ocheje, Paul D. 2018. "Norms, Law and Social Change: Nigeria's Anti-Corruption Struggle, 1999–2017." *Crime, Law, and Social Change* 70 (3): 363–381.

Odebrecht. 2015. "Receita da Odebrecht S.A. totaliza R$107,7 bilhões, um crescimento de 11%, sobretudo nas operações no exterior." https://www.odebrecht.com /pt-br/comunicacao/releases/receita-da-odebrecht-sa-totaliza-r-1077-bilhoes-um -crescimento-de-11-sobretudo.

Odilla, Fernanda. 2019. "Oversee and Punish: Understanding the Fight Against Corruption Involving Government Workers in Brazil." Unpublished PhD diss., Faculty of Social Science and Public Policy, King's College London.

Odilla, Fernanda. 2020. "Oversee and Punish: Understanding the Fight Against Corruption Involving Government Workers in Brazil." *Politics and Governance* 8: 140–152.

O'Donnell, Guillermo. 1999. "Horizontal Accountability in New Democracies." In Andreas Schedler, Larry Diamond, and Marc F. Plattner, eds. *The Self-Restraining State*, 29–51. Boulder, CO: Lynne Rienner Publishers.

O'Donnell, Guillermo. 2003. "Horizontal Accountability: The Legal Institutionalization of Mistrust." In Scott Mainwaring and Christopher Welna, eds. *Democratic Accountability in Latin America*, 34–54. Oxford: Oxford University Press.

OECD. 2012. "OECD Integrity Review of Brazil: Managing Risks for a Cleaner Public Service." OECD Public Governance Reviews, at www.oecd-library.org.

OECD. 2019. "Brazil Must Immediately End Threats to Independence and Capacity of Law Enforcement to Fight Corruption." November 13. https://www.oecd.org /brazil/brazil-must-immediately-end-threats-to-independence-and-capacity-of -law-enforcement-to-fight-corruption.htm.

O Estado de S. Paulo. 2003. "Justiça quebra sigilo de 26 no caso Banestado." July 11.

O Estado de S. Paulo. 2011. "Sem apoio, demissão de Palocci foi acertada com Dilma." June 8. https://politica.estadao.com.br/noticias/geral,sem-apoio-demissao -de-palocci-foi-acertada-com-dilma,729506.

O Estado de S. Paulo. 2020. "Dossiê contra opositores: veja a cronologia do caso e recuos do ministro da Justiça." August 13.

O Estado de S. Paulo. 2021. "Após escândalo do 'tratoraço,' Governo muda regra no Orçamento de 2021." May 25. https://politica.estadao.com.br/noticias/geral ,apos-escandalo-do-tratoraco-governo-muda-regra-do-orcamento-de-2021 ,70003726255.

O Globo. 2009. "PF omitiu PT de investigação sobre doações." March 31.

O Globo. 2015a. "Delatores relatam propina na construção da Ferrovia Norte-Sul." April 2.

O Globo. 2015b. "Fraude anulou licitação da Ferrovia Norte-Sul em 1987." April 2.

O Globo. 2015c. "O que são Operação Zelotes e Carf." April 7. https://oglobo .globo.com/economia/o-que-sao-operacao-zelotes-carf–15801384.

O Globo. 2017a. "Ferrovia norte-sul: longo histórico de corrupção." May 26. https://oglobo.globo.com/brasil/ferrovia-norte-sul-longo-historico-de-corrupcao –21392482.

O Globo. 2017b. "Protógenes e a Operação Satiagraha: Entenda o caso." March 31.

O Globo. 2019. "A cronologia do caso Queiroz." May 9. https://oglobo.globo.com /brasil/a-cronologia-do-caso-queiroz–23663199.

Oliveira, Adriano. 2019. *Qual foi a influência da Lava Jato no comportamento do eleitor? Do lulismo ao bolsonarismo*. Curitiba: CRV.

Oliveira, Mariana. 2013. "Supremo determina prisão imediata do deputado Natan Donadon." *G1 Política*, June 26.

Oliveira, Mariana. 2015. "Ministro do STF arquiva ação contra senador Jader Barbalho." *G1*, May 12.

Oliveira, Mariana. 2016. "Gilmar Mendes suspende nomeação de Lula como ministro da Casa Civil." *G1*, March 18.

Oliveira, Mariana, and Rosanne D'Agostino. 2019. "STF condena Geddel a 14 anos de prisão e irmão Lúcio a 10 anos no caso das malas de dinheiro." *G1*, October 22.

Oliveira, Temistocles Murilo de., Jr. 2019. "Cultura do escândalo e a 'ortodontia' da accountability em democracias recentes: as reformas anticorrupção no Brasil na 'Era Lava Jato.'" *Revista da CGU* 11 (18): 1053–1074.

Olivieri, Cecília. 2010. *A lógica política do controle interno: o monitoramento das políticas públicas no presidencialismo brasileiro*. São Paulo: Annablume Editora.

Olivieri, Cecília, Maria Rita Loureiro, Marco Antonio Carvalho Teixeira, and Fernando Abrucio. 2015. "Control and Public Management Performance in Brazil: Challenges for Coordination." *International Business Research* 8 (8): 181–190.

Orta, Charles. 2017. "How Odebrecht Profited from Corrupting Latin American Political Elites." *InSight Crime*, August 9.

Ortega, Pepita, and Fausto Macedo. 2019. "Lava Jato abre nova fase da investigação sobre fim da Castelo de Areia e faz buscas em escritórios de advocacia em São Paulo e Brasília." *O Estado de S. Paulo*, November 29.

Ortega, Pepita, and Fausto Macedo. 2020. "Lava Jato Rio procura 12 por desvios na Eletronuclear e mira ex-ministro Silas Rondeau." *O Estado de S. Paulo*, June 25.

Osborn, Catherine. 2017. "Brazilian Business Goes Global—Here Comes the Culture Shock." OZY, June 7. http://www.ozy.com/fast-forward/as-public-offerings-heat -up-for-brazilian-companies-they-show-off-a-culture-shift/78856.

Oswald, Vivian, Cristiane Jungblut, and Ramona Ordoñez. 2012. "Partidos se irritam com mudanças feitas por Graça na Petrobras." *O Globo*, April 26.

Paludo, Januário, ed. 2011. *Forças-tarefas: direito comparado e legislação aplicável*. Brasília: Escola Superior do Ministério Público da União (Manuais de Atuação).

Pangalangan, Raul C. 2010. "The Philippines' Sandiganbayan: Anti-Graft Courts and the Illusion of Self-Contained Anti-Corruption Regimes." In P. Nicholson and A. Harding, eds. *New Courts in Asia*. London: Routledge.

Pârvulescu, Radu A. 2021. "Decoupled Rationalisation: Judicial Anticorruption and Fragmentation of Parliament and the Magistracy." *SocArXiv*, March 23.

Pavão, Nara. 2018. "Corruption as the Only Option: The Limits to Electoral Accountability." *Journal of Politics* 80 (3): 996–1010.

Pavão, Nara. 2019. "Corruption, Courts, and Public Opinion in Brazil." In Robert I. Rotberg, ed. *Corruption in Latin America: How Politicians and Corporations Steal from Citizens*, 93–126. Cham, Switzerland: Springer International.

Pearson, Samantha. 2017. "Brazil, Widening the Hunt for Corruption, Finds It Under Every Rock." *Wall Street Journal*, March 7.

Pei, Minxin. 2018. "How Not to Fight Corruption: Lessons from China." *Daedelus* 147 (3): 216–230.

Peixoto, Maria Andrade de Godoy. 2014. "A análise econômica do direito no Tribunal de Contas da União: um estudo a partir da fiscalização da Petrobras." PhD diss., Universidade Federal de Pernambuco.

Pereira, Carlos, Lucio R. Rennó, and David J. Samuels. 2011. "Corruption, Campaign Finance, and Reelection." In Timothy J. Power and Matthew M. Taylor, eds. *Corruption and Democracy in Brazil: The Struggle for Accountability*, 80–99. Notre Dame, IN: University of Notre Dame Press.

Pereira, Daniel. 2012. "Com saída de Gabrielli, Planalto retoma controle da Petrobras." *Veja*, January 23.

Pereira, Daniel, and Sergio Ruiz Luz. 2020. "Frederick Wassef diz que escondeu Queiroz para 'proteger' Bolsonaro." *Veja*, June 26.

Pereira, Joelma. 2018. "Aécio Neves vira réu na Lava Jato por corrupção passiva e tentativa de obstruir a Justiça." *Congresso em Foco*, April 17.

Pérez-Liñán, Aníbal. 2007. *Presidential Impeachment and the New Political Instability in Latin America*. Cambridge: Cambridge University Press.

Persson, Anna, and Bo Rothstein. 2015. "It's My Money: Why Big Government May Be Good Government." *Comparative Politics* 47: 231–249.

Persson, Anna, Bo Rothstein, and Jan Teorell. 2013. "Why Anticorruption Reforms Fail: Systemic Corruption as a Collective Action Problem." *Governance* 26 (3): 449–471.

Peruzzotti, Enrique, and Catalina Smulovitz, eds. 2006. *Enforcing the Rule of Law: Social Accountability in Latin America*. Pittsburgh: University of Pittsburgh Press.

Peterson, Jonathan. 1997. "U.S., Brazil Reach Accord on Crime, Environment." *Los Angeles Times*, October 15.

Picci, Lucio. 2011. *Reputation-Based Governance*. Stanford: Stanford University Press.

Picci, Lucio. 2012. "Reputation-Based Governance and Making States 'Legible' to Their Citizens." In Hassan Masun and Mark Tovey, eds. *The Reputation Society: How Online Opinions Are Reshaping the Offline World*, 141–150. Cambridge: MIT Press.

Pimenta, Raquel de Mattos. 2019. "Reformas Anticorrupção e Arranjos Institucionais: O Caso dos Acordos de Leniência." PhD diss., Faculdade de Direito, Universidade de São Paulo.

Pimenta, Raquel de Mattos. 2020. *A construção dos acordos de leniência da Lei Anticorrupção*. São Paulo: Editora Edgard Blucher.

Pimentel, Matheus. 2019. "Quais os efeitos políticos da operação contra Luciano Bivar." *Nexo*, October 15.

Pinto, Paulo Silva, Douglas Rodrigues, and Ludmylla Rocha. 2021. "Empresas investigadas na Lava Jato deixaram de faturar R$563 bilhões." *Poder360*, July 6.

Pires, Breno. 2021a. "Bolsonaro cria orçamento secreto em troca de apoio do Congresso." *O Estado de S. Paulo*, May 8.

Pires, Breno. 2021b. "'Tratoraço' atropelou leis orçamentárias e veto de Bolsonaro." *O Estado de S. Paulo*, May 9.

Pires, Breno, and André Shalders. 2021. "Orçamento secreto inclui outros três ministérios, e negociação ocorreu até por WhatsApp." *O Estado de S. Paulo*, June 29.

Pitombo, João Pedro, and Camila Mattoso. 2017. "PF prende Geddel após descoberta de 'bunker' com R$ 51 milhões." *Folha de S. Paulo*, September 8.

Pizzorno, Alessandro. 1992. "La corruzione nel sistema politico." In Donatella Della Porta, ed. *Lo scambio occulto*. Bologna: Il Mulino.

Polícia Federal. 2002. *Relatório de Atividades—2002*. http://www.pf.gov.br/institucional/acessoainformacao/acoes-e-programas/relatorio-anual-pf/RA%202002.ppt/view.

Polícia Federal. 2014. "Operação Lava Jato desarticula rede de lavagem de dinheiro em 7 estados." March 17. http://www.pf.gov.br/agencia/noticias/2014/03/operacao -lava-jato-desarticula-rede-de-lavagem-de-dinheiro-em-7-estados.

Pontes, Felipe. 2021. "Força-tarefa da Lava Jato no Paraná deixa de existir, informa MPF." Agência Brasil, February 3. https://agenciabrasil.ebc.com.br/justica/noticia /2021-02/forca-tarefa-da-lava-jato-no-parana-deixa-de-existir-informa-mpf.

Popova, Maria. 2006. "Watchdogs or Attack Dogs? The Role of the Russian Courts and the CEC in the Resolution of Electoral Disputes." *Europe-Asia Studies* 58 (3): 391–414.

Popova, Maria. 2012. "Why Doesn't the Bulgarian Judiciary Prosecute Corruption?" *Problems of Post-Communism* 59 (5): 35–49.

Popova, Maria. 2017. "Putin-Style 'Rule of Law' and the Prospects for Change." *Daedalus* 146 (2): 64–75.

Popova, Maria, and Vincent Post. 2018. "Prosecuting High-Level Corruption in Eastern Europe." *Communist and Post-Communist Studies* 51 (3): 231–244.

Portal da Transparência Estadual. 2016. "Relação de Servidores." http://www .transparencia.sp.gov.br/BuscaAdmDirInd.html.

Porto, Mauro P. 2011. "The Media and Political Accountability." In Timothy J. Power and Matthew M. Taylor, eds. *Corruption and Democracy in Brazil: The Struggle for Accountability*, 103–126. Notre Dame, IN: University of Notre Dame Press.

Powell, G. Bingham. 2000. *Elections as Instruments of Democracy: Majoritarian and Proportional Visions*. New Haven: Yale University Press.

Power, Timothy J., and Matthew M. Taylor, eds. 2011. *Corruption and Democracy in Brazil: The Struggle for Accountability*. Notre Dame, IN: University of Notre Dame Press.

Praça, Sérgio. 2011. "Corrupcão e reforma institucional no Brasil 1988–2008." *Opinião Pública* 17: 137–162.

Praça, Sérgio. 2013. *Corrupção e reforma orçamentária no Brasil 1987–2008*. São Paulo: Anna Blume.

Praça, Sérgio. 2018. *Guerra à corrupção: lições da Lava Jato*. São Paulo: Évora.

Praça, Sérgio. 2021. "Por que Bolsonaro precisa de um 'orçamento secreto'?" *Revista Exame*, May 11.

Praça, Sérgio, and Matthew M. Taylor. 2014. "Inching Toward Accountability: The Evolution of Brazil's Anticorruption Institutions, 1985–2010." *Latin American Politics and Society* 56: 27–48.

Prado, Mariana Mota, Lindsey D. Carson, and Izabela Correa. 2015. "The Brazilian Clean Company Act: Using Institutional Multiplicity for Effective Punishment." *Osgoode Hall Law Journal* 53 (1): 107–163.

Prado, Mariana Mota, and Marta Rodriguez Machado. Forthcoming, a. "Turning Corruption Trials into Political Tools, with a Little Help from the Media, the Lava Jato Case." In Sandra Botero, Daniel M. Brinks, and Ezequiel González-Ocantos, eds. *The Limits of Judicialization: Progress and Backlash in Latin American Politics*. Cambridge: Cambridge University Press.

Prado, Mariana Mota, and Marta Rodriguez Machado. Forthcoming, b. "Using Criminal Law to Fight Corruption: The Potential Risks and Limitations of Operation Car Wash." *American Journal of Comparative Law*.

Prasad, Monica, Mariana Borges Martins da Silva, and Andrew Nickow. 2019. "Approaches to Corruption: A Synthesis of the Scholarship." *Studies in Comparative International Development* 54 (1): 96–132.

Procuradoria Geral da República (PGR). 2007. "Inquérito no. 2280." November 20. http://media.folha.uol.com.br/brasil/2007/11/22/denuncia_inquerito_n2280.pdf.

Procuradoria Geral da República (PGR). 2017. "Inquérito no. 4325." September 5.

Public Expenditure and Financial Accountability Program (PEFA). 2009. "Brazil: Federal Public Financial Management Performance." www.pefa.org.

Quah, Jon S. T. 2008. "Curbing Corruption in India: An Impossible Dream?" *Asian Journal of Political Science* 16 (3): 240–259.

Quah, Jon S. T. 2010. "Defying Institutional Failure: Learning from the Experiences of Anti-Corruption Agencies in Four Asian Countries." *Crime, Law and Social Change* 53 (1): 23–54.

Quah, Jon S. T. 2011. *Curbing Corruption in Asian Countries: An Impossible Dream?* Bingley, UK: Emerald Publishing.

R7 Notícias. 2009. "Entenda o escândalo do mensalão." October 8.

Ramalho, Renan, and Mariana Oliveira. 2018. "Ministério Público apresenta denúncia contra o ex-procurador Marcello Miller e o empresario Joesley Batista." *G1*, June 25.

Rebello, Márcia Miranda. 2015. "A dificuldade em responsabilizar: o impacto da fragmentação partidária sobre a clareza de responsabilidade." *Revista de Sociologia e Política* 23: 69–90.

Recondo, Felipe, and Luiz Weber. 2019. *Os onze: o STF, seus bastidores e suas crises.* São Paulo: Companhia das Letras.

Reddy, Karthik, Moritz Schularick, and Vasiliki Skreta. 2020. "Immunity." *International Economic Review* 61: 531–564.

Reis, Bruno P. W. 2013. "Sistema eleitoral, corrupção e reforma política." *Revista do Centro Acadêmico Afonso Pena* 19 (1): 11–22.

Reis, Bruno P. W. 2017. "A Lava Jato é o Plano Cruzado do combate à corrupção." *Blog Novos Estudos Cebrap*, January 9. http://novosestudos.uol.com.br/a-lava-jato-e-o-plano-cruzado-do-combate-a-corrupcao/.

Rennó, Lúcio R. 2011. "Corruption and Voting." In Timothy J. Power and Matthew M. Taylor, eds. *Corruption and Democracy in Brazil: The Struggle for Accountability*, 56–79. Notre Dame, IN: University of Notre Dame Press.

Rennó, Lúcio R. 2020. "The Bolsonaro Voter: Issue Positions and Vote Choice in the 2018 Brazilian Presidential Elections." *Latin American Politics and Society* 62 (4): 1–23.

Reporters Without Borders. 2020. "2020 World Press Freedom Index." https://rsf.org/en/ranking.

Reuters. 2010. "Brazil's Lula to Leave with Record-High Popularity." December 16. https://www.reuters.com/article/us-brazil-lula-poll/brazils-lula-to-leave-with-record-high-popularity-idUSTRE6BF4O620101216.

Rey, Beatriz. 2021. "Understanding Bolsonaro's 'Secret Budget' Scandal." *Brazilian Report*, May 17.

Richard, Michelle. 2014. "Brazil's Landmark Anti-Corruption Law." *Law and Business Review of the Americas* 20: 357–362.

Richter, André. 2016. "Supremo confirma decisão sobre prisão do ex-senador Luiz Estevão." *Agência Brasil*, November 18.

Ríos-Figueroa, Júlio. 2006. *Judicial Independence: Definition, Measurement, and Its Effects on Corruption.* Unpublished PhD diss., New York University.

Ríos-Figueroa, Júlio. 2012. "Justice System Institutions and Corruption Control: Evidence from Latin America." *Justice System Journal* 33 (2): 195–214.

Rodan, Garry, and Caroline Hughes. 2014. *The Politics of Accountability in Southeast Asia: The Dominance of Moral Ideologies.* Oxford: Oxford University Press.

Rodrigues, Alex, Yara Aquino, and André Richter. 2017. "JBS ajudou a financiar campanhas de 1.829 candidatos de 28 partidos." *Agência Brasil*, May 19.

Rodrigues, Douglas, Paulo Silva Pinto, and Ludmylla Rocha. 2021. "Estado deixa de arrecadar R$41,3 bilhões de empresas envolvidas na Lava Jato." *Poder360*, July 6.

Rodrigues, Fabiana A. 2019. "Operação Lava Jato: aprendizado institucional e ação estratégica na justiça criminal." Unpublished master's thesis, Universidade de São Paulo.

Rodrigues, Fabiana A., and Rogério Bastos Arantes. 2020. "Supremo Tribunal Federal e a Presunção de Inocência: Ativismo, Contexto e Ação Estratégica." *Revista de Estudos Institucionais* 6 (1): 21–54.

Rodrigues, Fernando. 2012. "Dilma tem aprovação recorde, mas Lula é favorito para 2014." *Folha de S. Paulo*, April 22.

Rodrigues, Fernando. 2014. "Conheça a história da compra de votos a favor da emenda da reeleição." *Blog do Fernando Rodrigues*, June 16.

Rodrigues, Lino, Ronaldo D'Ercole, and Liana Melo. 2012. "Juiz federal condena envolvidos no escândalo Marka e FonteCindam." *O Globo*, March 29.

Rodrigues, Lorenna, and Breno Pires. 2021. "Governo destina R$ 2,1 bi via orçamento secreto para Saúde." *O Estado de S. Paulo*, July 4.

Roland, Gérard. 2001. "Ten Years After . . . Transition and Economics." IMF Staff Papers, Special Issue, 29–52.

Rose-Ackerman, Susan. 1999. *Corruption and Government: Causes, Consequences and Reform*. Cambridge: Cambridge University Press.

Rosenberg, Gerald N. 1992. "Judicial Independence and the Reality of Political Power." *Review of Politics* 54 (3): 369–398.

Rosenn, Keith S. 2014. "Recent Important Decisions by the Brazilian Supreme Court." *Inter-American Law Review* 45: 297–334.

Rosenn, Keith S., and Richard Downes. 1999. *Corruption and Political Reform in Brazil: The Impact of Collor's Impeachment*. Boulder, CO: Lynne Rienner Publishers.

Rossi, Marina, Regiane Oliveira, and Paula Bianchi. 2019. "'O barraco tem nome e sobrenome. Raquel Dodge,' o retrato da procuradora-geral segundo a Lava Jato." *El País Brasil*, August 10. https://brasil.elpais.com/brasil/2019/08/08/politica/1565296861_511506.html.

Rotberg, Robert I. 2017. *The Corruption Cure: How Citizens and Leaders Can Combat Graft*. Princeton: Princeton University Press.

Rothstein, Bo. 2011. "Anti-Corruption: The Indirect 'Big Bang' Approach." *Review of International Political Economy* 18 (2): 228–250.

Rothstein, Bo, and Jan Teorell. 2015. "Getting to Sweden, Part II: Breaking with Corruption in the Nineteenth Century." *Scandinavian Political Studies* 38 (3): 238–254.

Roussel, Violaine. 1998. "Les magistrats dans les scandales politiques." *Revue Française de Science Politique* 48: 245–273.

Roussel, Violaine. 2002. "Changing Definitions of Risk and Responsibility in French Political Scandals." *Journal of Law and Society* 29 (3): 461–486.

Roussel, Violaine. 2003. "Les magistrats français, des cause lawyers malgré eux?" *Politix. Revue des Sciences Sociales du Politique* 16 (62): 93–113.

Ryder, Ernest, and Stephen Hardy. 2019. *Judicial Leadership: A New Strategic Approach*. Oxford: Oxford University Press.

Sacramento, Ana Rita Silva, and José Antonio Gomes de Pinho. 2016. "The Process of Implementing Answerability in Contemporary Brazil." *Revista de Administração Pública* 50: 193–213.

Sadek, Maria Tereza. 1990. "A Justiça Eleitoral no processo de redemocratização." In Bolivar Lamounier, ed. *De Geisel a Collor: o balanço da transição*. São Paulo: Editora Sumaré.

Sadek, Maria Tereza. 1995. *A Justiça Eleitoral e a consolidação da democracia no Brasil*. São Paulo: Konrad-Adenauer-Stiftung.

Sadek, Maria Tereza. 2008. "Ministério Público." In Leonardo Avritzer, Newton Bignotto, Juarez Guimarães, and Heloisa Maria Murgel Starling, eds. *Corrupção: ensaios e críticas*. Belo Horizonte: Editora UFMG.

Sadek, Maria Tereza, and Rosângela Batista Cavalcanti. 2003. "The New Brazilian Public Prosecution: An Agent of Accountability." In Scott Mainwaring and Christopher Welna, eds. *Democratic Accountability in Latin America*, 201–227. Oxford: Oxford University Press.

Sá e Silva, Fábio de. 2020. "From Car Wash to Bolsonaro: Law and Lawyers in Brazil's Illiberal Turn (2014–2018)." *Journal of Law and Society* 47 (S1): S90–S110.

Salles, João Moreira. 2008. "O caseiro: de como todos os poderes da República— Executivo, Legislativo, Judiciário, polícia, imprensa, governo, oposição—moeram Francenildo dos Santos Costa." *Revista piauí* 25 (October).

Salminen, Ari. 2013. "Control of Corruption: The Case of Finland." In Jon S. T. Quah, ed. *Different Paths to Curbing Corruption: Lessons from Denmark, Finland, Hong Kong, New Zealand and Singapore*, 57–78. Bingley, UK: Emerald Publishing.

Salomão, Karin. 2017. "Além da Lava Jato: as investigações que envolvem JBS e J&F." *Revista Exame*, May 18.

Samuels, David. 2001. "Money, Elections, and Democracy in Brazil." *Latin American Politics and Society* 43: 27–48.

Santiso, Carlos. 2009. *The Political Economy of Government Auditing: Financial Governance and the Rule of Law in Latin America and Beyond*. New York: Routledge.

Sardinha, Edson. 2012. "Entenda o caso: o que foi a Operação Sanguessuga." *Congresso em Foco*, February 28.

Sardinha, Edson. 2015. "A 'lista de Janot' agora é official: os politicos que serão investigados na Lava Jato." *Congresso em Foco*, March 6. https://congressoemfoco .uol.com.br/especial/noticias/os-politicos-que-serao-investigados-na-lava-jato-2/.

Sardinha, Edson, and Larissa Calixto. 2019a. "No novo Senado, um em cada três senadores responde a acusações criminais. Veja a lista." *Congresso em Foco*, May 24.

Sardinha, Edson, and Larissa Calixto. 2019b. "Quem são os deputados acusados de crime." *Congresso em Foco*, May 31.

Scharpf, Fritz W. 1988. "The Joint-Decision Trap: Lessons from German Federalism and European Integration." *Public Administration* 66 (3): 239–278.

Schedler, Andreas. 1999. "Conceptualizing Accountability." In Andreas Schedler, Larry Diamond, and Marc F. Plattner, eds. *The Self-Restraining State*, 13–28. Boulder, CO: Lynne Rienner Publishers.

Schleiter, Petra, and Alisa Voznaya. 2018. "Party System Institutionalization, Accountability and Governmental Corruption." *British Journal of Political Science* 48 (2): 315–342.

Schreiber, Mariana. 2016. "Pedido de impeachment da OAB contra Dilma é por 'conjunto da obra,' diz presidente da ordem." BBC Brasil, March 28.

Schreiber, Mariana. 2020. "Como aproximação com Bolsonaro e inquérito polêmico fragilizaram STF na gestão Toffoli, segundo juristas." BBC Brasil, September 8.

Schütte, Sofie A. 2016a. "Specialised Anti-Corruption Courts: Indonesia." *U4 Brief*, no. 4 (July).

Schütte, Sofie A. 2016b. "Two Steps Forward, One Step Backwards: Indonesia's Winding (Anti-) Corruption Journey." In Ting Gong and Ian Scott, eds. *Routledge Handbook of Corruption in Asia*. New York: Routledge.

Schütte, Sofie A., and Matthew C. Stephenson. 2016. "Specialised Anti-Corruption Courts: A Comparative Mapping." *U4 Issue*, no. 7 (December).

Schütte, Sofie A., and Simon Butt. 2013. "The Indonesian Court for Corruption Crimes: Circumventing Judicial Impropriety?" *U4 Brief*, no. 5 (September).

Schwartsman, Hélio. 2018. "STF, a hipótese alucinógena." *Folha de S. Paulo*, April 27.

Secretaria Nacional de Justiça. 2012. "ENCCLA: Estratégia nacional de combate à corrupção e à lavagem de dinheiro: 10 anos de organização do estado brasileiro contra o crime organizado." Secretaria Nacional de Justiça, Departamento de Recuperação de Ativos e Cooperação Jurídica Internacional (DRCI). Brasília: Ministério da Justiça.

Segal, David. 2015. "Brazil's Great Oil Swindle." *New York Times*, August 9.

Seidl, Antonio Carlos. 1998. "Ferrovia Norte-Sul: Caso vai a Brasília, ao RJ, volta e é arquivado." *Folha de S. Paulo*, December 31.

Senado Federal. 1988. "Relatório Final da CPI da Corrupção." https://legis
.senado.leg.br/sdleg-getter/documento?dm=4484303&ts=1568662726350&
disposition=inline.

Senado Federal. 1997. "Relatório Final, Comissão Parlamentar de Inquérito dos Títulos
Públicos." https://legis.senado.leg.br/sdleg-getter/documento?dm=44415---67&ts
=1586468841294&disposition=inline.

Senado Federal. 1999. "Relatório Final, Comissão Parlamentar de Inquérito do Sistema Financeiro Nacional." http://www2.senado.leg.br/bdsf/bitstream/handle/id
/82020/CPI_Bancos_.pdf?sequence=7&isAllowed=y.

Senado Federal. 2020. "Nova República: Presidentes do Senado Federal durante a
Nova República (a partir de 1985)." https://www25.senado.leg.br/web/senadores
/nova-republica.

Senado Notícias. 2016. "Delcídio do Amaral foi o primeiro senador a ser preso no
exercício do mandato." May 10. https://www12.senado.leg.br/noticias/audios
/2016/05/delcidio-do-amaral-foi-o-primeiro-senador-a-ser-preso-no-exercicio-do
-mandato.

Senters, Kelly, Rebecca Weitz-Shapiro, and Matthew S. Winters. 2019. "Continuity and
Change in Public Attitudes Toward Corruption." In Barry Ames, ed. *Routledge
Handbook of Brazilian Politics*, 15–38. New York: Routledge.

Serapião, Fabio, and Fábio Fabrini. 2017. "Lula vira réu por venda de MP de incentivos fiscais a montadoras." *O Estado de S. Paulo*, September 19.

Shores, Nicholas, and Lucas Mendes. 2021. "Em vídeo, Luis Miranda mostra registro
de negociação da Covaxin por preço menor." *Poder360*, July 5.

Silva, Marcos Fernandes da. 1999. "The Political Economy of Corruption in Brazil."
RAE: Revista de Administração de Empresas 39: 26–41.

Silveira, Rose Ane. 2004. "Relatório da CPI do Banestado pede 91 indiciamentos."
Folha Online, December 14.

Sims, Kimberly. 2011. "Judges Without Borders? Transnational Networks of Anti-
Corruption Prosecuting Judges in Europe." PhD diss., Northwestern University.

Slater, Dan. 2004. "Indonesia's Accountability Trap: Party Cartels and Presidential
Power After Democratic Transition." *Indonesia* 78 (October): 61–92.

Smulovitz, Catalina, and Enrique Peruzzotti. 2003. "Societal and Horizontal Controls:
Two Cases of a Fruitful Relationship." In Scott Mainwaring and Christopher
Welna, eds. *Democratic Accountability in Latin America*, 309–332. Oxford:
Oxford University Press.

Soares, Ronaldo. 2001. "Desvio de dinheiro teria conexão em duas cidades." *Folha
de S. Paulo*, March 18.

Souza, Cíntia Pinheiro Ribeiro de. 2013. "A evolução da regulação do financiamento
de campanha no Brasil (1945–2006)." *Resenha Eleitoral—Tribunal Regional
Eleitoral de Santa Catarina* 3.

Souza, Leonardo. 2008. "Após desgaste, Lula exonera Lacerda da direção da Abin."
Folha de S. Paulo, December 30.

Souza, Renato. 2019. "Ministro do Turismo é denunciado pelo MP pelo laranjal do
PSL." *Correio Braziliense*, October 5.

Souza, Rodrigo Telles de. 2020. "The Continuing Controversy over the Destination of
the Petrobras Penalties: The Coronavirus Crisis Has Ended One Debate, but May
Start Another." *Global Anticorruption Blog*, April 10. https://globalanticorruption
.blog.com.

Sparrow, M. K. 2008. *The Character of Harms: Operational Challenges in Control*.
Cambridge: Cambridge University Press.

Speck, Bruno Wilhelm. 2002. "Perspectivas para o futuro." In Bruno Wilhelm Speck,
ed. *Caminhos da Transparência*, 479–482. São Paulo: Editora da Universidade
Estadual de Campinas.

Speck, Bruno Wilhelm. 2006. "Reagir a escândalos ou perseguir ideais? A regulação
do financiamento político no Brasil." *Elecciones* 5 (6): 133–162.

Speck, Bruno Wilhelm. 2011. "Auditing Institutions." In Timothy J. Power and Matthew M. Taylor, eds. *Corruption and Democracy in Brazil: The Struggle for Accountability*, 127–161. Notre Dame, IN: University of Notre Dame Press.

Speck, Bruno Wilhelm. 2012. "O financiamento político e a corrupção no Brasil." In Rita de Cássia Biason, ed. *Temas De Corrupção Política*, 49–98. São Paulo: Balão Editorial.

Staton, Jeffrey K., Christopher M. Reenock, Jordan Holsinger, and Staffan I. Lindberg. 2018. "Can Courts Be Bulwarks of Democracy?" V-Dem Working Paper, no. 71. https://ssrn.com/abstract=3213165.

Stauffer, Caroline. 2016. "Brazil Graft Crackdown Spurs Work for Lawyers, Corporate Change." Reuters, March 24.

Stein, Ernesto, Mariano Tommasi, Koldo Echebarría, Eduardo Lora, and Mark Payne. 2006. *The Politics of Policies: Economic and Social Progress in Latin America.* Washington, DC: Inter-American Development Bank.

Stephenson, Matthew. 2016. "Specialised Anti-Corruption Courts: Philippines." *U4 Brief*, no. 3 (July).

Stephenson, Matthew. 2019. "The Incredible Shrinking Scandal? Further Reflections on the Lava Jato Leaks." *Global Anticorruption Blog*, June 17. https://globalanticorruptionblog.com/2019/06/17/the-incredible-shrinking-scandal -further-reflections-on-the-lava-jato-leaks/.

Stephenson, Matthew C. 2020. "Corruption as a Self-Reinforcing Trap: Implications for Reform Strategy." *World Bank Research Observer* 35 (2): 192–226.

Sunstein, Cass R. 1996. "Social Norms and Social Roles." *Columbia Law Review* 96 (4): 903–968.

Supremo Tribunal Federal (STF). 2014. "Emenda Regimental No. 49." June 5. http://www.stf.jus.br/ARQUIVO/NORMA/EMENDAREGIMENTAL049-2014.PDF.

Supremo Tribunal Federal (STF). 2017. Habeas Corpus 126292. http://portal.stf .jus.br/processos/detalhe.asp?incidente=4697570.

Supremo Tribunal Federal (STF). 2018. Recurso Extraórdinario 593727. http://portal .stf.jus.br/processos/detalhe.asp?incidente=2641697.

Supremo Tribunal Federal (STF). 2020. Ação Penal n. 307. http://portal.stf.jus.br /processos/detalhe.asp?incidente=1565721.

Tahyar, Benjamin H. 2010. "The Politics of Indonesia's Pengadilan Tipikor." In Andrew Harding and Penelope Nicholson, eds. *New Courts in Asia*. London: Routledge.

Talento, Aguirre. 2019. "Grupo da Lava-Jato na PGR pede demissão coletiva em protesto contra Raquel Dodge." *O Globo*, September 4.

Tavits, Margit. 2007. "Clarity of Responsibility and Corruption." *American Journal of Political Science* 51 (1): 218–229.

Taylor, Matthew M. 2006. "A Justiça Eleitoral." In Leonardo Avritzer and Fátima Anastasia, eds. *Reforma Política Brasileira*, 147–152. Belo Horizonte: Editora UFMG/PNUD.

Taylor, Matthew M. 2009. "Institutional Development Through Policymaking: A Case Study of the Brazilian Central Bank." *World Politics* 61: 487–515.

Taylor, Matthew M. 2011. "The Federal Judiciary and Electoral Courts." In Timothy J. Power and Matthew M. Taylor, eds. *Corruption and Democracy in Brazil: The Struggle for Accountability*, 162–183. Notre Dame, IN: University of Notre Dame Press.

Taylor, Matthew M. 2017. "Corruption and Accountability in Brazil." In Peter Kingstone and Timothy Power, eds. *Democratic Brazil Divided*, 77–96. Pittsburgh: University of Pittsburgh Press.

Taylor, Matthew M. 2018. "Getting to Accountability: A Framework for Planning and Implementing Anticorruption Strategies." *Daedalus: Journal of the American Academy of Arts and Sciences* 147: 63–82.

Taylor, Matthew M. 2019. "The Troubling Strength of Brazilian Institutions in the Face of Scandal." *Taiwan Journal of Democracy* 15: 91–111.

Taylor, Matthew M. 2020. *Decadent Developmentalism: The Political Economy of Democratic Brazil.* Cambridge: Cambridge University Press.

Taylor, Matthew M., and Vinicius Buranelli. 2007. "Ending Up in Pizza: Accountability as a Problem of Institutional Arrangement in Brazil." *Latin American Politics and Society* 49: 59–87.

Teixeira, Lucas Borges. 2020. "O que se sabe sobre o Caso Queiroz." *UOL*, June 24.

Teixeira, Marco Antonio, and Mário A. Alves. 2011. "Ethos organizacional e controle da corrupção: O TCU sob uma ótica organizacional." *Cadernos Adenauer* 12: 75–98.

Teixeira, Matheus. 2020. "PGR denuncia Aécio sob acusação de receber R$ 65 milhões em propina." *Folha de S. Paulo*, May 5.

Telles, Helcimara de Souza. 2015. "O que os protestos trazem de novo para a política brasileira?" *Em Debate* 7 (2): 7–14.

Teorell, Jan, and Bo Rothstein. 2015. "Getting to Sweden, Part I: War and Malfeasance, 1720–1850." *Scandinavian Political Studies* 38: 217–237.

Tortato, Mari. 2003. "Ex-dirigentes do banco Araucária são acusados por lavagem de dinheiro." *Folha de S. Paulo*, September 12.

Transparency International. 2017. Global Corruption Barometer, 9th ed. https://www.transparency.org/en/gcb/global/global-corruption-barometer–2017.

Traumann, Thomas. 2020. "O Centrão chegou para proteger Michelle Bolsonaro." *Veja*, August 17.

Treisman, Daniel. 2000. "The Causes of Corruption: A Cross-National Study." *Journal of Public Economics* 76 (3): 399–457.

Treisman, Daniel. 2007. "What Have We Learned About the Causes of Corruption from Ten Years of Cross-National Empirical Research?" *Annual Review of Political Science* 10: 211–244.

Treisman, Daniel. 2014. "What Does Cross-National Empirical Research Reveal About the Causes of Corruption?" In Paul Heywood, ed. *Routledge Handbook of Political Corruption*, 109–123. New York: Routledge.

Tribunal de Contas da União (TCU). 2016. "Fiscobras: 20 Anos." Brasília: TCU.

Tribunal Regional Federal da 1ª Região. 2020. Processo n. 0035229-36.2003.4.01 .3400. https://processual.trf1.jus.br/consultaProcessual/processo.php?proc=352 293620034013400&secao=JFDFL.

Tribunal Regional Federal da 2ª Região. 2020. Nota de esclarecimento do relator da Operação Furna da Onça na 1ª Seção Especializada do TRF2. May 17. https://www10.trf2.jus.br/portal/nota-de-esclarecimento-do-relator-da-operacao -furna-da-onca-na-1a-secao-especializada-do-trf2/.

Truffi, Renan. 2017. "CPI da JBS conclui que PGR orientou gravações." *O Estado de S. Paulo*, December 7.

Tsebelis, George. 2002. *Veto Players: How Political Institutions Work.* Princeton: Princeton University Press.

Twitter. 2020. "Deltan Dallagnol @deltanmd." https://twitter.com/deltanmd?lang=en.

UOL Notícias. 2009. "Entenda a operação Satiagraha da Polícia Federal." March 19. https://noticias.uol.com.br/politica/2009/03/19/ult5773u850.jhtm.

UOL Notícias. 2012. "Relembre o que é o mensalão, veja os envolvidos e o que pode acontecer." July 30. https://noticias.uol.com.br/infograficos/2012/07/30/o-escandalo -do-mensalao.htm.

Uribe, Gustavo. 2020. "Bolsonaro sanciona transferência do Coaf para o Banco Central." *Folha de S. Paulo*, January 7.

Valarini, Elizangela, and Markus Pohlmann. 2019. "Organizational Crime and Corruption in Brazil: A Case Study of the 'Operation Carwash' Court Records." *International Journal of Law, Crime and Justice* 59: 1–15.

Valente, Fernanda. 2020. "Absolvição de nove réus no TRF–1 sinaliza desmanche da Zelotes, dizem defesas." *Consultor Jurídico*, April 29.

Valente, Rubens. 2013. *Operação Banqueiro: as provas secretas do caso Satiagraha*. São Paulo: Geração Editorial.

Valente, Rubens. 2016. "Em diálogos gravados, Jucá fala em pacto para deter avanço da Lava Jato." *Folha de S. Paulo*, May 23.

Valente, Rubens, and Lilian Christofolleti. 2004. "Sonegadores enviam R$ 4,3 bi ao exterior." *Folha de S. Paulo*, February 2.

Valfre, Vinícius, and Breno Pires. 2021. "Oposição só teve 4% do 'orçamento secreto' do governo Bolsonaro." *O Estado de S. Paulo*, May 17.

Valor. 2020. "Governo Bolsonaro dá a primazia aos militares." February 6. https://valor.globo.com/opiniao/noticia/2020/02/06/governo-de-bolsonaro-da-a-primazia-aos-militares.ghtml.

Vanberg, Georg. 2015. "Constitutional Courts in Comparative Perspective: A Theoretical Assessment." *Annual Review of Political Science* 18: 167–185.

Vannucci, Alberto. 2009. "The Controversial Legacy of 'Mani Pulite': A Critical Analysis of Italian Corruption and Anti-Corruption Policies." *Bulletin of Italian Politics* 1 (2): 233–264.

Vannucci, Alberto. 2016. "The 'Clean Hands' (Mani Pulite) Inquiry on Corruption and Its Effects on the Italian Political System." *Em Debate* 8: 62–68.

Vasconcellos, Fábio. 2021. "Qual é o tamanho do Centrão? Um recorte entre 2002 e 2021." *Fábio Vasconcellos: Sobre dados, política e tudo mais*. August 10. https://fabiovasconcellos.com/2021/08/10/qual-e-o-tamanho-do-centrao-um-recorte-entre-2002-e-2021/.

Vasconcelos, Frederico. 2013. "Combate à corrupção será prioridade na gestão do Procurador Geral da República." *Interesse público* (blog), October 9. https://blogdofred.blogfolha.uol.com.br/2013/10/09/quem-e-quem-na-equipe-convocada-por-janot/.

Vassallo, Luiz. 2019. "Procuradoria cobra R$ 3 bi de Geddel, Henrique Alves, Cunha e mais 14 por fraudes na Caixa." *O Estado de S. Paulo*, July 29.

Vaz Ferreira, Luciano. 2016. *Corrupção e negócios internacionais: como o Brasil pode controlar o suborno praticado por empresas transnacionais*. São Paulo: Paco Editorial.

Vaz Ferreira, Luciano, and Fabio Costa Morosini. 2013. "The Implementation of International Anti-Corruption Law in Business: Legal Control of Corruption Directed to Transnational Corporations." *Austral: Brazilian Journal of Strategy and International Relations* 2: 241–260.

V-Dem Institute. 2020. *Autocratization Surges—Resistance Grows: Democracy Report 2020*. Gothenburg: V-Dem Institute.

Veja. 2011. "Se Dilma Rouseff mantiver a coerência, demitirá Pimentel." December 7.

Veja. 2012. "Caso dos Sanguessugas entra para a Rede de Escândalos." June 13.

Veja. 2016a. "13 de março: protesto sem precedentes contra Dilma e PT não indica que líder pode emergir da crise." March 14.

Veja. 2016b. "Na mira da PF, ferrovia foi idealizada no governo Sarney e está longe de ser concluída." February 26.

Veja. 2017. "Dallagnol: 2018 será 'batalha final' da Operação Lava Jato." November 27.

Vieira, Oscar Vilhena. 2018. *A batalha dos poderes: da transição democrática ao malestar constitucional*. São Paulo: Editora Companhia das Letras.

Vogl, Frank. 2012. *Waging War on Corruption: Inside the Movement Fighting the Abuse of Power*. Lanham: Rowman and Littlefield.

Wang, Juan. 2018. "What's Wrong with Corruption? Messages from Confessions in China." *Crime, Law and Social Change* 69 (3): 447–463.

Watts, Jonathan. 2017. "Operation Car Wash: Is This the Biggest Corruption Scandal in History?" *Guardian*, June 1.

Wibowo, Richo A. 2018. "When Anti-Corruption Norms Lead to Undesirable Results: Learning from the Indonesian Experience." *Crime, Law and Social Change* 70 (3): 383–396.

Williams, Andrew. 2014. "A Global Index of Information and Political Transparency." University of Western Australia Discussion Paper 14.07.

Winters, Matthew S., and Rebecca Weitz-Shapiro. 2014. "Research Note: Partisan Protesters and Nonpartisan Protests in Brazil." *Journal of Politics in Latin America* 6: 137–150.

Wolffenbüttel, Andréa. 2007. "O que é? Contas CC5." *Revista Desafios do Desenvolvimento*, February 5.

Zamprogna, Carlos Alberto D. 2019. "A Competência Eleitoral na 'Lava Jato.'" *Migalhas*, March 29.

Zhu, Jiangnan, and Dong Zhang. 2017. "Weapons of the Powerful: Authoritarian Elite Competition and Politicized Anticorruption in China." *Comparative Political Studies* 50 (9): 1186–1220.

Zucco, Cesar, Jr. 2009. "Ideology or What? Legislative Behavior in Multiparty Presidential Settings." *Journal of Politics* 71 (3): 1076–1092.

Index

271

About the Book

Brazil's democracy has repeatedly suffered major cor-ruption scandals, despite numerous reforms designed to overcome entrenched patterns of illicit behavior. Why? What has caused corruption scandals to recur across some four decades of presidential administrations? And what are the implications of Brazil's experience for efforts to enhance accountability elsewhere?

Addressing these questions, Matthew M. Taylor and Luciano Da Ros provide a framework for evaluating the bottlenecks to effective accountability in Brazil and analyze the successes and failures of anticorruption efforts from the early days of the democratic transition through the demise of the massive *Lava Jato* investigations.

Luciano Da Ros is assistant professor of political science at the Federal University of Santa Catarina. **Matthew M. Taylor** is associate professor of international relations at American University.